DATE DUE

DEMCO 38-296

SYRIA AND ISRAEL

SYRIA AND ISRAEL

From War to Peacemaking

MOSHE MA'OZ

CLARENDON PRESS · OXFORD

n Street, Oxford OX2 6DP

ν York

ok Bogota Bombay

e Town Dar es Salaam

ng Istanbul Karachi

Kuala Lumpur Madras Madrid Melbourne
Mexico City Nairobi Paris Singapore
Taipei Tokyo Toronto
and associated companies in
Berlin Ibadan

Oxford is a trade mark of Oxford University Press

Published in the United States by
Oxford University Press Inc., New York

© Moshe Ma'oz 1995

First published 1995

British Library Cataloguing in Publication Data
Data available

Library of Congress Cataloging in Publication Data
Ma'oz, Moshe.
Syria and Israel: from war to peace? / Moshe Ma'oz.
Includes bibliographical references.
1. Syria—Relations—Israel. 2. Israel—Relations—Syria.
3. Jewish–Arab relations—1949– . I. Title.
DS95.6.I75M36 1995 327.569105694'09'045—dc20 95-5775
ISBN 0-19-828018-1

3 5 7 9 10 8 6 4 2

Printed in Great Britain
on acid-free paper by
Biddles Ltd, Guildford and King's Lynn

For Ettie

PREFACE

No Arab–Israeli war is possible without Egypt, and no Arab–Israeli peace is possible without Syria. This view, widely held among Middle Eastern analysts, has gained special importance since the late 1970s, when Egypt made peace with Israel and the Arab–Israeli conflict became, in many respects, a Syrian–Israeli conflict. For, apart from Egypt, Jordan has maintained *de facto* peaceful relations with Israel for decades, and in October 1994 the two countries signed a formal peace treaty. Iraq has in practice departed from its conflict with Israel since 1980, when it became involved in two successive, devastating wars in the Gulf.

It is true that the Palestinian problem has been at the core of the Arab–Israeli conflict, although the Palestinians constituted only a political challenge to Israel, never a military threat. Their antagonism has greatly diminished since the PLO's recognition of Israel late in 1988 and the PLO–Israel agreements in September 1993 (Oslo) and in May 1994 (Cairo). Only Syria has manifested a consistent political and ideological hostility to the Jewish entity since the 1920s, and a military threat to Israel's security since 1948.

Israel, for its part, has considered Syria an implacable and brutal foe, publicly committed to its destruction. Syria has voiced anti-Zionist and anti-Jewish doctrines and has used the Golan Heights to harass Jewish villages and jeopardize Israel's water resources, all of which led to the eruption of the 1967 war. In reaction—sometimes without previous provocation—Israel launched vigorous military operations against Syrian positions, both before and after the 1967 war. That war consolidated the zero-sum conflict between Damascus and Jerusalem, leading, *inter alia*, to the 1973 war, which, in turn, deepened their mutual hostility and intensified their struggle over Lebanon and the Palestinians. Although Israel mended fences with Sadat's Egypt, during the mid-1970s it rejected several suggestions by Asad for a political settlement. In 1981 it formally annexed the Golan Heights which had been occupied during the 1967 war; and during the 1982 Lebanese war, it attacked the Syrian army in Lebanon without provocation. Syria was subsequently able to bring about Israel's departure from Lebanon by means of its Shi'i guerrilla surrogates and to establish control in Beirut. Simultaneously Asad, with massive Soviet military help, promoted his doctrine of strategic balance, aiming at single-handedly confronting Israel, primarily to deter it from attacking Syria.

However, Asad failed to achieve this strategic-military balance, and faced severe difficulties owing to changes in Soviet policy, the Iraqi challenge, and the domestic economic crisis. Therefore, since 1988, Asad has given priority to a diplomatic rather than a military strategy. Seeking rapprochement with Egypt, and particularly with the United States, Syria, for the first time and with American backing, has been prepared to make peace with Israel in return for the entire Golan Heights, as well as for an acceptable settlement of the Lebanese and Palestinian problems.

But, at the same time, Syria has continued its military build-up as well as its alliances with Iran, the Hizballa in Lebanon, and several militant Palestinian organizations, all of whom vehemently oppose the peace process. All this, in order to negotiate from a position of military strength, or to sabotage the peace process if Syria is left out of it.

The Israeli Likud government, in power since 1977, refused to give up the Golan Heights (let alone the West Bank and the Gaza Strip) even in return for peace with Syria. This government continued to hold that same position even during the 1991 Madrid peace conference. A similar stance was declared by the Israeli Labour Party, until its advent to power in the June 1992 elections. Subsequently, however, Israel's new prime minister, Yitzhak Rabin, adopted a flexible policy aimed at achieving a peaceful settlement with Syria (as well as with the PLO and Jordan). Thus, with active American mediation, and despite significant obstacles the peace-making process between Jerusalem and Damascus gradually advanced during 1993–4.

The purpose of this book is to trace and analyse Syrian–Israeli relations from the 1948 war until early 1995, when the peace negotiations entered a crucial phase. It will explain the factors influencing their relations, the regional and global ramifications of their interactions, and the effect of domestic policies on both their relations. It will also show the crucial importance of Syrian–Israeli relations for the strategic posture of both countries, for the outcome of the Lebanese and Palestinian problems and for the prospects of an overall Middle East peace settlement.

Among the major issues to be discussed are: ideological concepts and political developments in Syria, notably under the Ba'th regime, regarding Zionism and Israel; Arab unity, Greater Syria, and Palestine; the interplay between these concepts and domestic issues—nation-building, Muslim opposition, economic problems—and Syria's policies towards Israel; the evolution of Syrian political and military strategy towards

Israel, notably Asad's doctrine of strategic balance, and its linkage to relations between Damascus and the Arab world. The book will also dwell upon the linkage between domestic issues in Israel—party politics, public opinion, ideological concepts, nation-building—and its attitude towards Syria; Israel's attitudes and actions towards Lebanon and the Palestinians, and their effects on Israeli–Syrian relations; the role of the United States and the Soviet Union in Syrian–Israeli relations; the 1991 new Middle East and international configuration, and the peacemaking process between Syria and Israel since then.

ACKNOWLEDGEMENTS

I wish to express my gratitude to the institutions and persons that helped me in the various stages of my research. The United States Institute of Peace in Washington, DC, initially provided me with a major grant; subsequently I received a stipend from the Leonard Davis Institute for International Relations at the Hebrew University, Jerusalem, and finally I was awarded a fellowship at Rand, Santa Monica. I am grateful to Mrs Mary Morris, Associate Director of the Greater Middle East Studies Center, Rand, for enabling me to complete my study in a scholarly and stimulating environment, and to Prof. Muhammad Muslih, Dr Avraham Sela, and Dr Avi Shlaim for reading the manuscript and making useful remarks.

I wish also to thank my research assistants who devotedly helped me to gather materials from different sources: Oren Barak, Matthew Berkowitz, Uri Bitan, and Amira Zeira; Esther Porath for efficiently typing the manuscript and Mira Reich for editing it. I am indebted also to the managements and staffs of the archives that enabled me to gather important documents for my study: the Public Record Office, London; the National Archives, Washington, DC; Israel State Archives, Jerusalem; Israel Defence Forces Archives; the Ben Gurion Archives, Sde Boker.

CONTENTS

ABBREVIATIONS

APR	*Arab Report and Record*
DD	Declassified Documents (US)
DMZ	Demilitarized Zone
DOS	US Department of State
FBIS	Foreign Broadcast Information Service
FRUS	*Foreign Relations of the US*
GOI	Government of Israel
IDF	Israel Defence Force
ISA	Israel State Archives
MAC	Mixed Armistice Commission
MECS	*Middle East Contemporary Survey*
MER	*Middle East Record*
MK	Member of the Knesset
NA	National Archives, Washington
NSC	National Security Council (US)
OFNS	Observer Foreign News Service
PLA	Palestine Liberation Army
PLO	Palestine Liberation Organization
PNC	Palestine National Council
PPS	Syrian Nationalist Party
SLA	Southern Lebanese Army
SSNP	Syrian Social Nationalist Party
UAR	United Arab Republic
UNEF	UN Emergency Force
UPI	United Press International
U.S.G.	US government

The Historical Setting: Dialogue and Conflict between Two Nationalist Movements

The Jewish-Zionist national movement, which launched its activities in the early 1880s, aroused vehement opposition among most Arabs in Palestine from the turn of the century onwards. At about the same time, however, Arab leaders in Syria, the emerging centre of the Arab national movement, conducted talks and reached agreements with the Zionist movement which indicated their recognition of Jewish national aspirations in Palestine. Thus, for example, in 1911, before the collapse of the Ottoman empire, two Zionist officials met in Istanbul with the leaders of the Arab cultural-nationalist association *al-Muntada al-Arabi* ('The Arab Club'); among them was a Syrian politician, Faris al-Khuri. Reportedly they reached an agreement confering, *inter alia*, a central role on the Jews in Palestine, within the framework of a future all-Arab political configuration. Two years later, in 1913, Sami Hochberg, a representative of the Zionist bureau in Istanbul, was invited to attend the first Arab Congress in Paris, where he established some rapport with Arab leaders, including several Syrian political figures.[1]

Further dialogues between Zionist leaders (such as Sokolov and Ussishkin) and Arab nationalist figures, including the Syrians Jamil Mardam and Abd al-Rahman Shahabandar, took place on the eve of the First World War; but the outbreak of war caused a meeting between larger groups of Arab and Jewish representatives, scheduled to convene on 1 July 1914, to be suspended. Yet, in the aftermath of the war, Jewish-Zionist leaders, notably Chaim Weizmann, and Amir (later King) Faysal, commander of the Arab forces and first ruler of the semi-independent Syria (1918–20), resumed the Arab–Jewish dialogue at the highest level. Weizmann was equipped with the Balfour Declaration of 2 November 1917, which granted a 'National Home' to the Jewish people in Palestine, while Faysal enjoyed the backing of his father, Sharif Hussein of Mecca, the leader of the 'Arab Revolt' (who acknowledged the Balfour Declaration and in March 1918, through his official organ *al-Qibla*, called upon the Palestinian Arabs to welcome the Jews from Europe as brothers).[2] With British inducement Faysal met Weizmann near Aqaba in June 1918, and subsequently other Zionist leaders in London, to discuss Arab–Jewish co-operation. As a result, on 3 January 1919, Faysal and Weizmann signed a historic agreement, which for the first time officially expressed Arab recognition of Jewish nationhood in Palestine. Referring in the preamble to 'the racial kinship and ancient bonds existing between the Arabs and the Jewish people', this unique document stated that 'the surest means of working out the consummation of their national aspirations is through the closest possible collaboration in the development of the Arab state and [Jewish] Palestine.' It also undertook the task of 'carrying into effect the British Government's [Balfour] Declaration of 2nd November 1917 [favouring the establishment in Palestine of a national home for the Jewish people]' (Article 3). The agreement also stipulated that 'all necessary measures shall be taken to encourage and stimulate immigration of Jews into Palestine on a large scale, and as quickly as possible to settle Jewish immigrants upon the land' (Article 4).

In the same vein, Faysal wrote in March 1919 to Judge Felix Frankfurter, a prominent American Zionist: 'We Arabs, especially the educated among us, look with the deepest sympathy on the Zionist movement ... We are working together for a reformed and revived Near East, and our two movements complete one another. The Jewish movement is national and not imperialist. Our movement is national and not imperialist, and there is room in [Greater] Syria for us both.'[3]

Similar expressions of sympathy for the Zionist movement, and of support for a Jewish national home in Palestine and for Jewish immigration to it were made in 1919 and 1920, also by Syrian Arab nationalists associated with Faysal, namely, members of the Syrian delegation to the post-war Paris Peace Conference, as well as representatives of the Syrian Nationalist Party (*al-Hisb al-Watani al-Suri*), both composed of Damascene notables. The Syrian Nationalist Party, for example, signed an agreement in 1920 with the Zionist movement, acknowledging the separation of Palestine from Syria and the creation of a 'national home' for the Jewish people there.[4]

On the other hand, however, the majority of Arab nationalists in Syria (let alone in Palestine), mostly young people, strongly rejected the notion of a Jewish national home in Palestine, and of Jewish immigration into it. These anti-Zionist attitudes were particularly manifested during 1918–20, when most Arab nationalists in Palestine designated their country as

'Southern Syria', expecting to realize their national aspirations through a union with the 'independent' Arab state of Syria. Partly under the impact of Palestinian activities in Nablus, Haifa, Jerusalem, and Damascus (where a 'Palestinian Arab Society' was formed by Amin al-Husayni and Arif al-Arif), and partly following their own ideological motives, a growing number of Syrian Arab nationalists, organized in *al-Nadi al-Arabi* (the 'Arab Club', based in Damascus), actively helped their fellow Arabs in Palestine to fight the Zionists. This meant financial and propagandist assistance, the organization of anti-Zionist petitions and demonstrations, sending armed bands to Palestine, and providing a haven for Palestinians who fled to Syria. Even more significant was the fact that Faysal's sponsored representative assembly, or the 'Syrian Congress', which claimed to represent the Arab population of 'Greater Syria' (including Palestine and Lebanon) expressed anti-Zionist positions that contradicted the Faysal–Weizmann agreement. At its first meeting on 1 July 1919, demanding the complete independence of Greater Syria, the Congress repudiated the Zionist claim in Palestine as well as the Balfour Declaration.[5]

The nationalist parties which controlled the Syrian Congress, notably *al-Fatat*, as well as Palestinians who served in the Syrian government, were also highly critical of Faysal's relations with the Zionist movement and exercised pressure on him to back out of his commitments to the Zionist Jews (although they indicated their willingness to accept non-Zionist Jews as equal citizens in the Syrian Arab state).

Partly under this pressure, Faysal, following his agreement with Weizmann, displayed a cooler and more reserved attitude towards the Zionist leaders and their requests. On several occasions he stressed that Palestine was an integral part of (Greater) Syria and warned against the establishment of a Jewish state in Palestine lest it provoke an Arab–Jewish conflict.

Further, even without pressure from his militant nationalist comrades, Faysal had added a reservation to his agreement with Weizmann, as follows:

If the Arabs attain their independence as we demanded in our memorandum dated 4 January 1919 addressed to the British Foreign Office, I shall approve of the articles contained in this [document]. If the slightest change or adjustment is made I shall not be bound by a single word in this contract, which will be null and void and of no account and no validity, and I shall not be answerable in any way.[6]

To be sure, although he might have felt a personal affinity with the Jewish people, Faysal agreed to sign this extraordinary document essentially out of political calculation and interest. Apparently he believed that the Zionists, in addition to representing a potential economic asset to Syria, possessed great influence with the world's major power, Great Britain (from whom they had already gained the Balfour Declaration). Since the Zionist movement also carried some weight in the United States (which was involved in the post-war peace conference), it could, in Faysal's thinking, help him achieve his grand aim, namely, Arab independence under his leadership, backed by Britain and recognized by the international community. To realize this goal and to nullify France's claim to control Syria, Faysal conditionally agreed to the creation of the Jewish national home in Palestine (as a separate entity or, according to another version, as part of his Syrian dominion). But as his ambitions did not materialize, and he was ousted from Syria by the French army in July 1920, Faysal subsequently denied that he had signed any agreement with Weizmann.

The Mandatory Period

This ambivalent connection between Faysal and the Syrian nationalists on the one hand, and Weizmann and the Zionist Jews on the other, may indicate the complex pattern of relations which developed between these two nationalist movements in the subsequent decades.

As far as the Syrian Arab nationalist movement is concerned, it identified ideologically with the struggle of the Palestinian Arabs against the Zionist movement; and as a pan-Arab movement it also regarded Palestine as part of 'Greater Syria'. However, the policies and actions pursued by the different factions of Syrian Arab nationalists towards the Zionists in Palestine during the 1920s and 1930s did not reflect, in many cases, this official ideology. These policies and actions were mostly pragmatic and certainly more moderate than those of the Palestinian Arab leadership. Indeed, the attitudes of the Syrian nationalists towards the Zionist–Palestinian conflict were partly, or largely, determined by a variety of other factors, namely, the interplay between pan-Arab and local Syrian nationalism, relations with the regional powers, France and Britain, and personal and factional rivalries, as well as economic and financial considerations.

The most moderate positions towards the Zionist movement were again adopted by Syrian leaders who had been associated with Faysal and were pro-Hashemite and pro-British. Partly operating outside Syria, after Faysal's defeat, several of these politicians belonged to the 'Party of Syrian

Unity' and the 'Syrian Palestinian Congress', both established in Cairo, in 1918 and 1920, respectively. In talks held in 1921 and 1922 with Zionist representatives in Cairo and London, these Syrian leaders, including Ishan Bey al-Jabiri and Riad al-Sulh (from Lebanon), were prepared to recognize the national rights of the Jews in Palestine, even in the form of a national home. They also undertook to try and convince Palestinian nationalists to reach a political settlement with the Zionist movement (but provoked angry reactions from the Palestinians). In return, these Syrian leaders requested Jewish help in achieving—with British help—independence and unity for the Arab countries, while preventing France from officially obtaining a mandate over Syria.[7] However, the draft agreement between the Syrian and Zionist parties was not implemented, owing, *inter alia*, to the inability of either party to fulfil its side of the deal.

Less than a decade later, in 1929 and 1931, Faysal himself, then the King of Iraq, again suggested a settlement for the Zionist–Palestinian conflict, by granting the Jews a restricted form of national home in Palestine within a larger Arab unity, namely, the 'Fertile Crescent' union (comprising Iraq, Syria, Lebanon, Transjordan, and Palestine) under his personal monarchal rule.[8] Apparently Faysal believed that by making these concessions to the Jews in Palestine, he could win British support for his 'Fertile Crescent' plan, which, in turn, was to be accepted by the nationalist movement in Syria and Palestine for the sake of Arab unity. Faysal was wrong. Apart from the British government, which did not welcome his plan, many Arab nationalists in Syria and in Palestine, in any case rejecting the idea of a monarchal regime, strongly resented the notion of a national home for the Jews in Palestine.

Faysal's failure did not discourage his brother, Abdallah, the Amir (later King) of Transjordan from trying in the late 1930s to unify under his crown 'Greater Syria' (consisting of Syria, Palestine, Lebanon, and Transjordan). In a series of talks, he offered Zionist representatives autonomous Jewish regions within a 'Greater Syria' unity, with rights of unlimited immigration to, and land purchase in, Palestine. To be sure, Abdallah's propositions were not only directed towards winning the co-operation of the powerful Zionist movement, but, more important, towards obtaining through the Zionists Great Britain's vital backing for his plan. But, like Faysal's 'Fertile Crescent,' the 'Greater Syria' scheme was not implemented, mainly because of strong British reservations as well as extensive opposition in Syria to Abdallah's design.[9]

It should be noted at this point that apart from the co-operation of the moderate Nashashibi faction in Palestine, Abdallah also enjoyed the support of the prominent Syrian nationalist leader Abd al-Rahman Shahabandar, who founded the 'People's Party', subsequently rebelled against the French in 1925–7, and was exiled by them. (Other Abdallah supporters in Syria were Alawites, Druze, and also Faris al-Khuri, who in 1928, together with other Syrian nationalists, formed the 'National Bloc' (*al-Kutla al-Wataniyya*) and later became Speaker of the Syrian parliament.)

Like other moderate Syrian nationalists, during the mid- and late 1930s Dr Shahabandar conducted talks with Zionist representatives regarding a peaceful settlement of the Jewish–Palestinian conflict and the integration of Palestine within a larger (Hashemite-led) Arab Federation. Dr Shahabandar, however, did not muster many followers in Syria for his pro-Hashemite orientation and certainly not for his pragmatic attitude towards the Zionists. Indeed, even had he reached an agreement with the Zionist movement (which he did not), he almost certainly would not have been able to win much approval from the majority of Syrian nationalists, who were then more anti-Zionist than anti-Hashemite.

Still, despite the anti-Zionist feelings of most Syrians, during the 1920s the Syrian nationalists' support of the Palestinian struggle against the Zionists was insignificant; it was verbal and vocal, more than material. The nationalist press periodically criticized Zionist activities in Palestine, and a few public demonstrations were held in Syrian towns in response to critical developments in Palestine. The largest popular manifestation of Syrian backing for the Palestinian cause appeared during the 1929 (Wailing Wall) Arab–Jewish strife in Jerusalem. But even then only several commercial strikes and public demonstrations erupted in Syrian cities as an expression of solidarity with the Palestinian Arabs.[10]

The reasons for this limited Syrian help for the Palestinians were not only related to the constraints imposed by the new international boundaries which separated Syria and Palestine. More important, the Syrian nationalists were engaged at that time in a crucial struggle for independence against the French mandate. In particular the 1925–7 Syrian revolt against the French absorbed the attention and energy of the Syrian nationalists (who as a matter of fact received help during those years from their Palestinian fellow nationalists, in the form of moral and material support, and refuge for Syrian rebels).

Another relevant and highly significant reason for the relatively mild support extended by Syrian nationalists to their Palestinian comrades since the late 1920s was associated with the growing debate among the *Kutla* leaders regarding the equilibrium between their pan-Arab ideological commitments and their Syrian national interests. Interwoven in this debate was the growing dichotomy between the moderate veteran leaders and the militant young cadres of the Syrian nationalist movement. The moderate faction of the *Kutla*, headed by Jamil Mardam, assumed leadership of this bloc in 1928 and developed a 'Syria first' doctrine, that is, devoting its entire efforts to gaining independence for Syria, while deferring all other issues, including the Palestinian cause, which might disrupt these efforts. This doctrine entailed, on the one hand, a strategy of 'honorable co-operation' with the mandatory authorities in order to secure a political agreement with France and, on the other hand, an attempt to win the diplomatic support of Britain, the major power in the region, and a potential ally against the French mandate.

Accordingly, during the 1929 Arab–Jewish eruption in Palestine the *Kutla* leaders discouraged anti-British reactions among the Syrian public for fear of jeopardizing any future British support against France. Similarly, in the summer of 1931 these nationalist leaders deliberately avoided appearing at several large Syrian public rallies organized in solidarity with Palestine. Later on, in December, the *Kutla* also failed to send an official delegation to the Islamic Congress in Jerusalem convened to mobilize Islamic support for the Palestinian cause.[11]

However, towards the mid-1930s, *Kutla* leaders modified this cautious policy for a while and became more openly supportive of the Palestinian cause and hostile to the Zionist movement. The reasons for this new position were related to domestic calculations as well as to fresh developments in Palestine. To begin with, Jamil Mardam and his colleagues were disappointed with their futile negotiations with the French, which failed to produce the expected bilateral treaty in 1933. They thus had to raise pan-Arab issues, notably the Palestinian cause, in order to repair their damaged public image of collaborators with France and reinforce their wavering position as nationalist leaders who had not neglected their pan-Arab commitments. To be sure, Mardam's pragmatic Syrian-oriented policies were challenged during that period by the radical pan-Arab *Istiqlal* faction within the *Kutla* headed by Shukri al-Quwwatli, and by the newly created pan-Arab 'League of National Action' (which was also influenced by Quwwatli). These two groups, as well as various Islamic organizations, during the 1930s expressed *inter alia* the growing support of many Syrians, mostly young people, of the Palestinian struggle against the Zionist Jews. For the large waves of Jewish immigration to Palestine, coupled with the strengthening of the Jewish *Yishuv* (population or community) during that period, alarmed not only Palestinian Arabs. More and more Syrians had come to regard these developments not merely as a danger to Arab and Islamic Palestine, but also as a potential threat to pan-Arab unity as well as to the Syrian national economy.[12] Consequently, increasing numbers of Syrians became actively involved in the Palestinian struggle against the Zionists and the British, particularly during the Arab revolt in Palestine of 1936–9. Large demonstrations and strikes took place in Syrian towns in solidarity with Palestine, or 'Southern Syria'; money and jewellery were contributed and arms were smuggled to the Palestinian rebels. Hundreds of Syrians, among them several ex-military officers, infiltrated Palestine, participating in and leading armed operations against the British and the Jews. The most prominent Syrian military commander to participate in the Arab Revolt in Palestine was Fawzi al-Qawuqji, one of the heroes of the 1925 Syrian revolt and a former Syrian army officer. Coming from Iraq and recruiting hundreds of Syrians (and Iraqis), Qawuqji declared himself the 'commander-in-chief of the Arab Revolution in Southern Syria'. Other Syrian personalities who inspired or helped the Palestinian rebellion were Shaykh 'Izz al-Din al-Qassam, a Syrian Muslim fundamentalist who already in the early 1930s organized and in 1935 led a Palestinian armed band around Haifa, and Shaykh Muhammad al-Ashmar, another Syrian Muslim who commanded a Palestinian rebel group in the 1936–9 rebellion.[13]

Most, if not all, Syrian military, financial, and propaganda help for the Palestinian Arabs was co-ordinated by the 'Palestine Defence Committee' based in Damascus. In addition to organizing a Syrian boycott on Jewish products, in 1937 this committee sponsored a major pan-Arab Congress in Bludan (eastern Syria) which adopted extreme anti-Zionist resolutions, while taking further measures to help the Palestinians fight for their cause.[14]

To be sure, although this important Syrian committee was officially a non-governmental organ, it was in fact controlled and directed by Shukri al-Quwwatli and his pan-Arab *Istiqlal* faction within the Syrian *Kutla*. In addition to genuinely supporting the Palestinian cause, Quwwatli used the Palestinian issue to challenge Jamil Mardam's pragmatic leadership of this bloc.

In order to neutralize Quwwatli's challenge, and in reaction to the negative French position, Jamil Mardam had to demonstrate his interest in the Palestinian problem as well as to advance Syria's pan-Arab ties. Thus already in 1934 the *Kutla*, under Mardam's leadership, established the 'first significant propaganda organization in the Arab world, the National Bureau of Propaganda'. Headed by Fakhri al-Barudi, a member of the Quwwatli-led *Istiqlal* faction, this bureau devoted itself mainly to serving the Palestinian cause, particularly during the Arab revolt in Palestine. In addition, while trying to prevent Syrian landowners from selling their holdings to Jewish organizations, the *Kutla*, which then ran the Syrian government, in 1937 granted political asylum to many Palestinians who escaped from British-dominated Palestine and continued to conduct the rebellion from Damascus. Around the same time two prominent *Kutla* leaders, Lutfi al-Haffar and Nabih al-ʿAzma, as well as other party activists, participated (together with 400 Arab delegates, 160 of them from Syria) in the pan-Arab anti-Zionist Bludan Congress, and played a leading role in its organization and deliberations.

Nevertheless, alongside these pro-Palestinian and anti-Zionist actions, Jamil Mardam and the pragmatic *Kutla* leaders were careful not to support and encourage the Arab revolt in Palestine openly and officially; they also endeavoured to curtail Syrian help to the Palestinian rebels and to put a stop to anti-Jewish actions in Syrian towns. Apart from the heavy economic losses inflicted on Syrian merchants associated with the *Kutla* by the rebellion in Palestine (which was a most valuable export market for Syrian goods), the motives for Mardam's displeasure with the Palestinian revolt stemmed again from Syria's national interests. Mardam feared that the rebellion might jeopardize his negotiations for a bilateral treaty with France, and that Syria's support for the rebellion in Palestine might alienate Britain, which could be most helpful in promoting Syrian independence.

Thus not only did Premier Mardam accept certain British suggestions towards restraining the Palestinian Arab rebellion, but in October 1937, while in Paris, he publicly deplored the 'terrorism' going on in Palestine, adding that the Syrian government in concert with the French and British authorities 'was taking all steps to prevent arms smuggling and rebels into Palestine'.[15]

Moreover, this unique statement (reported only in the French-language paper in Damascus) which Mardam made despite the violent anti-Zionist feelings prevailing in Syria, had been preceded by several talks he had held during 1936–7 with Zionist leaders, including Chaim Weizmann, regarding Syrian–Zionist accord over the Palestine problem. Like Faysal in 1919, Jamil Mardam basically believed, in the mid-1930s, that Weizmann and the Zionist movement could facilitate Syria's negotiations with the newly elected French Socialist premier, Léon Blum, who was Jewish and pro-Zionist. As Weizmann reported to his colleagues, Jamil Mardam had offered 'to tell the Arabs in Palestine to lay off if we

would help them in Syria; the assumption being apparently that we had
Blum in our pockets'.[16] On another occasion Mardam reportedly told
Zionist officials that 'between the two nations, the Jewish and the
Arab . . . apart from friendship, there exist concrete interests that require
peaceful relations.'[17]

Mardam was not the only Syrian national leader to negotiate with the
Zionists in 1936–7. Most significantly, even the radical pan-Arab pro-
Palestinian leader, Shukri al-Quwwatli—who was greatly respected by
Palestinian nationalists for his deep commitment to 'the liberation of
Palestine from Zionist colonization'—even he, in his capacity as acting
president of the *Kutla*, held official talks with Zionist representatives in
the summer of 1936 at Bludan. In this meeting (as well as in other talks,
which included top Syrian and Zionist leaders) Quwwatli said to the
Zionist representatives: 'We sincerely wish that we may come to an
understanding with you on our own accord and not by means of cannon
and fire.'[18] He also suggested that the Zionist leaders 'help us in every way
to gain . . . independence . . . [and] if Syria were to get its independence
first then it could devote its attention to the question of Arab independence and an Arab–Jewish entente', provided the Zionist movement did
not intend 'to make of Palestine a Jewish National Home', to which 'we
are categorically opposed'. But if the idea is 'to make a Jewish National
Home in Palestine . . . then we are ready . . . to find a solution to the
mutual advantage of both parties.'[19]

Quwwatli, like Mardam, apparently believed that the Zionist movement could help Syria gain independence as a step towards pan-Arab
unity, and in return he was perhaps prepared to consider a Jewish national
entity in Palestine, within a larger Arab federation. In other words, even
the most pro-Palestinian Syrian leader, Shukri al-Quwwatli, was possibly
ready in 1936 to compromise his radical ideological principles regarding
Arab Palestine in order to advance Syrian and pan-Arab aspirations and
perhaps also his personal ambitions. Such an ambivalent position was also
evident where Quwwatli's personal economic interests were involved. For
example, in 1934 he invested much effort in attempting to prevent a large-
scale sale of Syrian-owned land near Tiberias to the 'Jewish National
Fund', in order to 'preserve the wealth of the country [Syria] in the hands
of her children', and block 'Zionist penetration into Syria'. Yet at the end
of 1935 Shukri al-Quwwatli himself visited Palestine to explore the possibility of establishing branches of his canning company and 'to win Jewish
clients'.[20]

Still, in the long run, Quwwatli remained basically committed to pan-Arabism and to the Palestinian cause, both out of ideological conviction and because of political considerations. Not only was he later actively involved in helping the Palestinian rebels, but in 1938 he resigned from Mardam's cabinet because he disagreed with the Syrian government's reticent policy toward the Palestinian revolt. Quwwatli took this step also because he wished to strengthen his credibility as a devout pan-Arab in the eyes of the young nationalists, the emerging new radical forces which at that juncture were threatening the traditional Syrian political leadership. Rather than allowing himself to be swept aside by these fresh forces—the militant *Istiqlalis* and the members of the 'League of National Action'—Quwwatli staked his political future on their support.

However, these Syrian pan-Arab radical groups, which had also formed the backbone of the 'Palestine Defence Committee', by late 1938 became more and more preoccupied with domestic Syrian politics rather than with the Palestinian revolt (despite the fact that early in 1938 Palestinian rebels who had fled to Damascus established there the 'Revolt (or *Jihad*) Central Committee' aiming at continuing the Arab struggle in Palestine— or 'Southern Syria', as they renamed it).[21] The Syrian committee's leader, Nabih al-ʿAzma, for example, reportedly diverted funds intended for Palestine to his radical Syrian comrades, to fight Mardam's government. Indeed, early in 1939, these Syrian radicals, through their mounting pressure, contributed to the collapse of Mardam's government as well as to the partial disintegration of the *Kutla*. And while the pro-Palestinian infrastructure in Syria totally collapsed by 1939—partly because of suppressive French measures, but mainly owing to the defeat of the Arab revolt in Palestine—Shukri al-Quwwatli became the new *Kutla* leader. His rival, Jamil Mardam, had been discredited because of the failure of his national policies, and the pro-Hashemite potential competitor, Abd al-Rahman Shahabandar, was assassinated in 1940.[22] Following the 1943 national election, Quwwatli became the first president of the newly emerging Syrian Republic, and was determined to renew his struggle against Jewish Zionist national aspirations in Palestine.

To sum up the relations between the Syrian Arab and the Jewish Zionist national movements, it would appear that some senior Syrian nationalist leaders shared a common position regarding the Zionist movement. Although ideologically they objected to the Zionist venture, and identified with the Palestinian Arabs' demands and aspirations, in practice these Syrian leaders were periodically ready to acknowledge Jewish national rights (or national home) in parts of Palestine, and negotiate Arab–Jewish accords with Zionist leaders.

Yet, it is evident that, just as in the case of the Faysal–Weizmann episode, Syrian nationalist leaders were not essentially keen to reach any accord with the Zionist movement as such, but only on condition that this would facilitate British (and French) support for Syrian independence. The Jewish Zionist leaders were likewise primarily interested in sustaining British backing for the Jewish national home in Palestine, but they sought agreements with Syrian Arab representatives (and it was mostly the Zionists who took the initiative) in order to overcome the resistance of the Palestinian Arabs to the Zionist venture. For as long as the process of Jewish immigration to, and settlement in, Palestine proceeded uninterruptedly, most Zionist leaders would not make any special effort to seek an accord with Palestinian, Syrian, or other Arab representatives. Only when the Zionists realized that the Palestinian Arab opposition to the Jewish national enterprise was violent and/or effective, and that a Zionist–Palestinian agreement was impossible to achieve, did they approach Syrian leaders. Aiming at outflanking Palestinian antagonism, and perhaps also at mitigating it, the Zionist leaders tried to enlist the help of non-Palestinian Arab leaders, notably Syrian Arab nationalists. With Syria being the hotbed and the major centre of the Arab nationalist movement, and Palestine being regarded as the southern part of Greater Syria, the Zionists assumed that an agreement with senior Arab leaders in Damascus would be effective and binding also vis-à-vis the Palestinian Arabs. In addition to financial and economic aid, the Zionists offered to help the Syrian nationalist leaders achieve their national goals (although it is doubtful whether the Zionist movement would have been able to deliver on such promises).

In return, the Zionist representatives insisted that Palestine should become a Jewish national home, or a political entity, whereas the Palestinian Arabs would be part of a larger Arab framework centred on Damascus.

To be sure, most Syrian nationalist leaders still regarded Palestine as 'Southern Syria', as is evident from the *Kutla*'s 1928 draft constitution, as well as from its position during the 1936–9 events in Palestine. (They rejected, for example, the 1937 recommendation of the Peel Commission to divide Palestine into Arab and Jewish Zones.) Yet, much as these leaders objected to the creation of a separate Palestinian entity, or state, they were even more strongly opposed to turning Palestine into a Jewish national home or state. They were possibly ready to accept, or tolerate, a limited form of Jewish autonomy, or self-rule, in a small part of Palestine, within a large federation, but they rejected the creation of a fully independent Jewish entity in Palestine without any restrictions on immigration and land purchases—issues which were non-negotiable demands of the Zionist movement. The Syrian leaders feared that such a Jewish entity in Palestine could become a serious obstacle or threat to Arab unity, as well as a potential danger to Syrian interests.[23] But even assuming that those veteran Syrian leaders were ready to accept a Jewish national entity in Palestine, they would have had either to obtain the consent of, or face a fierce resistance from, two important groups: the mainstream of the Palestinian Arab nationalist movement and the militant stance of Syrian pan-Arab nationalism.

As we know, both these groups denied Jewish national rights in Palestine and vehemently rejected any political settlement with the Zionists.[24] The Palestinian nationalists, led by the Mufti of Jerusalem, al-Hajj Amin al Husayni, had developed a strong sense of nationalism during the mandatory period and under no circumstances were they inclined to comply with any request or pressure by Syrian leaders regarding a Jewish national home in Palestine. Similarly, the radical pan-Arab nationalists in Syria (the *Istiqlal* faction), like their comrades in Palestine, uncompromisingly insisted that an Arab Palestine, and by no means a Jewish Palestine, should be part of an all-Arab unity. By the late 1930s these Syrian militants, young members of the *Istiqlal* faction of the *Kutla*, and of the League of National Action, had become the most powerful pressure group in Syrian politics and an important power-base for Shukri al-Quwwatli, the newly emerging leader of the Syrian Arab nationalist movement.

Thus it would seem that to the extent that a slight chance existed for a Syrian–Zionist accord over Palestine during the period of the French Mandate, it was totally eliminated at the end of the Mandate, when Syria became an independent republic in 1946, under the leadership of President Shukri al-Quwwatli, a prominent pan-Arab politician. If this was not enough to end the Syrian–Jewish dialogue, the Zionist movement, for the first time in 1942, officially stated its new goals, not only of pursuing free Jewish immigration to Palestine, but also of the establishment of a 'Jewish commonwealth' there. This resolution—the 'Biltmore programme'—was adopted under the impact of the annihilation of Jewish communities in Europe by Nazi Germany; and in the following years, the Jewish Zionist *Yishuv* in Palestine was indeed engaged in absorbing hundreds of thousands of Jewish refugees from Europe, as well as solidifying the infrastructure for the future state of Israel.

NOTES

1. For details of these meetings, as well as other Jewish–Arab dialogues before and after the First World War, see Y. Luntz, 'The Diplomatic Contacts between the Zionist Movement and the Arab Nationalist Movement' [Hebrew], *Hamizrah Hehadash*, 12 (1962), 212–29; N. J. Mandel, *The Arabs and Zionism before World War I* (Berkeley, 1976), 141 ff.
2. Luntz, 'Diplomatic Contacts', 219; F. Khouri, *The Arab–Israeli Dilemma* (Syracuse, NY, 1970), 9.
3. For texts of the Faysal–Weizmann Agreement, the Balfour Declaration, and the letter to Frankfurter, see W. Laqueur (ed.), *The Israel–Arab Reader* (London, 1968), 17–21.
4. Y. Porath, *The Emergence of the Palestinian Arab Nationalist Movement* (Hebrew; Tel Aviv, 1970), 62. Porath quotes various Arab and Jewish sources.
5. A. L. Tibawi, *A Modern History of Syria* (London, 1969), 197; G. Antonius, *The Arab Awakening* (London, 1961), 440–8, citing the text of the Congress declaration; P. S. Khoury, *Urban Notables and Arab Nationalism* (Cambridge, Mass., 1983), 84. See also memo by the Congress to the King–Crane Commission, 2 July 1919, in Laqueur, *Israel-Arab Reader*, 31–3; Khayriyya Qasmiyya, *al-Hukuma al-arabiyya fi Dimashq* (Cairo, 1971), 109 ff.; Walid al-Mu'alim, *Suriyya, 1918–1958* (Damascus, 1985), 6 (hereafter cited as al-Mu'alim); Amin Sa'id, *al-Thawra al-arabiyya al-kubra* (Cairo, 1934), 51 ff.
6. Tibawi, *A Modern History*, 291. For a slightly different and shorter version, see Laqueur, *Israel–Arab Reader*, 20. See also an interpretation by Ali Sultan, *Ta'rikh Suriyya 1918–1920* (Damascus, 1986), 72 ff., 201.
7. Porath, *Emergence*, 91–3.
8. On the subsequent formulation of this union, see M. Khadduri, 'The Scheme of Fertile Crescent Unity', in R. A. Frye (ed.), *The Near East and the Great Powers* (Cambridge, Mass., 1951), 137 ff.
9. On Abdallah's plans, see Y. Porath, *Bemivhan hama'ase hapoliti* (Jerusalem, 1985), 26 ff; see also *Al-Kitab al-Urduni al-Abyad* (Amman, 1947); on the Syrian reaction, see *Kalimat al-Suriyyin wa-al-Arab fi Mashri' Suriyya al-Kubra* (Damascus, 1947).
10. S. H. Longrigg, *Syria and Lebanon under French Mandate* (London, 1958), 184–6; P. S. Khoury, *Syria and the French Mandate* (Princeton, 1987), 538.
11. P. S. Khoury, 'Divided Loyalties? Syria and the Question of Palestine, 1919–1939', *Middle Eastern Studies*, 21 (1985), 326–7.
12. For details, see ibid. 329.
13. Ibid. 333. Y. Arnon-Ohana, *Falahim bamered ha'aravi be-Eretz Yisrael, 1936–1939* (Tel Aviv, 1978), 51; M. G. Fry and I. Rabinovich (eds.), *Despatches from Damascus* (Tel Aviv, 1985), 162, 172. For details on the role of Qawuqji, see

Khayriyya Qasmiyya (ed.), *Falastin fi mudakkirat Fawzi al-Qawuqji* (Beirut, 1975), *passim*.

14. See E. Kedourie, 'The Bludan Congress on Palestine, September 1937', *Middle Eastern Studies*, 17 (1981), 107; Fry and Rabinovich, *Despatches*, 189.
15. Khoury, 'Divided Loyalties?', 338–40.
16. N. Caplan, *Futile Diplomacy*, i (London, 1983), 49.
17. E. Sasson, *Baderech el hashalom* (Tel Aviv, 1978), 45; and cf. p. 130.
18. Khoury, *Syria*, 284; idem, 'Divided Loyalties?', 336–7.
19. Cited in Khoury, 'Divided Loyalties', 336–7; cf. Sasson, *Baderech*, 44.
20. Khoury, *Syria*, 449–50 and 284.
21. Y. Porath, *From Riots to Rebellion* (Hebrew; London, 1976), 174–5. On the revival of the 'South Syria' notion by the *Istiqlal* faction in Palestine, see also pp. 125 ff.
22. All these pragmatic leaders apparently tried in vain to recover their nationalist image by stating their opposition to the 'Jewish terror' in Palestine in 1939. See Sasson, *Baderech*, 167–8; cf. *Mudhakkirat al-za'im al-shahid al-duktur Abd al-Rahman Shahabandar* (Amman, [1947?]), 128–31.
23. Khoury, 'Divided Loyalties?', 328–9; cf. Luntz, 'Diplomatic Contacts', 226–7.
24. Porath, *Bemivhan*, 72.

2

The 1948 War, Armistice, and Peace Offers

THE 1948 WAR: BACKGROUND, MAJOR OPERATIONS, AND CONSEQUENCES

By the mid-1940s, then, the positions of both Syria and the Zionist movement had become crystallized and were highly antagonistic. The Jewish Zionist community in Palestine was determined to create its own state in part of Palestine and to secure American and British support for this policy. Zionist leaders also hoped to gain the backing of some Arab leaders, particularly King Abdallah of Transjordan, as well as prominent Egyptian personalities, like the prime minister, Ismail Sidqi.[1]

Syria, however, was excluded as a possible partner in Arab–Jewish understanding because of the anti-Zionist position of its outspoken pan-Arab and pro-Palestinian leader, al-Quwwatli (who had also acquired a record of association with Nazi Germany). True, in 1946 a few prominent Syrian figures such as Taj al-Din al-Hasani (a former president) and Husni Barazi (a former premier) advocated the establishment of a Jewish state in Palestine,[2] but those moderate leaders had lost their influence on Syrian politics, notably on policy concerning the Jewish *Yishuv*. Indeed, unlike the mandatory period, during the mid-1940s, the newly emerging Syrian Republic became the most anti-Zionist Arab state in the Arab East. The previous dichotomy between the pragmatic leadership and the radical nationalists regarding the Palestine question had now given place to a wide consensus, namely, an unequivocal commitment to fight the Zionist entity in Palestine. This ideological stance was no longer mitigated, as in the past, by nationalist leaders who possessed certain pragmatic interests, both domestic and external. On the contrary, such interests now converged with the ideological position of the government. For example, on the domestic scene the new Syrian regime was confronted with a series of critical political, social, and economic problems which threatened to shatter the stability and perhaps the very existence of the state. The most urgent of these issues were the centrifugal tendencies of the minorities, particularly the Druze and the Alawites; and the growing socio-economic gap between the old class of landlords, merchants, and industrialists and the lower classes of peasants and workers. In addition, the persistent drive of the new, modern middle class towards upward mobility contributed a threat to the old socio-political status quo which had been maintained by the current rulers of Syria, like Quwwatli and his associates.[3]

President Quwwatli, thus, while announcing Syria's intention to eliminate Zionism and rescue Palestine, apparently used the Palestinian–Zionist issue as an outlet for domestic pressures and as an instrument for strengthening his own political position. Interwoven with these considerations were the regional interests of the Quwwatli regime, which largely contributed to promoting its anti-Zionist, pro-Palestinian policies. Indeed, the new and fragile Syrian Republic was faced with the threat of a takeover by the neighbouring Hashemite regimes, notably Transjordan, which became an independent monarchy in 1946. Backed by a strong military force, King Abdallah was pressing for his Greater Syria scheme, primarily aimed against Damascus. Reportedly, at that juncture Abdallah also sought Zionist help in implementing the scheme.[4]

To counterbalance these pressures and defend itself from Hashemite ambitions, Syria badly needed the help of the other Arab states, particularly Egypt—the leading Arab country—and Saudi Arabia, the important Islamic and Arab factor. Syria thus enthusiastically adhered to the pan-Arab, anti-Zionist policies of the newly established Arab League (1945), which were largely formulated by Egypt and Saudi Arabia. Damascus strongly supported the Arab League-sponsored 'Supreme Arab Committee' for the Palestinians, and assumed a leading role (alongside Iraq) in a fierce opposition to any plan by the United Nations and other international organs to divide Palestine between Jews and Arabs. Syria was also the first Arab state to implement the Arab League's anti-Zionist policies, in addition to initiating its own militant measures against the Jewish *Yishuv*. For example, it was the first Arab country to enact and impose, in 1946, strict economic boycott laws against the Jewish *Yishuv* and to prevent Jewish immigrants from Europe (as well as local Jews) from travelling to Palestine via Syria. Damascus was also the first, in October 1947, to mobilize troops along the Palestine border, in accordance with the Arab League resolutions.[5]

Simultaneously, while public committees and the association for the 'Defence of Arab Palestine' were being formed in Damascus (and in other Arab capitals) and Jews were attacked and killed in Aleppo (and sub-

sequently also in Damascus),[6] late in 1947 the Syrian government started
to smuggle arms to the Palestinian Arabs, to deploy its troops in the
Golan, and to organize an irregular volunteer force for military intervention in Palestine.[7] Such actions were taken not only in order to help the
Palestinians against the Jewish *Yishuv*, but also to prevent the Transjordanian army from occupying Palestine, or part of it. Led by Fawzi al-
Qawuqji, the Syrian military commander who had operated in Palestine
during the 1936 Arab revolt, this force, the 'Liberation Army', was composed of Syrians, Palestinians, Lebanese, and Iraqis, trained by Syrian
officers and equipped in Syrian army bases. Damascus in fact became, late
in 1947, the headquarters of the Arab League's 'military committee',
which supervised the Arab states' preparation of irregular military forces
in order to prevent the creation of the Jewish state in Palestine recommended by the United Nations partition resolution of 29 November
1947.[8]

Under the *de facto* direction of the Syrian government (nominally
under Arab League control), the Liberation Army, commanded by Syrian
regular army officers (including Adib Shishakli), moved into Palestine late
in 1947, and again early in 1948, with a public proclamation 'to nullify
the United Nations partition resolution, to eliminate any remains of
Zionism . . . and to secure the Arabness of Palestine'. Subsequently these
forces attacked Jewish *kibbutzim* in the north and centre of the country,
but were repelled.

To be sure, this irregular army was hastily organized and dispatched
by Syria not only to fight the Jews but at the same time to forestall
Transjordan's strong regular army and possibly also to prevent Palestinian forces from occupying parts of Palestine without co-ordination with
the 'military committee' controlled by Syria. (Qawuqji is even said to have
suggested collaborating with the Jewish Haganah against the Palestinian
forces led by the Jerusalem Mufti and supreme Palestinian leader, al-Hajj
Amin al-Husayni.)[9]

However, the failure of the Syrian-sponsored irregular Liberation
Army in Palestine (although it helped, in early May 1948, to defend Arab
regions near Jerusalem) paved the way for the invasion of Palestine by five
regular armies on 15 May 1948. The invasion resulted *inter alia* in the
occupation of parts of Arab Palestine by the Transjordanian army, a gain
which Syria had greatly endeavoured to prevent. This surely represented
a setback to Syria's war efforts, to its political prestige, and to its aspirations to prevent the creation of a Jewish state. As a matter of fact, the
regular Syrian army which invaded Palestine—some 3,000 troops—was

itself not well prepared for the war, partly because of bad organization and intelligence, and partly owing to deficiencies in both the quantity and quality of its weapons. A significant amount of supplies had been transferred to the Liberation Army, while some of the remaining arms were allegedly defective.[10] Consequently the major Syrian offensive against a Jewish border area south of Lake Tiberias (Zemach village and the *kibbutzim* Degania A and B) was repulsed in May 1948 by the Jewish defenders, who were very poorly equipped; but the Syrian army was subsequently able (in June 1948) to occupy another strategic border area north of that lake (Kibbutz Mishmar Hayarden) and repel Israeli counter-attacks. It also assumed control over a strip of land east of the lake which had been allocated to Israel in the 1947 UN resolution.[11]

Apart from these two operations, the Syrian army remained by and large inactive during the 1948 war and essentially entrusted the irregular Liberation Army with the task of carrying on its attacks on Jewish villages in Galilee (until late 1948, when this irregular force was defeated). The static posture of the Syrian army during the war can be attributed partly to its severe shortage of arms and ammunition, and partly to the government's fear that further Syrian attacks could provoke fierce Israeli retaliation against Damascus, and thus undermine Quwwatli's regime. Syria was afraid to be exposed alone to an Israeli threat since it could not rely on military support from other Arab armies: the Egyptian army was too far away, the Lebanese army was much too weak, the Iraqi army was not dependable because of Baghdad's Hashemite regime, while the Transjordanian army continued to be suspected of collaborating with Israel.

Nevertheless, the Syrian government, despite its military passivity, demonstrated a tough diplomatic position towards Israel. For example, it objected to arranging a truce, and for a long time refused to sign an armistice agreement with the new Jewish state.[12] Again, the Syrian prime minister declared on 27 December 1948 that Syria would continue to give priority to the liberation of Palestine and would refuse to recognize the 1947 partition resolution as well as the Jewish state.[13] To be sure, these militant expressions were essentially geared to secure the survival of the Syrian regime, which had by then become rather vulnerable.

Indeed, this parliamentary regime, initially headed by President Quwwatli and Prime Minister Mardam, was subjected to severe public criticism for the negligence and corruption in which it had been involved during war preparations against Israel, including the case of Captain Fuad Mardam, a nephew of the prime minister, who had allegedly allowed a Czechoslovak arms consignment shipped from Italy to be intercepted by

Israel.[14] To cover up such misdeeds, as well as to obscure the initial failure of the Syrian army in the 1948 war, these veteran Syrian leaders made fiery speeches and adopted militant positions against Israel and in support of the Palestinian Arabs.

In addition, in late May 1948, Mardam made sweeping changes in the military command and the Defence Ministry, personally assuming the portfolio of defence minister and replacing the chief of staff by Colonel Husni Za'im, who had led the Syrian attack south of Lake Tiberias. When all these measures and gestures failed to calm the angry mobs (who, for instance, fiercely demonstrated against the government and attacked Jewish synagogues during 1948), Mardam resigned in December 1948.[15] Subsequent attempts by President Quwwatli to stabilize his regime totally failed. Colonel Husni Za'im, indignant at public accusations that the army had performed badly in the war, seized power on 30 March 1949 in a bloodless military coup which signified for the first time the army's intervention in Syrian national politics, notably on the issue of the conflict with Israel.

SYRIAN PEACE OFFERS TO ISRAEL?

The Israeli issue indeed played a major role in the agenda of the new military leaders, notably Colonels Husni Za'im and Adib Shishakli, who ruled Syria almost successively from 1949 to 1954. Significantly, each of these two dictators adopted pragmatic attitudes towards Israel and sought to conclude political agreements with the new Jewish state rather than to fight it. During the armistice negotiations in the spring of 1949, Za'im surprisingly suggested that instead of an armistice agreement, Syria should sign a full peace treaty with Israel which would include open borders and an immediate exchange of ambassadors, as well as economic and military co-operation. Furthermore, he also offered to settle between 250,000 and 300,000 Palestinian refugees in the Jazira region of Syria as part of the peace agreement, but insisted that Israel should make territorial concessions and that he and Ben Gurion, Israel's prime minister, should meet to discuss the peace agreement. But Ben Gurion refused to meet Za'im as long as Syria would not make a commitment to evacuate the territories it had occupied during the 1948 war and return to the international border.[16]

Consequently, no peace treaty was concluded between Syria and Israel, but an armistice agreement only was signed on 20 July 1949 between the two parties. On 14 August 1949 Colonel Zaʿim was overthrown by Colonel Sami Hinnawi, who in turn was toppled by Colonel Adib Shishakli in December 1949. Shishakli, who held the reins of power in Syria until February 1954, also offered, early in 1952, to sign a 'peace agreement' with Israel, which in fact meant a non-belligerency agreement, devoid of diplomatic and economic relations. Shishakli and his chief ally, Fawzi Silu, were also willing to absorb about half a million Palestinian refugees in the framework of this agreement, but insisted, like Zaʿim, that Israel should concede to Syria half of Lake Tiberias as well as some other small areas. However, Israel's prime minister, David Ben Gurion, refused to make any territorial concessions to Syria in return for a non-aggression agreement, and apparently not even in return for a full peace treaty. Hence the 1949 armistice agreement remained the legal basis for Syrian–Israeli relations. But as this agreement was ambiguous in certain respects, it could not prevent the violent disputes and clashes which erupted periodically along the armistice lines from the early 1950s, becoming a zero-sum struggle in 1953–4 and culminating in the June 1967 war.

Following this brief outline, it is interesting to examine the various causes and circumstances which led Zaʿim and Shishakli, the authoritarian leaders of this anti-Israeli nation, to make their peace offers to the new Jewish state. Were these offers credible and viable in the face of the popular ideological rejection of Israel? Or were they tactical moves, aimed at gaining time and strategic positions for a renewed military offensive against Israel?

Similarly, it is highly significant to enquire why Ben Gurion rejected these peace offers, despite the more conciliatory attitudes of Foreign Minister Moshe Sharett and his aides. Did Ben Gurion let slip these rare opportunities to make a deal with Syria, or did he have a more realistic approach than Sharett regarding Syrian–Israeli relations?

Starting with Zaʿim's bold peace offer, it would be useful first to identify his motives. Husni Zaʿim was a professional French-trained soldier of Kurdish origin, who apparently did not harbour any ideological commitment to pan-Arab nationalism. Rather, he aimed at establishing his personal rule in Damascus, while turning Syria into a cohesive nation-state and playing an independent role in Middle East politics. Zaʿim thus perceived his relations with Israel not in ideological terms but within the sphere of regional power politics. Being aware of Israel's military strength, he initially (unsuccessfully) sought to conclude a military pact with Iraq in

order to defend Syria's borders against 'Zionist aggression',[17] but subsequently he strengthened his ties with Egypt and Saudi Arabia, to counterbalance the potential threat from Iraq (and Jordan).[18]

Za'im's peace offer to Israel was thus possibly aimed at neutralizing
its military threat, gaining strategic assets along the Syrian–Israeli border,
and perhaps also using Israel to counterbalance Iraq. No less important
was Za'im's aspiration to win American political, military, and economic
help in his attempts to consolidate his control in Syria and reform its
socio-economic conditions. Za'im was said to have staged his coup with
American co-operation and presumably wished to cultivate further
United States support by suggesting a peace agreement with Israel.[19]

In addition to his strategic considerations, Za'im was apparently also
motivated by personal greed. For example, in his plans to settle Palestinian refugees in Syria with American financial assistance, Za'im allegedly
intended to put some of the money in his private pocket. (He also had a
record of embezzling money during the French era.[20]) Similarly, during
the 1948 war Za'im reportedly secretly asked Israel for one million dollars
to help him topple the Syrian government, put an end to the war and
bring about a change in Syria's policy towards Israel.[21]

The latter episode may partly explain why Ben Gurion rejected Za'im's
peace proposal as well as his offer to meet him personally. Ben Gurion
was possibly aware of Za'im's shady reputation as an adventurer, 'money
embezzler . . . opportunist, and megalomaniac, emotionally somewhat
unstable and easily inflamed';[22] and he doubted whether Za'im really
represented Syria. Another partial explanation for Ben Gurion's refusal to
meet Za'im is that the American State Department objected to such a
meeting and suggested that Syrian–Israeli negotiations be conducted only
at the Lausanne peace conference (1949).[23]

Furthermore and more crucial, the concessions that Za'im requested
from Israel in lieu of a peace treaty (*inter alia* in order to justify this
proposal in Syria itself) were presumably too high a price to pay for a
dubious agreement: Za'im demanded that Israel give up important strategic areas in Lake Tiberias and the Hula valley as well as in al-Hamma—
all of which the 1947 United Nations resolution had assigned to Israel.
Ben Gurion insisted that Syria must first sign an armistice agreement on
the basis of the existing international border and withdraw its forces from
the areas it had occupied within the Israeli side of this border; only then
would he agree to meet Za'im personally and discuss a peace agreement
between Israel and Syria. As Ben Gurion told an American journalist in
reaction to Za'im's peace offer: 'Although I am prepared to get up in the

middle of the night and sign a peace agreement, I am not in a hurry and I am prepared to wait ten years. We are under no pressure to do anything.'[24]

Ben Gurion's negative reaction to Zaʿim's offer has led a few Israeli 'new historians' to conclude that in 1949 Israel missed a chance for peace with Syria. In particular, Dr Shlaim has criticized Israel's reaction as a 'short-sighted' policy which 'maintained that time was on Israel's side and that Israel could manage perfectly well without peace with the Arab states and without a solution to the Palestinian refugee problem'; and that Israel's negative response to Zaʿim's offer 'was characteristic of Ben Gurion's general preference for force over diplomacy as a means of resolving disputes between Israel and the Arabs'.[25]

It is indeed true that Ben Gurion believed in the importance of power in determining Israeli–Arab relations and possibly also reshaping the Middle East. Thus, for example, following Israel's victory in the 1948 war, Ben Gurion wrote in his diary in a state of some exhilaration: 'when we have broken the force of the Arab Legion we shall annihilate Transjordan and then Syria will fall.' And at a meeting held on 12 April 1949 at the Ministry of Foreign Affairs, he said: 'In order to make peace with the Arabs, it is necessary that they should have the sense that we have power. This would influence them to establish peaceful relations with us.'[26] Subsequently, during the Syrian–Israeli armistice negotiations, Ben Gurion considered launching a military operation to 'expel the Syrians' from the territories they had occupied during the 1948 war; and in fact some military action was taken by Israel during the negotiations in order to substantiate its political claims.[27]

Apart from United Nations and United States senior officials, high-level Israeli diplomats, such as Moshe Sharett and the Israeli ambassador to the United Nations, Abba Eban, expressed themselves with some reserve regarding Ben Gurion's refusal to meet Zaʿim, but neither of them would (or could), at that juncture, oppose Ben Gurion's line.[28] Only Elias Sasson, the Syrian-born Israeli Arabist and diplomat, was unequivocally opposed to the policy of using military force rather than diplomacy in settling the conflict with the Arabs. Already in late 1948 he declared that Israel should choose between two options—either living by the sword as a state in conflict with its Arab neighbours, or attempting to integrate into the region. Sasson certainly advocated the latter alternative, which would entail making territorial compromises. Apparently he continued to adhere to this line during the negotiations with Syria in June 1949,[29] but was unable to change Ben Gurion's attitude.

Upon examining Ben Gurion's position it seems possible that his refusal to meet Zaʿim and negotiate a peace treaty with him did not stem
merely from his concept of power politics vis-à-vis the Arabs. Rather it
might have reflected his long-term strategic thinking and his deep convictions concerning Israeli–Syrian relations. In other words: Ben Gurion was
not prepared to make important strategic concessions to Syria in return
for a formal peace treaty signed by an unpredictable and corrupt Syrian
dictator, who might not be willing or able to fulfil Syria's peace commitments to Israel in the future. Zaʿim himself was a member of a small
minority group, opposed by the mainstream of the Syrian Arab nationalist
community, which remained hostile to Israel.[30] Ben Gurion's calculation,
if indeed he made it in these terms, proved correct. On 14 August 1949
Zaʿim was overthrown and executed in a military coup led by Colonel
Sami Hinnawi; being pro-Iraqi and anti-Israeli, the new regime worked
towards a union with Iraq, *inter alia* in order to face the 'Zionist menace'
and 'liberate Palestine'.[31]

Nevertheless, one cannot help questioning Ben Gurion's outright rejection of Zaʿim's bold offer; at the least it might perhaps have been worth
his while to meet Zaʿim and examine his proposal. For not only was Zaʿim
himself devoid of anti-Israeli ideology, he had also appointed as prime
minister and foreign minister Muhsin Barazi, another Syrian Kurd who
also upheld a pragmatic position towards the Israeli–Palestinian question.
Moreover, at that juncture, not a few Syrian Arab officers and politicians
had negotiated an armistice agreement with Israel in a flexible and constructive manner.[32] Even the senior Arab nationalist leader, Khalid al-
ʿAzm, was ready to negotiate with Israel in spring 1949, while serving as
prime minister, after other Arab states had signed agreements with Israel
and Syria was left confronting it alone. Al-ʿAzm claimed then that 'Syria
by herself and even with her sisters, will be unable to rescue Palestine.
Moreover, Syria will even be unable to defend her own lands if the Zionist
forces should attack her.'[33]

It is noteworthy that even those Syrian officers and politicians who
toppled Zaʿim did not censure him for his readiness to sign a peace treaty
with Israel, or for his approval of the armistice agreement with the Jewish
state (although he was accused of many other 'crimes'). This was so
because the Syrian leaders, in the period after the 1948 war, realized that
the new Jewish state was militarily powerful and thus could endanger
Syrian security as well as their own rule. In order to contain this potential
danger and consolidate their control while tackling their severe domestic

problems, they had to reach at least an armistice agreement, which was positively accepted by the Syrian public as an Arab achievement.[34]

The other Syrian options would have been to continue the state of war with Israel or to sign a full peace treaty. Obviously Syria was then unable to face Israel single-handedly and needed the military support of either the Hashemite states—Jordan and/or Iraq—or Egypt. But, whereas Egypt had been badly defeated by Israel in 1948 and was still militarily weak (and geographically remote), Jordan and Iraq—each possessing a strong army—still harboured ambitions to dominate Syria—within their respective schemes of Greater Syria and the Fertile Crescent. Relying on the military help of either of these Hashemite states might have led Syria to lose its independence.

The other alternative—full peace with Israel—could have been pursued only by a Syrian dictator, such as Za'im, who was not ideologically committed to Arabism and anti-Zionism, and was courageous enough to disregard the Arab nationalist sentiments of his fellow countrymen. Za'im was willing to take such a far-reaching step only if he could be assured of strategic territorial (and economic) gains along the Israeli border, notably half of Lake Tiberias. Such gains might also justify a peace treaty with Israel in the eyes of his domestic nationalist opposition.

Israel, for its part, was not prepared at that point to make such strategic concessions, even for peace with Syria, which did not seem to be a real and viable option. Ben Gurion and other Israeli leaders did not view peaceful relations with Syria as a vehicle for integration in the region and/or for assuming a role in inter-Arab rivalry, for example by siding with Za'im against Hashemite attempts to 'swallow Syria'.[35] Ben Gurion was concerned about the deep Arab hostility to Israel and was reluctant to make any concessions lest these should be interpreted as Israeli weakness and invite further Arab demands to cede more territory and accept Palestinian refugees. Ben Gurion was rather satisfied with the armistice agreement with Syria (and with other Arab states) and did not consider peace as a high priority. More important for him was absorbing the new Jewish immigrants and moulding a cohesive nation-state.

In sum, the wide gap in the positions of Ben Gurion and Za'im constituted the major obstacle to a political settlement between Damascus and Jerusalem after the end of the 1948 war. Both parties were contented with an armistice agreement, which was concluded about a month before Za'im's downfall, following similar agreements between Egypt, Lebanon, Jordan, and Israel. And although future peaceful relations between Israel and Syria were anticipated in this agreement, in fact it was not able to prevent violent disputes and clashes between the two adversaries, during the period of Shishakli's rule and afterwards. Before discussing Shishakli's peace offer to Israel in 1952 and Ben Gurion's negative reaction, let us briefly consider that agreement and its initial repercussions.

TENSE ARMISTICE AND BORDER DISPUTES

The Israeli–Syrian General Armistice Agreement was signed on 20 July 1949,[36] on the mutual understanding that it would 'facilitate the transition from the present truce to permanent peace in Palestine' (preamble):

The two parties have undertaken not to resort 'to military force in the settlement of the Palestine question' and agreed also that 'no aggressive action by the armed forces—land, sea or air—of either party shall be undertaken, planned or threatened, against the people or the armed forces of the other' (Article I) . . . 'No element of the land, sea or air, military or para-military forces of either party, including non-regular forces, shall commit any warlike or hostile act against the military or para-military forces of the other party, or against civilians in territory under the control of that party, or shall advance beyond or pass over for any purpose whatsoever the Armistice Demarcation Line . . .' (Article III) . . . 'The Armistice Demarcation Line shall follow a line midway between the existing truce lines . . . where the existing truce lines run along the international boundary between Syria and Palestine, the Armistice Demarcation Line shall follow that boundary line . . . where the Armistice Demarcation Line does not correspond to the international boundary between Syria and Palestine, the area between the Armistice Demarcation Line and the boundary, pending final territorial settlements between the parties, shall be established as a Demilitarized Zone from which the armed forces of both parties shall be totally excluded, and in which no activities by military or para-military forces shall be permitted. This provision applies to the Ein Gev and Dardara sectors which shall form part of the Demilitarized Zone' (Article V) . . . 'The execution of the provisions of this Agreement shall be supervised by a Mixed Armistice Commission . . . whose chairman shall be the United Nations Chief of Staff of the Truce Supervision Organization' (Article VII).

Thus the agreement. To quote Bar Ya'acov on the subject: 'Among the four Armistice Agreements between Israel and her neighboring Arab states, the Israeli–Syrian stands out as regards both the nature of the disputes relating to its implementation and the frequency of clashes between the armed forces of the parties.'[37]

Without going into the details of these disputes (which can be found in the studies of Bar Ya'acov, Khouri, and Shalev) it can be said that most of the disputes and armed clashes along the Syrian–Israeli line basically stemmed from the struggle between Syria and Israel for virtual control of the three Demilitarized Zones (as well as of the north-eastern bank of Lake Tiberias). From Israel's point of view, these zones were clearly situated within its sovereign territory as delimited by the United Nations partition resolution of 1947, and thus could be exploited for economic development and other civilian activities, without any restrictions. Syria, on the other hand, which had occupied these zones during the 1948 war and evacuated them under the 1949 Armistice Agreement, not only denied Israel's sovereignty over these areas, but claimed a *locus standis* (or a recognized authority of intervention) in the Demilitarized Zone (DMZ). To all intents and purposes, Syria demanded a veto power on Israeli civilian activities in these areas, which, in its view, were likely to tip the local strategic balance in Israel's favour.

Initially, following the Armistice Agreement and until early 1951, Israel took steps to 'create facts', by means of *Nahal* units (farmer-soldiers). Syria, then too weak to resist these actions, lodged a complaint with the Mixed Armistice Commission (MAC) and moved soldiers, disguised as civilians, into other parts of the DMZ. It also virtually took control of the 10-metre-wide strip of the eastern shore of Lake Tiberias, which formally belonged to Israel.[38]

The Hula Conflict

But by early 1951, under the strong rule of Adib Shishakli, Syria decided not to tolerate any longer Israel's unilateral actions in the DMZ. Israel was then embarking on a big development project: the drainage of Lake Hula, designed to reclaim 15,000 acres for cultivation, and to eradicate malaria from the area. Although the lake itself was outside the DMZ, the first stage of this project involved work on a portion of Arab-owned land in the DMZ. Syria objected to the undertaking on the grounds that it would effect topographical change by obliterating a natural military obstacle, thus granting Israel a military advantage. In addition, Syria claimed that the Arab landowners strongly opposed the execution of the project on their lands and would not accept compensation.

Major-General Riley, chairman of the MAC, ruled that, in draining Lake Hula, 'the Israelis will not enjoy any military advantage, not equally applicable to the Syrians', and that Syria would also benefit, from a sanitary point of view, through the elimination of malaria in the area.[39] However, he also ordered that work should cease within the DMZ until Syria and Israel reached mutual agreement on compensation for the Arab-owned lands. Rather than settling this dispute by agreement, Israel adopted a 'brinkmanship policy' towards Syria and continued operations after a few days; Israeli workers were then fired at by local Arabs, apparently Syrian proxies or soldiers. The situation deterioriated further, with more exchanges of fire between the two parties, apparently adopting 'extreme positions'. Israel, in particular, 'hardened' its stance and late in March 1951 forcibly evacuated the inhabitants of two Arab villages in the DMZ.[40] A few days later, Israel, for the first time since the 1948 war, dispatched a patrol to al-Hamma village which was nominally under Israeli sovereignty but in fact under Syrian domination. The Syrian army shot and killed seven Israeli soldiers (formally policemen) of that patrol. And, although certain Israeli officials, notably Sharett, felt that the Israel Defence Forces (IDF) action had been 'a calculated provocation', Israel nevertheless reacted by bombing a Syrian military outpost and a police station near al-Hamma, as well as by destroying several Syrian villages inside the DMZ. Two women were killed and six men wounded in the air attack.[41]

Instead of acting as a deterrent, this massive Israeli retaliation provoked large-scale clamour for war in Syria and the Arab world. Although Shishakli might have opted to solve this conflict by diplomatic means, he was now forced to react against Israel on a military level. In early May 1951, his troops occupied Tall al-Mutilla, a strategic hill north of Lake Tiberias, one mile within the Israeli side of the border (i.e. not in the DMZ). Israel subsequently recaptured Tall al-Mutilla in a poorly executed attack, involving heavy losses: twenty-five killed and dozens wounded. This discomfiture painfully affected morale among Israeli troops for some time, while Israeli leaders, notably Ben Gurion, were more convinced than before that the conflict with Syria was a zero-sum struggle, and that Israel should unilaterally pursue its development projects without trying to secure Syrian consent. Israel consequently completed the Hula project, in accordance with the Security Council resolution, but did not use the disputed Arab lands in the DMZ.

SHISHAKLI'S POLICY TOWARDS ISRAEL

Despite these armed clashes, or perhaps because of them, a year later, in May 1952, Adib Shishakli made a peace offer to Israel which was influenced by, and contained, certain factors similar to those of Za'im's offer. Like Colonel Za'im, Colonel Shishakli, who seized power from Colonel Hinawwi on 19 December 1949, initially tried to consolidate his control in Damascus and contain the potential Israeli threat to his country and his rule. Indeed, having participated in the 1948 war as a deputy commander of the Liberation Army, Shishakli had experienced the defeat of his forces in Upper Galilee and was also aware of the poor performance of the Syrian regular army during that war. Since seizing power in Damascus, Shishakli consequently engaged in systematically building a modern army for Syria. He wanted his new army to help him turn Syria into a 'fortress of steel', a 'Prussia of the Arab states'. Yet he realized that a vital pre-requisite for achieving this goal was the elimination of sources of political instability and social friction, and the creation of a cohesive political community. He needed the army primarily to dismantle the centrifugal centres (notably the Druze) and to impose law and order, as well as to safeguard the socio-economic reforms that he introduced in Syria for the first time.

These were indeed Shishakli's first priorities, and consequently the conflict with Israel was relegated *de facto* to a secondary position, at least for the time being. Shishakli also realized at that juncture that apart from Israel's military superiority, Syria faced another serious constraint: the three powers—Britain, France, and the United States—in May 1950 issued a Tripartite Declaration opposing the use of force between any of the states in the area and making the supply of arms conditional on an undertaking of non-aggression. As a result, while for several months the Israeli–Palestinian issue was not widely discussed in the Syrian Parliament, the negotiations between Syrian and Israeli officers within the Armistice Commission were conducted in a pragmatic and constructive atmosphere and resulted in several minor agreements.[42]

In February 1951, prior to the armed clashes over the Hula works, Shishakli also initiated a compromise proposal regarding the DMZ and in late March even personally participated in direct negotiations with the Israeli deputy chief of staff, Mordechai Makleff.[43] Shishakli suggested dividing the DMZ between Syria and Israel along the River Jordan, and the eastern shores of Lakes Tiberias and Hula. Israel, however, rejected this proposal because it involved giving up lands west of the international boundary which were formally under Israel's sovereignty and vital to its national irrigation and development projects. Instead, Israel offered to expand the negotiations with Syria beyond the proposed changes in the Armistice Line, and discuss a peace treaty, or at least a non-aggression agreement which would include economic and political issues as well. The

Syrian negotiators did not accept Israel's peace offer, but made other suggestions along their previous lines.[44] Despite the essential disparity between the positions of the parties and the armed clashes that occurred periodically, both sides continued negotiations in ten more meetings, until May 1953. Although from time to time each side made fresh proposals and both parties arrived at certain understandings, the deliberations came to a halt without reaching any result.[45]

The failure of these negotiations, which were held on a senior military level outside the MAC deliberations, was apparently linked to and influenced by Shishakli's vain attempt, following his assumption of direct rule in Syria in late 1951, to negotiate a political agreement with Israel, by way of the United States. Even though, unlike Za'im, he was an Arab nationalist, Shishakli, like Za'im and like several other Syrian leaders, adopted a pro-Western, notably a pro-American orientation aimed at obtaining both American military equipment and economic assistance. Shishakli continued his search for financial aid, to carry out his ambitious socio-economic reforms, and for modern weapons, to safeguard his rule against domestic enemies, and to protect Syria against a possible Israeli attack.[46] In return for the required American help, Shishakli was prepared, like Za'im previously, to enter a Western alliance vis-à-vis the Soviet Union and also to make peace with Israel in accordance with the American demand. However, Shishakli and his chief associate, Fawzi Silu (defence minister and subsequently prime minister), in their talks with American (and French) diplomats, made it clear that by 'peace' with Israel they in fact meant a non-belligerency agreement which would not entail commercial (and political) relations, but would terminate the armed clashes along the border and contribute to removing the Israeli issue from the Syrian political agenda. Subsequently (in Silu's evaluation), with the continuous acknowledgement of Israel's existence, a peace treaty with Israel might be expected in the future, provided Israel could be persuaded to drop its 'provocative tactics'. The Syrian leader also said that, within the non-belligerency agreement, Syria would be willing to absorb about half a million (Palestinian) refugees from Jordan, Gaza, and Lebanon, in addition to the 80,000 refugees already living in Syria—on condition that Syria would receive $200 million for economic development.[47]

Alas, although the United States welcomed this Syrian initiative and was ready to deliver certain types of weapons to Syria, Shishakli's government did not sign any military or economic agreement with the Americans, mainly owing to intense domestic opposition by Syrian 'doctrinaire neutralists', such as Akram Hawrani and others, 'to whom any agreement with the West was a betrayal', since the West allegedly had created Israel and strengthened it.[48]

At the other end of the Syrian political spectrum, Dr Maʿruf al-Dawalibi, minister of national economy in the early 1950s, who unofficially represented the Muslim Brethren movement, vehemently rejected an alleged American attempt to bring about an Arab–Israeli peace. Such an agreement, he declared, would lead to 'Judaizing the rest of the sons of the Arab people [following the occupation of Palestine by the Jews] and the Arabs would a thousand times prefer to become a Soviet republic rather than become prey to the Jews'.[49] Dawalibi's position was widely reported also in the Beirut press and *Bayrut al-Masa* commented: 'We hate Russia, but we hate Zionism more.'[50]

MUTUAL PERCEPTIONS AND ATTITUDES

If this was the attitude of many Syrian politicians towards an agreement with the United States, which they considered to be under 'Jewish influence',[51] it is not surprising that Shishakli was not in a position to sign a full peace agreement with Israel, the arch-enemy of many Syrians and other Arabs. Indeed, various Syrian politicians (and certainly the Syrian media) continued to manifest—particularly during periods of armed clashes—sentiments of hatred and violence towards the Jewish state and the Jews. For example, senior Syrian leaders—including prime ministers—publicly attacked the 'wicked Jews', 'the selfishness and fanaticism of Jews, the enemies of the world', and promised 'to settle accounts with the Jews in due course'.[52] Even Adib Shishakli and Fawzi Silu, who were inclined to reach an agreement with Israel, had periodically to make anti-Jewish statements. Silu, for instance, said in July 1952: 'As the Jews misled their people as well as the world with their propaganda, it has become the duty of Syria, which is on the lookout for tyrannical Israeli ambitions, to expose Zionist deceit by all possible means.' A month later, Shishakli said, in a public speech:

Syria, always the leader of the Arab people, [should] impose her will and recover her rights by force [in Palestine]. The Middle East is not big enough to hold the Arabs and the Jews; either the Arabs would be fleeing back into the desert and the sea or the Jews would return to their homes in the various parts of the world.

This declaration followed an earlier statement by Shishakli that Syria's independence was threatened as long as Israel existed.[53] Certainly, these and previous hostile statements against Israel largely reflected the various historical, nationalist, and religious causes and motives for the intense Syrian (and Arab) animosity to Israel (which are fully discussed by Harkabi). Yet at this juncture it is important to point out also the deep sense of fear—justified or not—among many Syrians of what they considered Israeli aggression and expansionism since 1948. To quote British diplomatic reports from Damascus during the early 1950s: [There had been] 'an increasing fear of the growing power of Israel and the threat which that involves';[54] 'Syria's external affairs may be summed up as acute fear of Israel . . . Syrians are obsessed with the danger of Israeli expansion'; and, according to a senior Syrian leader: 'In the eyes of the Syrian people as a whole, Israeli aggression was Syria's danger No. 1.'[55]

To be sure, various Syrian leaders and parties cultivated and/or exploited the public's fear of Israel to sustain their positions and/or propagate their ideological and political orientations. The supporters of an Iraqi–Syrian merger, led by the 'People's Party', continued to argue that 'only such a union could make an effective stand against Israeli expansionism', whereas their rivals, leaders of the 'National Party' and other politicians, advocated the Egyptian-proposed Arab collective security pact and asked for Egyptian military assistance and Saudi financial help.[56]

These regional orientations were manifested for instance in 1951, when Israel unilaterally started work on the Hula project in the DMZ, which led to armed clashes with Syrian troops. Syrian pro-Iraqi politicians used those events to press again for a union with Iraq 'as a sole defence against Israel's menace'; and when the Israeli–Syrian clashes resumed during April–May 1951, Egypt pledged air support to Syria, while Iraq in fact sent troops and anti-aircraft batteries to help Syria 'against Zionist air aggression'.[57]

Apart from the Syrian leaders' exploitation of the alleged Israeli danger to advance their own agendas, Israel itself, both directly and indirectly, contributed to the intimidation of the Syrian population. Thus, the victory over several Arab states in the 1948 war, followed by the huge wave of immigration of about 700,000 Jews to Israel during 1949–52, alarmed many Syrians (as well as many other Arabs), lest Israel should further expand at their expense, allegedly 'from the Euphrates to the Nile'.[58]

Contemporary Israeli experts on Arab affairs in the Ministry of Foreign Affairs were aware of, and reported on, this Syrian fear of Israeli expansion, but had little impact on the government.[59] Indeed, Israeli leaders, notably Ben Gurion, hardly attempted to mitigate this Syrian Arab fear, but rather helped to substantiate it by both words and deeds. Thus, for example, in an interview with *Time* magazine of 16 August 1948, repeatedly quoted by Arab spokesmen, Ben Gurion said: 'I can quite imagine a Jewish state of ten million.' When asked if that many could be accommodated within the United Nations partition boundaries of Israel, Ben Gurion had replied, 'I doubt it . . . we would not have taken on this war merely for the purpose of enjoying this tiny state.'[60]

In 1952 Ben Gurion made a similar statement whose major part was subsequently cited by Arab writers: 'The State of Israel has been established only in part of Eretz Israel [Palestine] and even one who questions the existence of historical boundaries . . . cannot doubt that the state's borders are anomalous.' (Ben Gurion's statement, however, contained another part which was not cited by those Arab writers: 'But [concerning] these borders, Israel has committed itself in the Armistice Agreements with its neighbours to maintain these borders as long as it would not be attacked again, and Israel keeps its commitments.'[61]

Another relevant announcement by Ben Gurion, early in 1951, prompted a Syrian minister to voice his country's 'fear' of Israel 'in view of Mr. Ben Gurion's recent pronouncement that Israel could put 200,000 troops into the field'. The minister also declared that his fellow countrymen feared an Israeli military assault and added that in such a case Jewish influence in the United States and Britain could prevent those countries from implementing the Tripartite Declaration regarding the defence of Syria.[62] Although no major Israeli offensive against Syria was launched at that time, Israeli unilateral actions in the Hula region—including the deportation of local Arabs and building new Jewish villages in the DMZ, as well as armed clashes with Syrian troops—all these contributed to corroborating the aggressive and expansionist image of Israel in Syrian eyes. This image was further enhanced by Israel's harsh retaliatory actions against Jordan and Egypt, notably the Qibya raid in 1953 (see below).

The Syrian perceptions of Israel represented a mirror image of Israeli perceptions of Syria. Indeed, most Israeli Jews were obsessed with fear of Syrian (and pan-Arab) belligerency and its declared intention to destroy the Jewish state. For, in Syrian (and other Arabic) media and textbooks, as well as in public speeches by Syrian (and other Arab) leaders stringent anti-Israeli, anti-Zionist, and anti-Jewish expressions periodically figured, alongside calls to eliminate Israel by force.[63]

But apart from these written and oral utterances, which frightened many Israeli Jews, notably survivors of the Nazi Holocaust, Arab demands at the United Nations that Israel should allow the Palestinian refugees to return to their homes in Israel and that Israel should withdraw to the 1947 partition lines were interpreted by many Jews, and even by some Arab leaders, as a means 'to eliminate the State of Israel'.[64] Similarly, hostile actions against Israel, such as the all-Arab economic boycott, Egypt's blockage of Israeli ships in the Suez Canal and, frequently, of all naval traffic to Eilat through the Straits of Tiran—all such actions clearly signified Arab intentions to strangle Israel economically.[65]

Syria in particular had a large share in such anti-Israeli activities, becoming the headquarters of the Arab boycott against Israel, threatening Israeli irrigation and land reclamation projects, and killing Israeli soldiers in border incidents, as well as potentially being part of a larger and stronger Arab unity aimed at fighting Israel.[66] Thus, among the belligerent Arab states bordering Israel, Syria has been regarded by most Israeli Jews since 1948 as the most hostile and dangerous. Israeli perceptions of hostile Syrian intentions (as well as Syrian perceptions of Israel) are reflected in a Foreign Office research paper, written in late 1952:

Of all Arab states, Syria has always stood out in the first line in its attitude and action against Zionism and Israel. This extreme approach—which is not typical only of Shishakli's Syria, has stemmed from several basic reasons . . . Syria has been the cradle of the Arab nationalist movement . . . hence its Arab-racial and Muslim sensitivity and intense opposition to European colonization and to its extensions, either real or imaginary in the Arab and Islamic East . . . The ambition to implement the union of 'Natural Syria', is one of the most important causes for Syria's extreme attitude towards Israel . . . The Syrian nationalists are worried about a Christian–Jewish (and anti-Muslim) association [i.e. between Lebanon and Israel] . . . hence Syria's interest in the Galilee, and its ambition is to sever it from Israel . . . cutting off . . . the water sources in the north from Israel. Syrian politicians . . . believe that Israel will not be satisfied with its territory and present boundaries . . . the enhanced immigration to Israel . . . the economic difficulties and the scarcity of land and water sources . . . would prompt Israel in the not so far distant future to look for new living space. Its expansionist tendency would be northward . . . the fear of Israel in Syria is great and hence its extremism and the strong desire to harm Israel and hasten its defeat . . . Syria regards itself—and justly—as the only Arab country that had not been defeated in the war against Israel . . . Syria demands today . . . to divide the DMZ by . . . delimiting the Jordan, Lake Tiberias and the Hula as the border [and this would] give Syria an opportunity to intervene in Israel's water projects and disrupt [them] . . . The transfer of part of the territory of Mandatory Palestine to Syria would promote the prestige of the rulers and would help to strengthen their position in Syria . . . Shishakli's insecure position forces him to adopt extremism and to use many anti-Israeli slogans and threats . . . The chances for a real peace between Syria and Israel are very slim, for according to objective geographic factors, the very existence of Israel poses a security problem, and hurts Syrian national feelings and the chances for Arab unity.[67]

Conclusion

To sum up this discussion of mutual Syrian and Israeli perceptions and attitudes during the early 1950s, it is useful to begin by citing excerpts from a private conversation between Elias Sasson, an Israeli diplomat and Arabist, and Shukri al-Quwwatli, former (and future) Syrian president, which took place in Geneva in September 1951:

As to the existence of the State of Israel, in the middle of all this, El Kuwetli termed the fact as 'a bone which sticks in the throat'. He confessed to me quite spontaneously that he wishes there were no State of Israel. But since it is there . . . the existence of Israel [has] been necessary for the Arabs for more than one reason: it has roused up their patriotic feelings and has stimulated their nationalism even outside the frame of their animosity to Israel. Their united hatred and action against Israel has brought about a fusion of their divergences . . . He did not conceal that many . . . including himself—envisage the destruction of Israel . . . Objectively speaking, El Kuwetli added, Israel's fate . . . will not only depend on the Arabs but mainly on itself. If Israel succeeds in winning over the Arabs' confidence and in making them understand that its existence is necessary and useful for them, it can become a kind of Switzerland in the Orient . . . El Kuwetli himself . . . looks forward to the repetition of ancient history when the Jews were a small community gently serving the Arabs and getting along with them beautifully. Such an atmosphere could be restored . . . El Kuwetli said, with a weakened State of Israel living as a helpful community perhaps larger and more profitable than in ancient times. Israel could supply the Arab world with experts, technicians etc., El Kuwetli said.[68]

In contrast, Ben Gurion, as we know, had maintained that 'in order to make peace with the Arabs, it is necessary that they should have the sense that we have power', while General Moshe Dayan, the powerful chief of staff, reportedly said in April 1954: 'The Arabs were born blackmailers, and the more one conceded to them, the more they would demand. There is no hope of their giving anything in return.'[69]

It can thus be concluded that, despite Shishakli's pragmatic attitude towards Israel and Ben Gurion's declared desire to make peace with Syria, a Syrian–Israeli peace agreement could not have been achieved during the early 1950s. The traumatic experience of the 1948 war still lingered among both Israelis and Syrians, and was compounded by mutual fear, distrust, and prejudice. Whereas Israeli Jews felt threatened by Syrian (and inter-Arab) belligerency and the declared intention to eradicate Israel, Syrian Arabs were afraid of Israeli military aggression and territorial expansionism. Thus, on the Syrian side, the feelings of fear, enhanced by deep ideological and political antagonism to Zionism and Israel and by the all-Arab opposition to peace with Israel, greatly contributed to constraints on Shishakli from offering full peace (although he himself probably sought such a solution).[70]

Indeed, although he was a dictator, Shishakli was not strong enough to conclude a peace agreement with Israel. Instead, he suggested, in a series of secret negotiations, an alternative agreement involving territorial concessions from Israel which could improve Syria's strategic position vis-à-vis Israel and thus perhaps be accepted by the anti-Israeli Syrian public. It would seem that even his offer to sign a non-belligerency/non-aggression agreement with Israel was a bold step; for, despite the antagonistic attitudes at that time between Arab states and Israel, Shishakli was the only Arab leader who dared then to attempt to come to terms with Israel.[71] But, having failed to reach an understanding, he conversely used 'the threat from Israel, however real . . . [as] a powerful argument in support of . . . [his] military dictatorship'.[72]

Ben Gurion, on his part, was by no means willing to make any territorial concessions in the DMZ, which he considered to be under Israeli sovereignty, let alone give up half of Lake Tiberias and of Lake Hula as had reportedly been requested by Shishakli. He would not make even minor territorial concessions to Syria in return for peace, let alone for a non-aggression agreement which, he claimed, was already included in the Armistice Agreement.[73] However, a few Israeli officials held different views.

Apart from the United States, which favoured a new *modus vivendi* in the DMZ, Moshe Sharett argued that if Syria would be content with minor Israeli concessions, 'it would be worth while for us to pay this price in order to do away with the issue of the DMZ.'[74] In contrast to Ben Gurion, Sharett also observed that 'the Syrians endeavoured to solve the problem in a practical and simple way, while the Israelis complicated the matter with legislative pedantry.'[75] And when, in May 1953, Syrian–Israeli negotiations finally failed, Major-General Riley, chairman of the Mixed Armistice Commission (who was depicted by the Syrian press as pro-Jewish) criticized the Israeli delegation for that failure, while the

American minister in Damascus declared that the Israelis, not the Syrians, had ruined the negotiations. Even Brigadier (ret.) Shalev—who at that time represented Israel in the Israeli–Syrian MAC and who has recently published a comprehensive study of those negotiations—expresses some criticism of the Israeli position. While holding both Syria and Israel responsible for failing to reach an agreement, Shalev adds: 'It is a pity that an agreement was not achieved, which would have brought about a certain tranquillity along the border and perhaps also would have advanced relations between the two countries.'[76]

If there had indeed been some possibility under Shishakli's authoritarian rule of concluding a Syrian–Israel agreement, such an opportunity no longer existed under the short-lived new Syrian parliamentary regime. While the Ben Gurion–Dayan hard line towards Syria (and other Arab states) continued to predominate over Sharett's more flexible position, Syria's attitudes towards Israel became, after 1954, more militant, owing to significant domestic political changes, as well as to regional and global factors.

As will be discussed presently, these attitudes on both sides created a zero-sum conflict between Jerusalem and Damascus.

NOTES

1. Caplan, *Futile Diplomacy*, i. 142 ff.; A. Sela, 'The Question of Palestine in the Inter-Arab System', Ph.D. diss. (Hebrew University, Jerusalem, 1986), 302 ff. (hereafter cited as Sela).
2. Sela, 246; A. H. Podet, 'Husni Al-Barazi on Arab Nationalism in Palestine', in E. Kedourie and S. Haim (eds.), *Zionism and Arabism in Palestine and Israel* (London, 1982), 173–7.
3. On these issues, see my article 'Attempts at Creating a Political Community in Modern Syria', *Middle East Journal*, 22 (1972), 389–404; P. Seale, *The Struggle for Syria* (London, 1965), 24 ff. (hereafter cited as Seale, *Syria*).
4. Caplan, *Futile Diplomacy*, i. 145. See also Sasson, *Baderech*, 382.
5. For a detailed survey, see Sela, 228, 239, 325 ff., 369, 384 ff., 436 ff.
6. H. Cohen, *The Jews in the Middle Eastern Countries* (Hebrew; Jerusalem, 72), 50–1. Jews were attacked in Damascus in 1935, in 1948, and in 1949 because of the Zionist actions in Palestine.
7. At the same time, however, the government prevented other forces, such as Ba'th Party volunteers, from operating against the Jewish *Yishuv*. See *Nidal al-Shʿab*, i. *1943–1949* (Beirut, 1963), 221, 224, 227.

8. Sela, 362 ff., 421–4, 426. Cf. Great Britain, Public Record Office, FO 371/75527, Damascus, 31 Jan. 1949; see also T. Mayer, 'Arab Unity of Action and the Palestine Question, 1945–8', *Middle Eastern Studies*, 22 (1986), 331 ff.

9. Sela, 443, 472; for details regarding military activities see pp. 445 ff. It should be noted, however, that a prominent Palestinian leader asserted that Syria was the only Arab country which tried to rescue Palestine although it was not well prepared; see ʿArif al-ʿArif, *al-Nakbah* (Beirut, 1956), i. 339–40.

10. Seale, *Syria*, 33; G. H. Torrey, *Syrian Politics and the Military* (Columbus, Oh., 1964), 103 ff.; A. Sela, 'Syria and the Palestine Question' [Hebrew], *Maʿarachot* (July 1984), 46 ff.; Khalid al-ʿAzm, *Mudhakkirat* (Beirut, 1973), i. 278, 383 (hereafter cited as al-ʿAzm).

11. For details, see Ch. Herzog, *The Arab–Israeli Wars* (New York, 1982), 23 ff.; A. Nafuri, 'The Syrian Army in the 1948 War' [Hebrew translation], *Maʿarachot* (May–June 1981), 30–2.

12. On the armistice agreement and its repercussions, see N. Bar Yaʿacov, *The Israel–Syrian Armistice* (Jerusalem, 1967), 26 ff.

13. FO 371/75529, Damascus, 27 Dec. 1948. Cf. similar declaration in early 1948, Torrey, *Syrian Politics*, 104, quoting *The Times*, 12 Jan. 1948.

14. Seale, *Syria*, 33. Mardam was sentenced to death for allegedly selling those arms to Israel, but Israel sent a secret message to Syria denying any contact with Mardam. For further criticism see *Nidal al-Shʿab*, 278–9.

15. Al-Muʿalim, 89 ff.; FO 371/75528 Damascus, 17 Jan. 1949; cf. FO 371/121892 London, 28 Apr. 1956, citing a memo by the Anglo-Jewish association.

16. *Documents on the Foreign Policy of Israel*, iii, ed. Y. Rosenthal (Israel State Archives (ISA): Jerusalem, 1983), 581–2; full details in A. Shlaim, 'Husni Zaʿim and the Plan to Resettle Palestinian Refugees in Syria', *Journal of Palestine Studies*, 15 (1986), 68 ff.; I. Rabinovich, *The Road Not Taken* (Hebrew; Jerusalem, 1991); 59 ff.; A. Shalev, *Co-operation under the Shadow of Conflict* (Hebrew; Tel Aviv, 1989), 56 ff.

17. Al-Muʿalim, 108; al-ʿAzm, ii. 203; FO 371/82821, Damascus, 12 Jan. 1950; FO 371/75077, Damascus, 18 Jan. 1949.

18. However, Syrian sources claim that, when serving as chief of staff, Zaʿim had developed secret ties with King Abdallah regarding the 'Greater Syria' scheme; al-Muʿalim, 99.

19. Cf. M. Copeland, *The Game of Nations* (New York, 1969), 50; al-Muʿalim, 104; Rabinovich, *Road*, 72–9; al-ʿAzm, i. 375, 381.

20. Cf. al-Muʿalim, 98–9; al-ʿAzm, ii. 180; Shlaim, 'Husni Zaʿim', 69–70.

21. Shlaim, 'Husni Zaʿim', 69–72; Rabinovich, *Road*, 84–5.

22. Seale, *Syria*, 43–4; Shlaim, 'Husni Zaʿim', 69 and 79; Rabinovich, *Road*, 84, quoting ISA.

23. ISA, File 2447/5, 31 July 1949 (this reference has been given to the author by Dr Z. Shalom of the Ben Gurion Research Centre at the Ben Gurion University).

24. Ben Gurion's diary for 18 July 1949 quoted in Shlaim, 'Husni Zaʿim', 77.

25. Ibid. 78–9; see also Y. Nimrod, 'Suria—Yok' [Hebrew], *Monitin* (Tel Aviv) (Feb. 1984), 88–9.

26. See respectively I. Pappe, *The Making of the Arab-Israeli Conflict, 1947–51* (London and New York, 1992), 141, citing Ben Gurion's diary, and *Documents on the Foreign Policy of Israel*, ii, ed. Y. Freundlich (Jerusalem, 1984), 571.

27. Rabinovich, *Road*, 62, quoting Ben Gurion's diary; Y. Harkabi, 'The Armistice Agreements—in Retrospect' [Hebrew], *Maʿarachot* (July 1984), 4.

28. Rabinovich, *Road*, 63 ff., 82 ff.; Nimrod, 'Suria—Yok', 89; Shalev, *Co-operation*, 57.

29. *Documents on the Foreign Policy of Israel*, ii. 241–3, 320 ff.; iv, ed. Y. Rosenthal (Jerusalem, 1986), 135; Nimrod, 'Suria—Yok', 89.

30. Cf. Rabinovich, *Road*, 84 ff.

31. Torrey, *Syrian Politics*, 155; al-Muʿalim, 119.

32. Shalev, *Co-operation*, 52, 71, 77–8.

33. Al-ʿAzm, i. 379. See also Rabinovich, *Road*, 189–90; FO 371/75529, Damascus, 3 Jan. 1949; FO 371/75528, Damascus, 14 Mar. 1949.

34. FO 371/75528, Damascus, 4 Aug. 1949; cf. Rabinovich, *Road*, 91; al-ʿAzm, i. 380.

35. T. Arazi (New York) to the Middle East Department, Israel Ministry of Foreign Affairs, 30 Apr. 1949, reporting on his talk with Ambassador Malik from Lebanon. (This document is in the possession of the author.)

36. Full text of this agreement in *Documents on the Foreign Policy of Israel*, iii. 723 ff. See also F. J. Khouri, 'Friction and Conflict on the Israeli-Syrian Front', *Middle East Journal*, 17 (1963), 15–16.

37. Bar Yaʿacov, *Israel–Syrian Armistice*, 9.

38. Details in Shalev, *Co-operation*, 109 ff.

39. The quotations and details respectively in Bar Yaʿacov, *Israel–Syrian Armistice*, 10; Khouri, 'Friction and Conflict', 22; Shalev, *Co-operation*, 154–5; FO 371/91706, Tel Aviv, 14 Apr. 1951.

40. Shalev, *Co-operation*, 167; cf. FO 371/98785, Tel Aviv, 27 Feb. 1952 (Annual Report for 1951); Khouri, 'Friction and Conflict', 19.

41. Shalev, *Co-operation*, 173–4. Cf. Sami al-Jundi, *Arab wa-Yahud* (Beirut, 1968), 133–4; al-Muʿalim, 145–6.

42. Shalev, *Co-operation*, 118 ff. Cf. FO 371/82785, Damascus, 5 and 24 Jan. 1950, reporting on deliberations in the Syrian parliament, which did not discuss the Israeli problem at all.

43. See interviews with Makleff, *Maʿariv*, 27 Apr. 1962, 2 Oct. 1964, and 3 Mar. 1978.

44. Israel Ministry of Foreign Affairs, Memos of 22 Sept. 1952 and 26 Mar. 1953, ISA, Group 13002, File 22, Box 2408; FO 371/98486, Damascus, 30 June 1952, and Tel Aviv, 13 Oct. 1952.

45. For a highly detailed survey of these negotiations, see Shalev *Co-operation*, 193 ff. See also FO 371/104765, Damascus, 22 and 30 Jan. 1953; ISA/Syria/MAC, 2434/3, 13 Apr. 1953 and 27 Aug. 1953.

46. FO 371/91849, Damascus, 11 Nov. 1951; FO 371/98167, Damascus, 26 Feb. 1951. Cf. al-Muʿalim, 155 ff.

47. Shalev, *Co-operation*, 189–90, citing documents from the US National Archives; FO 371/98914, Damascus, 6 May 1952; FO 371/98511, Damascus, 15 May 1952.

48. Seale, *Syria*, 128; FO 371/104755, London, 26 May 1953, citing the Syrian Ambassador.

49. Al-Muʿalim, 137–8; al-ʿAzm, ii. 233–5. Cf. FO 371/81918, Damascus, 15 and 19 Apr. 1950.

50. FO 371/81918, Damascus, 19 Apr. 1950.

51. FO 371/91852, Damascus, 8 Feb. 1951.

52. FO 371/91849, Damascus, 11 Nov. 1951; FO 371/91867, Damascus, 26 Feb. 1951; FO 371/104753, Damascus, 26 Dec. 1952; ISA/Syria, 2408/22, 3 Feb. 1952, citing an anti-Israeli speech by Ahmad Shuqayri, Syria's UN representative.

53. See respectively, FO 371/98916, Damascus, 23 July and 22 Aug. 1952; FO 371/98914, Damascus, 14 Mar. 1952; ISA/Syria, 2408/22, 17 Aug. 1952.

54. FO 371/82782, Damascus, 13 Jan. 1950. For a highly detailed study of Arab hostility to Israel, see Y. Harkabi, *The Arabs' Position in their Conflict with Israel* (Hebrew; Tel Aviv, 1968) (hereafter cited as Harkabi), *Conflict*; al-ʿAzm, ii. 235–6.

55. FO 371/98913, Damascus, 8 Mar. 1952; FO 371/91867, Damascus, 18 June 1951. Cf. FO 371/104755, London, 19 May 1953; *Nidal al-Sh'ab*, 229–30.

56. For more details, see Seale, *Syria*, 84 ff. and 90; al-Muʿalim, 134 ff., 139–44.

57. Seale, *Syria*, 107–8; FO 371/91852, Damascus, 10 Apr. 1951. According to al-Muʿalim (p. 146), Egypt sent one air squadron and Iraq two. See also Salah al-Aqqad, *al-Mashriq al-arabi, 1945–1958* (Cairo, 1966), 114–15.

58. Cf. FO 371/91852, Damascus, 10 Dec. 1951; FO 371/98913, Damascus, 8 Mar. 1952; FO 371/104753, Damascus, 12 Mar. 1953; Cf. *al-Hayat*, 15 May 1954, cited in Harkabi, *Conflict*, 83; *Nidal al-Sh'ab*, 229–30, 234–7, 240; FO 371/11590, Damascus, 12 Nov. 1955.

59. 'The Syrian Policy towards Israel', 22 Sept. 1952, p. 2; ISA, Record Group 13002, File 22, Box 2408.

60. Cited in Khouri, *The Arab–Israeli Dilemma*, 83–4.

61. Cited in Harkabi, *Conflict*, 84.

62. FO 371/91852, London, 8 Feb. 1951; cf. FO 371/91867, Damascus, 26 Feb. 1951.

63. See e.g. FO 371/98914, Damascus, 14 Mar. and 6 May 1952; FO 371/11069, Damascus, 18 Jan. 1954; FO 371/104753, Damascus, 26 Dec. 1952; cf. *al-Hayat*, Jan. 1950 and *al-Difaʿ* (Jordan), 11 Mar. 1954 in Harkabi, *Conflict*, 96 and 77; *Hamizrah Hehadash* (Israel Oriental Society), 4 (1953), 283.

64. Muhammad Salah al-Din, Egypt Foreign Minister, in *al-Masri* (Cairo), 11 Oct. 1949, cited in Harkabi, *Conflict*, 37; cf. Shukri al-Quwwatli to Elias Sasson, in a diplomatic dispatch by Sasson, Istanbul, 3 Sept. 1951, ISA Record Group 13002, File 22, Box 2408; FO 371/104774, citing *The Times*, 2 Oct. 1953.

65. ISA/Syria, 2408/22, 4 Mar. 1951, citing Damascus Radio, 25 Feb. 1953; cf. C. D. Smith, *Palestine and the Arab–Israeli Conflict* (New York, 1988), 152; *Hamizrah Hehadash*, 4 (1952), 102–4. Cf. FO 371/111070, 22 Apr. 1954.

66. Cf. FO 371/82790, Washington, 17 Jan. 1950; FO 371/91851B, London, 17 May 1951; FO 371/91849, Damascus, 17 Aug. 1951; FO 371/98914, Damascus, 9 Oct. 1952.

67. 'The Syrian Policy towards Israel'; cf. FO 371/104757 Damascus, 25 Nov. 1953.

68. E. Sasson to W. Eytan, Istanbul, 3 Sept. 1951, ISA Record Group 13002, File 22, Box 2408.

69. See *Documents on the Foreign Policy of Israel*, ii. 571; FO 371/111070 Tel Aviv, 6 Apr. 1954; cf. ISA/Syria, 2569/1A, 4 Dec. 1952.

70. Cf. Shishakli's conversation with Sasson, ISA, 18 Apr. 1956, cited in Shalev, *Co-operation*, 192. FO 371/91842, Damascus, 16 June 1951; FO 371/104753, Damascus, 2 Jan. 1953.

71. Shalev, *Co-operation*, 249, quoting the Syrian Ambassador in the US. See also p. 252. Cf. FO 371/104753, Damascus, 2 Jan. 1953; ISA/Syria, 2569/1A, 4 Dec. 1952.

72. FO 371/111137, Damascus, 12 Feb. 1954. See also FO 371/111139, Damascus, 3 and 9 Feb. 1954; ISA/Syria 2564/25, 18 May 1954. *Foreign Relations of the United States* (hereafter *FRUS*), ix. *1952–1954* (Washington, 1986), 1042–4, Damascus, 6 Nov. 1952.

73. Ben Gurion to Sharett, 26 Oct. 1952, ISA, Group 13002, File 11, Box 2446; *FRUS*, ix. 1042–4, cable from Damascus to the State Department, 6 Nov. 1952; ISA/Middle East, 2564/24A, 10 Oct. 1952.

74. Sharett to Ben Gurion, 30 Oct. 1952, ISA, 571/52, cited in Shalev, *Co-operation*, 223. On the American position, see idem, 217. Cf. Nimrod, 'Syria—Yok', 87.

75. ISA, 21 Oct. 1952, 142/52, in Shalev, *Co-operation*, 433–4 n. 56. On Ben Gurion's position, see ISA 13002/11, Box 2446, 26 Oct. 1952.

76. Shalev, *Co-operation*, 247–8, quoting UN and US archives, and 253.

3

A Zero-Sum Conflict: Domestic, Regional, and Global Factors

A ZERO-SUM CONFLICT

Broadly speaking, Syrian attitudes towards Israel became increasingly hostile after 1954 because of domestic instability, ideological and political radicalization, the growing fear of Israel military action or aggression, as well as owing to Syria's new alliances with the USSR and Egypt. In turn, Syria's militant attitude to Israel, and its Soviet and Egyptian orientations, coupled with Egypt's increasing belligerency, deepened Israel's sense of siege and fear, and contributed as well to strengthening Ben Gurion's hardline stance, leading to serious military operations against Syria and Egypt. Consequently, while a series of armed clashes periodically erupted between Israel and Syria, their mutual antagonism was further aggravated.

To begin with Syria, after Shishakli's overthrow in late February 1954, political unrest in Syria further deteriorated: five governmets succeeded one another within a year, while the political and military establishments were torn by inter-group struggles.[1] Significantly, Syrian leftist and radical forces grew stronger than the conservative and rightist parties and developed an intense neutralist anti-Western and anti-Israeli orientation. These developments stemmed from socio-economic and political changes in Syria itself and were also influenced by the 1952 Egyptian revolution and the new Soviet penetration of the region, on the one hand, as well as by the growing threat from Syria's pro-Western neighbours—Iraq, Turkey and Israel—on the other.

Thus, in the free democratic elections of September–October 1954, the leftist radical Ba‘th Party, led by Michel Aflaq, Salah al-Din al-Bitar, and Akram Hawrani, won 22 seats (out of 142; as against 1 out of 114 seats in the 1949 elections); a veteran Communist, Khalid Baqdash, became the first Syrian Communist deputy, while Khalid al-‘Azm, the leftist millionaire, won many votes in Damascus and subsequently formed a large neutralist bloc in the parliament.[2] Although not commanding an absolute parliamentary majority, the radical leftist forces were highly motivated and organized, energetic and well co-ordinated; they also mustered growing support among the younger army officers—the emerging power centre in Syrian politics.[3] Adhering to an anti-Western foreign policy, these new forces successfully foiled attempts by Iraq and pro-Iraqi Syrian parties—notably the People's Party—to enlist Syrian participation in the British-engineered Baghdad Pact of February 1955 (between Iraq and Turkey and subsequently also Great Britain, Pakistan, and Iran).[4] The radical Syrian anti-Western, anti-Iraqi campaign was obviously inspired and backed by the newly established Nasserite regime in Egypt (1954)—with whom the Baʿth Party developed close links—as well as by the Soviet Union, with whom the 'two Khalids', Baqdash and al-ʿAzm, worked closely.

Yet with regard to Israel, the new Syrian leaders—conservative and radical alike—showed 'more nervousness and more fear vis-à-vis the Israeli danger than Shishakli';[5] but they made sharp anti-Israeli statements, apparently in order to compete with their rivals and gain popularity.[6] Prime Minister Faris al-Khuri, for example, declared in late 1954 that Syria would not make peace with Israel even if Israel should implement United Nations resolutions regarding Palestine, the refugees, etc.:

As long as the Jews reside amongst us there will be hostility between us and them. The first round [the 1948 war] was not successful. Undoubtedly the Arabs should prepare for the second round [against Israel] . . . the Jews should be ousted from Palestine only by war . . . in the same way that we expelled the Crusaders.[7]

In February 1955 Prime Minister Sabri al-Asali declared: 'Our enemy no. 1 is the criminal Zionist . . . the usurped part of Palestine is an integral part of the Arab homeland and therefore the Syrian government rejects any thought of peace.'[8] Similar announcements were subsequently made by radical Syrian leaders, such as Foreign Minister Khalid al-ʿAzm[9] and even—for the first time—by Khalid Baqdash, the leader of the Communist Party, which had previously avoided dealing with the Palestinian problem (apparently following Soviet recognition of Israel).[10]

But, in addition to these anti-Israeli declarations, the new parliamentary regime in Damascus not only continued to lead the all-Arab economic boycott against Israel,[11] but also breached the Armistice Agreement with Israel in various ways: seizing and/or controlling territories east of Lake Tiberias and the River Jordan which were *de jure* under Israeli sovereignty or situated in the DMZ; firing at Israeli fishermen and police boats on the lake, as well as at Israeli farmers in nearby *kibbutzim*, sometimes causing serious casualties.[12] These attacks—partly provoked by Israeli actions— also worried many Israelis on account of Syria's topographical advantage and domination from the Golan Heights, its previous military gains in Tall al-Mutilla, and its attempts to obstruct Israel's national development projects in the Hula drainage scheme and the Jordan–Negev water carrier (see below). The aggressive image that Syria represented in the eyes of most Israelis reached some kind of peak by late 1954, when four Israeli soldiers were captured by Syrian troops while carrying out an intelligence mission within Syrian territory. One of the soldiers committed suicide in a Syrian jail, allegedly under torture, while for a long time Syria refused to release the three others.[13] This 'barbaric' Syrian conduct shocked and enraged Israeli Jews who considered Syria the most vicious of their enemies. (In retaliation, Israeli air force planes in December forced a Syrian commercial plane to land in Israel, but released it two days later.) Furthermore, militant Syrian conduct at that period was seen by Israel as part of an inter-Arab endeavour to beseige the Jewish state, this by means of the Egyptian blockade of Israeli navigation through the Suez Canal and the Gulf of Aqaba, as well as by the activities of Palestinian *fida'iyyun* who infiltrated from the Gaza Strip and the West Bank and attacked Israeli citizens.[14]

In this respect, even more crucial in Israel's view were the strengthening political and military relations between Syria and Egypt, as well as the developing military and diplomatic links between Syria and Egypt on the one hand and the Soviet bloc on the other. As we shall elaborate later, Syria was the first Arab state to sign, late in 1954, a small arms deal with Czechoslovakia, which was followed by large arms deals with Prague and Moscow; at the same time, following the fall of Shishakli in early 1954, Syria developed close relations with Nasser's Egypt, signing a military alliance with Cairo in October 1955 which provided for a joint command under an Egyptian officer.

To be sure, these deals and agreements were essentially aimed at defending Syria against alleged or real military threat from its pro-Western neighbours, Turkey, Iraq, and Israel. Yet Syrian leaders singled out Israel as the major enemy against whom their new alliances were primarily directed. Thus, for example, after a new pro-Soviet cabinet was formed in Damascus in February 1955, Khalid al-ʿAzm, 'the dominant figure in the new government', pointed out: 'We felt we needed the support of a group of nations which had no preconceived notions on the Israeli issue . . . This was the reason we became pro-Russian, deriving great moral and material support from the eastern bloc.'[15] Later on, in September 1956, Nazim al-Qudsi, the Speaker of the Syrian Parliament, told a visiting Soviet parliamentary delegation that the Arabs would be grateful to a country that would support them 'in the elimination of Israel'.[16] In May 1955 and later on, American Embassy reports from Damascus indicated that the 'basic features of Syrian political situation are . . . universal resentment against Israel and corollary resentment against us as the power primarily responsible for Israel's existence.'[17]

Similarly, Prime Minister Sabri al-Asali 'went further than any previous prime minister in declaring his hatred of Israel and desire for revenge in Palestine'. He also tried to assure both Turkey and Iraq that the military treaty with Egypt was not directed against them but 'was aimed at Israel'.[18] President Nasser also declared at the ratification ceremony of the 1955 treaty:

This agreement is a prelude to a new future. History shows that if Syria and Egypt unite, they will protect the eastern world from all dangers that may threaten it. This is what happened at the time of the Crusades. When Syria allied itself with Egypt, together they protected the Islamic world from the dangers that it feared. Today Syria and Egypt will protect the Arab world against Zionism.[19]

As will be discussed later, the Syrian–Egyptian pact of October 1955 constituted a major inducement for the fierce Israeli raid of December 1955 on Syrian positions north-east of Lake Tiberias. The raid was apparently aimed, *inter alia*, at exposing the Syrian–Egyptian pact as not likely to be implemented and possibly also at provoking Syria into a war with Israel.

ISRAELI ATTITUDES AND ACTIONS: BEN GURION VS. SHARETT

Indeed, the year 1955 signified a crucial point in the zero-sum conflict which had developed between Israel on the one hand and Syria and Egypt on the other, not only because of increasing Arab hostility. No less crucial was the predominance of Ben Gurion's activist, hawkish approach over Sharett's moderate, diplomatic line regarding Israel's attitudes towards these Arab states. Ostensibly both leaders repeatedly stated their desire to make peace with the Arab nations on the basis of the 1949 Armistice lines. But whereas Sharett considered this Israel's first priority and advocated the use of diplomacy, Ben Gurion relegated it to a secondary position while continuing to employ force against the Arabs.[20]

Examining Ben Gurion's attitude to the Arabs, his biographer writes:

Ben Gurion remained all his life extraneous to the Arabs. He did not know them well, neither understood nor liked them. He did not speak their language, had no interest in their customs, and did not associate with them. Gradually he became aware that the Arabs would not make peace with Israel in our time. He was convinced that the Arabs' wish to exterminate Israel . . . their recognition or non-recognition of Israel did not depend at all on Israel's behaviour.

According to Shlaim's analysis,[21] Ben Gurion regarded 'the Arabs as an implacable enemy . . . [and] only by the repeated and vigorous application of force . . . could Israel demonstrate its invincibility and in the long run compel the Arabs to come to terms with her existence as an independent sovereign state in the Middle East. Advocating self-reliance and distrust of the world's willingness to protect Israel, Ben Gurion repeatedly said: 'Our future does not depend on what the Gentiles say, but what the Jews do.'[22]

In contrast, Moshe Sharett, who was well versed in Arab history, culture, and politics, 'was much closer to the Arabs. His approach to them was much more sympathetic . . . he emphasized that they are human beings, not only enemies . . . he believed in Israel's ability to modify Arab hostility by a conciliatory policy' (Bar Zohar). He

attached considerable value to patient and imaginative diplomacy, to gestures of good will and to mobilization of the international community in an all-out effort to whittle down Arab hostility and to prepare the ground for peace . . . To this end, he deemed it necessary . . . to refrain from actions which would alienate the international community, antagonize the Great Powers, and increase the tensions in Israel's relations with her neighbors. (Shlaim)

However, Sharett, as foreign minister, had by and large little support for his views in the Israeli cabinet. For example, Golda Meir, a member of the cabinet, later remarked:

Sharett thought that the best way to deal with [Arab] infiltration across the borders was to press the superpowers. . . . He was sure that well-written protests to the UN . . . would eventually succeed. . . . But Ben Gurion thought that his responsibility was primarily to the [Israeli] citizens who were subject to Arab attack and not towards the Western politicians. . . . Another consideration was important to Ben Gurion: it was necessary to teach the Israeli citizens—a mixture of people, languages, and cultures—that the government, and *only* it, was responsible for their safety.[23]

Consequently, contrary to Sharett's conciliatory approach, Ben Gurion and his followers, notably Moshe Dayan, the chief of staff, adopted, particularly from 1953, a policy of tough and prompt military actions in response to the actions of Arabs who crossed the Armistice lines from Jordan, Syria, and Gaza to carry out acts of theft, killing, espionage, and sabotage inside Israel.

Yet some of these reprisals, which were carried out on a large scale under Dayan's dynamic leadership, aimed not only at reinstilling a sense of confidence among fearful Israelis, but also at forcing the Arab governments to curb infiltration from their territory into Israel, and possibly also to 'create a situation of such gravity that it would force the Arab states to take up open battle with Israel'.[24]

Nevertheless, these military reactions, whatever their motives, were disproportionate in scale to the foregoing Arab action and thus significantly contributed to intensifying the conflict. To quote General Harkabi, chief of Military Intelligence in the mid-1950s:

As far as the retaliatory action had been directly related to the previous event, there certainly had been a disproportion between the [Arab] inducement and the [Israeli] reaction. It had stemmed from Israel's feelings of weakness, of isolation, of fear regarding the future. . . . [There was] a war over all sorts of tiny pieces of territory which later on, it became clear, were not needed. [There were] small disputes which eventually produced the [1967] Six Day War.[25]

Among the IDF's conspicuous retaliatory operations was the attack in October 1953 on Qibya, in the Jordan-held West Bank, where about fifty Palestinian inhabitants were killed. This attack, led by then Major Ariel Sharon, came in reaction to the killing of an Israeli woman and two children.[26]

Still, Ben Gurion's main concern at that juncture was not so much the threat from Jordan or even from Syria, which were both rather small and weak, but from Egypt. It was indeed the biggest Arab country, ruled by a revolutionary, yet stable regime, and by a strong, charismatic leader, Nasser, who aspired to unite the Arab world, ostensibly against Israel. As Ben Gurion said in mid-1954 to one of his aides: 'If a snake lies by your feet and a fly bothers your head, which do you take care of? The fly is more troublesome but not dangerous. This is Jordan. You have to hit the snake; this is Egypt.'

He indeed believed that Egypt aimed *inter alia* at pushing Israel back to the United Nations partition lines, cutting off the Negev and subsequently eliminating the Jewish state through an all-Arab war. Conse-

quently, Ben Gurion, in opposition to Sharett, was determined to intimi-
date and deter Nasser from attacking Israel, by ordering retaliatory actions.[27] Thus, on 28 February 1955 the IDF carried out a large-scale attack
on an Egyptian military camp in Gaza, killing some forty Egyptian soldiers. Officially Israel claimed that the operation was undertaken in reaction to acts of terrorism, espionage, and murder by Egyptian soldiers who
had come from Gaza. According to two Israeli historians, Shamir and
Shlaim, prior to the Israeli attack Moshe Sharett, Israel's new prime
minister, had started secret talks with Egypt designed to pave the way for
an understanding between the two countries. But the Gaza raid, initiated
by Ben Gurion soon after he had assumed the defence portfolio in
February 1955, contributed, together with other factors, to halting those
talks. Further, rather than intimidating Nasser, this raid 'further
aggravated matters', and 'brought about, as Nasser repeatedly claimed, a
shift in Egypt's priorities . . . toward greater and more aggressive involvement in the Arab–Israeli conflict.'[28] Apart from stepping up *fidaʾiyyun*
activities against Israel, Nasser was apparently prompted by the Gaza raid
to acquire new weapons, and in September 1955 he concluded his arms
deal with Prague. Using the Israeli threat, Nasser also signed, as we know,
the October 1955 military alliance with Syria essentially to enhance his
pan-Arab leadership, notably vis-à-vis Israel, and to counter the Iraqi
ambition to incorporate Syria in the Baghdad Pact.[29] In October 1956
Jordan joined this alliance, which aimed at presenting a united front
against Israel.

   These developments led Ben Gurion and Dayan to the conclusion that
Nasser (with Syria and Jordan) was preparing a 'second-round' military
offensive against Israel, and that the Israeli army should therefore acquire
the military capacity to launch a pre-emptive strike against Egypt, in the
hope of causing Nasser's downfall.[30] Israel thus stepped up its endeavours
to obtain modern arms from the West, notably to counter the Egyptian—
and Syrian—arms deals with the Soviet bloc. Since the United States
refused to sell it arms, Israel obtained new weapons from France, which
then regarded Nasser as the main supporter of the anti-French Algerian
rebellion.

   In the spring and winter of 1955 Ben Gurion submitted to the Israeli
cabinet proposals to capture the Gaza Strip and the Straits of Tiran
respectively, but these were rejected by the cabinet under the leadership
of Sharett, who was prime minister from late 1953 until late 1955.[31]
Nevertheless, Ben Gurion, as defence minister, persuaded the cabinet to
order the launching, on 31 August 1955, of an attack on an Egyptian police

station in Khan Yunis in the southern part of the Gaza Strip. This raid, reportedly claiming the lives of 17 Egyptians and wounding 45 others, was followed by another on the Egyptian border post of Kuntila (near the Sinai–Negev line, north of Eilat (Aqaba)), killing 10 Egyptians and capturing 29.[32] In November 1955 Ben Gurion formed a new government, replacing Sharett as prime minister and also retaining the position of defence minister. Sharett agreed to stay on as foreign minister for a while, but resigned in June 1956, apparently since he strongly disapproved of the large-scale retaliatory actions against Egypt and Syria, which were likely to provoke a war with either or with both of these states.

Indeed, Sharett resigned, or rather was forced to resign, not only because of his objection to Ben Gurion's preparations (already in late 1955) to launch a preventive war against Egypt in 1956;[33] but essentially owing to his criticism of the large-scale operation against Syrian positions near Lake Tiberias in December 1955. This operation, which impressed Sharett as 'bloodthirsty and provocative', was ordered by Ben Gurion without his previously consulting Sharett or the cabinet. In his personal diary Sharett cited an editorial in *Ha'aretz*, the leading Israeli paper, entitled, 'A Dictatorship of the Prime Minister?' The article pointed out: 'Ben Gurion who serves as prime minister and defence minister, and in these days also as acting foreign minister, did not ask the opinions of the cabinet members regarding the Kinneret [Lake Tiberias] operation.' Following this citation, Sharett remarked: 'Defence Minister Ben Gurion has consulted Foreign Minister Ben Gurion and obtained a confirmation from Prime Minister Ben Gurion.'[34]

To be sure, Sharett's indignation with Ben Gurion's conduct of the Kinneret operation was a culmination of his (mostly feeble) objection to Ben Gurion's rigid line towards Syria, which had started during Za'im's rule and continued under Shishakli's regime.

LAKE TIBERIAS AND DMZ INCIDENTS

Shooting incidents between Syrian military positions on the eastern shore of Lake Tiberias and Israeli police boats and fishermen occurred periodically from the early 1950s, and particularly during 1954 and 1955. Most of these exchanges, which involved casualties, were caused by the following factors: on the one hand, attempts by Syrian troops (who controlled the 10-metre strip of Israel's territory on the north-eastern shore of the lake) to prevent Israeli fishing in this part of the waters; and on the

other, attempts by Israeli police boats to prevent Syrians from fishing in
the north-eastern part of the lake without Israeli permits.[35] A compromise
proposal in late 1950 which might have settled the dispute was rejected by
Israel; according to Shalev this was a 'miscalculation'.[36] Shalev also reveals
that in early 1954 the Israeli chief of staff decided 'to react in an aggressive
manner in each case affecting Israeli fishing in the Kinneret [Lake
Tiberias]', the entire lake being formally under Israel sovereignty.

Indeed, Ben Gurion, while prime minister and defence minister, unilaterally adopted harsh and occasionally provocative actions against Syria
in Lake Tiberias and the DMZ. As General Makleff, chief of staff in the
mid-1950s, frankly admitted later:

On the Syrian front we represented a rousing [provocative] element by wishing to
fill a vacuum in the DMZ, by establishing Israeli settlements there and evicting
them [the Syrian peasants] from the region . . . very harsh things occurred then;
fields were divided; they sowed in winter and came to harvest in summer. We
reaped their fields or burnt them. They infiltrated. We mistakenly regarded every
infiltrator as a *fida'iyyun* [guerrilla fighters] and saw it [the infiltration] as a deliberate action.

Shalev puts it more abstractly: 'In contradiction to the common
opinion, the two countries—not only Syria—were responsible for the
tensions and the violent confrontations that periodically occurred between
them. Israel was not always the innocent sheep and Syria the wolf.'[37]

Sharett, as we know, while foreign minister, advocated a moderate,
diplomatic approach towards Syria, but was overruled by Ben Gurion.
Only when he was prime minister was Sharett able to thwart, in February
1954, a suggestion by Defence Minister Lavon, backed by Ben Gurion
and Dayan, that Israel should exploit the confusion created in Syria
following Shishakli's overthrow, in order to occupy the DMZ and the
surrounding hills.[38]

In May 1955 Ben Gurion suggested that in case of an Iraqi invasion of
Syria, Israel should intervene in Lebanon, occupy the area south of the
River Litani and help establish a strong Christian state in Lebanon which
would be allied with Israel. Sharett rejected this idea—which had been an
old dream of Ben Gurion's—arguing that it would bring about a war with
Syria.[39]

But when in late 1955 Ben Gurion again became prime minister and
defence minister, he perhaps tried to provoke a major battle with Syria
over its attempts to fish in Lake Tiberias and disrupt Israeli fishing.
According to General Burns, chairman of the Syrian–Israeli MAC, who

rejected Syrian claims to fishing rights in the lake: 'These [Israeli] police boats, whether they escort fishing craft or not, often cruise close to the shore . . . Such cruising has been considered provocative by nearby Syrian positions, and there have been from time to time exchanges of fire.' He indicated that the Syrian chief of staff, Shawkat Shuqayr, tried to 'avoid incidents and situations which might involve Syria in active hostilities, for he realized his army's weakness in the face of the Israelis' superior armament, training, and organization'.[40]

Burns also argued that on a certain occasion an Israeli police boat had possibly been sent deliberately to provoke the Syrians into opening fire in order to give Israel a pretext to launch a massive attack on Syrian positions along the north-eastern shore of Lake Tiberias. He was referring to the shooting incident of 10 December 1955, when a Syrian position on the shore of the lake fired with small arms and bazookas and hit an Israeli police boat patrolling in the lake about 70 metres from the shore. (The Syrians later claimed that two Israeli boats had first fired at two Syrian farms.) In retaliation Israeli armed forces, reportedly supported by armoured vehicles, aircraft, and artillery, on the night of 11 December 1955 attacked several Syrian positions in Kursi and Butayha, killing 37 Syrian soldiers, as well as 12 civilians, and taking 30 prisoners.

To be sure, the Israeli Kinneret/Tiberias raid was aimed not merely at punishing Damascus for alleged aggressive actions in the lake area. It was particularly directed at exposing Syria's (and Egypt's) military weakness and warning it that its military pact with Egypt could become a liability rather than an asset. As the *Jerusalem Post* commented at that juncture: 'We hope that the Israeli raid has convinced many Syrians that the military pact with Egypt has increased the danger to Syria instead of guaranteeing Syria's defence.'[41]

However, this massive Israeli raid (which was severely critized by many cabinet and Knesset members), while failing to deter Syria, or Egypt, further aggravated the Israeli–Syrian conflict, and in certain other respects also turned out to be a serious liability to Israel itself. Referring to this Israeli doctrine of massive retaliation, including the case under discussion, Gideon Rafael, one of Israel's senior diplomats, wrote:

But the application of overdoses of the prescribed remedy, instead of curing the malady, caused in quite a number of cases severe affliction to the dispenser. It usually produced harmful international repercussions, strengthening the Arab position and encouraging them to pursue their hostile campaigns against Israel with greater virulence. Most of the difficulties arose from ill-timed and ill-conceived actions. Sometimes their scope exceeded the planned proportions and in other cases their timing completely ignored the effect on wider political and regional developments of foremost significance to Israel and its friends.[42]

Indeed, the Kinneret/Tiberias raid ('Operation Olive Leaves'), which was carried out with excessive zeal by Major Ariel Sharon, greatly affected Israel's international and regional relations. According to Abba Eban, Israel's ambassador to the United Nations, 'it presents a shocking vision of a massacre, making almost no attempt to alert world public opinion regarding its necessity and magnitude.' Apart from the severe condemnation by the Security Council, Secretary of State Dulles promptly stopped his talks with Sharett in Washington on Israel's request for American arms and security guarantees. Sharett, who felt that he had been 'stabbed in the back' by Ben Gurion, later remarked: 'Satan could not have chosen a worse timing' (for the Kinneret operation), and that he 'would never be able to look Mr. Dulles in the face again'. Sharett also suspected that Dayan had carried out the Kinneret operation in order to provoke Syria into a full-scale war with Israel and thus disrupt Syrian efforts to absorb the new Soviet weapons.[43]

As it happened, already at the end of 1953 the Soviet Union tried to win the goodwill of the Arabs, particularly the Syrians, at the expense of Israel and in reaction to the Western move to establish anti-Soviet regional security organizations in the Middle East. Thus, in January 1954, the USSR for the first time cast a veto in Syria's favour at the Security Council debate on Israel's initial attempt to divert the Jordan waters.[44] Several months later Syria became the first Arab country to sign a minor arms deal with the Soviet bloc, followed by bigger arms deals in 1955 and 1957.[45]

TOWARDS A SYRIAN–EGYPTIAN UNION

Despite Soviet military and diplomatic help, Syria was, nevertheless, not provoked into launching a full-scale war against Israel in reaction to the Kinneret operation, nor did Egypt come to its help in spite of the October 1955 military pact between Cairo and Damascus. Syria, like Egypt, was militarily too weak and still unprepared for a large-scale offensive against Israel.[46] The Israeli raid, however, further induced Syria to strengthen its military forces, purchase more Soviet arms, entrench its military and political ties with Egypt, and seek a military alliance with Jordan and Lebanon, while continuing to make more vehement anti-

Israeli statements and occasionally engage in shooting incidents along the Israeli border.

Thus, following the Tiberias raid, the Syrian government decided to increase its military budget for the following year by about $18 million and also assign a $10 million Saudi loan to the army, while continuing to obtain many more arms from the Communist bloc, including T-34 Soviet tanks.[47] Damascus, and subsequently also Cairo, exercised pressure on Lebanon during 1956 to sign a military pact with Syria and permit Syrian troops to enter the strategic Biqaʿ valley in case of an Israeli attack against Syria.[48] Simultaneously, in May 1956 Syria reached an agreement with Jordan to establish a joint military committee which would conduct consultations in case of war with Israel; and on 23 October 1956 Jordan joined the 1955 Egyptian–Syrian military pact.[49] In accordance with this pact, Syrian forces reportedly prepared to attack Israel on 30 October 1956, soon after the IDF started its Sinai campaign against Egypt. But the Egyptian commander-in-chief, General ʿAmr, ordered the Syrian army to hold fast for fear that Britain and France would invade Syria.[50] The only actions that Syria took during the Sinai/Suez war were shooting down a British plane which flew over Syria, blowing up the British-owned Iraqi oil pipeline which passed through Syrian territory, and cutting off diplomatic relations with Britain and France.[51]

Whether or not Syria would have attacked Israel at that juncture, had it obtained Egyptian approval, remains an open question. However, it would appear that Damascus, as during the December 1955 raid, was still afraid to face Israel on the battlefield, owing to Israel's military superiority and its British and French backing. Hence, the Syrian government preferred, as in the past, and mostly for domestic consumption, to launch vehement verbal attacks on Israel, whose assumed alliance with the imperialist powers was now clearly exposed.[52] Syrian leaders continued to make fiery anti-Israeli and anti-Zionist speeches, calling for 'revenge' against, and the 'elimination' or 'destruction' of Israel, 'the Zionist serpent'.[53] Syria's prime minister, Sabri al-Asali, for example, announced in July 1957, in a radio broadcast: 'Israel cannot exist in the Middle East area and the Arabs will fight to liberate the conquered parts of Palestine.'[54] But, in addition to these rhetorical propaganda campaigns, Syria periodically initiated shooting incidents along the Israeli border, or reacted with force to Israel's attempts to carry on the Jordan waters development project, possibly in order 'to divert Syrians' attention from their internal problems' and strengthen the prestige of the leftist radical elements.[55]

Indeed, as already indicated, Syrian political and military leaders, notably from the Ba'th Party, used *inter alia* the Israeli threat to reinforce their positions and enhance their prime ideological goals—Arab unity, or more specifically, union with Egypt. These Syrian leaders were also convinced by 1957 that union with Egypt was the best guarantee for the security and integrity of Syria. This, vis-à-vis the growing threat from Turkey, Iraq, and Israel externally,[56] and from the Muslim Brethren and particularly the Communists, internally.

Indeed, during 1957, the Communists gained strength both in the government and in the army, while the military was placed under the virtual control of a newly formed leftist Revolutionary Council which included the new pro-Communist chief of staff, Afif al-Bizri. These developments were taken very seriously by Western and pro-Western governments and widely reported in the press, giving the impression that Syria was 'going Communist' and becoming a Soviet satellite. Syria, indeed, emerged as a source of concern, even alarm, in the region and in the Western world, notably in the United States and Britain as well as in Turkey, Iraq, Saudi Arabia, Jordan, Lebanon, and Israel. Thus, according to American estimates of late 1956 and early 1957, 'the U.K., France, Turkey, Israel and Iraq all have strong incentives to intervene to retrieve the situation in Syria;.' 'The British are believed to favor active stimulation of a change in the present regime in Syria in an effort to assure a pro-Western orientation on the part of future Syrian governments.'[57] In 1956 Hashemite Iraq reportedly initiated, in league with Britain and the United States, a scheme to topple the radical regime in Damascus. Following the collapse of that Iraqi conspiracy and the establishment of a radical-leftist government in Jordan late in 1956, President Eisenhower announced his new doctrine early in 1957, aiming at filling the 'power vacuum' in the Middle East which had been left by Britain, strengthening the pro-Western Arab regimes in Saudi Arabia, Lebanon, and Jordan and combating the expansion of Communism in Syria and Egypt.

In August 1957, according to official Syrian sources, the United States master-minded a plot to overthrow the Syrian government and replace it with a pro-Western regime. This new regime was allegedly to receive a large sum of money from the Americans, *inter alia*, as an inducement to make peace with Israel.[58]

Following the exposure of this supposed American plot, a top State Department official, Loy Henderson, was dispatched to Ankara in order to mobilize Turkey, Iraq, Lebanon, and Jordan against their 'dangerous' neighbour, Syria. Turkey indeed threatened Syria by concentrating troops along the Syrian border both before and after Henderson's visit. A Soviet newspaper was not slow to declare that the concentration of Turkish troops on the Syrian border was a stage in 'a diabolical American plot' to invade Syria; according to this report, the other parties to this plot were Israel and Iraq.[59]

Whether or not there was any American plot to overthrow the Syrian regime with Turkish, Iraqi, and Israeli participation, the Syrian sense of vulnerability to such external threats was one of the main factors leading to union with Egypt in February 1958. Another major cause for the union was, as we know, the growing concern of Ba'thist and nationalist leaders (and also of Egypt) about the growing strength of the Communists in the army and in the country.[60] The Ba'thists indeed believed that the best way to neutralize the Communist influence, to safeguard Syria against Western threats, to consolidate their own position in the state, and to implement their pan-Arab ideas—was to unite Syria with Nasser's Egypt.[61]

To be sure, Nasser's prestige and popularity had reached a peak in Syria in the mid-1950s and was substantially stronger and wider than that of the Soviet Union on account of his spectacular victories against 'Western imperialism' and his immensely inspiring vision of pan-Arab solidarity. In April 1954 he attended the Bandung Conference of Afro-Asian states and emerged as one of the leaders of the neutralist bloc; and in July 1956 he nationalized the Western-controlled Suez Canal. In October 1956, he skilfully turned his defeat in the British, French, and Israeli-engineered Suez–Sinai war into a great political gain for Egypt.[62]

These impressive achievements indeed invested Nasser with the status of an all-Arab leader and hero among many sections of the Syrian population and consequently brought Syria under growing Egyptian influence. Already, on 17 April 1956, Syria's independence day, an Egyptian contingent joined Syrian troops in the traditional march-past in Damascus, and several weeks later the Egyptian government contributed $14,000,000 to the Syrian army.[63] The Ba'th Party continued to call for a complete union between Syria and Egypt and in July 1956 the conservative Premier Asali formed a three-man ministerial committee to conduct negotiations for union with Egypt.

Syria's association with Egypt reached a peak during the second half of 1957, in reaction to the Eisenhower Doctrine and the alleged plots and threats by Syria's pro-Western neighbours. Syrian President Shukri al-Quwwatli made several demonstrative visits to Cairo and declared in

August 1957 that 'Syria's dearest wish was to achieve a union with Egypt which would serve as the nucleus for universal Arab unity'.[64] In September Syrian military leaders discussed with their Egyptian counterparts plans for Egyptian military intervention in Syria, apparently to face Turkish and Iraqi threats; and in October 1957, invoking the 1957 treaty, Egyptian troops landed at Latakia to take up battle positions vis-à-vis Turkey. Finally, on 12 January 1958, with Ba'th encouragement, fourteen Syrian officers, headed by General Bizri, the chief of staff, flew to Egypt, urging Nasser to agree to a full union with Syria, practically on his own terms.[65]

Significantly, once the union with Egypt became imminent, Syrian leaders made new threatening statements against Israel, such as:

Time is now on the Arabs' side. A small state with but a million and a half inhabitants, like Israel, surrounded on all sides by enemies . . . cannot be stronger than Egypt . . . [it] will be swallowed up in the twinkle of an eye by the Syrian army.[66]

But, in any event, the Damascus union with Cairo in February 1958 did not bring about a joint Syrian–Egyptian war against Israel, although Israeli leaders felt threatened by the establishment of the new union (United Arab Republic—UAR) and by the growing Soviet military backing it was receiving.

NOTES

1. Al-Mu'alim, 177 ff.; Seale, *Syria*, 141 ff., 164 ff.
2. Seale, *Syria*, 182–4. For a comprehensive and excellent survey of Syrian politics at that period, see ibid. 164 ff. See also T. Petran, *Syria* (London, 1972), 107–8; *FRUS*, xiii. *1955–1957*, 530 ff.
3. Cf. *FRUS*, xiii. 554, 618.
4. Texts of the pact in J. C. Hurewitz, *Diplomacy in the Near and Middle East* (Princeton, 1956), ii. 390–5; on the struggle in Syria against the Baghdad Pact, see also *FRUS*, xiii. 514 ff., 527–8, 530 ff.; al-Mu'alim, 179 ff.; al-Aqqad, *al-Mashriq al-arabi*, 158 ff.; al-'Azm, iii. 85 ff.
5. Israel Ministry of Foreign Affairs, May 1954, ISA/Syria 2408/20/A and 2569/9, 15 July 1955; *FRUS*, xiii. 555.
6. Cf. conversation between a Syrian and a Dutch diplomat, cited in ISA/Syria, 2569/1/B, 6 Sept. 1954. Also Quwwatli's private remarks, ISA/Syria, 2564/

24, 3 Dec. 1954; FO 371/111076, Damascus, 25 Oct. 1954; FO 371/121725, Damascus, 3 Feb. 1956.

7. Damascus Radio, 4 Nov. 1954, cited in ISA/Arab–Israeli Relations, 2410/10; *al-Ahram*, 27 Sept. 1954; FO 371/111138, Damascus, 7 Dec. 1954—report on events in Nov. 1954. Cf. FO 371/104754, Damascus, 27 Mar. 1953 and 13 May 1953; FO 371/111092, Damascus, 15 Mar. 1954.

8. *Falastin* (East Jerusalem), 23 Feb. 1955, cited in ISA/Syria, 2569/1/B; Torrey, *Syrian Politics*, 278, 280; cf. *Hamizrah Hehadash*, 5 (1953/4), 217–18; *FRUS*, xiii. 515.

9. Damascus Radio, 23 Mar. 1955; ISA/Syria 2569/1/B and 2569/2; cf. *FRUS*, xiii. 525. Cf. al-ʿAzm, ii. 247.

10. Al-Aqqad, *al-Mashriq al-Arabi*, 136 ff.; ISA/Arab–Israeli Relations, 16 Dec. 1955. Cf. *New York Times*, 14 Mar. 1955, cited in *Hamizrah Hehadash*, 6 (1955), 234.

11. *Alif Ba*, 17 May 1955; ISA/Arab Boycott, 2427/7; FO 371/111076, Damascus, 13 Nov. 1954.

12. *Hamizrah Hehadash*, 5 (1953–4), 218, 302; 6 (1954–5), 58–9; ISA/Border Disputes, May, June, July 1954, File 2439/9; ISA/Armistice Commission, 15 Mar. 1954, File 2434/8; 20 Dec. 1954, File 2434/6; 5 Dec. 1955, File 2434/7/II.

13. E. L. M. Burns, *Between Arab and Israeli* (London, 1962), 108–9; *Hamizrah Hehadash*, 6 (1954–5), 235; FO 371/115850, Jerusalem, 7 Jan. 1955, citing *New York Herald Tribune*, 7 Jan. 1955. But see Sharett's version—that the soldiers were not tortured: *Yoman Ishi* (Hebrew; Tel Aviv, 1978), iii. 648–9, 814–15.

14. ISA/MAC/Syria, 2434/7/5, 14 July 1955; ISA/Arab–Israeli Relations, 2410/10, 13 Feb. 1955; ISA/Kinneret incident, 2440/5, 14 Dec. 1955; *Hamizrah Hehadash*, 6 (1954–5), 155, 218.

15. Quoted in Seale, *Syria*, 219. For full details and a good analysis of Syrian reactions to the Baghdad pact, see ibid. 213 ff. See also *FRUS*, xiii. 515 ff.

16. FO 371/121867, Damascus, 18 Sept. 1956.

17. *FRUS*, xiii. 525. Cf. ibid. 535–6, 555; FO 371/115950, Damascus, 3 Mar. and 21 Sept. 1955.

18. Torrey, *Syrian Politics*, 278, 280. See also ISA/Syria, 2569/2, 1 and 8 Nov. 1955.

19. *Al-Ahram*, 9 Nov. 1955, quoted in al-Muʿalim, 193–94; cf. D. Ben Gurion, 'Toward Fateful Events', *Davar*, 15 July 1966.

20. ISA/Arab–Israeli Affairs, 2446/6, 1 Oct. 1952. But see also Ben Gurion Diary (IDF Archive), 29 Mar. 1953; and Z. Shalom, 'Hitnagdut Ben-Gurion ve-Sharett . . .', *Iyunim Bitkumat Israel*, 2 (1992), 203; G. Sheffer, *Resolution versus Management of the Middle East Conflict: A Reexamination of the Confrontation between Moshe Sharett and David Ben Gurion* (Jerusalem, 1980), 12 ff., 36–7.

21. See respectively M. Bar Zohar, *Ben Gurion* (Hebrew; Tel Aviv, 1968, here-after cited as Bar Zohar), ii. 968; A. Shlaim, 'Conflicting Approaches to Israel's Relations with the Arabs: Ben Gurion and Sharett 1953–6', *Middle East Journal*, 37 (1983), 181. See also M. Brecher, *The Foreign Policy System of Israel* (London, 1972), ch. 12; Smith, *Palestine*, 157 ff.; Shalev, *Co-operation*, 259–61; G. Sheffer, 'Inclusive Solutions versus Moderation', in *Zionism and the Arab Question* (Hebrew; Jerusalem, 1979); Y. Shavit, 'Meshihiyut, utopia ve-pesimiyut . . .', *Iyunim Bitkumat Israel*, 2 (1992), 58 ff.

22. See respectively FO 371/111070, Tel Aviv, 6 Apr. 1954; Shlaim, 'Conflicting Approaches', 183; Sheffer, 'Inclusive Solutions', 12.

23. See respectively Bar Zohar, ii. 968; Shlaim, 'Conflicting Approaches', 182–3; Golda Meir, *My Life* (Hebrew; Tel Aviv, 1975), 208. See also Shabtai Teveth, *Moshe Dayan* (Hebrew; Jerusalem, 1973), 427 ff.; D. Ben Gurion, 'Toward Fateful Events', *Davar*, 15 July 1966.

24. Cf. G. Rafael, *Destination Peace* (New York, 1981), 30; Shalev, *Co-operation*, 260. Cf. Bar Zohar, iii. 1136–7. Cf. Moshe Dayan's speech cited in NA/DOS 683.84/1–457, 55, Tel Aviv, 15 July 1957. For a comprehensive study, see B. Morris, *Israel's Border Wars* (Oxford, 1993).

25. Cited in Y. Hameiri, 'The Question of the DMZ along the Israeli-Syrian Border, 1949–1967', MA thesis (Hebrew; Haifa University, 1978), 108. Cf. Sheffer, 'Inclusive Solutions', 41, 45.

26. Smith, *Palestine*, 158; *Hamizrah Hehadash*, 5 (1953–4), 105. Cf. 371/111070, 22 Apr. 1954; FO 371/111073, Amman, 10 Aug. 1954. Cf. S. Shamir, 'The Collapse of Project Alpha', in W. M. R. Louis and R. Owen (eds.), *Suez 1956* (Oxford, 1989), 73 ff.; *The Times*, 25 Nov. 1954; cf. FO 371/111075, Tel Aviv, 5 Oct. 1954; cf. Bar Zohar, iii. 1136–7.

27. See respectively Bar Zohar, iii. 1136–7; M. Dayan, *Avney Derekh* (Tel Aviv, 1967), 155; cf. Shlaim, 'Conflicting Approaches', 187–8; FO 371/121725, Tel Aviv, 19 Mar. 1956; FO 371/121727, Amman, 28 Apr. 1956; cf. FO 371/12090, Tel Aviv, 12 Jan. 1957; Ben Gurion Diary (IDF Archive), 9 Sept. and 19 Oct. 1956.

28. See respectively Shamir, 'Collapse', 79; Shlaim, 'Conflicting Approaches', 188. Cf. Memo by American Secretary of State, 21 Aug. 1957, DD 1710 (1985); Sharett, *Yoman*, v. 1316.

29. Smith, *Palestine*, 167–8; Seale, *Syria* 235–6, 284. Cf. ISA/Syria, 2569/2, 1 and 8 Nov. 1955.

30. Shamir, 'Collapse', 100; M. Bar-On, *Gaza Gates* (Hebrew; Tel Aviv, 1992), 59 ff.; Smith, *Palestine*, 168. Shlaim, 'Conflicting Attitudes', 194; Bar Zohar, iii. 1136–7. Sh. Peres, *Qela David* (Jerusalem, 1970), 142–3; Ben Gurion Diary (IDF Archive), 15 Jan. and 19 Oct. 1956; Ben Gurion's article in *Davar*, 13 May 1966.

31. Shlaim, 'Conflicting Attitudes', 189–93; Bar-On, *Gaza Gates*, 63; Sheffer, 'Inclusive Solutions', 44.

32. *Hamizrah Hehadash*, 7 (1956), 36, 124; Shlaim, 'Conflicting Attitudes', 192. Cf. Ben Gurion's letter to Eban, 19 Dec. 1955, Ben Gurion Archives.

33. Cf. Sharett, *Yoman*, v. 1392 ff. Cf. FO 371/121722, Tel Aviv, 3 Jan. 1956.

34. *Yoman*, v. 1307–10; see also pp. 1315, 1318.

35. For details see Bar Ya'acov, *Israel–Syrian Armistice*, 214 ff.; Shalev, *Co-operation*, 281 ff.; Dayan, *Avney Derekh*, 168; Ben Gurion in *Davar*, 6 May 1966.

36. Shalev, *Co-operation*, 284, 285. Cf. ISA/Armistice Commission, 2434/6, 17 Nov. 1954.

37. See respectively interview with Uri Milshtein in *Ma'ariv*, 3 Mar. 1978; Shalev, *Co-operation*, 298.

38. Ben Gurion Diary, 27 Apr. 1954; Sharett, *Yoman*, ii. 374–7. But in Feb. 1955 Sharett, as prime minister, himself contemplated similar actions. See ISA/Syria, 2569/1/B, 13 Feb. 1955.

39. Sharett, *Yoman*, iv. 996–9. Cf. Ben Gurion's letter to Sharett, 27 Feb. 1954, Ben Gurion Archives.

40. Bar Ya'acov, *Israel–Syrian Armistice*, 218–19; cf. Burns, *Between Arab and Israeli*, 110, 118; Damascus Radio (in Hebrew), 22 Oct. 1955; FO 371/111091, Damascus, 30 July 1954; FO 371/111092, Damascus, 15 Mar. 1954; Khouri, 'Friction', 24; cf. Sharett, *Yoman*, v. 1346–7. But see Ben Gurion's version in *Davar*, 6 May 1966.

41. Quoted in Seale, *Syria*, 254. Cf. Burns, *Between Arab and Israeli*, 118–19; ISA/Kinneret Incident, 2440/5, 14 Dec. 1955, guidelines from Israel Ministry of Foreign Affairs; al-Mua'lim, 194. See also Dayan, *Avney Derekh*, 169–70; Bar Zohar, iii. 1186.

42. Rafael, *Destination Peace*, 30. Cf. ISA 13002/22, 12 Dec. 1955; Teveth, *Dayan*, 427–8. See also Bar-On, *Gaza Gates*, 77 ff. For details of the military operation, see U. Even, *Arik—Darko shel Lohem* (Hebrew; Tel Aviv, 1974), 132 ff.

43. See respectively A. Eban, *Pirkey Haim* (Tel Aviv, 1978), 186–7; Rafael, *Destination Peace*, 48; Sharett, *Yoman*, v. 1295–1318; FO 371/121722, Tel Aviv, 29 Dec. 1955; Burns, *Between Arab and Israel*, 119–20; NA 683 84A, 697, Tel Aviv, 10 Jan. 1956; *FRUS*, xiii. 560. But see also Ben Gurion's letter to Eban, 19 Dec. 1955, Ben Gurion Archives.

44. See speech by the Soviet UN delegate Vishinski, in Y. Ro'i, *Policies and Interests of the USSR in the Middle East, 1945–66* (Tel Aviv, 1969–70; hereafter cited as Ro'i), part 2, 263 ff. Cf. FO 371/115942, London, 4 Apr. 1955; NA/DOS 683.84/1-457, 2633, 3 May 1957; al-Mu'alim, 195.

45. American Embassy, Damascus to DOS, 8 Nov. 1956, Declassified document [DD] 882 (1989); NA/683.00/10-657, 1496, 22 Nov. 1957. Seale, *Syria*, 233 ff.; al-Mu'alim, 195–6; E. Karsh, *The Soviet Union and Syria* (London, 1988), 3; 'Soviet Statement on Security in the Near and Middle East: 16

Apr. 1955', in *Soviet News*, 19 Apr. 1955, cited in Ro'i, 263 ff.; al-ʿAzm, iii. 4–6.

46. Cf. FO 371/121862, Damascus, 13 Apr. 1956. Ben Gurion, however, told NBC (26 Dec. 1955—Ben Gurion Archives) that the Arab countries, notably Egypt, were well armed and were about to attack Israel.

47. ISA/Kinneret Incident, 2440/5, citing Syrian Radio broadcasts. FO 371/121862, Damascus, 13 Apr. 1956; FO 371/121867, Damascus, 30 Oct. 1956; Dayan, *Avney Derekh*, 186; Bar Zohar, iii. 1318–19; NA/683.00/10–657, 1496, 22 Nov. 1957.

48. NA/68300/10-657, DOS 797, 17 Jan. 1956, and 557, 11 Sept. 1956; ISA/MAC 2434/9, 3 Jan. 1956.

49. Bar Zohar, iii. 1241, 1259–60. Cf. al-Muʿalim, 197–8; see also FO 371/128219, Damascus, 15 Nov. 1957.

50. Seale, *Syria*, 262; FO 371/12156, Tel Aviv, 13 Dec. 1956; NA/68300/10-657, DOS 179, 17 Dec. 1956; al-Muʿalim, 203.

51. FO 371/121867, Damascus, 30 Oct. 1956; Seale, *Syria*, 262; Bar Zohar, iii. 1297; Dayan, *Avney Derekh*, 291.

52. Cf. FO 371/121867, 30 Oct. 1956, a joint Syrian–Soviet statement; FO 371/128236, Damascus, 19 Jan. 1957; NA/68384A/8-257, DOS 259, Damascus, 5 Dec. 1957.

53. FO 371/121867, Damascus, 18 Sept. 1956; FO 371/121727, Tel Aviv, 23 Apr. 1956; FO 371/128236, Damascus, 14 Jan. 1957; FO 371/134312, Damascus, 24 Dec. 1957; ISA/Kinneret Incident, 2440/5, 13 Dec. 1955, and 6 Jan. 1956.

54. FO 371/128159, 22 July 1957; NA/683.84A/8-257, referring to 15 July 1957; cf. a previous statement by al-ʿAsali. FO 371/121858, Damascus, 27 June 1956.

55. NA/683.84/1-457, 1460, 27 July 1957; 76, 10 July 1957; 1235, DOS, 19 Apr. 1957; 2565, 26 Apr. 1956; FO 371/128159, Tel Aviv, 18 Nov. 1957; FO 371/134303, New York, 30 Jan. 1958; ISA/DMZ, 2953/11, 12 July 1956; Bar Zohar, iii. 1318–19; Dayan, *Avney Derekh*, 179–80.

56. NA/683.00/10-657, 13, 6 Oct. 1957; cf. FO 371/121867, Damascus, 27 June 1956; FO 371/121862, 7 July, 7 Sept., and 7 Dec. 1956. Cf. Amin Saʿid, *al-Jumhuriyya al-arabiyya al-muttahida*, i (Cairo, 1959), 25.

57. Special National Intelligence estimate 36.7-56, 20 Nov. 1956, DD 790 (1983); Document of 21–3 Mar. 1957, DD 283 (1985). See also Memo by Secretary of State Dulles, 2 Sept. 1957, DD 1886 (1984); *FRUS*, xiii. 561, 567, 575 ff., 638, 642; FO 371/121858, Teheran and Damascus, 10 and 15 Mar. 1956; FO 371/121802, Beirut, 10 Dec. 1956. American Embassy, Beirut, to DOS, 28 Aug. 1957, DD 2095 (1989).

58. American Embassy, Damascus to DOS, 17 Aug. 1957, DD 71G (1977); White House Records, 12 Apr. 1960, DD 926 (1983); Radio Damascus, 13 Aug. 1957, quoted in Torrey, *Syrian Politics*, 360.

59. Seale, *Syria*, 301–2; *FRUS*, xiii. 681 ff., Bulganin to Menderes, 10 Sept. 1957, in Ro'i, 355–7; al-ʿAzm, iii. 15–16.

60. Cf. *FRUS*, xiii. 525; Copeland *The Game of Nations*, 220 ff.; al-ʿAzm, iii. 35–6; White House Records, 22 Apr. 1960, DD 926 (1983).

61. Cf. FO 371/121867, Damascus, 27 June 1956; for a detailed account of the process leading to this union, see F. A. Sayegh, *Arab Unity* (New York, 1958), 171 ff.; al-Muʿalim, 225 ff. See also al-ʿAzm, iii. 111, criticizing the Syrian motives.

62. For comprehensive accounts, see Louis and Owen, *Suez 1956* (Oxford, 1989); S. I. Troen and M. Shemesh (eds.), *The Suez–Sinai Crisis 1956* (New York, 1990); see also American Embassy, Damascus to DOS, 3 Aug. 1957, DD 71E (1977); CIA Report, 30 Sept. 1958, DD 772 (1983).

63. Seale, *Syria*, 256; al-Muʿalim, 202. Cf. Memo to the US Joint Chiefs of Staff, 17 June 1957, DD 471B (1981).

64. Seale, *Syria*, 305; cf. NA/68384/1-457, DOS 13, 10 July 1957. White House Records, 18 Aug. 1960, DD 926 (1983). But see also al-ʿAzm, iii. 111 ff., harshly criticizing the Syrian leaders' motives and Nasser's intentions.

65. Seale, *Syria*, 305–6; Sayegh, *Arab Unity*, 173.

66. See respectively FO 371/134312, Tel Aviv, 3 Jan. 1958, citing Radio Damascus, 2 Dec. 1957; Tel Aviv, 6 Jan. 1958; Radio Cairo, 8 Dec. 1957, quoting the Syrian COS, General Bizri. Cf. 371/128219, Damascus, 15 Nov. 1957; NA/783.00/1-258, DOS 58, 7 Jan. 1958; NA/68384/1-457, DOS 13, 10 July 1957.

4

Israel Confronts the USSR, the USA, and the UAR

SOVIET ANTI-ISRAELI POLICY

Indeed, since late 1956 Ben Gurion and Dayan were becoming more and more concerned about the growing military threat from Syria, not only in conjunction with Egypt, but also in view of increasing Soviet military assistance to Syria, as well as to Egypt. Moreover, they were worried not merely about the continued supply of modern Soviet weapons to Syria, but more particularly about the possibility of the direct involvement of Soviet troops, disguised as volunteers, in a Syrian/Arab attack on Israel. Such a danger appeared imminent soon after the Suez–Sinai operation, when the Israeli Mossad (intelligence service), the CIA, NATO, and other sources reported that, in addition to weapons and 'volunteers', Soviet pilots and military aircraft were arriving in Syria, with the intention of bombing Israel. These reports, which later proved to be false, followed a very severe warning by the Soviet prime minister, Nikolai Bulganin, on 5 November 1956, that Israel was about to jeopardize its own existence as a state if it did not immediately stop the war with Egypt and withdraw from occupied Sinai.[1] Bulganin's threatening letter (apparently alluding to the use of 'terrible' new weapons against Israel) was described by Ben Gurion as one that could have been written by Hitler, and it in fact influenced Israel's decision to withdraw from Sinai early in 1957. This hostile attitude, coupled with growing Soviet military aid to Syria, led Ben Gurion to express a concern, late in 1957, that Israel might be 'attacked by Russia through Syria'.[2] It should be noted that Ben Gurion and other leaders appealed to the Soviet government in an attempt to refute the allegations against Israel, stressing its desire to coexist peacefully with the Arab nations, and deploring Soviet anti-Israeli propaganda and military supplies to Syria and Egypt.

Thus, in an October 1957 dispatch to the Soviet ambassador in Tel Aviv, apparently prepared by Ben Gurion, the Ministry of Foreign Affairs indicated, *inter alia*:

The Ministry of Foreign Affairs views with deep concern the harsh propaganda campaign against the State of Israel which has been conducted for a while by the Soviet press and radio, totally overlooking proven facts and publishing things that have no existence . . . Soviet newspapers of 6 October 1957 reached a kind of climax in the anti-Israeli propaganda campaign when they printed a 'Tass' cable from Damascus [regarding] . . . a plan to attack Syria by American and Israeli armies on 27 September 1957 from Israeli soil . . .

Israel has no aggressive intentions against Syria . . . Israel's Prime Minister declared on 18 July 1957 . . . [that] with the approval of the Knesset, the government has formulated the paragraph: to work toward a Jewish–Arab alliance, economic, social and political cooperation with the neighbouring countries . . . cooperation between the Hebrew nation and the independent Arab nations is an historical necessity. . . . Jewish–Arab peace, real peace is one of the major aims of the State of Israel. . . .

'During the first days of our independence we too enjoyed the moral assistance of the Soviet Union and the tangible help of Czechoslovakia, and we see, with sorrow and astonishment, that these two states have become in recent years, without any justification, the sharpest adversaries of Israel. . . . This Soviet propaganda . . . encourages the most aggressive and extremist circles in the Arab world in their ambition to eliminate the State of Israel . . . [it is] relevant to the massive supply of heavy weapons to Syria and Egypt by the Soviet Union . . . these weapons . . . could be used in an all-out attack on Israel.'[3]

Moshe Dayan, then chief of staff, also referred in a speech (in July 1957) to Soviet allegations of Israeli plans of aggression against Syria (supposedly in co-ordination with the United States, Turkey, and Iraq). He openly invited Russian delegates to visit the border areas in the north to see for themselves that Israel was not engaged in hostile preparations against Syria. But he added that the Russians were not interested in the truth, but were only 'looking for a tune to please the riffraff in Damascus'.[4]

Even though Dayan was sceptical about American willingness to help Israel against a possible Soviet–Arab threat, Ben Gurion and other ministers sought American action to neutralize this alleged threat, and prevent Syria from turning into a 'Soviet satellite'. Further, it can be argued that Ben Gurion used the growing Soviet support of Syria and Egypt at that juncture in order to influence United States policy towards Israel and obtain greater American backing and assistance in its conflict with the Arabs.

AMERICAN–ISRAELI RELATIONS AND
THE SYRIAN ISSUE

American policy regarding the Arab–Israeli conflict since 1949 had by no means been compatible with Israel's positions. To quote a CIA report of July 1950:

At present US and Israeli policies toward the three major issues in Palestine differ widely. On the territorial issue, Israel insists on keeping all the territory it now occupies, while the US supports a settlement based on the 1947 UN partition plan, unless Israel and the Arab states agree on some other resolution. On the question of the Arab refugees, Israel refuses to accept any responsibility while the US endorses the December 1948 UN resolution that those refugees wishing to return to their former homes in Israel be permitted to do so and that those not wishing to return be compensated by Israel for their losses. On the question of Jerusalem, Israel favors limited UN supervision of the holy places, while the US supports some form of international regime for the whole city. . . . Until they are reconciled . . . Israel will probably be considered an increasingly poor credit risk, and its relations with the US government will rest on an uneasy basis.[5]

Thus, although committed 'to the existence of the State of Israel', and rendering it financial and moral support, the United States consistently refused to supply arms to the Jewish state, in order to maintain a neutral position on the Arab–Israeli conflict and possibly 'to retain the good will and friendship of the Arab states'.[6]

This impartial American policy—notably during the Eisenhower–Dulles administration—which occasionally had also been critical of various Israeli actions towards the Arabs, did not essentially change with the advent of Soviet influence and arms to Syria and Egypt. And when Israel, in conjunction with France and Britain (the Americans had been kept in the dark), captured Sinai from Egypt in late October 1956, the Eisenhower administration condemned Israel (as well as France and Britain) and demanded total withdrawal from Sinai, indicating its intention to adopt sanctions against Israel.[7]

At that juncture Ben Gurion was more concerned about this unfriendly American attitude than about the Soviet military threat,[8] remarking that, according to the opinion expressed in the White House, he (Ben Gurion) had almost caused a global war out of his own head, and that the existence of Israel disrupted normal relations between the United States and the Arab world. Consequently, Ben Gurion tried very hard not only to justify the Sinai operation and to persuade the American administration (and other Western countries) to help safeguard Israel's freedom of navigation through the Suez Canal and the Straits of Tiran, but in particular to mend fences with the United States and to use the menace of Soviet influence in Egypt and Syria to generate American–Israeli co-operation within the framework of the new Eisenhower doctrine (early 1957). Countering the Soviet–Arab alliance, the hoped-for American–Israeli coalition would first aim at toppling the Egyptian and Syrian regimes. As Ben Gurion already suggested on 10 November 1956, in his communications to the United States, Britain and other Western countries:

... The danger of the Soviets taking control in the whole of the Middle East with the aid of the Egyptian dictator and the Syrian president Shukri al-Quwwatli, who has just returned from Moscow as a Soviet instrument. Should this Soviet take-over not be stopped shortly (and the most efficient means to do this is to remove Nasser and Quwwatli from power) the whole continent of Africa will fall into Soviet hands in the near future. There exist in the Arab world—inside Egypt as well as in Syria—many forces and persons who oppose the rule and the aspirations of Nasser and Quwwatli, but they need the active assistance of the free world in order to be rid of these two malignant people.[9]

On 23 August 1957 Ben Gurion wrote to Secretary of State Dulles:

Turning Syria into a base of international Communism is one of the most danger-ous events which is occuring these days in the free world. . . . All depends on the assertion and bold position of the USA. If this position should be taken, Syria's neighbours—except for Israel—would certainly take action together with rebel-lious elements in Syria in order to uproot the danger to the independence, free-dom and security of the region.[10]

Israeli and American Plans to Topple the Pro-Soviet Regime in Damascus

Already during the summer of 1955 Israeli diplomats were apparently involved in the first futile plan to overthrow the new leftist radical regime in Syria. Husni Barazi, a Syrian pro-Hashemite/pro-Western politician and former prime minister, initiated a meeting with Israeli officials in Zurich in July 1955. He asked Israel's help in mobilizing American sup-port for his plan to establish a pro-Western democratic regime in Syria, under his leadership. A senior Israeli diplomat, Gideon Rafael, advised Barazi how to find 'a way to the hearts of the Americans' and never heard from him again.[11]

In January 1956 an American officer serving as a United Nations ob-server in the Syrian–Israeli MAC unofficially asked an Israeli member of the Commission whether Israel would object if Shishakli were to be reinstated as ruler of Syria; presumably, in order to block the pro-Soviet trends in Syria. This American query might have been linked to the discussions then going on in the State Department over whether or not the United States should help Shishakli and the Syrian Social Nationalist Party (SSNP) in their plan to topple the Syrian government.[12]

On 27 June 1956 the American Assistant Secretary of State for Near Eastern Affairs wrote a memo to Dulles, with the following conclusions:

Adib Shishakli falls clearly short of the type of leader we should like Syria to have, but he might be better than some other potential candidates. . . . Consequently, we should bide our time and await developments before taking any positive position relative to his possible return to power.[13]

Dulles apparently did not respond to this memo. Subsequently in early July 1956 a messenger from Shishakli informed an Israeli diplomat in Geneva that a Shishakli-led coup would be launched in Damascus between 15 and 20 July, and asked that Israel should not take any action except on the actual day of the coup—when the Israeli army should engage the Syrian positions along the border for several hours. The messenger also reported that Shishakli had been encouraged by the American military attaché in Switzerland to carry out his plan and to make contact with Israel. However, on 21 July 1956 Shishakli suddenly arrived in Geneva and reported to the Israeli diplomat that owing to certain new circumstances he had decided to postpone the coup. For a while Shishakli attempted no further action, whereas Israel (and also Iraq) lost several thousand dollars which they had advanced him.[14] In November 1956 and the summer of 1957 respectively, Shishakli was apparently again in touch with the French and American governments regarding further planned coups, which never took place. In August 1957 the United States was allegedly engaged in an anti-Syrian 'conspiracy' aiming at installing Shishakli and subsequently concluding peace between Syria and Israel.[15]

In conclusion, to the extent that the American government secretly planned to topple the pro-Soviet regime in Damascus, during 1956 and 1957, it worked with Turkey and Iraq and with other pro-Western regimes in the Arab world, and was very cautious not to involve Israel and even to discourage Ben Gurion from taking any action against Syria.[16] Further, the American administration endeavoured, at that juncture, to disassociate itself from Israel and show its support of the pro-Western Arab states while criticizing the pro-Soviet regime in Syria. Thus, for example, in a personal letter to King Saud of Saudi Arabia, President Eisenhower wrote in September 1957, *inter alia*:

We have, moreover, never been an important supplier of arms to Israel, nor are we now. You, of course, know that we are sending arms to Saudi Arabia, Iraq, Jordan and Lebanon. . . . Should Israel attempt to conquer any Arab state, the United States would, as it did last October, take action to prevent this.

Similarly, in a circular to American embassies in the Middle East, Secretary of State Dulles suggested the following guidelines:

a) [S]tress firm U.S. opposition to Israeli expansion at expense its neighbors . . . b) give publicity to U.S. arms already sent and still going to friendly Arab states; c) make discreet mention any complaints from Israel or pro-Israel sources about U.S. military and economic aid to Arab states; d) present Soviet support Arab states as purely tactical and motivated by desire increase influence in M.E., point out that Soviet Bloc supported establishment Israel and partition Palestine, furnished arms to Israel during Palestine war, and switched views only recently in hope establishing beachhead in M.E. . . . [and that] pro-Soviet regime in Syria does not have support of Syrian people, opposition to present Syrian regime is led by 'free' Arab countries who see their hard-won independence and their security threatened by traitors to nationalist cause, betraying Arabs to new foreign (Soviet) imperialism; 'free' Arab countries do not compromise their position with respect to Israel by cooperation with Free World.[17]

The growing co-operation between Syria and Egypt during 1957 and the establishment of the Syrian–Egyptian Union (UAR) in February 1958 did not essentially change American policy towards Israel's conflict with the Arab states, Syria included. For example, Dulles wrote to Eisenhower on the eve of the creation of the UAR: 'that the union was dangerous . . . that there was a strong possibility it was supported by the Russians and that if it materialized it would create danger that Jordan and Lebanon would be absorbed, putting Iraq and Saudi Arabia in peril'.[18] There was no mention in this memo of the danger to Israel, even though a military study by the Defense Department of May 1957 concluded *inter alia* that 'the increasing Communist influence in Syria and Egypt could stimulate either of them to actions which would result in a limited war against their neighbors, including Israel.'[19]

Moreover, the radical impact of the Syrian–Egyptian union which, in July 1958, inspired the collapse of the pro-Western regime in Iraq and the militant domestic opposition to the pro-Western governments in Lebanon and Jordan, did not induce the United States either to supply arms to Israel or to include it in a new American-sponsored regional alliance, as proposed by Ben Gurion. In contrast, it rushed arms shipments and marine units to Lebanon, and Britain, in concert with the United States, sent paratroopers to Jordan.

It would thus appear that at that juncture the American government assessed that Israel was militarily stronger than Syria and Egypt and was also likely to launch a pre-emptive military attack on its Arab neighbours. As a CIA report of September 1958 says:

We believe the Israel Defense Force is now more effective militarily than any combination of Arab forces likely to be opposed to it, and could probably defeat the Arab forces if Israel retained freedom of air action. . . . the growth of Arab military strength relative to that of Israel is increasing the chances of a deliberate resort to war [by Israel]. . . . [However] if Nasser's pan-Arab group believed it had achieved clear military superiority over Israel, it would be greatly tempted to blot out Israel.

This report concluded that 'an embargo on the flow of arms to the Arab–Israeli area would probably reduce the danger of war' but also remarked that 'the chances for such . . . cooperation [between the USSR and the USA regarding an embargo] are slim.' Consequently, while unable to halt Soviet arms shipments to Syria and Egypt and continuing to supply weapons to Jordan, Lebanon, and Saudi Arabia, the American administration carried on with the arms embargo on Israel. The reason for this was as follows: 'If significant military supplies are provided Israel by the U.S., prospects for re-establishment of good relations between the US and the bulk of the Arab area will be reduced.'[20]

Indeed, not only had Washington continued its efforts to please the conservative Arab allies, but it also developed a positive pragmatic policy toward the newly established nationalist, radical UAR (which itself did not wish to become too dependent on Moscow), while disregarding Israel's major defence concerns. Thus, a National Security Council (NSC) policy paper of November 1958 suggested *inter alia* the following guidelines:

Endeavor to establish an effective working relationship with Arab nationalism while at the same time seeking constructively to influence and stabilize the movement and to contain its outward thrust, and recognizing that a policy of U.S. accommodation to radical pan-Arab nationalism as symbolized by Nasser would include many elements contrary to U.S. interests . . . while seeking pro-Western orientation, accept neutralist policies of states in the area when necessary . . . continue limitation on shipments of arms to Israel except for the minimum numbers and types necessary for maintenance of internal law and order, and on a realistic basis for legitimate self defense. Solicit the assistance of other nations in implementing this policy of limitation.[21]

Nevertheless, this arms embargo policy was by no means intended by the United States to expose Israel to a UAR assault or to undermine its regional strategic position. For, apart from evaluating Israeli military capacity as superior to that of Egypt and Syria together, the Americans regarded their ties with Israel as 'close and friendly' and did not object to, perhaps even backed, Israel's new regional strategy—the 'periphery alliance'. Ben Gurion, who had designed this strategy, indicated in a memo of 22 July 1958 to Eisenhower:

Our aim is to form a group of several states, not necessarily a formal and publicized alliance, which would be able to firmly withstand the Soviet expansion via Nasser and could even result in Lebanon's freedom [independence] and perhaps, in time, that of Syria. This group would include two non-Arab Muslim states (Turkey and Iran), a Christian state (Ethiopia) and the State of Israel.

According to Ben Gurion, Dulles encouraged him to create this new alliance[22] and around the same time Israel co-ordinated with the United States the passage of 1,500 British troops over Israeli air space to help King Hussein defend his regime against an alleged Syrian (UAR) attempt to topple it.

Still, Ben Gurion was not satisfied with this limited understanding with Washington. He tried in vain to obtain a security guarantee against a possible all-out Arab attack, particularly an Egyptian–Syrian air assault. Alternatively, according to an American report, he planned to acquire 'nuclear weapons and ballistic missiles' in order to deter the Arabs from attempting to destroy Israel.[23] The US apparently objected to an Israeli nuclear capability.

ISRAEL AND THE UAR

Israel and the United States essentially disagreed about the role of Nasser and the UAR in Soviet–American rivalry as well as in the Arab–Israeli conflict. The United States believed that Nasser objected to Soviet–Communist expansion in the Middle East and was largely seeking the integration of Syria, and economic development within the UAR. Accordingly, American efforts to improve relations with the UAR were not considered by Washington to be carried on at Israel's expense. 'On the contrary [it was argued] we are endeavoring realistically to develop limited areas of mutual interest between the US and the UAR which will improve chances for gradual progress in overall area problems. We believe this policy is in the interests of Israel itself.'[24] Israel, however, regarded Nasser as a Soviet instrument who was endangering the security of the

Middle Eastern states, notably Israel, while his improved relations with the United States encouraged him to act against Israel, particularly on the Syrian front.[25]

Indeed, according to Israeli allegations and complaints, during the UAR period (1958–61) numerous attacks were made by Syrian troops against Israeli villages along the border as well as fishing and police boats on Lake Tiberias, namely: 100 attacks during 1958; 50 during 1959; 67 during 1960; and 25 during 1961.[26] These actions were periodically accompanied by strong anti-Israeli declarations by Syrian and Egyptian leaders as well as by the UAR refusal to permit Israeli ships to transit through the Suez Canal.[27] Thus, for example, UAR President Nasser and Syrian Ba'thist leaders Bitar and Hawrani vehemently attacked Zionism (and imperialism) and promised to 'spill Arab blood in order to free Palestine' (Nasser) and bring about 'the destruction of Israel'.[28]

In the same vein Egyptian and Syrian writers, like Muhammad Hassanein Haykal, wrote: 'Our delayed and inevitable war with it [Israel] was to have one single result, the defeat of Israel . . . as Saladin defeated the Crusaders, so will Gamal Abdul Nasser defeat the Zionists.'[29] Still, it should be noted that at least several of these verbal and military attacks against Israel were provoked by Israeli military assaults and actions against Syrian positions.

It is true that Foreign Minister Golda Meir and Prime Minister Ben Gurion appealed publicly in March and December 1959 as well as in November 1960 and July 1961 to the Arab leaders, notably Nasser, to negotiate a peace agreement.[30] These appeals, however, were rejected by Arab leaders, who declared that Israel was a usurper of Arab lands and an aggressor. And, like Israel, UAR/Syria filed many hundreds of complaints at the United Nations during 1958–61 against alleged Israeli provocative actions in the DMZ.[31] United Nations officers and other foreign observers were divided in their judgements regarding those Israeli actions. While some wrote that Israel acted during that period with 'great restraint' and 'unprovocatively',[32] others accused Israel of 'provocative actions' from Syria's viewpoint.[33]

A major case in illustration is that of the Syrian village of Tawafiq, near the southern part of the DMZ. Early in 1960 Israel decided to extend the cultivation of this area in order to prevent Syria from taking effective control there. Viewing this as an encroachment on their land, the Syrians fired at Israeli workers from their nearby positions in Tawafiq. In reaction, Israeli troops attacked Tawafiq on 31 January–1 February 1960 and destroyed it.[34] This assault was apparently aimed at deterring Syria from

further obstructing the land development and possibly also at challenging Nasser's leadership of the UAR. Nasser, for his part, regarded the
Tawafiq raid as a threat to Syria and the Union, and moved large Egyptian
military forces into Sinai, to the Israeli army's great surprise. Israel mobilized the reserves and also moved troops towards Sinai. This crisis was
eventually defused on the brink (and Nasser hailed it as a great Arab
victory),[35] while both the UAR/Egypt and Israel continued to acquire
more arms for the crucial showdown. While Egypt obtained modern
Soviet weapons, Israel was allegedly developing its nuclear capability,
with French help, and also getting modern Centurion tanks and Blood-
hound missiles from Britain.[36]

However, the possibility of a new Arab–Israeli war was deferred for
several years when Syria broke away from the UAR in late September
1961, thus inflicting a severe blow both to the ideal of Arab unity and to
the hope of all-Arab military strategy against Israel.[37] Syria, thus becoming regionally isolated and domestically weak, rendered Israel a clear
strategic service, as assessed by a contemporary CIA paper:

[I]ncreased disunity among the Arabs, particularly the dissolution of the UAR,
decreases the threat to Israel of simultaneous hostilities on two fronts, thus enhancing Israel's security position . . . We believe . . . that Israel will be able to
maintain its military superiority over its Arab neighbors—a superiority which the
Arabs recognize and which inhibits deliberate attack on Israel. . . . In its 13 years
of independence Israel has accomplished much. It has maintained a stable democratic system of government; it has made tremendous strides in economic development; it has absorbed a net flow of some 850,000 persons, more than doubling
its Jewish population.[38]

At that juncture, Israel utilized its strong position *inter alia* vigorously
to pursue its ambitious Jordan–Negev water carrier project—despite
intense Syrian/Arab opposition—to help absorb the new Jewish *olim*
(immigrants).

VIOLENT DISPUTES OVER THE JORDAN-NEGEV WATER PROJECT

Already in 1953 the Israeli government reached a decision to divert the
waters of the Upper Jordan river to the Negev desert region, which
comprised 60 per cent of Israel's uninhabited lands. (The Negev was
regarded, mainly by Ben Gurion, as the major agricultural settlement area
for the numerous but unskilled new Jewish immigrants.) The first phase

of the project included digging a canal from Bnot Ya'aqov bridge to Lake
Tiberias, and building a power station that would use the water flow in
the canal to produce electricity. Like the Hula project, a small part of the
newly designed canal was situated in the DMZ, but Israel, learning the
lesson of the Hula dispute (see above), made it clear that the project would
not involve the use of Arab-owned land in the DMZ.[39] Still, again as in the
Hula conflict, Syria objected to the Bnot Ya'aqov project mainly on the
grounds that the military balance in the area would be changed in favour
of Israel, owing to the topographical alterations, and that the project
would affect normal civilian life in the DMZ; Syria therefore had a right
to veto its implementation. It threatened to use military force and also to
divert the Banyas and Hasbani rivers—the Jordan tributaries—into Syria.
Major-General Bennike, the MAC chairman, supported the Syrian arguments and in September 1953 asked that Israel stop working on the
project. When Israel ignored this request, the United States threatened
Israel with economic sanctions, *inter alia* in order to launch its own
Johnston Jordan Valley project for the allocation of the Jordan and
Yarmuk waters among Israel, Jordan, Syria, and Lebanon. Against
Sharett's view, Ben Gurion initially rejected American pressure, but later
agreed to halt the work temporarily and to accept a compromise formula,[40]
which was contained in a joint Anglo-French-American resolution in the
Security Council. This resolution was vetoed by the Soviet Union, a
permanent member of the Security Council, casting its veto against Israel
for the first time.[41] Israel was thus obliged to stop working on this scheme,
and to divert its attention to preparing an alternative Lake Tiberias–
Negev water project.

   The UN Secretary-General initiated a water survey intended to settle
the dispute and enable Israel to divert the River Jordan without prejudic-
ing Syrian rights. The report by water experts J. W. Dixon and W. F.
Eysvoogel was secretly submitted in April 1954 but was not made public
owing to American pressure. The United States government preferred a
more comprehesive approach to the water problem, namely the four-
country Johnston Jordan Valley project. Ben Gurion objected to the
Johnston plan on the grounds that the River Litani in Lebanon was not
included in the project. He was also opposed to an American involvement
('American Mandate') in that issue for, in his view, the United States
supported the Arab side against Israel.[42] The Arab states, notably Syria,
likewise initially rejected the Johnston plan, 'since they oppose any
scheme which would give Israel a share of the Jordan waters. . . . They
also fear that the acceptance of the plan would imply acquiescence in the
existence of Israel.'[43]

Subsequently, however, persuaded by Sharett and Finance Minister Eshkol, the Israeli government approved a revised Johnston plan late in 1955, and so to all intents and purposes did Egypt and Jordan, although Syria maintained a determined opposition to the plan and thus caused its defeat. A senior United Nations official wrote later:

> The Johnston negotiation seemingly close to success was stalled by the obduracy of the Syrian politicians. They simply would not agree to anything that would benefit Israel, even if the Arab states would thereby achieve greater benefits. Syria also opposed anything implying recognition of Israel's right to exist.[44]

In October 1955 Johnston told Sharett that Nasser had asked for a two to three months' delay in order to have Syria join an agreement regarding the Jordan plan. Sharett agreed to wait four months until March 1956, stipulating that, if no agreement were reached, Israel would unilaterally start work to divert the River Jordan.[45] The Syrian government, on its side, threatened to use force if Israel started the diversion work. Egypt, Iraq, and Jordan declared that they would help Syria in such a case.[46] In reaction, 'Ben Gurion stated that if the Arabs did not agree to some plan for diverting the Jordan River soon, the work would be done whatever happens, and whoever interferes with them bears the consequences.'[47] Apparently to face possible Syrian action, Israel moved military forces into the area, 'slowly taking over the entire demilitarized zone' and 'creating new defensive positions'. Syria also moved more forces and weapons into defensive positions along the border; and for a long period incidents and exchanges of fire occurred in various border areas with each side accusing the other of provocation.[48]

Yet, apart from completing a small drainage canal in the Hula, Israel refrained from starting the major diversion of the Jordan near Bnot Yaʿaqov bridge, taking into account the American and United Nations objections to such work in the DMZ. Instead, Israel moved the site of the Jordan–Negev diversion to the north-west corner of Lake Tiberias, which was under full Israeli sovereignty, and started work in early 1958. Baʿth leaders in Syria, by then part of the UAR, urged Nasser to take action to halt the diversion, but he refused. Instead Syrian and Israeli forces continued to engage periodically in exchanges of fire—some of them sharp—resulting in not a few casualties among soldiers and civilians on both sides.[49] The most serious incident during the UAR period was that of Tawafiq in late January 1960 (as already described), but it was not related to the River Jordan diversion. From 1960 and particularly following the collapse of the UAR (in September 1961), the Syrian–Israeli conflict evolved mainly around the diversion project, as Israel stepped up work at the diversion site. The Arab League Defence Council was convened in June 1961 and adopted secret decisions to prevent the Israeli scheme from being carried out. Among the decisions taken was a plan to divert the headwaters of the River Jordan in Syria and Lebanon in order to prevent them from reaching Israeli-controlled territory. In fact, most Arab League members, including Egypt, were not prepared to carry out such a plan in practice. The short-lived new parliamentary regime in Damascus was obviously too weak to take any effective action against the Israeli diversion scheme. But, entangled in acute internal conflicts as well as harassed by Nasser and aiming at embarrassing him, this regime made show of a strong militant attitude towards Israel, making anti-Israeli declarations, shooting at Israeli boats on Lake Tiberias, and shelling villages around the lake.[50] In reaction, and apparently in order to deter the new Syrian regime from obstructing the Israel–Jordan River scheme, the Israeli army, in mid-March 1962, attacked and destroyed Syrian military positions in Nuqaib, near the north-eastern shore of the lake.[51] Israel was strongly condemned by the Security Council but continued to be engaged in periodic shooting incidents with Syria.[52]

Only after March 1963, following the Ba'th revolution and seizure of power in Damascus, did the new nationalist radical regime adopt bold actions against Israel's advanced work to complete the Jordan waters diversion scheme. The Ba'th Sixth National Congress, held in September 1963, resolved that Israel's Jordan–Negev diversion 'must be prevented by force',[53] while preparations were made by Syria to divert the headwaters of the River Jordan.

Vis-à-vis the new Syrian Ba'th militant regime, the new Israeli government formed in 1963 was headed by Levi Eshkol, a moderate, hesitant leader, who was urged by several ministers and army officers to adopt an activist policy towards Syria. Hence, a new and violent phase developed in the Syrian–Israeli confrontation, focusing mainly on the Jordan waters dispute and leading to the June 1967 war.

NOTES

1. Ben Gurion Diary, 7–8 Nov. 1956. Printed also in Troen and Shemesh, *Suez–Sinai Crisis*, 318. Cf. Bar Zohar, iii. 1272–3, 1292; Dayan, *Avney Derekh*, 186; Seale, *Syria*, 288; M. Zak, *Israel and the Soviet Union* (Hebrew; Tel Aviv, 1988), 189 ff.

2. Top Secret telegram from the American Embassy in Tel Aviv, 22 Aug. 1957, DD 2092 (1987). Cf. Dayan, *Avney Derekh*, 355–6; Bar Zohar, iii. 1318–19; FO 371/128090, Tel Aviv, 6 Sept. 1957; Ben Gurion Diary, 11 Oct. 1957.

3. Ben Gurion Archives, Oct. 1957. Cf. NA/68384A/1–457, DOS 930, Tel Aviv, 7 Feb. 1957; DD DOS 2092 from Tel Aviv, 22 Aug. 1957. On Soviet allegations, see al-Muʿalim, 220, citing a Soviet source.

4. FO 371/128090, Tel Aviv, 18 July 1957. See also *Divrey Haknesset* (Knesset Records, Hebrew; Jerusalem, 1958), 23. 2 (21 Oct. 1957); 179 (18 Nov. 1957), 485–6 (24 Dec. 1957).

5. CIA Report, 24 July 1950, DD 2504 (1986). Cf. 'Proposal by Secretary of State Dulles for a Settlement in the Arab–Israel Zone', 26 Aug. 1955, in Hurewitz, *Diplomacy*, ii. 395–8.

6. The quotations are from Dulles Papers, Memo, 30 Mar. 1956, DD 2564 (1982). Cf. N. Safran, *The United States and Israel* (Cambridge, Mass., 1963), 231–2; cf. Ben Gurion Diary, 22 Jan. 1952.

7. 'Ben Gurion's Diary: The Suez–Sinai Campaign', in Troen and Shemesh, *Suez–Sinai Crisis*, 320; Safran, *The United States*, 242–3. For the texts of the American-sponsored UN resolution, and for an excerpt from Eisenhower's broadcast of Feb. 1957, see C. H. Dodd and M. E. Sales (eds.), *Israel and the Arab World* (London, 1970), 124–8.

8. Zak, *Israel and the Soviet Union*, 195; Bar Zohar, iii. 1297.

9. Ben Gurion Diary, 10 Nov. 1956; also in Troen and Shemesh, *Suez–Sinai Crisis*, 319–20. Cf. American Embassy, Tel Aviv, 22 Aug. 1957, Report on a conversation with Ben Gurion, DD 2092 (1987).

10. Cited in Bar Zohar, iii. 1319. Cf. American Embassy, Tel Aviv to DOS, 28 Aug. 1957, DD 2093 (1987); Ben Gurion Diary, 16 Oct. 1957.

11. ISA/Israeli–Arab Relations, 2410/10, 3 Oct. 1955.

12. See respectively ISA/MAC, 130.02/22/2408, 11 Jan. 1956; *FRUS*, xiii. 563–4, from the American Embassy in Syria to the DOS. Cf. al-Muʿalim, 204–5.

13. *FRUS*, xiii. 579–81; cf. Seale, *Syria*, 270–2.

14. Dispatches: 81/192, 6 July 1956; 82/165, 8 July 1956; 93/219, 21 July 1956; 99/107 and 98/92, 22 Aug. 1956—between Israeli Ministry of Foreign Affairs and Israel's legation in Geneva (in the possession of the author). See also Ben Gurion Diary, 1 May 1957; al-Muʿalim, 205.

15. Cf. *FRUS*, xiii. 604; Seale, *Syria*, 294 ff.; al-Muʿalim, 216.

16. US Secretary of State to the President, Confidential, 20 Aug. 1957, DD 2094 (1987); US President to British Prime Minister, Top Secret 22 Aug. 1957, DD 2091 (1987); Bar Zohar, iii. 1318–19, citing Dulles's letter of 21 Aug. 1957 to Ben Gurion.

17. See respectively Presidential Handling, Secret, 11 Sept. 1957, DD 290 (1985); Circular, Secret, 25 Sept. 1957, DD 1544 (1989); cf. American Embassy, Tel Aviv to DOS, 28 Aug. 1957, Secret, DD 2093 (1987).

18. Memorandum for the President, Top Secret, 30 Jan. 1958, DD 1060 (1983).

On the UAR, see M. Palmer, 'The United Arab Republic: An Assessment of Failure', *Middle East Journal*, 20 (1966), 50 ff.

19. 'Military Study on the Defense of the Middle East', Top Secret, 29 May 1957, DD 155A (1980); NA/68384A/8-257, DOS 259, Damascus, 5 Dec. 1957.

20. 'Arab–Israeli Arms Problem—Relative Capabilities and the Prospects for Control, 30 Sept. 1958, DD 773 (1983); cf. 'Military Study', 29 May 1957; National Security Council [NSC], 'US Policy toward the Near East', 4 Nov. 1958, DD 386B. (1980).

21. NSC, 'US Policy', 4 Nov. 1958. Cf. Operations Coordinating Board, Washington, DC, Semi-Annual Appraisal of US Policy toward the Near East, 24 July 1959, DD 2566 (1989). Cf. al-ʿAzm, iii. 109; ISA/Middle East, 4 Jan. 1960.

22. Bar Zohar, iii. 1320–30; cf. 'Arab–Israeli Arms Problem', 3; Operations Coordinating Board, 24 July 1959, 8; Ben Gurion Diary, 10 Mar. 1958.

23. Ben Gurion Diary, 10 Mar. 1958; also Bar Zohar, iii. 1359 ff.; 'Arab–Israeli Arms Problem', 3; cf. FO 371/157765, 7 Mar. 1961; FO 371/157392, 20 Mar. 1961.

24. Position paper, 5 Mar. 1960, DD 493 (1992); cf. al-ʿAzm, iii. 108–9; ISA/ Middle East, 4 Jan. 1960.

25. Ben Gurion Archives, Resolutions of Mapai Party, 15 May 1958. Cf. 'Consultation Regarding the Middle East', 7 Jan. 1960, Ben Gurion Archives.

26. D. Ben Gurion, 'Syrian Attacks and Campaign in the UN', *Davar*, 27 Jan. 1967; [UN] *Year Book* 1959, 34–5; ibid., 1960 Suppl. 8–11, S/4264, 3 Feb. 1960, and 78, S/4843, 23 June 1961; FO 371/142324, 27 Oct. and 23 Nov. 1959.

27. US Operations Coordinating Board (July 1959), 6. Cf. *Divrey Haknesset*, 26. 1478 (16 Mar. 1959).

28. FO 371/150904, 3 Mar. 1960; FO 371/142324, 18 Dec. 1959; FO 371/134382, 6 Feb. and 13 Dec. 1958; FO 371/150904, 4 and 25 Feb. 1960; ISA/Arab propaganda, 5353/21, 2 Jan. 1961; [UN] *Year Book* 1960 Suppl. 3–5, S/4365, 1 July 1960; FO 371/157765, 25 July 1961.

29. FO 371/157765, 12 May 1961; FO 371/151204, 9 Feb. 1960. Cf. Ben Gurion Archives, 4 Feb. 1960. For a long list of anti-Israeli statements see *Middle East Record* [*MER*], i. *1960* (Tel Aviv, n.d.), 171 ff.; *MER*, ii. *1961* (Tel Aviv, n.d.), 180 ff. See also Saʿid, *al-Jumhuriyya*, 79.

30. FO 371/151166, 11 Nov. 1960; FO 371/157765, 14 July 1961; FO 371/157765, 11 July 1961; *Divrey Haknesset*, 26. 1703 (30 Mar. 1959); 28. 19 (16 Dec. 1959); *MER 1960*, 176; *MER 1961*, 183.

31. [UN] *Year Book* 1959, 34–5; ibid., 1960 Suppl. 4–5, S/4263, 3 Feb. 1960; 8– 11, S/4268, 18 Feb. 1960; NA/68384a/8-257, DOS 2086, 232, 2 Feb. 1958; 295, 31 Mar. 1958.

32. FO 371/151204, 3 Feb. 1960; FO 371/151201, 6 July 1960.

33. NA/68384a/8–257, DOS 2070, 30 Jan. 1958; ibid. 114, 19 Mar. 1959. See also F. Khouri, 'The Policy of Retaliation in Arab–Israeli Relations', *Middle East Journal*, 20 (1966), p. 452.

34. Khouri, 'The Policy', 442; FO 371/151200, 1 Feb. and 18 Feb. 1960; *Divrey Haknesset*, 28. 499 (1 Feb. 1966); *MER 1960*, 197 ff.

35. FO 371/151204, 9 Feb. 1960; Y. Rabin, *Pinkas Sherut* (Hebrew; Tel Aviv, 1979), 106–8; Ben Gurion Diary, 4 Feb. 1960; [UN] *Year Book* 1960 Suppl. 8–11, S/4268; ISA/UAR, 3344/50, 15 and 23 Feb. 1960. For full details, see *MER 1961*, 203–4.

36. FO 371/157765, 7 Mar. 1963; FO 371/157772, 10 Mar. 1961; FO 371/157793, 24 Mar. 1961; FO 371/157392, 20 Mar. 1961; FO 371/157744, 16 and 27 June 1961; *MER 1961*, 221 ff.

37. On the collapse of the UAR, Israeli reactions, and subsequent events in Syria, see FO 371/157826, 29 Sept. 1961; ISA/Middle East, 3325/42, Sept. 1961; Petran, *Syria*, 147 ff.; Palmer, 'The United Arab Republic'; al-ʿAzm, iii. 169 ff.

38. CIA Report (10), 5 Oct. 1961, Secret, DD 94 (1991).

39. Bar Yaʿacov, *The Israel–Syrian Armistice*, 114 ff. Shalev, *Co-operation*, 263 ff; F. Khouri, 'The Jordan River Controversy', *Review of Politics*, 27 (1965), 32 ff.

40. Ben Gurion Diary, 22 Oct. 1953; Bar Zohar, ii. 982–3; IDF Archive, 708/68/49. FO 371/104756, Amman, 30 Dec. 1953; Sharett, *Yoman*, 28 ff., 72 ff. Y. Bar Siman-Tov, 'The Limits of Economic Sanctions', *Journal of Contemporary History*, 23 (1988), 425 ff. For more details about the dispute, see FO 371/104772, Damascus, 14 Sept. 1953 and Tel Aviv, 24 Sept. 1953.

41. Khouri, 'Friction', 30–1; for the draft resolution, see DOS, 11 Nov. 1953, DD 2602 (1991).

42. Ben Gurion Diary, 26 June and 25 Aug. 1954; on the US initial position, see DOS from Damascus, 22 Oct. 1953, DD 375 (1984). For details, see Shalev, *Co-operation*, 273 ff; Y. Nimrod, *Mey Meriva* (Givat Haviva, 1966), 41 ff.

43. Dulles to Eisenhower, Confidential, 7 May 1954, DD 308 (1982).

44. See respectively Burns, *Between Arab and Israeli*, 113; Eric Johnston in *New York Times Magazine*, 10 Aug. and 19 Oct. 1958, cited in Bar Yaʿacov, *Israel–Syrian Armistice*, 135; Dulles to Eisenhower, 7 May 1954. For details, see Ben Gurion Diary, 22 May 1955; Sharett, *Yoman*, iv. 997 ff.; Nimrod, *Mey Meriva*, 52 ff.; Petran, *Syria*, 188 ff.

45. Sharett, *Yoman*, v. 1357; FO 371/121825, 2 Feb. 1956; cf. FO 371/121826, 21 Mar. 1956.

46. FO 371/121825, 30 Jan. and 1 Feb. 1956; FO 371/121826, 27 Feb. 1956; FO 371/121858, 14 Feb. 1956.

47. Memo, Joint Chiefs of Staff, Washington DC, DD 1984 (130) (1978).

48. Memo, Joint Chiefs of Staff, 8 Feb. 1957; Ben Gurion Diary, 11 June, 13 Aug. 1956 and 9, 10 July, 22 Oct. 1957; Sharett, *Yoman*, v. 1364–5; ISA/MAC/

Syria, 27, 29 June, 4 Sept., and 11, 12 Nov. 1956; [UN] *Yearbook, 1957*, Security Council, Suppl. 3/3815, 20 Apr. 1957; S/3827, 13 May; 3/3844, 1 July 1957; S/3945, 30 Jan. 1958; S/3946, 30 Jan. 1958.

49. [UN] *Yearbook, 1958*, 58–9; S/3985, 2 Apr. 1958, S/4123, 4 Dec. 1958. Ibid., 1959 Suppl. S/4151, 26 Jan. 1959; S/4154, 23 Jan. 1959; ibid. 1960, 182–3; Ben Gurion Diary, 18 Dec. 1958, 14 Feb. 1959; Khouri, 'Friction', 31; Petran, *Syria*, 190–1; Z. Schiff, 'Dispute on the Northern Border', *New Outlook*, 6, (1963), 10–19; ISA/MAC, 29 June 1960; Operations Coordinating Board, Washington DC, 29 July 1959; FO 371/157773, 26 June 1961.

50. On the Arab decision to divert the Jordan headwaters, see FO 371/157395, 12 June 1961; Khouri, 'Friction', 31–2. On the Syrian belligerent declarations and actions, see *Divrey Haknesset*, 33. 1850 ff. (10 Apr. 1962); *MER 1961*, 183, 210–12.

51. [UN] *Year Book* 1962, 135 ff., S/5093 and S/5098, 19 and 21 Mar. 1962; Khouri, 'Retaliation', 442–3; Ben Gurion, 'Syrian Attacks', *Davar*, 27 Jan. 1967; FO 371/157774, 7 Nov. and 12 Dec. 1961; Petran, *Syria*, 191. On the internal conflicts in Syria and its rivalry with Egypt, see Y. Bar Siman-Tov, *Linkage Politics in the Middle East: Syria between Domestic and External Conflict 1961–1970* (Boulder, Colo., 1983), 79 ff.

52. [UN] *Year Book* 1962, S/5111, 9 Apr. 1962, 137–8; ibid., Security Council, Suppl., Feb.–Mar. 1963, S/5258 and S/5261, 115, 131.

53. Petran, *Syria*, 191. For details about the Ba'th Congress and regime, see I. Rabinovich, *Syria under the Ba'th, 1963–66* (Jerusalem, 1972), 49 ff. (hereafter cited as Rabinovich, *Ba'th*). See also next chapter.

5

Ba'thist Extremism and Israeli Activism: The Road to War

The road to the 1967 war was indeed being paved, in many respects, from 1963, with the beginning of a new phase in Syrian–Israeli relations. In March 1963 a radical Ba'thist government was established in Damascus by means of a military coup. It was an ideological Arab nationalist and extremely anti-Zionist regime, its hostility to Israel highly motivated, also reinforced by Soviet support, intense rivalry with Nasser, and the need to channel domestic pressures towards an external enemy, Israel.

Israel, on the contrary, was from June 1963 headed by a new Labour Party leader, Levi Eshkol, a non-ideological, pragmatic, moderate politician, interested in domestic economic development and in peaceful co-existence with the Arabs. Yet his policy towards the belligerent Syrian attitude was influenced, on the one hand, by his assertive, activist colleagues, and, on the other, by the new American policy towards Israel.

The major cause for the Syrian–Israeli escalation into war was the diversion of the River Jordan, which Israel was determined to pursue and Syria to arrest. The issue was subsequently compounded by Syrian-sponsored Palestinian guerrilla operations inside Israel, Israeli retaliatory raids against Syria, Egyptian threats, and Soviet accusations—all of which eventually led to the 1967 Arab–Israeli war.

BA'THIST BELLIGERENCY AND ATTEMPTS TO DIVERT THE JORDAN RIVER SOURCES

Almost from its inception in the early 1940s, the Ba'th (Renaissance) Arab party was strongly anti-Zionist.[1] Affirming Arab unity above all else (and also freedom and socialism), the party considered the Jewish Zionist entity in Palestine as an integral part of the Arab fatherland that should be completely liberated.[2] Consequently the Ba'th strongly objected to Jewish immigration to Palestine during 1945–6 and particularly to the United

Nations partition resolution of November 1947 which recommended the establishment of a Jewish state in part of Palestine. The party indeed considered the establishment of a Zionist state as the 'greatest disaster in the modern history of the Arab people' for, according to Salah al-Din al-Bitar (the Ba'th co-leader alongside Michel Aflaq), that state could endanger Arab unity since the Zionists wished to expand from the 'Euphrates to the Nile'.[3]

In early 1948 the Ba'th Party demanded that the Syrian government arm its members and send them as volunteers to fight a holy war (*jihad*) in order 'to eliminate forever Zionism in Palestine'. The party itself organized a battalion of its members but was prevented by the government from reaching the battlefield.[4] Subsequently, however, the Ba'th continued to be highly concerned about the Palestine problem and the struggle against Israel, notably regarding the River Jordan issue.[5] The Ba'thists indeed considered the Jordan waters as the lifeline of Israel, which would enable it to develop further, by absorbing millions of Jewish immigrants in the Negev.[6] Consequently, the Ba'th Fourth and Sixth National Congresses, in 1960 and 1963 respectively, adopted strong resolutions on the need to prevent the Israeli diversion of the River Jordan, as well as to liquidate the State of Israel.[7]

Prior to the 1963 Congress and subsequently, the Ba'th regime in Damascus initiated a series of artillery attacks on Israeli diversion equipment, while the defence minister proclaimed that 'the Syrian army and people were ready to crush Israel'. In addition, numerous exchanges of fire occurred during 1963–5 between Syrian and Israeli troops along the border and on Lake Tiberias. For example, in July 1963 two serious incidents caused great tension: on 13 July the Syrians seized three Israeli and three Belgian citizens on the eastern shore of Lake Tiberias and jailed and tortured the Israelis for a long period, while on 19 July Syrian soldiers ambushed and killed two *kibbutz* members near Kibbutz Almagor.[8] However, the Syrian army was by no means ready to fight Israel alone. Those belligerent actions and proclamations largely reflected the need of the ruling Ba'th élite to demonstrate a strong Arab nationalist position and to score points in its fierce rivalry with President Nasser and his followers in Syria (concerning the 1963 unity talks between Egypt, Syria, and Iraq, as well as the position of the Nasserites in the new Syrian government). In the words of an Egyptian radio broadcast in June 1963:

The border incidents between Syria and Israel are an artificial crisis which is meant to keep the army busy . . . to divert public opinion from the failings of the

Ba'th regime and to dress up the Ba'th in a cloak of power and make it appear a force rejecting all compromise.[9]

Still, in order to embarrass Nasser and/or perhaps drag him into a war with Israel, the Syrian Ba'thist regime, in early December 1963, called for a meeting in Cairo of the Arab chiefs of staff to discuss its demand to check Israel's diversion project by force. Simultaneously, Damascus launched a propaganda campaign against Nasser's refusal to embark on a war against Israel over the diversion project. Akram Hawrani, a senior Ba'th leader and government minister, accused Nasser of 'collaborating with the US in an attempt to secure the peaceful implementation of the Israeli project', while a Ba'th organ warned Nasser that 'the people will punish all rulers who fail to carry out their duties against Israel.'[10]

Nasser, however, was not prepared to fight Israel over the River Jordan diversion. Forty thousand Egyptian troops had been engaged in a futile war in Yemen and he was reluctant to jeopardize aid from the United States (which supported Israel's project). He managed to outwit the Syrian Ba'th leaders by calling for a summit of the Arab heads of state to share responsibility for whatever decision was taken. The summit which convened in Cairo in January 1964 rejected Syria's demand to wage war against Israel, not even an Algerian type of war. Instead, a decision was taken to divert the headwaters of the River Jordan into Arab lands, to establish a joint Arab military command under Egyptian control, and to create a Palestinian entity.[11]

When Amin al-Hafiz, the dominating personality in Syria and head of the Ba'th National Command, came back from the Cairo summit, he was strongly assailed by the more militant members of the Ba'th Regional Command for his acceptance of the summit resolutions, thus deviating from the party's line. An internal circular by the Ba'th Regional Command of late January 1964 stated:

What we have to do is push the whole Arab people into entering the battle with all this means . . . entering the battle on the diversion of the Jordan on this basis will not only save our country from a grave danger . . . it will also enable our masses to expose the regimes which are hostile to it and conspire with Imperialism in the Arab homeland.[12]

Yet, rather than taking action against Israel's diversion project, the Ba'th regime, still immersed in conflict with domestic Nasserite elements and with Nasser himself, renewed its verbal attacks on Egypt in yet another attempt to drag Nasser into a military attack on Israel. Once again Nasser succeeded in isolating Damascus by convening a second Arab summit meeting in September 1964, which decided to start on the diversion of the Jordan headwaters at once. Frustrated and militant, Damascus was then endeavouring to use the newly emerging Palestinian Fath (or Fatah) liberation movement—led by Yasir Arafat—as a counter-weight to the Egyptian-sponsored Palestine Liberation Organization (PLO), which was first established in May 1964. Syria also intended to employ the Fath in guerrilla attacks inside Israel, to challenge Nasser's passivity, and to carry on a popular liberation war against Israel.[13] The first (futile) commando operation carried out by the Fath under Syrian directives on 1 January 1965 was aimed at damaging a section of the Jordan-Negev carrier in Lower Galilee. A few weeks earlier the Syrians had collected heavy equipment near the River Banyas, preparing to divert that Jordan tributary, and in early 1965, they started their River Banyas diversion works.[14] However, sharp Israeli military attacks soon resulted in the destruction of the diversion equipment (see below).

The Ba'th regime was consequently faced with a difficult dilemma: to fight Israel single-handedly and endure a severe defeat or to postpone the war as Nasser proposed, to a more propitious moment, and thus deviate from its ideological tenets and encounter domestic opposition.

ANTI-ISRAELI IDEOLOGIES AND POLICIES

The Syrian Ba'thist regime was indeed an ideologically charged anti-Israeli regime with a narrow social base, which urgently needed to channel its domestic Islamic popular opposition towards the Israeli enemy, and indoctrinate the Syrian public with anti-Zionist/anti-Jewish notions. The standard depiction of Israel in Ba'thist literature of the mid-1960s was as a Western colonialist-imperialist creation and instrument, aiming at destroying Arab nationalism and unity as well as at expanding from the Nile to the Euphrates.[15] According to this view Israel was a Zionist base which did not represent the Jews, who constitute a religion but not a nation, and have no specific homeland. Israel represented 'a foreign imperialist-Zionist invasion in order to conquer our fatherland . . . [it is] a state without an entity . . . an expanding pus which disseminates poisons of hatred and animosity.' In other Ba'thist publications Zionism was compared to Nazism as well as to the Crusades.[16]

Alongside these Zionist-imperialist stereotypes, Syrian Ba'thist organs also deployed Christian/European anti-Jewish/anti-Semitic epithets to depict Israel as a devilish enemy not only of the Arabs, but of human civilization as a whole. On the basis of the 'Protocols of the Elders of Zion' and similar European anti-Semitic writings, Jews were described as greedy and extortioners, the historic murderers of Jesus and, periodically, of Christians, whose final goal was to 'destroy Christianity' and humanity outside Zionism. In this connection it was proclaimed that 'Judaism is Zionism in itself'.[17]

This being the case, contemporary Ba'thist leaders and their propagandists unequivocally concluded that Israel must be destroyed by force; and that the Ba'th (Syrian) position should be based on 'extremism' in making 'sacrifices in blood, money, and sweat . . . we shall live in poverty, defer our growth . . . our future for the sake of Palestine.'[18]

But while some declared that Israel's destruction was the prior Arab goal, a precondition for Arab unity, others argued that Arab unity as well as proper military, social, and economic reform and preparation were first required in order to fight Israel to the end.[19] The latter position, which had been advocated by Nasser, was in fact adopted in 1965 by the Ba'thist regime under General Amin al-Hafiz (although publicly the government continued to criticize Nasser and to attack Israel). Thus, an internal circular by the National (all-Arab) command of the Ba'th Party stated, on 29 September 1965:

as regards Palestine, we aim at its liberation from conquering Zionism, the annihilation of the State of Israel and the return of the Palestinian Arab people to their fatherland. . . . Looking for the best way to achieve these aims, we should choose the path of revolution against our own reality as well as against conquering Zionism . . . the aim being the creation of a united, progressive force and socialist Arab society whose strength is based on itself. . . . However, taking into account the existence of Israel, its growing economic, political and military strength . . . our present resources are insufficient for the requirements of a war of liberation . . . against the Zionist aggression. . . . Every objectively truthful evaluation of the danger and power of Israel will have to concede that there is not one Arab state that could under present conditions face this danger single-handed, let alone liberate Palestine. It was therefore necessary to plan the strengthening of forces up to the point . . . considered the minimum requirement for an Arab victory.[20]

A similar evaluation was given by Sami al-Jundi, a senior Ba'th leader serving in the Syrian cabinet during 1963–4:

[W]e evaluated that the Syrian army, despite its good arms, experience and courage, was not in a position to hold out more than a few hours against any Israeli attack. . . . The Arab leaders attending several [summit] meetings . . . [regarding] the Palestinian problem . . . [and] the diversion of River Jordan . . . had to face the bitter truth. They were leaders of a nation of a hundred million Arabs who were hardly armed facing a country of a million and a half, which was fully armed.[21]

This position of the Ba'th National Command and government was criticized and challenged by the Ba'th Regional Command and Military Committee headed by General Salah Jadid. The Regional Command depicted (in a memo of 3 November 1965) the circular of the National Command as

> both dangerous and illogical if it implies the postponement of the liberation struggle to an indefinite future . . . we are now told that we shall continue with our non-revolutionary method. Thus we shall definitely lose the confidence of our people and of the rank and file of the party, unless we return to our principles and start a struggle that will be a real revolutionary experience, be it ever so cruel and costly in casualties. . . . It may well be that, as a state, we are unable, considering our present military capabilities, to liberate Palestine, but we are able to kindle the spark . . . we should not be fearful of losing the battle before we have started it.[22]

One way to 'kindle the spark', according to the Ba'th Regional Command, was by activating Palestinian armed groups as an avant-garde in guerrilla warfare inside Israel, which would 'lead to the final war'.[23] Thus the Fath organization was trained and instructed by Ba'thist military leaders, members or supporters of the Regional Command, to carry out guerrilla operations inside Israel. One of these Ba'thist leaders, Hafiz al-Asad, then the commander of the air force, allocated two training bases to Fath and helped it obtain arms from China—apparently without the knowledge of Amin al-Hafiz, the Syrian ruler.[24]

Indeed, the internal Ba'th debate regarding the struggle against Israel constituted one of the causes of the sharp power struggle between the radical Regional Command and the 'rightist' National Command during late 1965 and early 1966. Whereas the former used the Fath to reinforce its position, the latter allegedly created, in late 1965, an artificial crisis along the border with Israel in order to move troops loyal to the Regional Command out of the way.[25]

Eventually, however, the Regional Command, enjoying the support of senior military officers, seized power in Damascus on 23 February 1966 by means of a military coup, led by Salah Jadid, Hafiz al-Asad, and their comrades. The new Ba'th government called for a 'popular liberation war' to free Palestine and accordingly employed the Fath against Israeli targets. Simultaneously the new government resumed Syrian efforts to divert the River Banyas, thus triggering fierce Israeli retaliation.

NEW AMERICAN POLICIES AND ISRAELI
ACTIVIST POSITIONS

Israel considered the River Jordan diversion project not only as highly vital to its economic development but also as legitimate from the international point of view. As already indicated, under United Nations and United States pressure, Israel moved the site of the Jordan diversion scheme from the disputed DMZ, near Bnot Ya'aqov Bridge, to Lake Tiberias, which was fully under Israeli sovereignty. Israel also obtained the backing of the United States (and other Western powers) to divert the River Jordan, provided the work was compatible with Johnston's 'unified plan'. As American officials confirmed, with certain reservations, in their deliberations with Israel from 1962 to 1965:

On the Jordan waters diversion we have committed ourselves to stand by Israel's side during the time of gravest threat that it will have faced since its creation in 1948. . . . The United States has already given Israel some assurances on this, but the Arabs are going to be anxious. . . . The U.S. would not change its position, we had accepted the Johnston plan . . . U.S. reaffirms its support for Israel's water project within the quantities of the unified plan, and its opposition to Arab diversions contrary to this plan . . . [But] the U.S. simply could not accept Israel's military intervention against the Arab projects.[26]

Furthermore, Israel was very well aware that the Arab countries, notably Egypt, were not likely to go to war over the River Jordan diversion. Not only did the Arabs not have a case to attack Israel, but Nasser had candidly admitted that Egypt was unwilling and certainly unprepared to start a war over the Jordan.[27] Nasser even advised the Syrian leaders to refrain from getting involved in such a war lest Israel should 'bomb Damascus'[28] (although he also proclaimed that war was inevitable if Israel attacked Syria, Lebanon or Jordan, and he hoped to 'crush Israel within the present generation'[29]).

It can also be argued that at that juncture Israeli leaders were not really worried that Syria, although armed with modern Soviet weapons, could alone, or even with Egypt, successfully undertake a war against the Jewish state. Indeed, during the prolonged Jordan diversion crisis, 1962–5, Israel was militarily much stronger than Syria (and Egypt): according to an American estimate of May 1963 'Israel will probably retain its overall military superiority vis-à-vis the Arab states for the next several years.'[30] Israel possibly also felt more secure than ever before (without admitting it) owing to the significant change in American attitudes since the early 1960s. For, unlike Eisenhower, President Kennedy, after his election in

1960, publicly proclaimed his support for Israel and, in late 1962, assured Golda Meir that:

The United States . . . has a special relationship with Israel in the Middle East really comparable only to that which it has with Britain over a wide range of world affairs . . . we are in a position then to make clear to the Arabs that we will maintain our friendship whith Israel and our security guarantees . . . in case of an [Arab] invasion the United States would come to the support of Israel.[31]

In the same vein, according to an official US document, 'On October 30, 1963 President Kennedy wrote to Prime Minister Eshkol specifically affirming United States capability and preparedness to safeguard Israel. This letter in fact constitutes a security guarantee.'[32]

In addition to those assurances, the Kennedy administration also increased its economic assistance and, for the first time, provided significant military aid to Israel. As an official document of May 1964 stated:

We have made *generous arms sales* [to Israel] and *given extensive credit on military material short of major offensive weapons*; e.g. 106 mm recoilless rifles, sophisticated radar and communication equipment, $25 million Hawk [anti-aircraft missile] sales on credit. . . . We have *held secret talks with the Israelis in 1962 and 1963 to hear Israel's military concerns* in detail . . . Our *aid level* of about $75 million annually these last three years has been roughly $15 million over the 1948–60 average and *now totals over $1 billion* as compared to *$1.7 billion* of aid to all the Arab states.[33]

President Johnson, who succeeded Kennedy late in 1963, also felt great personal affinity with Israel (and developed a warm rapport with Eshkol), in addition to his perception of Israel as a buffer against Communism. He decided, therefore, to take an unprecedented step by also supplying Israel with offensive weapons:

in view of new Egyptian–Russian arms deal . . . henceforth U.S. undertakes to supply planes, tanks and other vital military equipment to Israel with a view to maintaining arms balance in the area. . . . and *provided the U.S.G. [US Government] and GOI [Government of Israel] agree that a disproportionate arms buildup on the Arab side is developing which cannot be otherwise met, the U.S.G. will make selective direct arms sales to Israel on favorable credit terms.* . . . [In conclusion] the U.S. has much good will for Israel and desires Israel to have an adequate deterrent [emphasis in original].[34]

It should be pointed out that the American government did not approve the development of an Israel nuclear deterrent (which had allegedly started in early 1960);[35] but encouraged Israel at that period (1964–5) to acquire more weapons 'from Western European sources'; and Israel indeed then obtained modern arms from West Germany.[36] In return for this significant support of Israel's military and economic capacities and the River Jordan diversion plan, the Kennedy and Johnson administrations alike insisted that Israel should by no means take any military action against the Arab diversion works lest this prejudice America's relations with its Arab allies in the Middle East.[37] In long conversations with Eshkol and Meir in February 1965, Special Ambassador Harriman repeatedly and sternly warned Eshkol against a pre-emptive military action and demanded 'an undertaking against the use of force' against Arab diversion projects. Initially Eshkol did not commit himself to such an undertaking and instead asked for a guarantee that Israel would get its 'share of the water'—a guarantee that Harriman would not undertake to promise. The American side suggested that the Arab diversion issue should be resolved by peaceful recourse through the UN—to which Eshkol reacted: 'Israel would be entitled to fight for its water if peaceful recourse failed.' In the draft memo of understanding which concluded that discussion, the American delegation suggested the following wording:

The GOI understands the U.S. cannot accept any military action against the Arab diversion works and the GOI agrees to have recourse to all peaceful means, including taking the problem to the United Nations where the U.S. would be prepared to support the principles of the Johnston plan.[38]

It is not clear whether or not the Israeli government approved this draft memo. At any rate, on 16 March 1965, shortly after the Harriman–Eshkol deliberations, Israel, reportedly exploiting Syrian-initiated firing, attacked the Syrian diversion works. On 13 May 1965, on the same plea, Israel again attacked the Syrian diversion site and completely destroyed the equipment, thus bringing the diversion works to a halt.[39] To be sure, these heavy attacks, which included the use of the air force, came after stringent Israeli warnings to Syria to refrain from diverting the Jordan headwaters.[40]

Most of the Israeli warnings were voiced by activist leaders such as Moshe Dayan and Shimon Peres, both Ben Gurion followers, as well as by Yigal Allon (and occasionally by Israel Galili) of the hawkish Ahdut Ha'avoda Party. They considered Ba'thist Syria as highly militant or, in Peres's words, as the 'extremist church' of the 'Arabs' secular religion— the hatred of Israel', and apparently pressed Eshkol to inflict a massive military blow on the Syrian regime.[41] (The execution of Eli Cohen, the Israeli master spy, by the Syrians in May 1965 possibly also contributed to deepen vindictive feelings among Israelis toward Damascus.[42]) But the moderate, pragmatic Eshkol, who had sought peaceful relations with the Arabs, and was also aware of the American position, opted for limited and specific operations against Syria for the 'useful purpose of demonstrating Israeli capability of interdicting the diversion works by measures short of full-scale war'.[43] Eshkol was possibly right, for on 31 May 1965, rejecting Syria's open call for military help, Nasser 'acknowledged that the Arab diversion plan could not be carried out and that the Arabs could not go to war in the foreseeable future'.[44] Nevertheless, the neo-Ba'th leaders who seized power in Damascus in the February 1966 coup managed to set the stage for the June 1967 Arab–Israeli war.

ESCALATION TOWARDS THE 1967 WAR

The neo-Ba'th regime obviously adopted a more militant line towards Israel than that of the previous Ba'th government and, indeed, represented the most extreme anti-Israeli policy since the beginning of the Syrian–Israeli conflict. For one thing, this new regime had the narrowest socio-political base and the most tenuous public legitimacy in modern Syrian history. It was in effect dominated by a group of officers, mostly members of the Alawite minority (12 per cent of the population), considered by many Syrian Muslims as religiously heretic and socially inferior. This unprecedented phenomenon in modern Syrian history, of a minority Alawite rule, was compounded by equally inhabitual and rigid secularist and socialist policies—all of which deeply hurt the religious beliefs and economic interests of large sections of the majority Muslim population.

These unpopular policies, which had already begun to be implemented under the previous Ba'th regime, provoked a series of anti-government demonstrations and disturbances which were brutally put down, thus exposing the sectarian, military nature of the regime. This was also how the new Ba'th rulers were already being seen and criticized by the veteran Ba'th leaders of the National Command on the eve of the 1966 coup. Michel Aflaq, the founder and ideologue of the Ba'th Party, said on 18 February 1966: 'Some of our friends in the armed forces have gone down the road toward factionalism and dominance over the party and the nation.'

A few months earlier, Dr Munif al-Razzaz denounced the 'sectarian grouping' of the Alawite officers.[45] Consequently, the new military rulers in Damascus, badly needing to acquire political legitimacy, neutralize public opposition, and demonstrate more pro-Palestinian and anti-Zionist positions than the veteran Ba'th leaders, embarked on a highly belligerent policy towards Israel in both word and deed. The neo-Ba'th proclamations, articulated by a group of young (non-Alawi) radical leftist ideologues, depicted Israel as the 'main base' of imperialism and colonialism in the region, and the Palestinian problem as 'the pivot of [Ba'th] internal, Arab, and international policy', and called for waging 'a people's war of liberation' against Israel.

Such war . . . with all the pain and sacrifice involved in it, is the sure way that can lead to the repatriation of the Arabs of Palestine as well as to the final liberation of the whole of the Arab homeland and to the achievement of a comprehensive Arab unity based on a people's socialism . . . after the elimination of Israel . . . we will direct our enormous resources towards economic development and prosperity.[46]

Based on these concepts, the neo-Ba'th regime designed a military strategy according to which the Palestinian Arab masses would be the pioneers of the people's war of liberation:

And when in response to the people's war of liberation, Israel will be forced to begin a conventional war, the Arab armies under progressive leadership must be ready to enter the struggle which will then be defensive, by protecting the bases of the *fida'iyyun* [guerrillas] who are the backbone of the people's war of liberation.[47]

Thus, while senior Syrian leaders repeatedly and publicly called, during 1966 and afterwards, for a popular liberation war against Israel, they reportedly initiated 177 border incidents and 75 Palestinian guerrilla actions inside Israel (mostly via Jordan) between 23 February 1966 and 15 May 1967.[48] There can be no doubt that those aggressive Syrian actions and declarations constituted one of the major issues leading to the June 1967 war, even according to neutral or pro-Syrian observers. For example, Patrick Seale, the well-known expert on Syrian affairs, alluded, in May 1966, to Syria's role in causing the 1967 war: 'By carrying terrorism into Israeli territory . . . it promotes guerrilla warfare and yet cannot protect itself against [Israeli] reprisals.' Another analyst, who supports the Syrian case, also concludes that

The increasing evidence of Syria's verbal aggressiveness more and more assumed the character of a calculated provocation, as the neo-Ba'th came to believe that the time had come to engage Israel in decisive battle. This provocative policy gave the Israeli activist clan precisely the pretext it needed to go to war to fulfil its territorial ambitions.[49]

As for Israeli reactions to Syrian verbal and military attacks, Jerusalem filed numerous complaints at the United Nations against hostile, anti-Israeli proclamations from Damascus, aggressive actions by Syrian troops, and 'terrorist' activities by Syrian-sponsored Palestinian organizations directed against Israeli civilian targets and persons.[50] Prime Minister Eshkol, while stressing that Israel was prepared to sign a permanent peace treaty with Syria, warned Damascus that the continuation of Syrian aggressive action would bring about Israeli reaction.[51] The Syrian government, however, interpreted Eshkol's warnings as 'warlike statements threatening Syria and neighboring Arab states', and especially complained about the statements of Israel's then chief of staff, Yitzhak Rabin. Reportedly in early May 1966

Rav-Aluf [Major-General] Rabin told correspondents that although Jordan was used as the base for recent El-Fatah [Fath] raids, it is Syria which openly supports these marauders. . . . We view each state as responsible for the activities [of Fath] launched from its soil. But this does not mitigate Syrian responsibility one iota, said the Chief of Staff.[52]

In September 1966 Rabin went further in his warnings or threatening statements: 'Israel's reaction against Syrian activities must be directed against those who carry out sabotage and against the rulers who support these acts. . . . Hence, the problem with Syria is basically one of a clash with the rulers.' Or, according to the Syrian version: 'The attacks that Israel is being forced to make in reprisal for the sabotage raids . . . are thus aimed at the regime in Syria. . . . Our aim is to change the Syrian Government's decisions and eliminate the cause of the raids.'[53]

Whether or not Rabin intended to cause the collapse of the neo-Ba'th regime, from July 1966 the Israel Defence Force certainly escalated its reaction to Syrian attacks, including the use of air power. This was indeed the position of General David Elazar, Northern Command [Israel . . . 'must perpetually escalate'], and of General Ezer Weizman, Chief of Operation Division, who, like Elazar, advocated the more extensive use of the air force against Syrian targets. Apparently under the influence of these officers and the pressure of his activist ministers and officials—notably Allon, Dayan, and Peres—on 14 July 1966 Eshkol permitted the use of air power against the Syrian Banyas diversion site.[54]

In reaction to these air attacks Syria also employed its air force on 15 August 1966 against Israeli targets, under the direction of General Hafiz al-Asad, the Air Force Commander and defence minister. A Syrian official communiqué of 15 August ran as follows:

[Syria] would not confine herself to defensive action but would attack defined targets and bases of aggression within the occupied area [Israel]. Syria has waited for a suitable opportunity to carry out the new policy . . . by means of her air force in order to prove to the Arab people . . . the untruth of the Israeli claim of air superiority.[55]

This communiqué was broadcast by Damascus Radio despite the fact that two Syrian MiG aircraft which had attacked Israeli boats on Lake Tiberias had been shot down by Israeli jets and ground fire. And although for a while Syria refrained from employing its air force against Israel, its leaders continued to make belligerent proclamations: 'We declare that we are continuing our preparations to launch a people's liberation campaign . . . no matter how heavy the casualties may be . . . until Palestine becomes Arab again.' Accordingly, Syria carried on further commando actions against Israel from its territory and allegedly directed Fath guerrilla operations from Jordan and Lebanon.[56]

While holding Damascus responsible for these actions, Israel also re-acted to guerrilla operations emanating from the Jordanian-held West Bank, by attacking police stations and other targets there. The most serious Israeli attack came on 13 November 1966; in retaliation for the derailment of a freight train near Jerusalem and the destruction of an army patrol vehicle by a land mine, Israeli forces massively attacked the village of Samuʿ and a nearby police station, killing fifteen Jordanian soldiers and three civilians.[57] This action possibly contributed to a further escalation of the Arab conflict with Israel and indirectly constituted one of the factors leading to the Egyptian–Syrian–Jordanian alliance against Israel on the eve of the June 1967 war. Indeed, for several years before 1967, Jordan had been at odds with Syria, Egypt, and the PLO, attempting to prevent Palestinian guerrilla actions against Israel from its territory. The Samuʿ raid provoked fierce domestic (Palestinian) riots against the Jordanian regime, as well as verbal attacks by Syria and Egypt—all of which contrib-uted to destabilizing the regime and subsequently to making it more susceptible to Egyptian–Syrian pressure to join forces in an anti-Israeli alliance.

It would appear that Israel chose to attack Jordan rather than Syria not only in order to put pressure on Amman effectively to check Palestinian raids against Israel, but apparently with the intention to deter Jordan from joining the newly signed Egyptian–Syrian Joint Defence Pact (of 7 November 1966), as well as to test this new Arab agreement.[58]

It should be pointed out that already on 12 October 1966, possibly in view of the Syrian–Egyptian rapprochement under Soviet influence (see below), King Hussein declared that, in case of war between Israel and Syria, Jordan would open a new front against Israel from the West Bank.[59] Although Hussein's statement was political and meant to demonstrate his pan-Arab position, the Israeli government was concerned and decided to warn the king. Hussein himself possibly considered the Samu' operation as a sign that Israel intended to conquer the West Bank.[60]

Yet, rather than coming to his assistance, Syria and Egypt continued their verbal attacks against Hussein, calling him a traitor and alleging that the Samu' operation had been orchestrated by Hussein, the CIA, and Israel in order to justify Jordan's anti-*fida'iyyun* measures.[61] Hitting back, Hussein taunted Nasser with hiding from Israel behing the screen of the United Nations forces in Sinai, while clandestine radio broadcasts from Jordan incited the Syrians to overthrow the Damascus government.[62]

Amidst these inter-Arab rivalries, Syria and Israel continued their mutual border clashes and had reportedly massed troops along the border by early 1967. This military build-up prompted the United Nations Secretary-General U Thant to try and settle the DMZ cultivation disputes through the Syrian–Israeli MAC, which had not convened since 1960.[63] In the first session of the MAC, on 25 January 1967, both sides agreed *inter alia* to refrain from further hostile acts, but under pressure from a radical Ba'thist faction and against Egypt's advice to refrain from military escalation, the Syrian government announced that it could not prevent guerrilla action against Israel by Palestinian *fida'iyyun*:

Revolutionary Syria has often declared that it cannot possibly act as a policeman entrusted with guarding the security and stability of the Zionists inside the occupied territory or resist the people's liberation struggle against Imperialism and its bases.[64]

In reaction to the Syrian position, Israeli activist Knesset members, notably Ben Gurion and Dayan, as well as the Israeli press, urged the government to withdraw from the United Nations-sponsored negotiations with Syria; or, in Ben Gurion's words: 'The Syrians really hate Israel . . . they claim that Palestine is part of southern Syria. The duty of every [Israeli] government is to defend its citizens, neither by words nor by the UN.' Moshe Dayan went further and, on 20 January 1967, warned: 'The Syrians want to hit us without being hit, and if they realized that the choice for them is either to stop acting against us or let the situation deteriorate toward war, they would prefer the latter.' Possibly in response to Ben Gurion and Dayan, Eshkol said, around the same time: 'Tranquility along our frontiers is of greater concern to us than the Israeli–Syrian M.A.C. . . . If tranquility is not maintained, we shall act with arms and methods of our choosing.' But he also added that Israel sought peace and was ready to sign a permanent peace treaty with Syria.[65] Consequently, with the continuing gap between the Syrian and Israeli positions in the MAC, the talks had reached a deadlock by early February 1967.[66]

Following the collapse of the talks, Syrian leaders resumed their verbal attacks on Israel. Hafiz al-Asad, Syrian defence minister and Air Force commander, said on 13 February 1967: 'The mere existence of Zionism in Palestine constitutes an aggression, and aggression and peace cannot co-exist in the same territory.' Muhammad al-Zu'bi, Syrian information minister, told a Lebanese paper at the end of March: 'There is no alternative for the Arabs but to liquidate Israel or be liquidated by her.'

Israeli leaders, in contrast, stated their desire for peaceful coexistence with Syria (and with other Arab states), but warned Syria against continuing its aggressive actions against Israel. For example, Moshe Carmel, minister of transport and 'Ahdut ha'Avoda leader, suggested on 23 March 1967 that 'the time may have come to act vigorously against Syria, whatever her relations with the Soviet Union.'[67]

Amidst further exchanges of fire and other incidents along the Syrian–Israeli border during February and March,[68] early in April 1967 Israel resumed the cultivation of a few controversial plots of land in the DMZ near Kibbutz Ha'On. On 7 April 1967 Syrian tanks fired at an Israeli armoured tractor in that zone, triggering a serious exchange of tank and mortar fire between the two sides. The Israeli Air Force went into action to silence Syrian guns, whereupon Syrian planes intercepted the Israeli Mirage fighters and in the ensuing battle six Syrian MiGs were shot down. Subsequently Israeli war-planes flew over Damascus.[69]

To be sure, this defeat did not discourage, indeed it possibly encouraged, Syria to carry on with the doctrine of 'popular liberation war', in practice mainly implemented by Palestinian *fida'iyyun*; Syrian leaders, whose prestige suffered great damage following the 7 April setback, recognized that this could or should develop into a full-scale war between Israel and the Arab regular armies. As Syrian chief of staff, General Ahmad Suwaydani, said in late April 1967:

I believe that Israel is not a state, but serves as a military base for the Imperialist camp. By means of this base we confront directly the Forces of Western Imperialism. . . . Can we hope to overcome these forces, on the ground, at sea and in the air? Certainly not . . . we must not, therefore, take the line of conventional warfare . . . we must take the line of popular liberation war . . . we shall see that the situation in Palestine is indeed similar to that in the Vietnam war, or in Algeria in the past. Should Israel react to the popular liberation war by conventional warfare, the Arab armies, under progressive command, must be ready to enter the battle, even if it is a defensive battle only, in order to safeguard the bases of the *fida'iyyun*. . . . This is why we believe that popular liberation war is the road not only towards the liberation of Palestine but also towards the liberation of the Arab homeland and towards its unification.

Asad apparently held a stronger view regarding the link between popular liberation war and a full-scale war: 'The people's revolution has decreed that the enemy shall be humiliated until zero hour strikes, after which . . . the Zionist bandits . . . cease to threaten us with aggression. Otherwise we shall carry out successive and continuous large-scale retaliation operations.'

Finally, the prime minister, Yusuf Zu'ayyin, while holding similar views, also believed that Israel was domestically weak and thus could be eliminated by a popular liberation war:

Israel is now in a state of internal collapse. Its regime is shaken and torn by power struggles, its economy is breaking down and racist domination and discrimination are prevalent. . . . Israel's military superiority is a legend which will not fool us.[70]

Whether or not Syria aimed at provoking a full-scale war against Israel, until early June 1967 it went on firing at Israeli villages and encouraging, or at least not discouraging, Palestinian *fida'iyyun* in attacking Israeli targets.[71] Simultaneously, Syrian leaders and media organs repeated their militant threats against Israel, such as: 'We are living in an atmosphere of imminent war which is bound to break out and which, when it does break out, will not be a limited one. The Arab masses are ready to sacrifice millions of dead for the liberation of Palestine.' (Radio Damascus, 20 April 1967); 'The Syrian forces are prepared to initiate . . . the blowing up of the aggressive Zionist existence' (Defence Minister Asad, 20 May 1967).[72]

Factors and Moves Leading to the June 1967 War

It would thus appear that on the eve of the June 1967 war most neo-Ba'th leaders sincerely believed that a popular liberation war could indeed lead to Israel's collapse, or, alternatively, should trigger a full-scale all-Arab conventional war against Israel, led mainly by Egypt and Syria. What, then, were their motives and calculations, and what were the other factors that led to the outbreak of hostilities?

Patrick Seale, writing for the London *Observer* at that juncture, depicted these Syrian leaders as 'a small group of sincere and devoted but not particularly wise or able men . . . They make great play with revolutionary war cries and left wing slogans. Their political minds were fashioned by the double talk, hysteria and lurid intrigue of Arab politics in the past decade. They have little experience in the outside world.'[73]

Yet, in conjunction with those characteristics and with their deep ideological commitment to fight Israel, the neo-Ba'th leaders were possibly influenced or motivated by other factors in adopting their belligerent policy against Israel in early 1967.

Syrian Domestic Conflicts

In early May 1967 a fresh wave of fierce Muslim religious demonstrations and disturbances erupted in Syrian towns in reaction to an unprecedented atheist article published in a military journal, *Jaysh al-Sh'ab*. It is possible that in an attempt to mitigate the public's fury and strengthen the regime's legitimacy, the Syrian leadership stepped up its anti-Israeli declarations and actions. Other internal conflicts, such as those between Druze officers and the Alawite-based regime, as well as between the two co-leaders, Salah Jadid and Hafiz Asad, may also have influenced militant anti-Israeli policies.[74]

Assumed Israeli Domestic Weakness and Military Threats

Certain Syrian leaders apparently interpreted unemployment, industrial strikes, and the absorption problems of the new immigrants as major weaknesses of Israeli society. They possibly believed that these difficulties, in addition to the Eshkol–Ben Gurion rivalry, were likely to cause Israel to collapse under the combined military pressure of Palestinian *fida'iyyun* and Arab armies.[75]

Other Syrian leaders, however, were concerned about Israeli military might, as a spearhead of 'Western Imperialism'; they were also put on their mettle by Israeli warnings or 'threats' and 'aggression'[76]—all of which led them to strengthen their ties with the Soviet Union and with Egypt, the two parties which greatly contributed to the outbreak of the June war.

The Soviet Union

The USSR indeed played a major role in the Syrian–Israeli escalation. Soviet–Syrian relations, which had been tense following the 1963 Ba'th revolution (because of the persecution of the Communist Party in Syria), improved since 1965, largely owing to the Baʿth decision to incorporate the Communists in the government.[77] The neo-Baʿth regime became definitely pro-Soviet (from February 1966) as it sought and got massive Soviet economic and military aid as well as political and diplomatic co-operation regarding 'solidarity with Palestinian Arabs and . . . support for their lawful rights in the just struggle against Zionism used by imperialistic forces.'[78]

Yet it would appear, even according to Syrian sources, that the Soviet Union by no means supported the Baʿth notion regarding the elimination of Israel, nor was Moscow interested in an Arab–Israeli war which could 'bring about a direct confrontation with imperialism and might lead to a world war, which the USSR does not want at this moment.'[79] Nevertheless, the Soviet Union possibly believed and certainly alleged that Israel, under the influence of 'extremist elements' (apparently Ben Gurion, Dayan, and Peres), was already in 1966 preparing 'aggressive plans . . . against Syria' and 'adopting its extraordinary belligerent attitude . . . [with] the support of the Western powers'.[80]

In August 1966 and again in May 1967 Moscow accused Israel of massing troops along the Syrian border with the purpose of overthrowing the Syrian government.[81] Whether or not these accusations were true (see below), the Soviets were aiming not only at deterring Israel from attacking Syria, but, more important, at demonstrating their support for the neo-Baʿth regime and increasing its dependence on Moscow. For the same reasons, and in order to group Syria and Egypt (UAR) together as Soviet allies in the region, Moscow used its allegations against Israel to involve Cairo in the May 1967 crisis, possibly without risking a full-scale war.[82] (But, according to an American evaluation, 'The Soviets overestimated the Arabs' ability to employ their substantial military strength against the Israelis, while the Arabs overrated their own strength and underrated the Israeli capability and determination to win.') In fact, Egyptian involvement in the crisis perhaps played a major role in the deterioration of the situation towards the 1967 war.

The Egyptian Involvement

As already discussed above, Egypt (UAR) since 1963 had foiled Syrian Baʿthist attempts to drag it into a full-scale war against Israel over the diversion of the Jordan headwaters and/or as a follow-up to the Palestinian-led popular liberation war. President Nasser, whose army had been engaged in a futile war in the Yemen since 1962, insisted that war against Israel needed proper preparation. Nasser reiterated this position following the rapprochement between Egypt and Syria in mid-1966 which culminated in their mutual defence pact of 7 November 1966. While now for the first time supporting the right of the Palestinian *fida'iyyun* to act inside Israel, Nasser said in February 1967: 'The battle with Israel is a decisive one, the Arab world cannot afford to enter a losing battle. We are the ones who will fix the time of the battle.' And as late as 15 May 1967 Nasser warned against Arab involvement in a 'premature war'.[83]

Significantly, the shooting down of six Syrian MiGs by Israel on 7 April 1962 did not provoke Egypt to invoke its mutual defence pact with Syria. Apart from rendering verbal support, Cairo suggested establishing an Egyptian air base in Syria, but Damascus turned down this offer.[84] Only on 14 May 1967 did Egypt decide to activate the defence pact with Syria and ordered its troops to move into Sinai in order 'to take a firm stand against the Israeli military threats and intervene immediately in case of any aggressive action taken by Israel against Syria'. Reasons for these steps of 14 May 1967 are given in an Egyptian army document (captured by Israel in the war):

It has appeared clearly in the course of the present year and since the beginning of May 1967 that Israel . . . urged on by Imperialism . . . is trying to direct military blows at the Arab people of Syria. In the past few days reliable reports have disclosed that there are huge Israeli troop concentrations on the Syrian borders. Their intention is to intervene on Syrian territory in order to overthrow the Arab liberated regime in Syria . . . This was supported by aggressive declarations . . . which were made by the Israeli PM and COS of the Israeli army.[85]

In an attempt to evaluate Nasser's bold action, several factors should be indicated:[86]

1. His strategy, which had sought to contain Syrian (and Palestinian) attempts to wage a popular liberation war against Israel, had damaged his prestige and Pan-Arab leadership. Vis-à-vis the growing criticism of his passivity in Egypt and in the Arab world, in early 1967 Nasser was not only pushed to voice his support of Syria and of the *fida'iyyi* activities against Israel, but by May 1967 he could no longer evade his obligations to Syria under their mutual defence pact, when Damascus was allegedly facing a massive Israeli attack.

2. Whether or not Nasser believed that Israel was about to attack Syria, he could not afford to remain idle in the face of such a possibility, thus also

throwing away the opportunity to regain his position of leadership in the Arab world.

3. By sending troops into Sinai, Nasser possibly intended to refute sarcastic Saudi and Jordanian allegations regarding his inaction vis-à-vis Israeli 'aggressiveness', as well as to disprove Israeli public statements that he was militarily too weak to help Damascus in its conflict with Jerusalem.

4. Nasser was also not in a position to ignore Israeli threats against Syria, and possibly used the dangerous Israeli–Syrian crisis to disengage his troops from the Yemeni quagmire and dispatch them into Sinai, thus initiating a new strategy in the struggle against Israel. Probably this strategy, reflected in the massing of troops in Sinai, was directed towards deterring Israel from attacking Syria, but without risking an all-out war against Israel.

However, further measures taken by Egypt in the eviction of the United Nations Emergency Force (UNEF) from Sinai and the closure of the Tiran Straits, as well as Nasser's highly belligerent declarations, against Israel,[87] together started the immediate chain of events that culminated in the June 1967 war.

While it is beyond the scope of this study to discuss in detail the Egyptian role in the outbreak of the war,[88] it should be noted that from Israel's point of view the Egyptian military challenge overshadowed the Syrian one, and possibly influenced Jerusalem's decisions regarding Damascus during the June war.

Israeli Threats and Moves

Further to his stiff warnings against the Syrian government in May and September 1966, the chief of staff, Yitzhak Rabin, issued fresh threats against the rulers in Damascus after the clash of 7 April 1967. While explaining the difference between the aims of Israeli retaliation against Jordan and Lebanon, and against Syria, he said on 14 May: 'In Syria the problem is different, because there it is the authorities who send out the saboteurs. Therefore the aim of action against Syria is different from what it ought to be against Jordan and Lebanon.' (Eshkol and Eban also warned Damascus against sending marauders into Israel and threatened to take measures against Syria 'no less drastic than those of 7 April'.)[89]

Syrian, Egyptian, and Soviet leaders, as well as a few Western sources, referred at that time to a statement made by Rabin on 12 May 1967, threatening to 'attack Damascus and topple the Syrian Government'.[90] Rabin and Israeli sources denied these allegations and several Western observers tend to accept these denials. A similar controversy exists with regard to Israeli troop concentration along the Syrian border by mid-May 1967. Whereas the Arabs and Russians accused Israel of massing troops in order to attack Syria, Israelis and most Western observers, including the United Nations, denied such troop concentration.[91] Ambassador Parker, who was political counsellor of the American Embassy in Cairo during the June 1967 war, investigated the issue and concluded in 1992:

The available evidence confirms Israeli assertions that the Soviet report that Israel was massing 10 to 12 brigades on the Syrian border was not true. . . . No countervailing evidence that the Israeli concentrations were actually in place has been presented to date and, with few exceptions, officials and scholars in Moscow today admit that the report was not true.

Concerning the question whether or not Israel was about to attack Syria in May 1967, Parker writes:

the Israelis under Prime Minister Levy Eshkol, who did not project a very warlike or resolute image, did not look like a people about to launch a war. There may have been Israeli hawks who maintained that a preemptive strike was necessary from time to time to keep the Arabs off balance, but they were not in control of the government.[92]

In point of fact, in late May 1967 Eshkol endeavoured to tone down his previous warnings and to reduce the tension. On 22 May 1967 he called on the Arab countries to participate with Israel 'in an effort to strengthen stability and to advance peace in our area'.[93] Reportedly he and other ministers, as well as some hawkish figures, were at that time reluctant to wage a war against Syria lest this should bring about Soviet military involvement and cause heavy Israeli losses.[94] Ben Gurion, for example, while sharply criticizing Eshkol for the escalatory measures taken against Syria on 7 April, was deeply worried in May about the outbreak of a war in which thousands of Israelis would die and public morale would be severely damaged.[95] (In contrast, Syrian leaders, notably Asad, continued in mid- to late May to call for a war against Israel.)[96] Undoubtedly one of the major reasons for Israel's endeavours during mid- to late May to reduce the tension and avoid war was the Egyptian troop concentration in Sinai, which took Israel by surprise. This sudden Egyptian measure, which was followed by the closure of the Tiran Straits, forced Israel to concentrate both diplomatic efforts and military preparations vis-à-vis the Egyptian threat, neglecting the Syrian front.

These Israeli diplomatic and military steps, as well as international and inter-Arab activities until 5 June, have been described and analysed in great detail elsewhere,[97] and need not be repeated here. Suffice it to point out that Israeli diplomatic action, backed by the United States, failed to lift Egypt's blockade on the Tiran Straits, as well as its troop concentrations on the Sinai–Negev line. Starting to mobilize on 16 May, Israel decided on 28 May, upon an American request, not to go to war and to postpone its decision for two weeks. In the mean time, further incidents occurred along the Egyptian and Syrian borders. Arab leaders, notably PLO chief Ahmad Shuqayri, made highly belligerent speeches directed against Israel and on 30 May King Hussein of Jordan signed a joint defence pact with Egypt, placing his forces under the command of an Egyptian general. As Arab troops were moving from Iraq into Syria (and later also Jordan) and from Saudi Arabia into Jordan, the Israeli public felt besieged by the Arab world, abandoned by the international community, and perturbed by Eshkol's hesitant posture.[98] Under pressure from his deeply alarmed public, Eshkol relinquished his Defence portfolio and appointed Dayan as minister of defence, and the 'Herut' leader, Menachem Begin, as minister without portfolio. Military action by Israel had now become imminent, not because of a wish to fight against Egypt and its Arab allies, but because the closure of the Tiran Straits constituted a *casus belli* and the concentration of Arab troops along the borders presented a serious threat to security. Israel could not be sure that the concentration of these troops was of only a defensive nature, aiming at deterring Israel from attacking Syria and procuring for Nasser a political and psychological victory in the Arab world.

Nasser was apparently aware that the massing of Israeli troops along the Syrian border had been Soviet–Syrian misinformation, but he believed that he could defeat Israel politically without resorting to war. His miscalculation certainly contributed to the outbreak of fighting. Moscow likewise was not interested in a war but contributed to it through its misinformation and propaganda campaign. Damascus, which supported and initiated the 'popular liberation war' against Israel, was the major contributor to the process of military escalation that led to the war, whereas Jerusalem was a minor partner in this escalation, through verbal threats and military actions against Syria. Finally, during the process of escalation, the United States had strongly objected to any large-scale Israeli attack on Syria and, until early June, also on Egypt. But, on 3 June 'the light from Washington shifted from red to yellow. It never turned green, but yellow was enough for the Israelis to know that they could take action without worrying about Washington's reaction.'[99]

THE 1967 WAR AND ITS AFTERMATH

On 5 June 1967, Israel launched an air strike on Egyptian air fields in Sinai and within three hours destroyed the bulk of the Egyptian air force. By 9 June it had occupied the entire Sinai and the Gaza Strip, defeating all Egyptian troops. On 5 June Israel appealed to King Hussein of Jordan to stay out of the fighting, but as Jordanian artillery began shelling Israeli towns and villages, including Jerusalem and Tel Aviv, the IDF launched a counter-attack, and after fierce fighting occupied the West Bank and East Jerusalem.[100] As for the Syrian front, originally two Syrian armoured columns were assigned to break through towards Tiberias and Upper Galilee respectively, but in fact Syrian troops conducted only two small ground attacks on two Israeli *kibbutzim* near the international boundary. Earlier, in the late morning hours of 5 June, Syrian planes attacked several targets in northern Israel, notably in the Haifa Bay area, and Tiberias. Israel shot down ten Syrian MiGs and subsequently attacked Syrian airfields, and destroyed two-thirds of the Syrian air force within one hour. Yet, despite Syrian shelling of *kibbutzim* from the Golan Heights for several days, starting at nightfall on 5 June (Radio Damascus announced on 6 June that the Syrian army was on its way to Tel Aviv), Israel refrained from attacking the Golan until 9 June. With the exception of Defence Minister Dayan, the entire Israeli cabinet, the chief of staff, as well as many *kibbutzim* in Galilee, wanted the army to take the Golan. And although the Americans reportedly did not object to such an action, Moshe Dayan was concerned about possible Soviet military intervention and the incurring of heavy losses among Israeli troops. He suggested occupying only a strip of 2–3 km. east of the Syrian–Israeli border but, after the Egyptian defeat, on 9 June Dayan ordered the occupation of the entire Golan Heights.[101] This proved to be a relatively easy operation, not only because the air force had gained complete control over the Golan skies, but also because the Syrian army was not well prepared for the battle. Many officers and soldiers fled from the field, and Damascus Radio prematurely announced, on behalf of the defence minister, that Qunaytra, the principal town of the Golan, had fallen.[102]

With the fall of Qunaytra, the road to Damascus (some 40 miles away) lay open, but Israel refrained from advancing towards the Syrian capital—

as General Elazar, chief of the Northern Command, advocated—because of American pressure and threats by the USSR, which broke off diplomatic relations with Israel on 8 June. The government also rejected a suggestion by Yigal Allon to occupy the Druze Mountain (Jabal Druze), about 60 miles south-east of Damascus and help establish an independent Druze state.[103]

Significantly, only a week after the Israeli–Syrian cease-fire (10 June), the Israeli Security Cabinet unanimously adopted (on 15 June) a resolution to the effect that

Israel stands for the conclusion of a peace treaty with Syria [and Egypt] on the basis of the international boundary . . . the conditions for a peace treaty are: (1) a total demilitarization of the Syrian [Golan] Heights, whose terms would be fixed in the peace treaty between Israel and Syria; (2) an absolute guarantee for free water flow from the River Jordan sources into Israel either by an alteration in the northern boundary, or by an agreement between the two countries.[104]

This resolution, which was intensely debated in the cabinet, was approved by it on 19 June, but was not published. Israel's declared position was made manifest in the Knesset resolution of 1 August 1967, adopted by the votes of all parties except the two Communist factions, which opposed it:

The Knesset confirms the government's stand that, by means of direct negotiations between Israel and the Arab countries, the conclusion of peace should be brought about; and until peace is achieved, Israel will continue to maintain fully the present situation.[105]

Yet the United States was informed by Eban of the decision of 19 June, and was asked to convey it to the Syrian government. According to Eban, the Americans

[H]ardly believed their ears. For just following victory Israel expresses readiness to give up all its gains in return for a simple condition, a permanent peace. It has been the most dramatic initiative ever adopted by Israel, and it has made a strong impression in the USA.

However, a few days later the Syrian reply came via Washington, rejecting Israel's offer and insisting on an unconditional Israeli withdrawal.[106] Indeed, Syrian leaders, accusing Israel of expelling most of the Syrian inhabitants of the Golan and committing atrocities, in late June 1967 and subsequently made such statements as: 'We will never agree to direct talks with Israel now or at any other time'; 'the Israeli enemy will be liquidated only by means of force.'[107]

This Syrian position was more recalcitrant than that of Egypt or Jordan, both of whom did not exclude a political solution with Israel. Damascus thus boycotted the Khartoum Arab Summit Conference (of 1 September 1967) whose resolutions stated *inter alia*:

The Arab heads of state have agreed to unite their political efforts at the international and diplomatic level to eliminate the effects of the aggression and to ensure the withdrawal of the aggressive Israeli forces . . . This will be done within the framework of the main principles by which the Arab states abide, namely no peace with Israel, no recognition of Israel, no negotiation with it, and insistence on the rights of the Palestinian people in their own country.[108]

Syria also continued to call for the resumption of war against Israel, notably a popular liberation war, and allegedly went on directing Palestinian *fida'iyyun* to carry on guerrilla activities against Israel.[109]

No wonder, then, that Syria, unlike Jordan and Egypt, also 'categorically and firmly' rejected UN Resolution 242 of 22 November 1967, which was largely based on American and British draft resolutions. The significant part of the resolution reads as follows:

Emphasizing the inadmissibility of the acquisition of territory by war and the need to work for a just and lasting peace in which every state in the area can live in security . . . the establishment of a just and lasting peace in the Middle East which should include the application of both the following principles: (i) Withdrawal of Israel armed forces from territories occupied in the recent conflict; (ii) Termination of all claims or states of belligerency and respect for and acknowledgement of the sovereignty, territorial integrity and political independence of every state in the area.[110]

In contrast to Damascus, Jerusalem reacted favourably to Resolution 242 (but accepted it formally only in 1968), while stressing that 'it is only within the establishment of a permanent peace with secure and recognized boundaries that other principles [i.e. withdrawal of Israeli armed forces] can be given effect.' Israel also emphasized its adherence to the original English text of the resolution, indicating the phrase: 'withdrawal of Israel armed forces, from *territories* occupied in the recent conflict' (and not from *the territories*).[111]

Nevertheless, Israel's position regarding the return of the Golan, albeit demilitarized, to Syria as part of a peace treaty, was eroded towards the end of 1967. This change, which was reflected by the government's decision in October 1968 to abolish its decision of 19 June 1967 and subsequently to establish Israeli settlements on the Golan,[112] occurred owing to three major factors: the continuing Syrian (and Arab) highly belligerent position, the sympathetic American attitude towards Israel, and Israeli domestic pressure to keep the Golan.

Consequently, in the aftermath of the June 1967 war, the historic dispute between Damascus and Jerusalem reached its highest point since 1948. For, in addition to its ideological antagonism, its commitment to the Palestinian plight, and its search for domestic legitimacy, the Syrian regime now had other crucial motives for its conflict with Israel: the painful defeat of the army, the loss of the Golan Heights, and the deployment of Israeli troops 40 miles from the Syrian capital. Syria was now facing a powerful army and state backed by the United States and determined to hold the Golan Heights (as well as Sinai, the West Bank and Gaza) until Syria (and other Arab states) would agree to sign a peace treaty—the anathema of Damascus.

NOTES

1. On the Ba'th Party and regime in Syria, see K. Abu Jaber, *The Arab Ba'th Socialist Party* (Syracuse, NY, 1966); J. F. Devlin, *The Ba'th Party: A History* (Stanford, Calif., 1976); Rabinovich, *Ba'th*; Michel Aflaq, *Fi Sabil al-Ba'th* (Beirut, 1959); Sami al-Jundi, *al-Ba'th* (Beirut, 1969); Munif al-Razzaz, *al-Tajriba al-murra* (Beirut, 1967); *Nidal al-Ba'th, 1943–1949* (Beirut, 1963); *Nidal Hizb al-Ba'th, 1943–1975* (Damascus, 1968). For a critical account, see Muta' Safadi, *Hizb al-Ba'th* (Beirut, 1964).

2. Cf. Devlin, *Ba'th* 26 and 347.

3. *Dirasat Tarikhiyya . . . li-Nidal Hizb al-Ba'th* (Damascus, 1972), 23; *Nidal al-Ba'th*, 222, 229 ff.; Devlin, *Ba'th*, 49–50; *Nidal Hizb al-Ba'th*, 20, 27.

4. *Nidal al-Ba'th*, 222 ff.; Devlin, *Ba'th*, 51; *Nidal Hizb al-Ba'th*, 27.

5. *Nidal Hizb al-Ba'th*, 43–4, 47; *Dirasat*, 41–5; al-Jundi, *al-Ba'th*, 164; Devlin, *Ba'th*, 87, 224.

6. *Al-Ma'rifa*, 26 (Apr. 1964), article by Salim al-Yafi; 27 (May 1964), article by Abdallah abd-al-Da'yin; cf. *New York Times*, 24 Jan. 1964; Peres, *Qela David*, 148, quoting al-Bitar's interview with *al-Safa* (Lebanon), 11 Mar. 1963; Damascus Radio, 15 Dec. 1963, cited in IDF Archives, 15 Jan. 1964.

7. *Dirasat*, 85; Devlin, *Ba'th*, 224.

8. *Divrey Haknesset*, 37. 40 (26 Aug. 1963); 38. 595–6 (25 Dec. 1963); *The Times*, 19 Aug. 1963; see also *New York Times*, 23 July, 21 Aug., 27 Aug. 1963; *New York Herald Tribune*, 2 Aug. 1963; [UN] *Year Book 1963*, 36, 53 ff.; ibid. *1964*, 173 ff.; Security Council Suppl. 1963, 115 ff. and 1964, 28 ff.; ibid., 1965, 217, Security Council Suppl. 185 ff.

9. Quoted in Bar Siman-Tov, *Linkage*, 131. For a detailed description and examination of the link between Syria's internal conflict and its conflict with Israel, see ibid. 117 ff. On the unity talks and the Syrian–Egyptian disputes, see M. Kerr, *The Arab Cold War* (London, 1965). Cf. Background paper, 22 May 1964, Johnson Library DD 193D (1979). See also M. Seymour, 'The Dynamics of Power in Syria', *Middle Eastern Studies*, 6 (1970), 35 ff.

10. See respectively Rabinovich, *Ba'th*, 96 (and p. 101); *New York Times*, 20 Dec. 1963. Cf. Bar Siman-Tov, *Linkage*, 136 ff. On Nasser's objection to waging war against Israel at that juncture, see *al-Nahar*, 20 Dec. 1963, cited in IDF Archives, 15 Jan. 1964; al-Jundi, *al-Ba'th*, 165.

11. For details, see A. Sela, *Unity within Conflict; the Arab Summit Conferences* (Hebrew; Jerusalem, 1982), 26–37; see also Petran, *Syria*, 191–2; *Guardian*, 14 Jan. 1964; *New York Times*, 16 and 19 Jan. 1964.

12. *Al-Thawra*, 21 Nov. 1968, cited by Rabinovich, *Ba'th*, 102–3; cf. Bar Siman-Tov, *Linkage*, 137.

13. H. Cobban, *The Palestinian Liberation Organization* (Cambridge, 1984), 32; M. Ma'oz and A. Yaniv, 'On a Short Leash: Syria and the PLO', in M. Ma'oz and A. Yaniv (eds.), *Syria under Assad* (New York, 1986), 192–3; *New York Times*, 19 Jan. and 11 July 1965.

14. *Daily Telegraph*, 12 Jan. 1965; *New York Times*, 19 Jan. 1965. Cf. *Divrey Haknesset*, 42. 1687 (29 Mar. 1965).

15. *Ba'd al-muntalaqat al-nazariyya*, the Ba'th Party's 6th National Congress, Oct. 1963 (Damascus, 1971), 51; *al-Ma'rifa*, 25 (Mar. 1964), 61–6; 40 (June 1965), 51–6, 49 (Mar. 1966), 10–20, 49–67, 75–84, 235–46. See also Ba'th Party internal circular, 29 Sept. 1965, cited in A. Ben-Tzur (ed.), *The Syrian Ba'ath Party and Israel* (Givat Haviva, 1968), 6.

16. See respectively a lecture by Dr Munif al-Razzaz, secretary-general of the Ba'th Party in the Palestine Week convention (Syrian Ministry of Information, Damascus 1965), 3–4; *al-Munadil* 5 (June 1966), cited in Ben-Tzur, *The Syrian Ba'ath Party*, 26; *al-Ma'rifa*, 49 (Mar. 1966), 186–93, 222–34 and 10–20.

17. *Al-Ma'rifa*, 29 (July 1964), 88–96; 49 (Mar. 1966), 224, 306–8, 309 ff., 323–32, 333–8.

18. Al-Razzaz, *al-Tajriba*, 8–9.

19. *Al-Ma'rifa*, 29 (July 1964), 49 (Mar. 1966), 15 ff., 60 ff., 186–93, 235–46, 247–53, 268–303; al-Razzaz, *al-Tajriba*, 16.

20. Ben-Tzur, *The Syrian Ba'ath Party*, 5–8. Cf. *New York Times*, 2 June 1965; *Egyptian Gazette*, 4 July 1965; *Dawn* (Lebanon), 18 June 1965.

21. Al-Jundi, *al-Ba'th*, 164–6.

22. Ibid. 8–10. Cf. *al-Ma'rifa*, 49 (Mar. 1966), 67.

23. *Al-Ma'rifa*, 49 (Mar. 1966), 67; cf. *al-Taqarir al-muqaddama ila al-mu'tamar al-qawmi al-thamin* (Damascus, 1967), 41 ff.; *al-Thawra*, 10 Aug. 1965; *al-Ba'th*, 27 Aug. 1965.

24. Abu Iyad, *Filastini bila hawiyya* (Kuwait, n.d.), 84–6. Cf. *al-Taqarir*, 41 ff., 54–6.

25. See Circular 1, 2 Mar. 1966, the Provisional Regional Leadership, in Ben-Tzur, *The Syrian Ba'ath Party*, 11–12. For more details, see Bar Siman-Tov, *Linkage* 135–6. See also *Sunday Times*, 31 Jan. 1966; *The Times*, 12 Dec. 1965.

26. See respectively Memo of Conversation with Israel Foreign Minister Golda Meir, 17 Dec. 1962, DD 193A (1979); Background paper, 25 May 1964, Prime Minister Eshkol of Israel, official visit, 1–3 June 1964, Lyndon B. Johnson Library, DD 193D (1979); United States Draft Memorandum of Understanding, 26 Feb. 1965, DD. 205A (1978); Memo of Conversation (with Eshkol and Meir), DOS 15 Feb. 1965. DD 204C and 204D (1978). Cf. IDF Archives, Memo by Y. Herzog, 2 Jan. 1964; *New York Herald Tribune*, 15 Jan. 1964.

27. IDF Archives, IDF Spokesman, 15 Jan. 1964; also quoting *al-Nahar*, 20 Dec. 1963; *New York Times*, 20 Dec. 1963.

28. Peres, *Qela David*, 148; cf. *New York Herald Tribune*, 15 Jan. 1964. *Divrey Haknesset*, 42. 1686–7 (29 Mar. 1965).

29. *The Times*, 8 Feb. 1964; *New York Herald Tribune*, 30 Apr. 1964; al-Jundi, *al-Ba'th*, 165.

30. Memo for the President, 2 May 1963, DD. 2320 (1986); cf. Background paper, 'The Situation in the Middle East', 22 May 1964, Lyndon B. Johnson Library, DD 193D (1979). Cf. al-Jundi, *al-Ba'th*, 165 ff.

31. Conversation with Israeli Foreign Minister Meir, 27 Dec. 1962, DOS, DD 193A (1979). See also Background paper, 22 May 1964.

32. Background paper, 22 May 1964.

33. Ibid.; cf. Memo of Conversation with Israel Foreign Minister, 27 Dec. 1962; cf. *New York Times*, 4 Apr. 1963, 16 Apr. 1964, and 11 Feb. 1965. Cf. E. Weizmann, *On Eagles' Wings* (New York, 1976), 176.

34. US Draft Memo of Understanding, 26 Feb. 1965; Memo of Conversation, 25 Feb. 1965. Cf. *Divrey Haknesset*, 42. 1665 (29 Mar. 1965); 45. 1469 (18 May 1965).

35. Rabin, *Pinkas Sherut*, 127, 129. Cf. Telegram from Tel Aviv to DOS, 16 May, 1964, DD 297A (1980). Cf. *New York Times*, 25 Apr. 1963, quoting Egyptian sources; Smith, *Palestine*, 185; Telegram from Tel Aviv to DOS, 16 May 1964, DD 297A (1980).

36. US Draft Memo of Understanding, 26 Feb. 1965; *New York Tiems*, 21 Jan. 1965; Rabin, *Pinkas Sherut*, 126.

37. Memos of Conversation, 27 Dec. 1962 and 25 Feb. 1965; Background paper, 22 May 1964; Rabin, *Pinkas Sherut*, 129.

38. US Draft Memo of Understanding, 26 Feb. 1965; Memo of Conversation, 25 Feb. 1965, DD 204C and 204D.

39. Bar Siman-Tov, *Linkage*, 139; *New York Times*, 8 and 18 Mar. 1965 and 27

May 1965; Incoming telegram, DOS 25 May 1965, DD 279D (1978); H. Bartov, *Dado, 48 Years and 20 Days* (Tel Aviv, 1978), 110–12.

40. Petran, *Syria*, 192; *The Times*, 27 Mar. 1965; see also *Daily Telegraph*, 18 Feb. 1963.

41. Peres, *Qela David*, 183–4; cf. A. Yaniv, 'Syria and Israel: The Politics of Escalation', in Ma'oz and Yaniv, *Syria under Asad*, 164; Khouri, *Arab-Israeli Dilemma*, 229; Background paper, 22 May 1964.

42. On the Eli Cohen affair see *Divrey Haknesset*, 43. 1864 (18 May 1965) and 2105–6 (9 June 1965); P. Seale, *Asad: The Struggle for the Middle East* (London, 1988), 114 (hereafter cited as Seale, *Asad*).

43. Incoming telegram, DOS 25 May 1965. Cf. *New York Times*, 25 Oct. 1963; Khouri, *Arab–Israeli Dilemma*, 223. *Divrey Haknesset*, 38. 2 (21 Oct. 1963); 45. 1468 (18 May 1965).

44. Petran, *Syria*, 193; Bar Siman-Tov, *Linkage*, 139; cf. al-Jundi, *al-Ba'th*, 165.

45. Cf. M. Ma'oz, 'Alawi Military Officers in Syrian Politics', in H. Z. Schiffrin, *Military and State in Modern Asia* (Jerusalem, 1976), 293; for detailed accounts of the opposition to the new Ba'th regime see Bar Siman-Tov, *Linkage*, 147 ff.; Rabinovich, *Ba'th*, 204 ff.; Petran, *Syria*, 172 ff. See also Seymour, 'The Dynamics of Power', 35 ff.; N. van Dam, *The Struggle for Power in Syria* (London, 1979), 51 ff.

46. Statement of the Regional Command of the Ba'th Arab Socialist Party on results of the party's Special Regional Congress, 10–17 Mar. 1966 (Damascus, Apr. 1966), 12, 42; Ben-Tzur, *The Syrian Ba'ath Party*, 20–1; see also *Resolutions of the 9th National Congress, September 1966* (Damascus, Ministry of Information, 1966), 125 ff., 150 ff. For details concerning the radical Syrian leaders and their views, see Seale, *Asad*, 104 ff.

47. *Jaysh al-Sh'ab*, 9 May 1967, cited in Ben-Tzur, *The Syrian Ba'ath Party*, 22; see also *Resolutions of the 9th National Congress*, 140–1. Cf. [UN] *Year Book 1967*, Security Council Suppl. S/7296, 16 May 1966.

48. Bar Siman-Tov, *Linkage*, 151–2; cf. [UN] *Year Book*, Security Council Suppl., S/7296, 16 May 1966; S/7326, 29 May 1966; S/7411, 14 July 1966; S/7460, 16 Aug. 1966; S/7485, 7 Sept. 1966, etc. etc.; *Financial Times*, 10 Jan. 1967; *New York Times*, 7 Mar. 4 Apr., and 10 May 1967. Cf. Devlin, *Ba'th*, 315; Observer Foreign News Service (OFNS), 2 June 1967.

49. See respectively Seale's report, OFNS, 19 May 1967; Petran, *Syria*, 195–6.

50. [UN] *Year Book 1966*, 167 ff., S/7572, 1 Nov. 1966, S/7573, 2 Nov. 1966; *Security Council Official Records 1967*, S/7296, 16 May 1966, S/7326, 29 May 1966, S/7411, 14 July 1966; *Financial Times*, 10 Jan. 1967.

51. [UN] *Security Council, 1967*, 119, OS S/7320, 29 May 1966, *Financial Times*, 18 Jan. 1967; *Divrey Haknesset*, 45. 1467–8 (18 May 1966).

52. See respectively [UN] *Year Book 1966*, 167, and [UN] *Year Book* Security Council Suppl. S/7320, 25 May 1966.

53. See respectively *MER 1967*, 161; [UN] *Security Council Official Records 1967*, S/7495, 15 Sept. 1966. Cf. Rabin, *Pinkas Sherut*, 121; al-Jundi, *al-Ba'th*, 169; Dayan, *Avney Derekh*, 392, recording his version of the events leading to the 1967 war, 391 ff.

54. Weizmann, *On Eagles' Wings*, 197; Yaniv, 'Syria and Israel', 165–6; *Davar*, 15 July 1966; [UN] *Year Book 1966*, 167–8; [UN] *Security Council Records*, S/7432, 26 July 1966.

55. [UN] *Security Council Records 1966*, S/7460, 16 Aug. 1966. Cf. Yaniv, 'Syria and Israel', 166–7.

56. [UN] *Security Council Records 1967*, S/7477, 26 Aug. 1966; see also S/7488, 11 Sept. 1966; S/7536, 10 Oct. 1966; S/7562, 23 Oct. 1966. Cf. *al-Thawra*, 4 Aug. 1965.

57. [UN] *Year Book 1966*, 173; *MER 1967*, 166; Dayan, *Avney Derekh*, 391.

58. *Ma'ariv*, 14 Nov. and 17 Dec. 1966; A. Ayalon in *Ma'arachot* (Mar.–Apr. 1978), 32, 36. For other comments, see *MER 1967*, 109, 166; Seale, *Asad*, 127.

59. *New York Times*, 12 Oct. 1966.

60. Cf. *Ma'ariv*, 18 Nov. 1966; Z. Bar-Lavi, *The Hashemite Regime 1949–1967 and its Position in the West Bank* (Hebrew; Tel Aviv, 1981), 45–6. Cf. [US] DOS, 90603, 23 Nov. 1966, DD (1983).

61. *Al-Ahram*, 18 Nov. 1966; Seale, *Asad*, 127; *MER 1967*, 109.

62. Petran, *Syria*, 196–7.

63. *MER 1967*, 170 ff. Cf. [UN] *Security Council Records 1967*, S/7572, 1 Nov. 1966; S/7668, 8 Jan. 1967; S/7688, 17 Jan. 1967; *New York Herald Tribune*, 26 Jan. 1967; *Financial Times*, 10 Jan. 1967.

64. Radio Damascus, 25 Jan. 1967, cited in *MER 1967*, 173. Cf. Radio Damascus, 11 Oct. 1966. [UN] *Security Council Records*, S/7704, 27 Jan. 1967. On the Egyptian position, see *al-Jarida*, 27 Jan. 1967; OFNS, 27 Jan. 1967; *New York Herald Tribune*, 27 Jan. 1967.

65. See respectively Hameiri, *The Question of the DMZ*, 115; *Financial Times*, 18 Jan. 1967; [UN] *Security Council Records 1967*, S/7769, 20 Jan. 1967; cf. M. Dayan, *The Story of My Life* (New York and London, 1976), 289.

66. *MER 1967*, 174; Seale, *Asad*, 127; *New York Times*, 17 Feb. 1967.

67. See respectively *MER 1967*, 162–5; [UN] *Security Council Records 1967*, S/7734, 10 Feb. 1967; S/7784, 23 Feb. 1967; S/7811, 7 Mar. 1967, S/7845, 9 Apr. 1967.

68. *New York Times*, 12 Feb. and 7 Mar. 1967; [UN] *Security Council Records 1967*, S/7734, 10 Feb. 1967.

69. *MER 1967*, 176–7; Seale, *Asad*, 127; *New York Times*, 8 Apr. 1967; [UN] *Security Council Records 1967*, S/7845, 9 Apr. 1967; S/7853, 14 Apr. 1967; Dayan, *Avney Derekh*, 391.

70. For references, see *MER 1967*, 159–60, 177. Cf. OFNS, 30 May 1965; [UN] *Security Council Records 1967*, S/7845, 9 Apr. 1967; S/7825, 16 Mar. 1967; S/7853, 14 Apr. 1967.

71. [UN] *Security Council Records 1967*, S/7880, 11 May 1967; S/7924, 2 June 1967; *MER 1967*, 177–8; Bar Siman-Tov, *Linkage*, 152.

72. See respectively *MER 1967*, 162; [UN] *Security Council Records 1967*, S/7901, 22 May 1967.

73. OFNS, 19 May 1967.

74. On these domestic conflicts and their possible effects, see M. Ma'oz, 'The Background of the Struggle over the Role of Islam in Syria', *New Outlook*, 6 (May 1973), 13 ff.; *al-Hayat*, 5, 6, 9 May 1967; Bar Siman-Tov, *Linkage*, 157–60.

75. Cf. Radio Damascus, 1 May 1967; *Nidal al-Fallahin*, 26 Apr. 1967, cited in *MER 1967*, 160, 177.

76. [UN] *Year Book 1967* 164; *MER 1967*, 179–80. Cf. Rabin, *Pinkas Sherut*, 137; *al-Taqarir*, 153.

77. Devlin, *Ba'ath*, 222–3; *Pravda*, 10 Jan. 1965, cited in Ro'i, 521.

78. 'Joint Soviet–Syrian Communiqué', Moscow, 23 Apr. 1966, cited in Ro'i, 534–5.

79. Secret circular by the Ba'th Party, Mar. 1966, cited in Ben-Tzur, *The Syrian Ba'th Party*, 23. Cf. al-Jundi, *al-Ba'th*, 168.

80. See respectively 'Soviet Comment on Syrian Regime', Moscow, July 1966, and speeches by N. Fedorenko at the UN Security Council, 25 July and 1 Aug. 1966, cited in Ro'i, 549 ff. Cf. [UN] *Year Book 1967*, 166, 170–1; A. Kapeliuk, in *Yediot Ahronot*, 17 Apr. 1992, citing Soviet-Communist documents from the 1960s.

81. Speeches by Fedorenko, cited in Ro'i, 550; *MER 1967*, 184; Dayan, *Avney Derekh*, 472–3.

82. 'Soviet Official's Comments on Soviet Policy on the Middle Eastern War', 8 June 1967, DD 280C (1981) Johnson Library; see also *MER 1967*, 184; cf. 'Soviet Objectives and Strategy in the Middle East', DOS, 8 Feb. 1963, DD 291D (1978); Peres, *Qela David*, 202; G. Rafael, *Besod Leumim* Jerusalem, 1981), 80, 112–13, 121–2. 'Israeli Objectives in the Current Crisis— Soviet Policy and Miscalculation', 6 June 1967, DD 416A (1981) Johnson Library.

83. Radio Cairo, 5 Feb. and 15 May 1967, cited in *MER 1967*, 160. Cf. R. B. Parker, 'The June 1967 War: Some Mysteries Explored', *Middle East Journal*, 46 (1992), 177.

84. For references from Arab sources, see *MER 1967*, 132–3.

85. Cited in *MER 1967*, 185; cf. *Guardian*, 25 May 1967; *New York Times*, 26 May and 10 June 1967.

86. For detailed discussions regarding Nasser's intentions, see Parker, 'The June 1967 War', 177 ff.; Seale, *Asad*, 121 ff.; *MER 1967*, 185; N. Safran, *From War to War* (New York, 1969), 266 ff. For more references, see *MER 1967*, 183.

87. [UN] *Year Book 1967*, 164 ff. *New York Times*, 26 May 1967.

88. For new accounts (and references) on the Egyptian role, see Parker, 'The

June 1967 War', 177 ff.; Muhammad Wajdi Qandil, 'Asrar 5 Yunyu' (The Secrets of 5 June), *al-Hayat*, 10 and 17 June 1992.

89. See respectively *MER 1967*, 179, 186; *Daily Telegraph*, 18 May 1967; [UN] *Security Council Suppl. 1967*, S/7901, 22 May 1967; *New York Times*, 14 May 1967.

90. *Sunday Times*, 21 May 1967; *The Times*, 16 May 1967; *MER 1967*, 180, 187–8, 190, quoting Arab and foreign sources, notably UPI. Cf. Parker, 'The June 1967 War', 179; Seale, *Asad*, 129.

91. [UN] *Year Book 1967*, 164; *New York Times*, 18 and 22 May 1967; *MER 1967*, 188 ff., quoting various sources.

92. Parker, 'The June 1967 War', 180–1, 177.

93. [UN] *Security Council Record 1967*, S/7901, 22 May 1967; *Daily Telegraph.* 23 May 1967; *New York Times*, 23 May 1967; *MER 1967*, 187.

94. *MER 1967*, 187; cf. Eban, *Pirkey Haim*, 319–20.

95. Bar Zohar, iii. 1587–90; cf. Teveth, *Dayan*, 560; Dayan, *The Story of My Life*, 290; cf. Rabin, *Pinkas Sherut*, 150.

96. *New York Times*, 21, 26 and 27 May 1967; *Financial Times*, 23 May 1967; *Guardian*, 25 May 1967; *MER 1967*, 196.

97. *MER 1967*, 192 ff., and a list of works on p. 183; [UN] *Year Book 1967*, 164 ff. See articles by Parker and Gera; and by W. B. Quandt, 'Lyndon Johnson and the June 1967 War', *Middle East Journal*, 46 (1992), 198 ff.; Qandil, 'Asrar 5 Yunyu'; Eban, *Pirkey Haim*, 322 ff.; Meir, *My Life*, 226 ff.; Dayan, *Avney Derekh*, 482 ff.

98. Dayan, *Avney Derekh*, 392, 396–7, 426; *MER 1967*, 203–4; Seale, *Asad*, 135–6.

99. Quandt, 'Lyndon Johnson', 199; cf. [UN] *Year Book 1967*, 192–3. See also Dayan, *Avney Derekh*, 429, 483; *MER 1967*, 196 ff.; Memo, 6 June 1967, DD 416B (1981) Johnson Library.

100. Details in *MER 1967*, 207 ff., 233 ff. [UN] *Year Book 1967*, 174 ff.; Weizmann, *On Eagles' Wings*, 211 ff.; Rabin, *Pinkas Sherut*, 185 ff.; Dayan, *Avney Derekh*, 430 ff.; al-Jundi, *al-Ba'th*, 172 ff.

101. Dayan, *Avney Derekh*, 430 ff., 441 ff.; 473 ff. Cf. CIA Memo, 10 June 1967, DD 110 (1991) Johnson Library. Y. Erez, *Conversations with Moshe Dayan* (Hebrew; Tel Aviv, 1981), 50–1; Rabin, *Pinkas Sherut*, 192–3; Eban, *Pirkey Haim*, 416 ff.; Bartov, *Dado*, 131 ff.; Teveth, *Dayan*, 579 ff. For text of the cease-fire, see [UN] *Security Council Record 1967*, 3.

102. Dayan, *Avney Derekh*, 479; Bartov, *Dado*, 145; Seale, *Asad*, 140–1; cf. Peres, *Qela David*, 202; OFNS, 2 June 1967. For full details, see Khalil Mustafa, *Suqut al-Jawlan* [The Fall of the Golan] (Amman, 1970)—a military account by a Syrian intelligence officer in the Golan before the war.

103. Bartov, *Dado*, 124–5; cf. *MER 1967*, 230, 247. See also Eban, *Pirkey Haim*, 416–19; Dayan, *Avney Derekh*, 480–1.

104. For further details, see M. Avidan, '19 June 1967. The Israeli government decides hereby', *Davar*, 2, 5, and 19 June 1987; cf. Rafael, *Destination*, 177;

Dayan, *Avney Derekh*, 491; Teveth, *Dayan*, 584; Memo, 6 June 1967, Johnson Library, DD 416B (1981); Rabin, *Pinkas Sherut*, 227.

105. Divrey Haknesset, 1 Aug. 1967, cited in *MER 1967*, 274; cf. Avidan, '19 June 1967', 5 June 1987.

106. Eban, *Pirkey Haim*, 430. See also [US] *National Intelligence Estimate: Israel*, 11 Apr. 1968, DD 412B (1981), 6; Dayan, *Avney Derekh*, 512.

107. The *Egyptian Gazette*, 25 June 1967; *al-Ba'th*, 31 Aug. 1967. See also *Financial Times*, 15 June 1967; *MER 1967*, 257; [UN] *Security Council Suppl.* 1967, S/7991, 15 June 1967; S/8030, 4 July 1967; S/8127, 18 Aug. 1967; S/8181, 4 Oct. 1967.

108. *MER 1967*, 264; also 139, 256.

109. *MER 1967*, 257, 266, 269, 271, 305, 307; *Guardian*, 1 Oct. 1967; [UN] Security Council Suppl. 1967, S/8181, 4 Oct. 1967; [US] *National Intelligence Estimate: Israel*, 11 Apr. 1968, DD 412B (1981), 6; [UN] *Year Book 1967*, 225–6.

110. Full text in [UN] *Security Council Record 1967*, 8–9; *MER 1967*, 272, citing Radio Damascus, 23 Nov. 1967.

111. [UN] *Year Book 1967*, 254; *MER 1967*, 277, 89.

112. Avidan, . . . '19 June 1967', 5 and 19 June 1987; cf. Bar Zohar, 1598; Teveth, *Dayan*, 595; [UN] Security Council Suppl. 1967, S/8178, 3 Oct. 1967.

6

From War (1967) to War (1973)

The further intensification of the Syrian–Israeli conflict following the June 1967 war planted *inter alia* the seeds of the October 1973 war between Egypt and Syria, and Israel. Israel, faced with continued Syrian belligerency and influenced by domestic pressures, abandoned its initial flexible post-1967 policy advocating the return of the Golan in exchange for a peace treaty, in favour of a status quo line: keeping the Golan and establishing new settlements there. Syria, meanwhile, attempted to undermine and destroy this status quo by means of Palestinian guerrilla warfare, mainly through Lebanese territory, and subsequently also by preparing its army for another war against Israel. Other factors which contributed to the aggravation of the Syrian–Israeli dispute and indeed to the outbreak of the 1973 war were Soviet and American backing of Syria and Israel respectively, and, crucially, the failure of Israel and Egypt to reach a political settlement despite American and United Nations diplomatic efforts.

ISRAEL'S STATUS QUO POLICY REGARDING THE GOLAN

Already on 30 October 1967, before the proclamation of UN Resolution 242 of 22 November 1967, Prime Minister Eshkol said in the Knesset: 'As for the Golan Heights, it is not possible that the pre-5 June situation should be reinstated, a situation that had carried destruction and loss to our settlements in the [Hula/Jordan] valley.'[1]

After the passing of Resolution 242, Israeli leaders stressed [and interpreted] its principles as follows: 'withdrawal of Israeli armed forces from *territories* occupied in the recent conflict' [to new] 'secure and recognized boundaries', in return for the 'termination of all claims or states of belligerency [by the Arab states] and respect for and acknowledgement of the sovereignty, territorial integrity . . . of every state in the area [including Israel] and their right to live in peace.'[2]

Yet, although repeatedly emphasizing Israel's desire for peace with its Arab neighbours, since early 1969 Eshkol and particularly his successor as prime minister (from March 1969), Golda Meir, declared that Israel would not give up the Golan (or East Jerusalem, the Gaza Strip, and Sharm al-Sheikh). Defence Minister Dayan, hero of the 1967 war, who shared this position, argued already in late 1967 and in mid-1968 that the Syrian leadership was not prepared to make peace with Israel, regardless of the Golan issue; and that, unlike Egypt and Jordan, Syria did not distinguish between the liberation of Palestine [Israel] and the recovery of the Golan.[3]

In 1968, Yigal Allon, minister of labour, and Israel Galili, minister without portfolio, both of the activist 'Ahdut ha'Avoda Party, proposed the annexation of the Golan Heights to Israel. They also facilitated, in late 1967, the establishment of two Israeli settlements in the Golan. Although the Israeli cabinet then objected to annexation, it approved the creation of new settlements and the maintenance of Israeli control in this area indefinitely.[4]

These new positions regarding the Golan stemmed from strategic and security considerations, also partly backed by the United States, in response to continuing Syrian belligerency in word and deed, as well as from domestic considerations. To begin with, Allon, one of Israel's chief strategic thinkers, repeatedly argued that:

our firm hold in the Golan Heights and the [Mount] Hermon shoulder is very vital not only in order to defend . . . the Hula valley from Syrian fire. . . . Our control over the [Golan] Heights . . . derives from Israel's overall strategy, since this means defending the chief water sources.[5]

To be sure, Israeli security requirements in the Golan region were acknowledged by both the Johnson and Nixon administrations, thus granting Jerusalem a certain backing in its policy regarding this region. For example, in a secret memo to the United States secretary of defense, General Wheeler, chairman of the Joint Chiefs of Staff, wrote on 29 June 1967 *inter alia*:

without regard to political factors . . . solely on military considerations from the Israel point of view . . . Israel must hold the commanding terrain [in the Golan] east of the boundary of 4 June 1967 which overlooks the Galilee area. To provide a defense in-depth, Israel would need a strip about 15 miles wide . . . inside the Syrian border [which] would give Israel control of the terrain which Syria has used effectively in harassing the border area. . . . This line would provide protection for the Israeli villages on the east bank of Lake Tiberias.[6]

A few months later, on 25 October, the United States State Department announced that the forty-eight A-4 Skyhawk jets agreed on in February 1966 would be delivered to Israel. And in January 1968 the Americans lifted the embargo on new arms shipments to Israel (and Jordan), which act led *inter alia* to the supply of fifty high performance F-4 Phantom jets. The latter arms deal was to be tied to withdrawal from Sinai, as part of an Israeli–Egyptian peace agreement. The Golan and Syria were not mentioned in this context (and in fact the Phantom deal had little influence on Israel's policy regarding Sinai).[7]

It is true that Washington expected that Israel would ultimately withdraw from most of the occupied Arab lands, including the Golan, except for minor border changes, in return for peace. In May 1968, for example, while warning Israel against 'being "too theological" in pressing for direct negotiations' with the Arabs, Undersecretary of State Rostow remarked:

We had also felt that any such agreement [between Israel and the Arabs] at this time must come from the parties to the conflict themselves. At the same time, we had not been talking about what the Israelis seem to have in mind—something akin to the Congress of Vienna in 1815 'with striped pants, a big peace treaty, and all the trimmings'.[8]

Nevertheless, American efforts and pressures on Israel regarding a political settlement between Israel and the Arab states continued to be directed during 1969–70 under the Nixon administration (the Rogers Plan), mainly towards Egyptian–Israeli and Jordanian–Israeli agreements, whereas Syria was to all intents and purposes left out.[9]

Indeed, since it regarded Syria as a hostile and dangerous state, Washington would not go out of its way to help Damascus regain the Golan. For not only did Syria reject UN Resolution 242, break off diplomatic relations with the United States—both in 1967—and subsequently strengthen its ties with the Soviet Union, but in June 1970, in contrast to Egypt, Jordan, and Israel, it rejected the Rogers initiative for the implementation of UN Resolution 242, and in September 1970 its armoured troops invaded Jordan—an American ally—in an attempt to help the rebellious Palestinian groups overthrow King Hussein. President Nixon depicted this invasion as follows: 'Syria created the gravest threat to world peace since this Administration came into office.'[10] Nixon then approved a joint American–Israeli plan (following a Jordanian appeal) for an Israeli air and land strike against the invading Syrian troops, this threat of massive intervention helped to save King Hussein's throne. The American president also authorized, during this crisis, $500 million in military aid for Israel and agreed to accelerate the delivery of eighteen F-4s.[11] In sum, as Dr Quandt puts it:

the crisis provided a convincing rationale for a policy based on arming Israel as a strategic asset for American policy in the Middle East. In an emergency, Israeli forces had been prepared to protect King Hussein, a task which would have been much more difficult for United States forces. By its mere presence, Israel had deterred the Syrian air force from entering the battle; Israeli armor massed in the Golan Heights must have helped convince the Syrians that they should withdraw.... The agreement hastily negotiated between Kissinger and Rabin, then ambassador in Washington, on September 21 was a remarkable testimony to the new strategic relationship that existed between the two countries. For the next three years US–Israeli relations flourished. Unprecedented levels of aid were provided by Washington.[12]

In addition to providing aid, notably arms, the Americans simultaneously continued their efforts, mainly through Ambassador Jarring, the United Nations representative, to bring about political settlements step by step between Israel, Egypt, and Jordan,[13] while disregarding the Syrians and the Palestinians, who consistently rejected any political negotiations with Israel.

Consequently, by the end of 1970, enjoying American diplomatic and military support and backed by the great majority of the Jewish population, Israeli leaders unequivocally considered the Golan *de facto* as part of Israel and continued to encourage the establishment of more Jewish settlements there.[14] To be sure, this position was largely a reaction to Syria's continuously highly belligerent attitudes. For, in addition to unremitting rejection of Resolution 242 and hostile anti-Israeli statements, Syria directed and/or encouraged, particularly during 1969 and 1970, guerrilla actions against Israel (see below), while preparing, with massive Soviet help, for another war. In addition, the Syrian government was allegedly persecuting the Jewish community in the country, and had detained two Israelis hijacked by Palestinian guerrillas on a TWA flight in November 1969, as well as two Israeli pilots whose planes had been shot down in June 1970.[15]

Israel's animosity to Syria (and to its Palestinian proxies) was so intense that even Eban, that eloquent and sophisticated diplomat, used extremely violent language toward Damascus-sponsored activities. During a debate in the Knesset on 25 February 1969, on the increasing terrorist action stemming from Syria, Eban held Damascus responsible for these raids and reacted thus to outside criticism of the Israeli air force attacks on the guerrilla/terrorist camps in Syria:

The human conscience should react to the [Israeli] blow that was struck on the [terrorist] camps in Syria as it should have reacted if a blow was struck on a [Nazi] SS camp, or on a training centre of the Auschwitz and Treblinka bullies during the Second World War. . . . they act . . . against peace, against liberation, against the State of the Jews . . . for the murder of Jews.[16]

In their antagonism to Syria, Israeli leaders, it would seem, did not always distinguish between 'the present leadership in Damascus . . . the Ba'th chiefs, or . . . another Syrian leadership that would ascend tomorrow' (in Dayan's words); and when Hafiz Asad seized power in Damascus on 16 November 1970, Meir interpreted that event as a sign of weakness and internal conflict in Syria. She acknowledged, though, that it reflected not only a personal contest for power but also 'an acute debate between diverse political trends including Syrian policy regarding the [Palestinian] saboteurs' actions and other adventurous schemes'.[17]

Yet, as it were, neither Moshe Dayan nor Golda Meir nor other Israeli leaders could or would perceive the change in Syrian strategy towards Israel under Asad's leadership (nor the significant shift in Egypt's policy under Sadat), namely: Asad's inclination to accept the principle of political settlement (UN Resolution 242) and, particularly and simultaneously, his strong determination and systematic preparations for waging another war against Israel.

ASAD VS. JADID: CONTINUITY AND CHANGE IN SYRIA'S POSITIONS

As already indicated, the Ba'th radical regime in Damascus, unlike the governments of Egypt, Jordan, and Israel, refused for several years to accept UN Resolution 242 calling for a peaceful solution to the Arab–Israeli conflict and the withdrawal of Israeli forces from territories occupied during the 1967 war. Syrian politicians and polemicists were engaged in a fierce anti-Israeli, anti-Zionist, and even anti-Jewish indoctrination and propaganda campaign, labelling Israel as 'racist', 'illegitimate', 'imperialist', 'expansionist', aiming at destroying the Arabs and controlling the Western world. Syrian leaders continued to declare their commitment to another war against Israel which would liberate the territories occupied in 1967, as well as the whole territory of Palestine, and eliminate the Israeli state.[18] This war, according to the radical Baʿthist leaders, should again be carried out mainly by Palestinian guerrilla organizations with the support of Syria. Thus, in addition to giving weapons, training, and safe haven to the Fath (amalgamated with the PLO since 1968 under Arafat's leadership), the 'Palestine Liberation Army', and other Palestinian groups, in late 1968 the Baʿth regime established its own guerrilla organization—*al-Saʿiqa* (the Thunderbolt)—made up of Palestinians from Syria, Lebanon, and Jordan and placed under the command of Syrian officers. With Syrian encouragement and direction, the various guerrilla groups carried out, particularly during the late 1960s, many military operations inside Israel (and Jordan), the West Bank, Gaza, and the Golan—from the territories of Lebanon, Jordan, and Syria. From mid-1969 Syrian troops also periodically attacked Israeli targets in the Golan.[19]

Israel retaliated partly by land raids but mostly by air attacks against guerrilla bases in Syria and Lebanon and, when confronted by Syrian military aircraft, the air force shot down several Syrian planes—for example, one MiG-21 on 12 February 1969, two MiG-17s on 24 February 1969, seven MiG-21s in July 1969, two MiG-17s, one MiG-21 on 17 December 1969. In August 1969, for the first time since 1967, Syrian artillery fired at Israeli positions in the Golan.

On 2 April 1970, Israel again reacted against guerrilla operations from the Syrian border and shot down three MiG-21s. On 8 and 24 June, Syrian forces attacked Israeli positions in the Golan and, in retaliation, the army attacked Syrian positions, on 26 June 1970, injuring and killing hundreds of Syrian soldiers, taking thirty-eight prisoners, and shooting down four more MiGs.[20]

Israeli air raids inside Syrian territory, the shooting down of Syrian MiGs, and indeed Syrian military strategy and operations against Israel—all these factors had an important impact on, and/or were influenced by, the struggle for power in Damascus between Salah Jadid and Hafiz Asad. Jadid, Syria's strong man since 1966, assisted by President Atasi, Prime Minister Zuʿayyin, and Foreign Minister Makhus and backed by the Baʿth Party, continued after the June 1967 war to visualize the struggle against Israel in terms of a 'popular war of liberation' and an 'armed struggle' to be launched by the Palestinian *fidaʾiyyun* with the backing of Syria, the 'stout fortress in the liberation campaign'.[21] The Syrian army itself should continue to be an 'ideological army' under Baʿth Party control, whereas socio-economic reforms should be given priority in government expenditure. Asad, the defence minister and commander of the air force, on the other hand, demanded priority for military reinforcement at the expense of economic development, in order to build a strong regular army. And, while questioning the effectiveness of the Palestinian guerrillas in the struggle against Israel, Asad insisted that they should be placed under strict army control, *inter alia* in order not to give Israel a pretext to attack Syrian positions. And, unlike Jadid, who denied the role of most Arab countries in the military struggle against Israel because of their alleged 'defeatist', 'rightist', or 'reactionary' regimes, Asad advocated co-operation with other Arab countries, regardless of their regimes, in the struggle against Israel. As he stated at the Baʿth convention in March 1969:

I have repeatedly stressed the importance of Arab military co-ordination—notably among the Arab states which border with Israel—regardless of the differences and the contradictions in their political positions, as long as it would serve the armed struggle . . . the defensive capability of the Syrian front is closely tied with the capability of other Arab fronts . . . and the same mistake prior to 5 June [1967] could be repeated and Israel would be able to strike at each of the Arab fronts separately one after the other. Therefore, the escalation and the continuation of the *fidaʾyi* [Palestinian guerrilla] action is largely tied up with the defensive capability of the Arab fronts.[22]

As far as the *fidaʾyi* action was concerned, both Asad and Jadid favoured surveillance of the various Palestinian guerrilla organizations in Syria, although the conflict between the two leaders prevented a systematic approach. Still, until early 1969, Damascus endeavoured to curtail guerrilla actions from the Golan line against Israel in order to avoid Israeli retaliation while the Syrian army was reconstructing its defence system there.[23] But during 1969, against the background of the Israeli–Egyptian war of attrition along the Suez Canal zone, Jadid's regime permitted, even encouraged, the *fidaʾyi* groups, notably Fatḥ-PLO and *al-Saiʿqa*, to operate against Israel.[24] Asad, more reserved regarding the guerrillas' contribution and aiming at diminishing Jadid's control of the various irregular military forces—notably *al-Saiʿqa*—had already placed these forces under his command, as defence minister, during 1968. And in early May 1969 he issued a special order regulating the modes of surveillance and the scope of activities of the various guerrilla forces.[25]

Furthermore, Asad apparently used the Israeli retaliatory air raids against *fidaʾyi* camps in Syria, which were exploited by Jadid to discredit him, to dislodge Jadid from power. Thus on 25 February 1969, one day after the Israeli raid on Faṭḥ bases in al-Hamma and Maysalun (near Damascus), Asad staged a 'mini-coup' against Jadid: army units took control of key buildings in Damascus, including Baʿth Party offices and Syrian media centres.[26] And, although he was still unable to depose Jadid, Asad continued his efforts to seize power in Damascus, largely using Syria's policy towards Israel as his motive (or pretext). Thus, for example, in March 1969 he forced the Baʿth emergency regional convention to adopt certain resolutions which were compatible with his strategy and contrary to Jadid's policy: that renewed efforts should be made to establish an Eastern command (with Iraq and Jordan) to co-ordinate between the Syrian front and other Arab fronts and to seek union with progressive Arab states—all in order to facilitate the struggle against Israel.[27]

In September 1970 Asad took yet another step to discredit his rival, Jadid, who was still in power. As defence minister and air force commander, Asad denied air cover to the armoured units dispatched by Jadid to Jordan to help the Palestinian guerrillas against King Hussein. Asad was apparently aware of the potential Israeli threat to these units as well as to the Syrian air force. Possibly he did not wish to alienate King Hussein, the leader of a strategically important 'confrontation' state, by supporting a Palestinian rebellion which was likely to fail in the event of American–Israeli intervention.[28]

Another crucial event which gave Asad a further pretext or motive finally to depose Jadid was the death, on 28 September 1970, of Egypt's president, Gamal ʿAbd al-Nasir (Nasser). This event could have further increased Syria's vulnerability vis-à-vis Israel, since Nasser had been committed, in Asad's view, to defending Syria against a major Israel offensive. In addition, Anwar Sadat, the new Egyptian president, shortly after his succession, decided to conclude a federal union with Libya and Sudan which Asad—but not Jadid—was anxious to join in order to strengthen Syria's strategic position in the face of Israel's military superiority.

Consequently, after taking measures against Jadid's chief supporters, Asad had Jadid and other senior Baʿth leaders arrested, seizing power in Damascus on 16 November 1970 by means of a bloodless military coup.[29]

ASAD'S NEW STRATEGY TOWARDS ISRAEL

Asad's first foreign policy decision, one day after he came to power (on 17 November 1970), was indeed to join the Federation of Arab Republics (with Egypt and Libya), which, in his words, was to be a stage towards a comprehensive Arab union from 'the Atlantic Ocean to the Arab Gulf', designed to face the 'aggressive and racist' Zionist entity, liberate the Arab territories occupied in 1967, and recover all Palestine.[30] To be sure, Asad's anti-Zionist/anti-Israel statements and rhetoric were at least as strong as those of his predecessors. Obviously, these statements and the accompanying anti-Israeli indoctrination reflected the ideological tenets of the Baʿth Party, which Asad was anxious to stress in order to demonstrate his Baʿthist convictions and leadership. Possibly, Asad's anti-Israeli expressions stemmed also from his own personal beliefs and feelings of anger caused by his country's severe defeat by Israel in 1967, when he was defence minister.

Since 1967, Asad indeed had greatly and systematically endeavoured to prepare his army for another war against Israel, to recover the Golan and Palestine, as well as heal his own wounded pride.

The need to fight another round was his obsession . . . He longed to wipe away the stain of defeat which had affected him personally and profoundly, restore the confidence of his troops, recover the land, and show the world that, given the chance, the Arabs could acquit themselves honourably.[31]

Yet, unlike Jadid, the doctrinaire Baʿthist who had refused to use any political or diplomatic moves in the struggle against Israel, Asad, the pragmatist leader, would not rule out such moves. Thus, although again advocating at two Baʿth Party conventions, in July and December 1970, the reaffirmation of Syria's rejection of UN Resolution 242, Asad subsequently changed his position: in February 1971 he indicated and in March 1972 he declared for the first time that he would no longer oppose the implementation of Resolution 242, provided it would entail Israel's withdrawal from the Arab lands occupied in 1967 and the realization of the [national] rights of the Palestinian people.[32]

What Asad possibly had in mind while adopting this new diplomatic step may be reflected in an interview he gave in March 1971:

Political activities could perhaps facilitate the military campaign . . . sometimes political manœuvres are important for the war effort in order, for example, to gain time or to acquire the sympathy of international public opinion.[33]

Indeed, at that juncture Asad had no faith in a political-diplomatic settlement with Israel regarding the Golan and the Palestinian issue. He believed that only Syria's military capacity would determine the struggle against Israel, since Israel openly rejected a political settlement by refusing to withdraw from the occupied Arab territories. Yet, even if Israel retired from the Golan and Sinai—Asad said—Syria would still continue to fight alongside the Palestinian people, as the 'Palestinian problem is the major issue' between the Arabs and Israel.[34]

Consequently, since coming to power, Asad not only continued to prepare his army, with massive Soviet help, for another round against Israel, but he also prepared the Syrian public for another war, by means of public statements and through media indoctrination. Simultaneously, he sought to establish a military axis with Egypt, the major Arab power, while looking for political co-ordination with, and economic assistance from, other Arab countries, radical and conservative alike.

Preparing for War

As Syria's ruler (since 1970) and president (since 1971), Asad continued to make forceful anti-Israel statements and inspired (or instructed) the Syrian media and press to carry out an indoctrination campaign along this line. This was done not only as part of the Baʿthist ideology, but also in order to gain legitimacy in the eyes of the Syrian public, neutralize the Islamic opposition, and prepare the people and army for war. Asad, and Syrian polemicists, thus depicted Israel as an extension of world Zionism and imperialism, a 'racist', 'colonialist', 'aggressive', and 'neo-Nazi' entity, a danger ('cancer') not only to the territorial integrity of the Arab world, but also to Arab society and civilization. Therefore, the struggle against Israel was inevitable. In Asad's words: 'it is a fatal confrontation, of life or death, of existence.'[35] Yet, in contrast to the anti-Jewish/anti-Semitic language which Syrian politicians and writers occasionally used during the Jadid period ('Jews wish to control the world', 'Judaism is Zionism itself', as well as other expressions from the 'Protocols of the Elders of Zion'), Asad made a distinction between Zionism and Judaism: 'We do not hate Judaism as a religion, but we hate Zionism as a colonialist, invading movement.'[36] Also, unlike the Jadid ideologues who frequently employed Soviet-Marxist terminology in their anti-Zionist writings, Asad refrained from stressing ideological links with the USSR, and chose to depict Moscow by and large as a strategic and political ally.

Indeed, Asad had been opposed since 1966 to the ruling Baʿth Party ideological link with Moscow, which had been promoted by his rival, Salah Jadid, in conjunction with the Syrian Communist Party. He also resented the growing dependence of Syria on the USSR and Moscow's backing of Jadid during their struggle for power during 1969–70. Thus, already in August 1969 Asad 'resolved to put relations with the Soviet Union on a business-like basis, free from doctrinal and emotional ups and downs. Only Moscow could supply the arms for the new-style army he planned to build . . . [Yet] arms transfers had to be set within the context of sensible political relationship.'[37]

During the period 1955–67 the Soviet Union had supplied Syria with $327 million worth of military aid (in addition to $234 million of economic aid). And, in view of massive American military assistance to Israel, Asad, particularly since coming to power, sought to increase greatly the level of Soviet military aid while allocating a larger share of Syria's annual budget to his military build-up. Thus, assigning over 70 per cent of the 1971 budget to the army, and endeavouring to mend fences with 'the friendly USSR', Asad paid his first official visit to Moscow as Syrian ruler, in February 1971. Agreeing with his hosts to continue their 'special relationship' and open a new 'era of close Soviet–Syrian co-operation', Asad apparently managed to secure a new Soviet arms deal; for in the spring and summer of 1971 began a steady flow of Soviet arms to Syria. During 1972 two or three arms deals were concluded between Moscow and Damascus, including a $700 million deal signed by Asad in July, upon his second visit to the USSR, now as Syria's president.[38] The Soviet arms deliveries consisted of MiG-21 fighter planes, SAM-2 anti-aircraft missiles, FRUG surface-to-surface missiles, and were accompanied by some three thousand Soviet military advisers.

During the spring and summer of 1973 more Soviet arms were delivered to Syria, including modern planes, T-62 tanks and SAM-6 anti-aircraft missiles. Consequently, on the eve of the October 1973 war, Syria had 2,000 Soviet tanks and 330 Soviet combat planes (in comparison to 430 tanks and 150 planes in 1968), as well as 135,000 troops (60,500 in 1963), thanks to the USSR and as an outcome of the substantial increase of Syrian military expenditure (from $268 million in 1965 to $384 million in 1970 and $427 million in 1971).[39]

Yet Asad was not content with his huge military build-up with massive Soviet help. To launch an effective war against Israel, he needed the military co-operation of Egypt as well as some degree of co-ordination with Jordan and Lebanon (Iraq continued to be at odds with Syria). On 26 November 1970, ten days after coming to power, Asad signed in Cairo a military agreement with Egypt, knowing very well that a two-front strategy against Israel was essential for a successful military campaign. By early 1971, according to Seale, Asad and Sadat began the secret planning of their joint strategy and by the end of 1971 the two leaders had taken soundings in Moscow, had appointed Egypt's war minister, General Sadiq, supreme commander of both armies, and had reached agreement on broad strategy vis-à-vis Israel.[40]

ISRAEL AND THE ROAD TO THE 1973 CAMPAIGN

Syria's massive military build-up since 1971 was closely monitored in Israel and evidently caused concern in the Israeli government.[41] This government, however, was more worried about the continued, and periodically increasing, activity of the Palestinian guerrilla organizations working from Syria and Lebanon. Following the liquidation of their bases in Jordan in September 1970, the Palestinian *fida'iyyun* considered Syria 'a strategic base for which there is no substitute', while Asad reiterated the Fath slogan that 'Syria is the lung through which Palestinian activity breathes.' Indeed, after the September 1970 disaster, most Fath regular and semi-regular forces moved to Syria, where the Fath headquarters, and the training and administrative networks, were also established. In addition to the *Sa'iqa* forces, all PLO units were located in Syria, whence arms and supplies were also delivered to the newly created *fida'yi* bases in southern Lebanon, which became the main launching centres for operations against Israel during the early 1970s. Thus, despite periodic friction resulting from Asad's attempts to control the *fida'iyyun*, during that period a certain co-ordination was achieved between Syria and PLO/Fath which even prompted Fath to declare in May 1973: 'The Pan Arab and national character of the Syrian regime . . . ensures preservation of close ties between Syria and the Palestinian Resistance. Syria is the chief active partner in the Arab struggle against the Zionist enemy.'[42]

In fact, during 1971–3 numerous *fida'yi* operations were undertaken against Israeli targets (also in other countries) from Syria and Lebanon, as well as from Jordan. Many of these were co-ordinated or directed by Damascus, while occasional Syrian artillery and air attacks on Israeli positions in the Golan were carried out in reaction to reprisals in Syria.[43] Many Israeli attacks, mostly in the form of air raids, were launched against *fida'yi* bases—and occasionally also against Syrian military and economic targets deep inside Syria and Lebanon—also involving the shooting down of Syrian combat planes. Israel's air raids—and Syrian reactions—intensified, particularly following the assault on the Israeli Olympic team in Munich (5 September 1972); for example, on 9 September three MiGs and again on 21 November 1972 seven planes were shot down by the

Israeli air force. On 8 January 1973 the air force attacked military and civilian targets in Latakia and Tartus in north-west Syria, killing and injuring 400 or 500 Syrian soldiers and civilians.[44]

It would appear that Israel's policy of military escalation was essentially aimed at forcing Damascus to curb or stop the Palestinian *fida'yi* actions— and this policy indeed proved effective by early 1973 when Asad 'ordered Palestinian commandos to halt their raids into the territory occupied by Israel'.[45] But it is also possible that Israel, being aware of the Soviet-aided military build-up in Syria, escalated military operations against Syria in order to teach Damascus a lesson, and warn and deter it from waging a new war against Israel.[46] At the same time, however, Israeli military leaders, particularly Dayan, trusting in Israel's strategic and military superiority—thanks also to newly arrived American weapons—calculated during 1972 and 1973 that neither Syria nor Egypt would be capable of fighting Israel for at least several years.[47]

Israel's calculation, or rather miscalculation, derived not only from a sense of superiority, perhaps of contempt, vis-à-vis Arab military capabilities, but also from a gross misinterpretation of Egypt's intentions and moves. Indeed, the Israeli cabinet, until late 1973, did not take Sadat's preparations for war seriously, for despite his repeated promises that 1971 would be a 'year of decision' in his conflict with Israel, by mid-1972 Egypt remained militarily idle. In July 1972 Sadat abruptly expelled more than 15,000 Soviet military personnel—advisers and experts—from Egypt on the grounds that the USSR had ceased to support Egypt's interests.[48] The Israeli prime minister, Golda Meir, considered this spectacular move as a 'significant fact' that might mark 'the hour of changes', and called on Egypt to enter into negotiations with Israel 'as equals' to make 'a supreme effort to arrive at an agreed solution', while the defence minister, Dayan, said that 'the withdrawal of Soviet troops from Egypt would enable Israel to alter its deployment of forces along the Suez Canal and reduce the call-up of reservists to active duty.'

Sadat, on his part, reacted to Mrs Meir's call for talks by saying that it was the 'same old tune' and subsequently told *Newsweek* on 31 July that American interests in the Arab world would 'shortly become part of the battle for the recovery of our land.'[49] In point of fact, Egypt and Syria stepped up their war preparations from the autumn of 1972. Following Asad's talks in Moscow, which included efforts to repair the Soviet–Egyptian rift, Soviet military aid to both Egypt and Syria 'rose to unprecedented levels' and continued also during 1973, consisting of more SAM-6 missiles, new SCUD missiles and the most modern T-62 battle tanks.[50]

In late January 1973 it was reported that Egypt's new war minister, General Ismail, was appointed commander-in-chief of the Syrian, Jordanian, and Egyptian fronts by the Arab Joint Defence Council convening in Cairo to draw up a plan for joint military action against Israel. Two weeks later Sadat announced Egypt's war budget to prepare for the resumption of war (reportedly in Suez and the Golan).[51] Earlier, in mid-December 1972, Asad told an Indian journalist that, if a political settlement was not achieved within six months, a war with Israel would be imminent. In mid-March 1972 the Lebanese weekly *al-Sayyad* reported from Damascus on intense military training and exercises, and urgent preparations in the civilian sector towards a new war.[52] In May 1973 the Lebanese press reported that King Hussein of Jordan had distributed a secret letter to his army officers telling them that several Arab countries were about to attack Israel. Around the same time the Israeli government received several messages (reportedly from King Hussein) that Egypt was about to attack Israel on 15 May 1973.[53] Israel reacted by a partial mobilization which was called off in mid-August 1973. Israeli leaders publicly warned Sadat against waging a new war lest Egypt suffer more than in 1967, since Israel was strong and the Egyptian army was in a difficult situation.[54]

At this juncture it is worth while to examine briefly the position of Moshe Dayan, the powerful and influential defence minister, who at that critical period shaped Israel's policy towards the Arab states. For a long time (since 1967, according to himself) he had assessed that Egypt and Syria would never resign themselves to Israel's occupation of Sinai and the Golan, and sooner or later they would renew the war against Israel. His strategy for preventing such a war was to reach an agreement with Egypt, even on a partial basis, in order to diminish its motivation to fight, and also to isolate Syria, evaluating that Syria would not go to war without Egypt. Consequently, already in August 1970, Dayan suggested a unilateral withdrawal from the Suez Canal to enable Egypt to reopen the canal for navigation and rebuild the ruined towns along it.[55] Although his proposal was not accepted by Meir, Dayan said again in August 1972 that Israel was ready for a 'peace by stages' with Egypt, and in November 1972 and March 1973 he said that Israel was ready to negotiate 'for a complete peace treaty, for interim, partial or any kind'.[56]

Yet although in 1973 he continued to assess that if there was no political settlement war would break out and the Israeli army should be prepared for war, Dayan (and other military leaders) also continued to adhere to the notion that war was not imminent, owing to Israeli military superiority which constituted an effective deterrence vis-à-vis the Arabs.[57] On 9

August 1973, in a lecture to the Defence Force Staff College, Dayan said *inter alia*:

The territories in our hands, Sinai, Judaea and Samaria, and the Golan constitute a great motivation for Egypt, Jordan, and Syria to fight us . . . the Arab states [were given] weapons, money, and professional assistance to strengthen and organize their armies . . . [but] the overall balance of power is in our favour, and this outweighs all other Arab motivations and calculations, and blocks the immediate resumption of the war . . . our military superiority is both a result of Arab weakness and our strengthening. Their weakness derives from factors that in my mind would not be over soon.

And on 10 September 1973, at a public meeting, Dayan stated: 'Six years have already passed since the Six Day War and we talk now about a period of four more years. We have become accustomed that every ten years we fight six days.'[58]

Apparently until mid-September 1973 Dayan had not altered his 'conception' despite further military preparations by Egypt and Syria during that period. In addition to the arrival of more Soviet arms in these countries, in July 1973 a second contingent of several thousand Moroccan troops reached Syria, following the first detachment in March 1973. In August 1973 Syrian and Egyptian military leaders secretly convened (on 21–3 August) in Alexandria, Egypt, and Bludan, Syria (on 26–7 August) for their final review of war plans. Around the same time Asad, Ba'th leaders and Muslim dignitaries attacked Israel fiercely, vowing they would shortly wage a crucial war against the 'Zionist enemy'. On 6 September 1973 the *Imam* (preacher) of the Great Mosque in Damascus called for a *jihad* (holy war) against Israel; and on 22 September the *International Herald Tribune* reported that Egypt had secretly told the Palestinians to expect a large-scale military operation along the Suez Canal in order 'to generate US pressure on Israel to soften its obstinate stand'. Significantly, King Hussein secretly and personally warned Prime Minister Meir, on 25 September 1973, that Syria and Egypt were about to attack Israel.[59]

Nevertheless, by late September (and beyond) Israeli (and American) intelligence did not envisage a co-ordinated offensive against Israel by Egypt and Syria, despite their accelerated military preparations. Yet, while the Israeli chief of staff and the chief of military intelligence considered Egyptian military activities along the Suez Canal as merely training exercises and the Syrian military deployment as manageable, Defence Minister Dayan, together with the Syrian section of military intelligence, as well as the Northern Command, became greatly concerned from mid-September about a possible massive Syrian attack in the Golan.[60] On 13 September 1973, following an Israeli air force reconnaissance flight over Syrian military installations, a big air battle developed over Syrian territory, in which thirteen Syrian MiG fighters were shot down (Israel lost only one Mirage plane). As this air battle constituted a severe blow to Syria, particularly to Asad himself, the former air force commander, Israeli military leaders expected a massive Syrian retaliation and thus watched that front more carefully.[61] And in fact, during late September and early October the Syrian military build-up along the cease-fire line grew stronger, with more troops, tanks, and missiles deployed.[62] Consequently the Syrian section of Israeli intelligence, as well as the Northern Command, again warned in late September that Syria was about to launch an attack in the Golan. Reportedly, however, these warnings referred to a limited operation and not to an all-out offensive. The chiefs of military intelligence evaluated on 3 October 1973 that 'Asad is a realistic, cool and balanced leader. . . . Syria won't go to war by herself. Asad is scared that the IDF will reach Damascus, war just would not make sense, and the Syrian deployment is apparently only because of fear of Israeli attack.' And since the Egyptian military deployment along the Suez Canal was merely a manœuvre and not related to the Syrian build-up, 'it is unlikely that a coordinated Egyptian–Syrian war will begin in the near future . . . not earlier than 1975'; and, in any case, if the Arabs were to attack, they would be badly defeated.[63]

While sharing the assessment that the Egyptians were not about to attack Israel, Moshe Dayan did worry about the Syrian deployment, fearing that the Syrians could occupy part of the Golan including some Jewish settlements. Consequently on 26 September he ordered a partial reinforcement of armour and artillery in the Golan as well as an air force stand-by. Still, despite further signs of an imminent Syrian–Egyptian offensive—including large-scale military movements and a hasty departure of Soviet families from Egypt—by 5 October the common Israeli assessment remained unchanged: an Egyptian–Syrian all-out war was not imminent and thus there was no need to call up the reservists; and even if an Egyptian–Syrian attack took place, the Israeli regular forces should be able to defeat the Arabs.[64] Nevertheless, on 5 October Dayan ordered the highest degree of alert in the standing army and air force, as well as more reinforcement of armoured brigades in the Golan. Deciding to take no further action until the cabinet meeting on Sunday, 7 October 1973 (a day after Yom Kippur), Meir closed her 'kitchen cabinet' meeting on Friday,

5 October saying: 'On Sunday we'll lay these problems before the cabinet, and please God, we won't have to. Meanwhile it would be good if we were able to send Asad to synagogue on Yom Kippur.'[65]

Asad was obviously not aware of Mrs Meir's condescending advice. He and Sadat were secretly preparing a Yom Kippur for the Israeli Jews which they would probably never forget. Indeed, Asad and Sadat had designed a grand plan of deception intended to lead Israel into believing that their massive military deployment was not aimed at an all-out offensive: the Egyptian deployment was designed to be considered as merely autumn manœuvres,[66] and the Syrian build-up as a defensive measure against a possible Israeli attack. The Syrian 'bait', partly 'swallowed' by Israeli military intelligence, possibly included *inter alia* provoking the air battle of 13 September 1973, in order to demonstrate Israel's 'aggressive' intentions against Syria and thus prompt Syria's military build-up along the cease-fire line in anticipation of further Israeli attacks.[67]

Yet, while both Asad and Sadat were engaged in deceiving Israel, Sadat, according to Seale, was deceiving Asad (and the Soviets) by leading him to believe that Egypt's offensive would be wider in scope than he ever intended, namely: Sadat agreed with Asad that 'the Egyptian objective was to reach the Sinai passes in the first stage before regrouping for the reconquest of the whole [Sinai] peninsula', whereas in fact he planned only to cross the Suez Canal and capture the narrow strip of land on the eastern bank. Sadat's duplicity, intended to enlist Syrian military pressure on Israel in the Golan while the Egyptian army crossed the canal, also reflected the divergence in the war aims of each of the Arab leaders. Whereas Sadat went into a limited war in order to shatter the status quo and generate American pressure on Israel to give up the entire Sinai, Asad envisaged the capture of the entire Golan (and Sinai) and subsequent pressure on Israel to give up the occupied Palestinian territories.[68]

It would seem that Asad's war aims were too ambitious and involved grave risks to himself and his country. For, in addition to the unreliability of Sadat's commitments (which he was still unaware of), Asad could not expect any significant military action against Israel from Jordan, Lebanon, or the Palestinians. In preparation for the October war, Asad (and Sadat) in September 1973 renewed diplomatic relations with Jordan (severed in July 1971 following Hussein's further suppression of the PLO). On the eve of the war Asad urged King Hussein to open a 'third front' against Israel, adding:

The road to Jerusalem is opened, why are you waiting? . . . you could rush to Jerusalem and liberate it and thereby win a splendid victory . . . but [Asad recalled] I did not succeed in convincing . . . I regret to say that Cairo pressured Jordan forcibly and emphatically not to participate in the war, being concerned over the fate of the East Bank . . . but . . . the king . . . chose to send his forces to the Golan [in fact this was a token force sent with Israel's tacit approval].[69]

Regarding Lebanon, another front-line Arab state, Asad did not expect this militarily weak country to attack Israel, but he intended to use its territory for two main purposes: first, to prevent an Israeli counter-attack via the Lebanese Biqaʿ valley and along the Beirut–Damascus highway; secondly, to have the PLO engage Israeli troops along the Lebanese–Israeli border in order to split the Israeli war effort even further. Presumably in August 1973 Asad obtained the Lebanese president's permission to move Syrian troops toward the Biqaʿ valley;[70] but as it turned out, the Israeli army did not attempt to launch its counter-offensive in October via the Biqaʿ, while the Palestinian guerrilla actions against Israel during the October war proved ineffective.

Finally, while preparing for war against Israel, Asad had to take into account seriously the position of the Soviet Union, Syria's major strategic ally and arms supplier. It stands to reason that Moscow was aware of the Syrian (and Egyptian) war preparations and rendered help by providing a great many new weapons and possibly also giving military advice to Syria (and Egypt). However, Asad and Sadat did not inform Moscow until 4 October that they were to attack on 6 October, so that the Soviets would be unable to obstruct the offensive. Indeed, although acknowledging Soviet support for the recovery of the Golan, Asad was possibly not sure how far Moscow was willing to go to help him implement his war aims, following Brezhnev's failure in July 1973 to persuade Washington to impose a political settlement on Israel.[71] Would the USSR send troops to the Golan in case of a Syrian defeat, or would it only impose, together with the United States, a cease-fire between Syria and Israel?[72]

Bearing all these uncertainties in mind, it would appear that Asad's firm determination to wage war against Israel was both hazardous and courageous, since he could expect a fierce and powerful Israeli counter-attack, including the possible use of nuclear weapons against Syria, or a major military thrust towards Damascus. Asad could also imagine that the Americans would not restrain Israel from severely punishing Syria, a Soviet ally and a United States adversary.

Asad indeed took this grave risk and was prepared for Syria to pay a high price if necessary. In addition to prearranging food and water supplies for the population, he ordered large graveyards laid out and had hotels converted into hospitals. He also systematically endeavoured to

forearm his people and army, psychologically and ideologically, and assumed the leading role in conducting the campaign against Israel. Consequently, despite his eventual military defeat, he achieved high prestige in
the Arab world as a new leader of the Arab struggle against Israel.

THE 1973 WAR AND ITS CONSEQUENCES

Without going into the details of the October 1973 war,[73] it can be briefly
said that for the first time since 1948 the Egyptian and Syrian armies
succeeded in surprising and defeating the Israeli forces, while storming
Israeli fortifications in both Sinai and the Golan and inflicting heavy losses
on the rather thinned-out Israeli troops, as well as their armoured re-
inforcements and the air force.

Syrian armoured and infantry divisions stormed the Golan plateau on
6 October afternoon and by 8 October they were stopped only several
miles away from the eastern shore of Lake Tiberias and the River Jordan,
reportedly aiming at advancing toward Nazareth. Syrian helicopter-borne
commandos simultaneously seized the strategic Israeli position on Mount
Hermon.

Obviously, Israeli leaders were deeply worried about the Syrian threat
because of its proximity to Jewish towns and villages inside Israeli territory; thus reportedly Dayan, the defence minister, on 8 October ordered
the deployment of nuclear missiles lest Syrian armour should cross the
international boundary.[74] Simultaneously the air force went into massive,
continuous action against the Syrian forces, while Israeli armoured divisions were engaged in repulsing the Syrian offensive. In retaliation for
Syrian ground-to-ground missile firing at air bases in the north of Israel,
the air force attacked strategic and economic targets deep inside Syria.
(Dayan reportedly rejected the chief of staff's proposal to launch ground-
to-ground missiles against Damascus.)[75] Following more fierce ground
battles, the Israeli forces pushed the Syrian troops back from the Golan by
10 October and subsequently advanced further inside Syrian territory,
some 25 miles south of Damascus.

The defeat of the Syrian army, which fought bravely and skilfully, was
due not only to the quick and effective Israeli recovery and domination of
the Golan skies; Egypt's defensive posture in Sinai, following the successful canal crossing, also enabled Israel to concentrate its efforts for several
days against the Syrian forces in the Golan. Asad, initially unaware of
Egypt's limited strategic aims, was deeply disconcerted by Sadat's 'du-

plicity' and his refusal (or inability) to fulfil his commitment to advance into Sinai and thus split Israel's war machine.[76] Only on 13 October, after the Israeli forces were half way to Damascus, did Sadat order his army to launch an attack into Sinai,[77] *inter alia* in order to honour his alliance with Syria and prevent the Israeli army from concentrating its main thrust on the northern front. But Sadat's order came too late, as Israel was now ready and able also to inflict a serious reverse on the Egyptian forces. The army crossed the Suez Canal westward on 15 October and, by 22 October, Israeli troops were deployed less than 70 miles west of Cairo, several hours before the United Nations cease-fire resolution went into effect. This Security Council Resolution 338, of 22 October 1973, reads as follows:

The Security Council calls upon all parties to the present fighting to cease all firing and terminate all military activity immediately . . . to start immediately after the cease-fire the implementation of Security Council Resolution 242 (1967) in all of its parts; decides that immediately and concurrently with the cease-fire, negotiations shall start between the parties concerned . . . aimed at establishing just and durable peace in the Middle East.[78]

Sadat, who had sought a cease-fire with Israel already on 16 October without consulting Asad, promptly accepted Resolution 338, as did Israel. Asad, however, feeling humiliated if not betrayed by Sadat and the Soviet Union, rejected the resolution, thus giving Israel a pretext to carry on fighting on the Syrian front, and recapturing the strategic Mount Hermon position on 22 October.[79] Only on 23 October did Syria reluctantly accept Resolution 338, spelling out its own understanding that the resolution called for total Israeli withdrawal from the occupied territories and the safeguarding of Palestinian rights.

Despite the cease-fire, hostilities continued between Israeli and Egyptian forces, causing great tension between the USSR and the United States, to the brink of nuclear confrontation. The two superpowers extended massive military supplies to their respective allies, sending huge airlifts to compensate for the heavy losses in tanks, aircraft, and various munitions incurred during the critical days of fighting. And while the Soviet Union made great efforts to achieve a cease-fire when the Egyptian and Syrian armies were being defeated, the American Secretary of State Kissinger held up Soviet cease-fire proposals for a few days in order to help the Israeli offensive, notably against Syria.[80]

Nevertheless, following the cease-fire, Kissinger prevented Israel from further attacking the Egyptians and thus humiliating Sadat, since Sadat was now ready to co-operate with the United States, rather than with the USSR, to bring about a political settlement to the Arab–Israeli conflict. Kissinger possibly also envisaged, as a first stage, paving the way for an agreement between Egypt and Israel, under American auspices, while cutting out the Soviet Union and deferring the Syrian–Israeli issue to a later stage.[81]

Accordingly, Kissinger embarked on a step-by-step strategy aiming at reaching interim political settlements between Egypt and Israel which would eventually lead to a full peace treaty between Cairo and Jerusalem. Thus, following the one-day Geneva peace conference on 21 December 1973, in Syria's absence, on 18 January 1974 Egypt and Israel signed their first 'disengagement of forces agreement' (Sinai 1) to be followed by the second disengagement accord on 1 September 1975 (Sinai 2), removing Israeli forces beyond the strategic Sinai passes and restoring Egyptian access to the oilfields in the Suez Gulf. These two agreements prepared the groundwork for the 1978 Camp David Accords (following Sadat's historic visit to Israel in November 1977) and the Egyptian–Israeli peace treaty of March 1979—all of which excluded Syria and turned it into the leading Arab adversary of Israel. For, unlike the fairly pragmatic Egyptian and Israeli attitudes, the positions of Damascus and Jerusalem in the post-war years were very far apart, rigid, and emotionally or ideologically charged. Asad initially demanded a full Israeli withdrawal from all Syrian territories acquired in the 1973 and 1967 wars as part of his disengagement agreement with Israel.[82] The Israeli government, charged with feelings of anger and revenge against Syria on account of its initial military gains and its subsequent 'criminal' treatment of Israeli prisoners of war, rejected Asad's demands. It was only ready to withdraw roughly to the pre-1973 war line.

Reportedly, Menachem Begin, leader of the opposition, and General Elazar, chief of staff, suggested during the war that the Israeli army should occupy Damascus.[83] The newly elected (in December 1973) government, under Mrs Meir, possibly had to demonstrate a tough position vis-à-vis Syria to counteract its loss of popularity among the Israeli public, reflected *inter alia* in the national elections. Consequently, the Israeli–Syrian negotiations for a disengagement of forces agreement, conducted indirectly by Kissinger's Jerusalem–Damascus 'shuttle', were slow and difficult and accompanied by frequent military clashes. Syria not only used the Israeli prisoners (and the Saudi oil embargo against the West) to pressure Israel, but during March–May 1974, Asad also initiated a war of attrition along the new cease-fire line, to back his diplomatic campaign against Israel. Asad's continuing military struggle was also aimed at strengthening his prestige and popularity in the Arab world, notably among his own people, who had suffered heavy losses during the war.[84] Eventually, after five months of extremely difficult negotiation underlined by bloody military action, on 31 May 1974, Syria and Israel reached a disengagement agreement whereby Damascus settled for only a fraction of its original demands, namely an Israeli withdrawal from the Syrian salient occupied during the war as well as from the town of Qunaytra and two hills in the vicinity which had been captured by Israel in the 1967 war. In Kissinger's evaluation, this 'outcome represented a Syrian gain over what a strict calculation of the existing balance of forces would have warranted'.[85]

Asad's small territorial gain of Qunaytra reflected his political and psychological achievements in the 1973 war, in which Syria was ultimately badly defeated. He indeed managed to turn this military reverse into a great victory in the eyes of many Syrians and other Arabs (although not a few Syrians who opposed his regime blamed him for losing the war). His bold conduct of the fighting, his decision to carry on without Egypt in a war of attrition against Israel, his tough and skilful negotiations with Kissinger—all these elevated Asad's prestige and popularity in Syria and beyond. Many Syrians and other Arabs now considered him the new pan-Arab leader, the worthy successor to Nasser, while several Arab states offered Syria military, diplomatic, and financial support, and various Western leaders, including Nixon, acknowledged his influential position in the Middle East.[86]

In contrast, despite its grand military victory, Israel emerged from the war—designated by Dayan 'an earthquake'—deeply shaken and hurt. First, its defence strategy collapsed, together with Dayan's 'conception', namely, the deterrence doctrine failed as Syria went to war against Israel despite its clear military weakness, especially in the air; the 'territorial depth' enjoyed by Israel on account of the Golan did not prevent the outbreak of the war and Syria's initial territorial gains; and the Israeli settlements in the Golan proved to be a liability rather than an asset to defence, since valuable time and energy had to be spend on evacuating them.[87] Secondly, despite its final military gains, Israel became diplomatically isolated in the international community and more dependent on the United States for military and economic assistance (the Israeli economy was also severely hit as a result of the war).

No wonder, then, that Israeli Jews blamed their government, especially Dayan, for the 1973 'blunder'—being palpably unprepared for the Arab offensive, which exacted thousands of casualties. (Yet the government was not blamed for holding on to the Golan and Sinai and establishing Jewish settlements there.) Consequently, worn out by public criticism and political infighting as well as economic difficulties, Meir resigned in April 1974, together with Dayan, and was succeeded by Yitzhak Rabin, former chief of staff and ambassador to Washington. His political arch-rival, Shimon Peres, succeeded Dayan as defence minister.[88]

A new chapter now began in Israel as well as in Syria. Both heads of state were former military leaders and war heroes—Rabin in 1967 and Asad in 1973. Asad's achievements in 1973 gave him the status of an unchallenged leader with all-Arab prestige. Rabin, the first Israeli-born prime minister, owed his ascendancy to his able conduct of the 1967 victory. Would their military background direct Asad and Rabin to rely more on military might in shaping their post-1973 policies towards each other; or would it conversely draw their attention to the limitations of military power in international relations and to the essential need to employ diplomacy and political measures in their confrontation? This also in view of the supreme role of the United States in achieving the disengagement agreement, and their own personal exposure to American diplomacy.

NOTES

1. *Divrey Haknesset*, 50. 4, 30 Oct. 1967.
2. Cf. speech by Eban, *Divrey Haknesset*, 50. 324–5, 5 Dec. 1967; 51. 1187–8, 26 Feb. 1968. See also 'Israeli Nine-Point Peace Plan, 10 October 1968', in Dodd and Sales, *Israel and the Arab World*, 187–91.
3. M. Dayan, *Mapa hadasha, yehasim aherim* (Tel Aviv, 1969), 47, 101; *Divrey Haknesset*, 54. 1523, 11 Feb. 1969; 2445, 19 Feb. 1969; 58. 2600–1, 25 May 1970; 60. 1857, 16 Mar. 1971; 3528, 27 July 1971; Rabin, *Pinkas Sherut*, 265; Meir, *My Life*, 270.
4. I. Galili, *Bemoqdey'asiya Ve-Hakhra'ah* (Tel Aviv, 1987), 206, 228, 249; Yigal Allon, *Kelim shluvim* (Tel Aviv, 1980), 117, 133–4; idem, *Behatira lashalom* (Tel Aviv, 1989), 47. Cf. *Divrey Haknesset*, 52. 2654, 10 July 1968.
5. Allon, *Kelim*, 117.
6. Memo, p. 2 and Appendix, p. 2: Subject: Middle East Boundaries Jcsm-373-67. Cf. D. Schoenbaum, *The United States and the State of Israel* (New York, 1993), 160. On Israel's sense of encouragement from the American position,

see *Divrey Haknesset*, 48. 324–5, 5 Dec. 1967 (Eban's statement); Rabin, *Pinkas Sherut*, 222, 257.

7. W. B. Quandt, *Decade of Decision* (Berkeley, 1977), 66–7. On the Israeli position and debate with the US, see Rabin, *Pinkas Sherut*, 236 ff.

8. Memo of Conversation, 17 May 1968, NSC Secret DD 1379 (1985), Johnson Library. See also Quandt, *Decade*, 63 ff. Cf. Schoenbaum, *The United States*, 162.

9. For a detailed analysis of these efforts, see Quandt, *Decade*, 81 ff. See also M. Gazit, *The Peace Process, 1969–73: Efforts and Contacts* (Jerusalem, 1983), 9 ff.; Rabin, *Pinkas Sherut*, 266 ff., 292 ff.; R. Nixon, *The Memoirs of Richard Nixon* (London, 1978), 477–80.

10. *U.S. Foreign Policy for the 1970's: A Report to the Congress by Richard Nixon, February 25, 1971* (US Embassy, Tel Aviv), 127.

11. Quandt, *Decade*, 114 ff.; Nixon, *Memoirs*, 483 ff.

12. Quandt, *Decade*, 122, 131; cf. Schoenbaum, *The United States*, 181–2. On Israel's role in the 1970 crisis in Jordan, see also *Divrey Haknesset*, 59. 146, 16 Nov. 1970 (Meir's statement); Rafael, *Destination*, 246–7; Dayan, *Avney Derekh*, 540; Allon, *Behatira*, 48; Rabin, *Pinkas Sherut*, 313 ff.

13. Quandt, *Decade*, 128 ff.; Gazit, *The Peace Process*, 57 ff. The Jarring mission had already started during the Johnson period. See also H. H. Saunders, *The Other Walls* (Princeton, 1991), 10–11; Smith, *Palestine*, 220 ff.

14. Meir's statements in the Knesset; *Divrey Haknesset*, 60. 1857, 16 Mar. 1971; 58. 2242, 29 June 1970. See also Allon, *Kelim*, 117; Bartov, *Dado*, 282 ff.; Smith, *Palestine*, 221, 229; *Arab Report and Record [ARR]*, (London, 1969), 132, 176.

15. *Divrey Haknesset*, 54. 1708, 20 Feb. 1969 (Eban's statement); 55. 2763 ff., 28 May 1969; 56. 379, 31 Dec. 1969; 57. 1859 ff., 26 May 1970 (Meir's statement); 58. 2498, 15 July 1970; 59. 1120, 26 Jan. 1971 (Dayan's statement).

16. *Divrey Haknesset*, 54. 1793.

17. See respectively, Dayan, *Mapa*, 47; *Divrey Haknesset*, 59. 147, 16 Nov. 1970.

18. See resolution of the 9th National Congress of the Baʿth Party, 17 Sept. 1967 in *MER 1967*, 491–2; *al-Baʿth*, 31 Aug. 1967; *al-Maʿrifa*, 66, (Aug. 1967), 4–18; 68, (Oct. 1967), 33–44; 71 (Jan. 1968), 79–81, 99–101, 140–5, 152, 162, 171–4. Cf. Petran, *Syria*, 201–2; Seale, *Asad*, 155; cf. *Divrey Haknesset*, 53. 1252, 22 Jan. 1969.

19. *Al-Anwar*, 31 Dec. 1968; *al-Hayat* 6 Oct. 1968; *al-Jarida*, 4 June 1969; Bartov, *Dado*, 160; *Skira Hodsheet* (Hebrew, IDF), Feb. 1969, 39; *ARR 1969*, 206, 214; *New York Times*, 3 Dec. 1968; 10 Aug. 1970; Dayan *Avney Derekh*, 549–50. For an examination of Syrian policy towards the various guerrilla organizations, see M. Shemesh, *The Palestinian Entity 1959–1974* (London, 1988), 113 ff.; W. B. Quandt, F. Jabber, and A. Mosely Lesch, *The Politics of Palestinian Nationalism* (Berkeley, 1973), 64 ff., 118 ff.

20. Details in Dayan, *Avney Derekh*, 549–50; *Skira Hodsheet*, Feb. 1969, 28–9, and Nov.–Dec. 1969, 49; Bartov, *Dado*, 160–1; Shemesh, *Entity*, 119; *New York Times*, 1 Mar. 1969.

21. Shemesh, *Entity*, 111, citing Syrian sources.

22. Ghalib Kayali, *Hafiz al-Asad—qa'id wa-risala* (Damascus, 1977), 31–3. For a detailed examination of Asad–Jadid rivalry during that period, see M. Ma'oz, *Asad, The Sphinx of Damascus: A Political Biography* (London and New York, 1988), 36 ff.; Seale, *Asad*, 144 ff.; Bar Siman-Tov, *Linkage*, 161 ff.; *Guardian* (London), 19 Oct. 1968.

23. *Al-Hayat*, 6 Oct. 1968; *al-Hurriyya*, 15 July and 16 Sept. 1968; *al-Jarida* (Beirut), 5 Oct. 1968; *Le Monde*, 23 Feb. 1968; cf. Shemesh, *Entity*, 118–21.

24. See e.g. Radio *Sawt al-'Asifa*, 8 June, 12 July, and 18 Aug. 1969; *Middle East News Agency*, 13 June and 17 July 1969; *al-Thawra*, 21 June 1969; *al-Jarida* 10 July 1969; Damascus Radio, 30 July 1969; *al-Difa'* 5 and 21 Aug. 1969; *Sawt Falastin* (Damascus), 8 and 27 Aug. 1969.

25. Shemesh, *Entity*, 120; Seale, *Asad*, 156.

26. Ma'oz, *Asad*, 36–8; Bar Siman-Tov, *Linkage*, 163. For a detailed description, see *New Middle East* [London], 28 (1971), 9 ff.

27. Damascus Radio, Apr. 1969; Ma'oz, *Asad*, 38, 84; Petran, *Syria*, 243; *New York Times*, 5 Mar. and 2 Apr. 1969; *Daily Telegraph*, 17 Mar. 1969; *New York Herald Tribune*, 24 Mar. 1969.

28. *New York Times*, 19 Oct. and 14 Nov. 1970. Ma'oz, *Asad*, 39, 116; cf. Quandt et al., *Palestinian Nationalism*, 126–7; Shemesh, *Entity*, 207–8; for a different interpretation, see Seale, *Asad*, 157 ff.

29. For details, see Ma'oz, *Asad*, 39–40; Seale, *Asad*, 162–5.

30. *Financial Times*, 17 Nov. 1970; Middle East News Agency (Cairo), 28 Dec. 1970; Asad speeches, Damascus Radio, 9 Dec. 1970. See also *Jaysh al-Sha'b*, 15 Dec. 1970; *New Middle East*, 28 (1971), 11; *Egyptian Gazette*, *The Times*, *Guardian*, 28 Nov. 1970.

31. Seale, *Asad*, 185; see also Ma'oz, *Asad*, 45 ff.

32. *Al-Nahar*, 17 Mar. 1971; Damascus Radio, 8 Mar. and 19 Dec. 1972; *Financial Times*, 10 Mar. 1973.

33. *Al-Nahar*, 17 Mar. 1971. See also Asad's interview with foreign journalists, Damascus Radio, 2 Apr. 1971, 17 Dec. 1972.

34. *Al-Nahar*, 17 Mar. 1971. Cf. Ma'oz, *Asad*, 86; Seale, Asad, 185.

35. Asad's speeches, Damasous Radio, 9 Dec. 1970, 17 Dec. 1971, 9 June 1973; *Jaysh al-Sha'b*, Dec. 1970; *Dirasat Ta'rikhiyya*, Apr. 1972, 109 ff., 120 ff.; *Flash of Damascus* (a monthly, Damascus), 24 (Sept. 1973), 1–2, 8–9, 21–3.

36. Asad's speeches, Damascus Radio, 9 Dec. 1970, 17 Dec. 1971. For anti-Jewish expressions during Jadid's period, see *al-Ma'rifa*, 49 (Mar. 1966), 353–63, 309–26; *The Fourth Conference of the Academy of Islamic Research* (Cairo, 1970), 527 ff.

37. See Seale, *Asad*, 148, citing Asad; also pp. 186–9; Karsh *The Soviet Union*, 4–5, 24 ff.; A. Levy and I. Rabinovich, *Soviet Policy, the Syrian Communists and Intra-Baʿthi Politics, 1963–1971* (Tel Aviv, 1979), 8 ff.

38. For quotations and details see Karsh, *The Soviet Union*, 8–9; cf. Seale, *Asad*, 187–9; Maʿoz, *Asad*, 86. For data on Soviet aid to Syria see 'Communist Foreign Aid to Arab Countries since 1955', NSC, 8 June 1967, DD 139E (1980).

39. Maʿoz, *Asad*, 58–9, 86, citing various sources; Karsh, *The Soviet Union*, 8–9; Dayan, *Avney Derekh*, 569; Bartov, *Dado*, 282.

40. Seale, *Asad*, 190–1. But cf. a different version in D. Kimche, *The Last Option* (Hebrew; Tel Aviv, 1992), 25 ff.

41. *Divrey Haknesset*, 61. 3532, 27 July 1971 (Dayan's statement); 62. 12, 26 Oct. 1971 (Meir's statement).

42. Shemesh, *Entity*, 201–3; but see also ibid. 213; Maʿoz, *Asad*, 121.

43. Details in Shemesh, *Entity*, 214–15; see also *Egyptian Gazette*, 16 Jan. 1972; *New York Herald Tribune*, 25 Jan. and 19 Sept. 1972; *Guardian*, 2 Mar. 1972; *Financial Times*, 16 Oct. and 22 Nov. 1972.

44. Details in Shemesh, *Entity*, 214–15; *Financial Times*, 16 Oct. and 22 Nov. 1972; Guardian, 31 Oct. 1972; *New York Times*, 10 Nov., 23 Nov. and 28 Dec. 1972; *Daily Telegraph*, 13 Jan. 1973; *Middle East Journal*, 26 (1972), 291; (autumn 1972), 430; (winter 1973), 56–68, 191–3.

45. *Middle East Journal*, 27 (1973), 192–3; Shemesh, *Entity*, 215–16.

46. Cf. Meir's warning, *New York Times*, 8 Dec. 1972; see also *New York Times*, 23 Nov. 1972.

47. *Guardian*, 4 Mar. 1972, citing Dayan; Eban, *Pirkey Haim*, 481–2, 489; Bartov, *Dado*, 282; Smith, *Palestine*, 229. Cf. D. Horowitz, *Israel's Concept of Defensible Borders* (Hebrew; Jerusalem, 1975), 25.

48. Karsh, *The Soviet Union*, 10; *Middle East Journal*, 26 (1972), 292; (autumn 1972), 431. Cf. *Skira Hodsheet*, Aug. 1973, 9–15.

49. *Middle East Journal*, 26 (1972), 431. Cf. ibid. 429.

50. Seale, *Asad*, 192–3; Maʿoz, *Asad*, 86–7; Bartov, *Dado*, 282; Dayan, *Avney Derekh*, 569–70.

51. *Middle East Journal*, 27 (1973), 192–3; *Guardian*, 16 Feb. 1973.

52. See respectively Radio Damascus, 19 Dec. 1972; *al-Sayyad* report cited in *Maʾariv*, 17 Mar. 1972; see also *Haʾaretz*, 9 Mar. 1973.

53. Bartov, *Dado*, 240; Dayan, *Avney Derekh*, 570; Z. Schiff, *October Earthquake* (Tel Aviv, 1974), 8; cf. Seale, *Asad*, 196.

54. Bartov, *Dado*, 240, 246, 259. *Daily Express* (London), 5 May 1973; cf. Eban, *Pirkey Haim*, 481–2.

55. Dayan, *Avney Derekh*, 569; Schoenbaum, *The United States*, 188–90.

56. *Middle East Journal*, 27 (1973), 55, 58. Cf. A. Barʾon, *Moshe Dayan and the Yom Kippur War* (Hebrew; Tel Aviv, 1992), 15.

57. Bartov, *Dado*, 235–7, 239; Eban, *Pirkey Haim*, 481–2, 489. Cf. *Middle East Journal*, 26 (1972), 429, quoting Dayan on 24 May 1972; Barʾon, *Dayan*, 20 ff.

58. See respectively *Ha'aretz*, 10 Aug. 1973; Bartov, *Dado*, 282. Cf. *Skira Hodsheet*, June 1973, 6, 22; Oct.–Dec. 1973, 5 ff. But cf. Bar'on, *Dayan*, 34–5.
59. See respectively Damascus Radio, 2 Aug. and 6 Sept. 1973; also, 4, 5 Aug. and 16, 25 Sept. 1973 regarding the *jihad*; on Hussein's warning see General (ret.) Zeira in *Yediot Ahronot*, 15 Sept. 1993; Z. Schiff, *Ha'aretz*, 15 Sept. 1993; Sh. Naqdimon, *Yediot Ahronot*, 29 Sept. 1993.
60. Dayan, *Avney Derekh*, 570–1; Bar'on, *Dayan*, 35 ff.; Bartov, *Dado*, 282–3; Ma'oz, *Asad*, 89. See also Eban, *Pirkey Haim*, 490–3; Meir, *My Life*, 305–6.
61. On the air battle and Israeli thinking see Bartov, *Dado*, 282–5; Dayan, *Avney Derekh*, 570–1; *New York Times*, 14 Sept. 1973; Bar'on, *Dayan*, 39–40.
62. Schiff, *October*, 2–4, 14–15; Bartov, *Dado*, 289; *Financial Times*, 4 and 5 Oct. 1973; Bar'on, *Dayan*, 42–3.
63. Quoted in Ma'oz, *Asad*, 89–90; cf. Bartov, *Dado*, 286 ff., 300; Bar'on, *Dayan*, 46 ff.
64. Meir, *My Life*, 306–7; Dayan, *Avney Derekh*, 571 ff.; Bar'on, *Dayan*, 54 ff., 75; Bartov, *Dado*, 289 ff., 320 ff. Sh. Gazit, former Chief of Military Intelligence, in *Yediot Ahronot*, 23 Sept. 1993.
65. Quoted in Ma'oz, *Asad*, 90. Cf. Bartov, *Dado*, 319; Dayan, *Avney Derekh*, 574; Bar'on, *Dayan*, 57 ff.
66. Bartov, *Dado*, 282, 300, 303, 312, 324; Eban, *Pirkey Haim*, 491–3.
67. Cf. Bartov, *Dado*, 286, 304, 310, 324; *Near East Report*, 30/9 (3 Mar. 1986), 36; *Daily Telegraph*, 15 Sept. 1973; *New York Times*, 15 Sept. 1973; *Egyptian Gazette*, 5 Oct. 1973.
68. Seale, *Asad*, 197–9; Ma'oz, *Asad*, 90. Cf. Kimche, *Option*, 30 ff.
69. See respectively Asad's interviews with *al-Sayyad*, 7 Mar. 1974 and with *al-Ray al-'am*, 18 Oct. 1975; Seale, *Asad*, 201; Ma'oz, *Asad*, 116.
70. Cf. *Jaysh al-Sh'ab*, 28 Aug. 1973.
71. On the Soviet attitude towards the Syrian–Israeli conflict before and during the 1973 war, see G. Golan, *Yom Kippur and After* (Cambridge, 1977), 56 ff.; Karsh, *The Soviet Union*, 10–12; Seale, *Asad*, 193. Ma'oz, *Asad*, 86–7.
72. Schiff, *October*, 1, 66; M. Heikal, *The Road to Ramadan* (New York, 1975), 213.
73. For detailed accounts see e.g., Schiff, *October*; Ch. Herzog, *War of Atonement* (Boston, 1975); Golan, *Yom Kippur*; Heikal, *The Road to Ramadan*; Seale, *Asad*, 202 ff.; Saad al-Shazly, *The Crossing of the Suez* (San Francisco, 1980); Dayan, *Avney Derekh*, 579 ff.; Bartov, *Dado*, 12 ff.; R. Eytan, *The Story of a Soldier* (Hebrew; Tel Aviv, 1985), 127–45. For the official Syrian account see *The political account submitted to the 12th National Congress of the Ba'th Party*, National Command, Damascus, 1975. (This document is in the author's possession.)
74. S. Aronson, *The Politics and Strategy of Nuclear Weapons in the Middle East* (Albany, NY, 1992), 143–6. Cf. Z. Schiff, *Peace with Security: Israel's Minimal Requirements in Negotiations with Syria* (Washington, 1993), 19.

75. Bar'on, *Dayan*, 130–2, 158; cf. Bartov, *Dado*, 120–1.

76. Cf. Seale, *Asad*, 207 ff.; Dayan, *Avney Derekh*, 608 ff.

77. Bar'on, *Dayan*, 163–4.

78. Cited in Saunders, *The Other Walls*, 170.

79. Cf. Seale, *Asad*, 222–3; Dayan, *Avney Derekh*, 661–2; Bar'on, *Dayan*, 229 ff. Cf. Ba'th 12th National Congress, 1975.

80. H. Kissinger, *Years of Upheaval* (Boston, 1982), 493 ff.; Quandt, *Decade*, 183–6, 190–1; Eban, *Pirkey Haim*, 506 ff.; Bartov, *Dado*, 160 ff., 208, 227, 280; Meir, *My Life*, 315; Bar'on, *Dayan*, 278; cf. Nixon, *Memoirs*, 920, 941, 1013; Karsh, *The Soviet Union*, 13–14.

81. On the American strategy see Quandt, *Decade*, 207 ff. For a different interpretation see Seale, *Asad*, 226 ff.

82. Kissinger, *Years*, 782–4; Quandt, *Decade*, 230.

83. Bar'on, *Dayan*, 156, 171; also 133, 155–6, 251, 340. See also Meir, *My Life*, 317; Eban, *Pirkey Haim* 533; also 563, 577. Cf. *al-Ard* (Damascus), 1/3 (21 Oct. 1973), 8–15; 1/4 (7 Nov. 1973), 35–6.

84. Cf. Ma'oz, *Asad*, 94–5; Seale, *Asad*, 240; Ba'th 12th National Congress, 1975.

85. Kissinger, *Years*, 781; also 1088–9, 1097–8. For more details, see Quandt, *Decade*, 235 ff. For the text of the agreement, see Dayan, *Avney Derekh*, 715–16; *ARR*, May 1974, 214.

86. Cf. Ma'oz, *Asad*, 96–7; Ba'th 12th National Congress, 1975.

87. Schiff, *Peace with Security*, 17–18.

88. H. M. Sachar, *A History of Israel*, ii (New York, 1987), 3–5. See also Eban, *Pirkey Haim*, 561–3, 567; Rabin, *Pinkas Sherut*, 410 ff.

7

Asad vs. Rabin

As might be expected, both Rabin and Asad lost no time in compensating for the heavy losses incurred by their armies in weapons and other equipment in the devastating October war. Thus, in addition to receiving massive arms airlifts during the war, Syria and Israel continued their efforts to obtain more weapons from the USSR and the United States, respectively.[1]

To be sure, both leaders deeply suspected each other's alleged aggressive intentions and gave high priority to rebuilding their armed forces in order to be prepared for another round of war. Simultaneously, however, both Rabin and Asad sought a political solution to their countries' conflict; and both—Asad, indeed, for the first time—endeavoured to gain the support of the Americans for their respective new strategic designs, which were obviously incompatible.

RABIN'S STRATEGY AND ISRAELI PERCEPTIONS

As for Rabin, in his first speech as prime minister, he envisaged

a full and comprehensive peace between Egypt and Israel, or another phase of partial settlement, under which Egypt would renounce the existence of the state of war with Israel. In contrast, there is no room for another interim settlement with Syria. If we are to achieve further progress with Egypt, it will be necessary to examine whether Syria is ready to sign a peace treaty with Israel. [But] . . . even with peace treaties, we would not withdraw to the lines of 4 June 1967, which are not defensible and encourage aggression against us, as has been proven in the past. We shall endeavour to achieve peace with Jordan based on the existence of two independent states: Israel with its capital, unified Jerusalem, and an Arab state east of Israel . . . a Jordanian–Palestinian state.[2]

In other words, Rabin sought further separate agreement, or agreements, with Egypt and Jordan, while delaying negotiations with 'extremist' Syria until after the 1976 American elections. During that year, in Rabin's evaluation, Israel would not be pressured into making territorial and political concessions, Egypt would remain weak and in conflict with Syria, and if Israel became stronger, its political position would improve. Israel should not 'descend' from the Golan Heights, not even within a state of full peace, but would be prepared to make 'only cosmetic and definitely insignificant adjustments' in the Golan line.[3]

In sum, Rabin, like his predecessor, Golda Meir, and like most Israelis, continued to consider Syria as Israel's most implacable and dangerous foe, and the Golan Heights as a vital area for defending Galilee and Israel's main water resources. Nearly all Israeli Jews, including political and military analysts, did not perceive the Syrian 1973 offensive as being motivated by Syria's ambition to recover merely the Golan Heights, but rather as a war aimed at capturing parts of northern Israel and, given the opportunity, eliminating Israel altogether. These perceptions derived not only from the collective memory of Syrian active belligerency prior to the 1967 war,[4] but also from the 'barbaric and inhuman crimes . . . of murder and mutilation committed on the persons of Israeli prisoners of war . . . during the October war'. Among the pieces of evidence for such crimes, Israel published an excerpt from the Syrian official *Gazette (al-Jarida al-Rasmiyya)*, no. 27, of 11 July 1974, which says:

In the course of a debate in the Syrian National Assembly [parliament] in December 1973, the minister of defence Mustafa Tlas cited the following incident as an example of 'supreme valour'. 'There is the outstanding case of a recruit from Aleppo who killed twenty-eight Jewish soldiers by himself, slaughtering them like sheep. All of his comrades in arms witnessed this. He killed three of them with an axe and decapitated them. . . . Need I single it out to award him the Medal of the Republic! I will grant this medal to any soldier who succeeds in killing twenty-eight Jews.'[5]

This image of a brutal anti-Jewish and anti-Israeli regime likewise emerged from the alleged harsh treatment of Syrian Jews by the Syrian secret services (*Mukhabarat*), as well as from Asad's refusal, during his negotiations with Kissinger for the disengagement agreement, to prevent Palestinian raids against Israel from the Golan.[6] And, although in practice Asad did not permit such raids from the Golan following the agreement, his continuous stringent anti-Israeli expressions were considered by most Israeli Jews as proof of his deep hatred and aggressive intentions towards the Jewish state.

Most Israelis did not change their attitude towards Syria (and other Arab nations) in subsequent years, even though Damascus publicly offered to sign a non-belligerency/peace agreement with Israel in return for total Israeli withdrawal from the Golan and the establishment of a

Palestinian entity/state in the West Bank and Gaza. Thus, for example, a CIA report of December 1976 indicated *inter alia*:

There is virtually no willingness anywhere [in Israel] to go along with a formal Arab–Israeli peace entailing the return of most or all the territories taken in 1967. The overwhelming bulk of Israelis insist on retaining East Jerusalem, some of the West Bank, the Golan Heights and Sharm el-Sheikh. . . . The Israeli public backs the military and civilian leaders' insistence on holding positions which would discourage or impede any conventional or guerrilla Arab attack. . . . There are deep-seated fears, suspicions and convictions in Israel that all Arabs are essentially hostile. Arab moderates, according to this point of view, differ from extremists only in which tactics to use to bring about Israel's destruction . . . while publicly proclaiming adherence to the aim of achieving a peaceful settlement through negotiations, the Rabin regime has in fact permitted Israelis in and out of the government to 'create facts'—such as settlements in the occupied territories [including the Golan]—which contradict that aim. . . . Rabin's privately expressed views can be hardline indeed . . . as he said to US officials . . . : 'An overall settlement is not attainable in the near future . . . Arab instability plus the deep emotions on the Arab–Israeli issues make full peace just a dream.'[7]

ASAD'S IDEOLOGY AND STRATEGY

Indeed, the ideological notions voiced by Asad and other Syrian leaders and Ba'thist organs, both before and after the May 1974 disengagement agreement, continued to be extremely hostile and militant towards Israel and Zionism. Thus, regarding Zionism, Judaism, and Israel, Asad, for example, stated on various occasions that:

(1) Zionism distorts the heavenly principles and misuses Judaism . . . it is an instrument to destroy existing societies in many countries of the world. . . . It is an ally of Nazism . . . it is an artificial, chauvinist phenomenon which manifests itself in the colonialist ideology, based on usurpation and expansionism in the region. . . . Israel has been seen by the world as a racist fascist state.

(2) I do not have any personal animosity against the Jewish religion or the Jew as a religious person. But the Jews in Israel, this is different. The Jews are our enemy . . . I feel about the Jews, the Israeli Jew . . . in the same way I feel about any people which comes and takes my land.

Again and again equating Israel with the Crusaders' state, Asad pointed out that

(3) Israel's age . . . is only one-sixth of the period of the Crusaders' dominion in our country. [He concluded that if Israel continued to occupy the Arab lands,

there would be a] fifth war against Israel . . . another October war [wherein] Syria would be the spearhead.

However, he qualified his statement regarding war against Israel by saying that

(4) if Israel withdraws to the original borders, we will not wage a war against it. We will accept the United Nations resolution of 1947 [for the partition of Palestine] in the interest of getting on with other important business and simply let nature take its course . . . [and then] we will work behind the scenes to overthrow the Zionist system in Israel and bring about a just return of Arab presence there, so as to make this land an integral part of the Arab world . . . once this problem is solved then I can say that the Jews will be able to live here [in Palestine] as Jews but not as Israelis.[8]

A long and full account of those ideological concepts, strategic goals, and tactical aims regarding Israel were presented to and endorsed by the 12th National Congress of the Ba'th Party in November 1975. The main points of this document were:

1. The Zionist entity in Palestine is artificial, racist, and expansionist. It constitutes the main attacking base of Imperialism and Zionism against the Arab Homeland, aiming at expanding from the Nile to the Euphrates.

2. The whole Arab national potential should be concentrated against the imperialistic, colonialistic, Zionist presence. The struggle against it is the major issue of the national liberation struggle.

3. The Arab–Zionist conflict is a fatal historical struggle, a struggle for life or death, to be or not to be. It is a long struggle and although there are periods of relative tranquillity and armistice, this struggle must end with the eternal elimination of Zionism and with the liberation of all occupied Arab territories, including the entire Arab Palestinian land.

4. In order to implement this strategy we have to formulate our interim tactical positions in the light of realistic considerations and in view of the Arab and international circumstances. The October war enabled the Arab nation, for the first time, to design interim goals without giving up the strategic aim of the full liberation of the Arab Palestinian land.

5. The first interim goal is to obtain the full withdrawal of Israel from the territories occupied in 1967, including the West Bank, Gaza, and Jerusalem. Then to assist the struggle of the Palestinian people and support its legitimate right to establish a national rule in the liberated territories. This as a step towards gradually uprooting the Zionist enemy from

the land through an armed struggle, and returning Arab sovereignty to the full Palestinian land, on the ruins of the Zionist entity.

Regarding the way to achieve the first interim goal, Asad (also Secretary-General of the Ba'th Party) made his concluding remarks to the 12th Congress in the rather sober words:

We are in the midst of the battle and the road is long, and we have to prepare ourselves militarily and act politically and economically to strengthen the military action . . . among our important and main weapons are . . . Arab solidarity, Arab unity . . . we have made efforts to establish positive relations . . . with the US . . . to gain its friendship in order to turn this power into a neutral one and to weaken this power's support to our direct enemy . . . to prevent creating new splits [among the Arabs] . . . I told Kissinger that we, the Arabs, are a nation that, more than any nation in the world, wants peace . . . but between us and peace there is apparently a very long way.[9]

ASAD'S PEACE OFFERS AND US INVOLVEMENT

Asad's post-1973 attitudes towards Israel may thus be summed up in Kissinger's words:

Asad would have liked to destroy the Jewish state but he recognized that . . . the cost of attempting it would hazard Syria's domestic structure, perhaps even its existence . . . He was as prudent as he was passionate, as realistic as he was ideological . . . he concluded that Syria was not sufficiently strong to unite the Arab nation, and needed to regain its own territory before it could pursue larger ambitions.

It would appear then that Asad saw two dimensions or stages in the conflict with Israel: the political one—to which he gave priority—aimed at liberating the Syrian (and Palestinian) territories occupied by Israel in 1967; and the ideological dimension—the continued struggle against Zionist Israel, to be carried out at the second stage, towards the total liberation of Palestine. And whereas the means of implementing the second-stage struggle were not clearly defined by Asad, those regarding the first stage were not only military but also political-diplomatic.

Asad was indeed inclined to try and employ diplomatic means to achieve his first goal, as he himself pointed out: 'If political action will give us back our lands, we would welcome it.'[10] This political action was directed mainly towards the United States and was first manifested by a bold and shrewd offer to make peace with Israel, as it were, in return for all Arab territories occupied in the 1967 war, and safeguarding the rights of the Palestinian people. Asad, indeed, made such offers during several talks and interviews given to American leaders and magazines in 1974, 1975, 1976, and 1977, while attempting to obtain goodwill (see also below). In early March 1974, before the disengagement agreement with Israel, he told *Time* magazine that he was not 'pessimistic' regarding peace prospects in the Middle East. Then on 1 June 1974, one day after the signing of the disengagement agreement, Asad said to *Newsweek* that that agreement was an integral part of a 'comprehensive and just settlement' and a step towards a 'just and durable peace' based on UN Resolution 338. Subsequently, on 25 February 1975, while Kissinger was working towards a second-stage agreement between Israel and Egypt, Asad gave a long interview to *Newsweek*'s Arnaud de Borchgrave, in which, for the first time, he indicated the option of signing a formal peace treaty with Israel ('This is not propaganda. We mean it seriously and explicitly'). According to Asad, such a peace treaty should be implemented in stages:

First we must end the state of belligerency. That means the implementation of United Nations Resolution 242. And the end of belligerency will mean the beginning of a stage of real peace. . . . If the Israelis return to the 1967 frontier and the West Bank and Gaza become a Palestinian state, the last obstacle to final settlement will have been removed . . . the actual duration of a [peace] treaty [with Israel] is a matter of procedure and it would be premature to discuss it at this stage.

Asad's words can be interpreted as an offer to sign merely a non-belligerency agreement with Israel in return for its withdrawal from all occupied territories and the recognition of Palestinian rights. Only subsequently, but not soon, would Syria consider signing a full peace treaty.[11] It can indeed be assumed that Asad, and most Syrians, were not psychologically and ideologically prepared to establish normal relations with Israel within a short time. As Asad himself indicated in conversations with Kissinger and with an American writer in 1974:

The Syrian difficulty is that people who have been nurtured over twenty-six years on hatred [towards Israel] can't be swayed overnight by our changing our course . . . There is a great struggle taking place between the heart and the mind. In our hearts we say 'No Israel—not on any terms'. In our minds we say 'we must turn to other things so let us give Israel a chance to withdraw to its original frontiers [of 1947], let us give it a chance to prove that it will no longer try to expand.[12]

As we know, and as Asad knew well, Israel was by no means willing to withdraw to the pre-1967 lines, let alone the 1947 partition lines, even in return for full peace with Syria, and certainly not for a non-belligerency agreement. Asad's peace offers were thus directed not towards Israel, but towards Egypt and the United States in an attempt both to prevent a further separate Egyptian–Israeli agreement and to formulate a joint Egyptian–Syrian post-war diplomacy towards Israel with American backing. He, indeed, made tireless efforts before the Sinai 2 agreement to bring Sadat back to the 'Arab fold' and reshape together a new Arab strategy towards Israel to be based on the Cairo–Damascus political–military axis, backed by Saudi financial power.[13] At the 1974 Arab summit in Rabat, Asad succeeded in mustering, for example, the support of the Arab states in rejecting partial solutions or separate steps (of Egypt towards Israel). And in April 1975, during another smaller summit meeting between King Khalid of Saudi Arabia, Sadat, and Asad, a decision was adopted that 'The political action during the next stage requires close co-operation between Syria and Egypt . . . as a basis for the common Arab action against the common enemy.'[14]

But despite these decisions, in September 1975, Sadat signed another separate disengagement agreement with Israel (Sinai 2). Consequently, Asad bitterly criticized Sadat's action as 'a breach in Arab solidarity . . . and a serious and dangerous attempt at foiling Arab struggles since 1948'.[15] Yet, although at public demonstrations in Syria Sadat was denounced as 'a traitor to the Arab cause', Asad was careful not to burn the bridges totally with Sadat, the leader of the strongest Arab country. In October 1976 Asad made a rapprochement with Sadat (with Saudi mediation) not only in order to secure Egypt's backing for Syrian intervention in Lebanon but also to design a new common Syrian–Egyptian strategy towards Israel, in anticipation of a fresh American administration in Washington. But, having reportedly 'much contempt for President Hafiz al-Asad', Sadat would not let the Syrian leader 'gain a veto power over his moves'.[16] He would rather have Asad adopt his own peace strategy towards Israel; and indeed on the very evening before his November 1977 journey to Jerusalem, Sadat went to see Asad in Damascus and reportedly said to him: 'Let us go together to Jerusalem! Or if you cannot come, then please keep silent.'[17] Of course, Asad neither went to Jerusalem nor remained silent. He declared 19 November an official day of mourning in Syria, while his state-controlled media attacked Sadat as a 'traitor' and 'trader in blood', and compared him with notorious collaborators such as Pétain, Quisling, Neville Chamberlain, and Rudolf Hess.[18]

But all in vain. Sadat chose to carry on his separate peace with Israel because he felt that by adopting a joint pan-Arab strategy with Asad, Egypt was likely to undermine its chances of getting back Sinai. Distrustful of the USSR, he was also influenced by Kissinger's step-by-step strategy which gave priority to an Egyptian–Israeli settlement.

The American Role

Alongside his endeavours to woo Sadat into a common strategy towards Israel, Asad tried very hard to gain American backing for his policy of comprehensive settlement, which would entail Israeli withdrawal from all Arab territories occupied in 1967. Asad was well aware that only Washington, with its effective leverage over Israel, was capable of helping him to regain the Golan (and the Palestinians to regain the West Bank and Gaza).

Already during his indirect negotiations for the disengagement settlement with Israel, Asad said to Kissinger that he wanted him to conduct the Syrian–Israeli settlement and told *Time* magazine that the United States was fulfilling an important function in the region. He also pointed out that he, Asad, 'was not a Soviet puppet'.[19] Following the signing of this agreement, in mid-June 1974, Asad welcomed President Nixon, on the first visit of an American president to Damascus; the two countries then resumed diplomatic relations. On the eve of this state visit, Asad gave his famous interview to *Newsweek*, where he called for a 'comprehensive and just settlement' based on UN Resolution 338, and requiring full Israeli withdrawal from the occupied territories and the safeguarding of Palestinian rights. Asad repeated this statement to Nixon while pointing out Syria's efforts both to achieve peace and to improve its relations with the United States.[20]

Nixon, highly impressed with Asad's personality, found him 'quite reasonable with regard to the various regional approaches we are making'. To encourage these approaches, Nixon promised financial aid to Syria. Moreover, in a private conversation between the two leaders, 'Nixon informed Asad that the United States favored the substantial restitution of the 1967 frontiers on the Golan Heights . . . within the framework of a general peace.' And when Asad said that Syria would never relinquish the Golan Heights, Nixon replied that 'the purpose of interim diplomacy . . . was to nudge the Israelis backwards upon the Heights, step by step until they reach the edge, then tumble over.'[21] Apparently Asad interpreted Nixon's words as a commitment to the search for a comprehensive settlement which would be linked to a total Israeli withdrawal from the occupied territories. Encouraged by this American position, Asad sought to 'open a page and begin a new phase . . . improve relations with the US' and deepen 'this American commitment' in an attempt to push a wedge between the United States and Israel and bring about American pressure on Israel. As Asad told the Egyptian *al-Ahram* newspaper, early in July 1974: 'This development [in the American position] is compatible with the interests of the American people and contradicts the interests of world Zionism.'[22] Later on, Asad stated in an interview with Geyelin of the *Washington Post*: 'None of the Arabs is talking now with Israel. We are talking with the US.'[23]

Unfortunately for Asad, American strategy in the Middle East was designed and carried out by Henry Kissinger, and was aimed at first securing an Israeli–Egyptian settlement (and subsequently an Israeli–Jordanian agreement), while deferring the Israeli–Syrian issue (and the Palestinian problem) to a later period, if not indefinitely. Kissinger himself admitted that 'during the May [1974] shuttle Asad had repeatedly asked me for a written assurance that we would support Syrian demands to regain all the Golan Heights. I had evaded it.' According to Seale, Kissinger also 'torpedoed' Nixon's intentions to bring about a comprehensive settlement.

The Israeli–Syrian disengagement agreement (of late May 1974) was reportedly accompanied by a secret American commitment to co-ordinate with Israel any future peace initiatives with Syria.[24] Earlier Kissinger persuaded Nixon to waive repayment of $1 billion of the $2.2 billion credit granted to Israel for arms purchases in the October war. Later on, a further $500 million was waived, and for the United States fiscal year 1976 Israel was allocated $2.25 billion by the Ford administration, which also promised to supply Israel with highly sophisticated combat planes.[25] Indeed, unlike Nixon, President Ford adopted a pro-Israeli line on the Golan issue as well and, while backing Kissinger's step-by-step strategy, he accepted Rabin's request that only 'cosmetic' changes should be made in the Golan line, within another interim agreement with Syria.[26]

On 1 September 1975, in a secret letter to Rabin, President Ford made the following undertaking: 'The US has not developed a final position on the borders. Should it do so, it will give great weight to Israel's position that any peace agreement with Syria must be predicated on Israeli remaining on the Golan Heights.' Ten months later, in July 1976, during the American election campaign, Ford told the *Boston Herald*: 'I don't think that Israel is going to relinquish to the Syrians direct control of the Golan Heights. I would not.'[27]

To be sure, while flirting with the Americans, Asad continued to maintain his strategic alliance and 'permanent friendship' with the USSR, and to seek further military and economic aid from Moscow. Soviet diplomatic backing was also sought by Syria, particularly in view of American support for the Egyptian–Israeli Sinai 2 agreement and its step-by-step strategy regarding the Arab–Israeli settlement. Vis-à-vis this strategy, Moscow and Damascus (only since May 1974) called for a comprehensive settlement to be achieved within the Geneva peace conference.[28] Yet, despite his deep disappointment with American policy, followed by the recovery in Syrian–Soviet relations, Asad could not afford to jeopardize his new rapprochement with the United States, which was rendering some economic aid to Syria and, more crucially, possessed a growing leverage on Israel. Syria indeed badly needed this American leverage in order to dissuade Israel, in spring 1976, from military intervention in Lebanon in reaction to armed Syrian involvement in the Lebanese civil war, which had broken out in 1975 (see below). In the event, Syria succeeded in obtaining American approval for its intervention in Lebanon, since this also served United States interests. Washington also persuaded Israel to agree tacitly to the Syrian military presence in Lebanon north of the Sidon–Jezzin line (the 'Red Line') in return for Syrian recognition of Israeli security interests in southern Lebanon. Significantly, this last understanding with Rabin was seen as so trustworthy that Asad felt able to withdraw most of his combat units from the Golan ceasefire line and dispatch them to Lebanon and to his troubled border with Iraq.[29]

Following the 'Red Line' agreement, Asad declared, during interviews with American journalists in late 1976 and early 1977, that Syria was willing to resume negotiations in Geneva and sign a peace treaty with Israel, but without exchange of people and goods with the Jewish state; this, provided Israel would withdraw from all territories occupied in 1967 and accept the creation of a Palestinian state in the West Bank and Gaza. Asad also implied that the United States should have a major role in mediating a political settlement in the Middle East.[30]

It would appear that Asad's statements regarding peace with Israel were again directed towards the newly elected president, Jimmy Carter, who initially believed that 'real peace between Arabs and Israelis could be achieved, and he [Carter] clearly wanted to play a role in bringing that about if possible.'[31] Asad was encouraged by the fresh positions of Carter's administration during the early months of 1977. In February, for example, the new American Secretary of State Cyrus Vance made his first trip to the Middle East to explore the possibilities for reconvening the Geneva Conference, which Carter now favoured. In March President Carter advocated in his famous Clinton speech the creation of a homeland for the Palestinians, rejecting around the same time Israel's request to purchase a certain kind of American cluster bomb. The state-controlled Syrian press was so elated by this new approach (Carter also regarded Asad as an important actor in Middle East politics) that *Tishrin* wrote, on 4 May 1977, that Carter 'tries to liberate American foreign policy from the Zionist dependency'. And during his meeting with Carter in Geneva, on 9 May 1977, Asad was pleased by Carter's repeated support for a Palestinian homeland as well as by his hint that the United States would endeavour to persuade Israel to withdraw to the pre-1967 borders.[32] Asad told Carter that in return for an Israeli withdrawal to the pre-1967 borders (including East Jerusalem) and the creation of a Palestinian entity (possibly also in confederation with Jordan), 'he would agree to an end of the state of belligerency [with Israel] as well as to certain security measures . . . Ending the state of belligerency would lead automatically to peace . . . [it] would solve many psychological problems.'[33]

If we attempt to examine Asad's proposal to Carter regarding a political settlement with Israel, it would seem that he continued to adhere to his post-1974 two-stage strategy: at the first stage he was ready to sign only a non-belligerency agreement (which he called a 'peace treaty') in return for all Arab territories occupied in 1967, including East Jerusalem, and the creation of a Palestinian state or entity. Regarding the second stage, which should be open-ended, Asad was much more ambiguous: on the one hand he reportedly indicated that it might lead to diplomatic and economic relations with Israel,[34] namely full peace. But on the other hand, Asad told Joseph Kraft of the *Washington Post* in November 1976:

It is my view that the UN resolutions should be implemented as they are. These resolutions stipulate among other things the withdrawal [of Israel] from the territories occupied since 1967, the [implementation of] the rights of the Arab people of Palestine and the end of the state of war [with Israel]. Ending the state of war means creation of a state of peace. The other issues raised by Israel . . . have no connection with the requirements of peace. . . . They [the Israelis] talk about diplomatic relations, economic, commercial and cultural exchanges etc. Such things may not exist between two countries which are not in a state of war.[35]

In the same vein, in a letter sent to Carter in August 1977 Asad stated his position regarding the settlement, indicating *inter alia* ' "ending the state of war" which would mean peace.' Dr Quandt, citing Asad's letter, remarks: 'The letter was not encouraging nor did Asad depart from his well known views.' Moreover, during his meeting with Carter, Asad expressed his deep hostility to Israel, which Carter recorded in his memoirs: 'I was troubled by his extremely antagonistic attitude toward Israel.'[36]

Yet, even assuming that Asad's hostile attitude towards Israel reflected his 'ideological' rather than his 'political' position, Israeli leaders as well as most Israeli Jews were reluctant to give up the Golan Heights and East Jerusalem and to accept a Palestinian entity in the West Bank and Gaza, in return for a peace treaty, let alone a non-belligerency agreement with Syria. Indeed, during his first meeting with Carter on 7 March 1977, Rabin expressed his desire for an Arab–Israeli peace, but said that Israel did not want to leave the Golan Heights, that it objected to dealing with the PLO and to a Palestinian state in the West Bank, as well as to a unified Arab delegation at Geneva (as Syria had requested).[37]

It is true that President Carter fully shared Israel's view regarding the definition of peace, namely that it would entail normal relations such as exchange of ambassadors, trade, open borders, tourism, and regional economic co-operation. But he equally insisted that Israel should eventually return to the 1967 lines, with only minor modifications, and that a Palestinian 'homeland' be created on the West Bank and Gaza. Consequently, the fact that Carter publicly voiced his views and openly spoke out against Israel on some points just before the Israeli elections of May 1977 not only antagonized the American Jewish community; it possibly also contributed to undermining the Israeli Labour Party in the May elections, which brought the hardline Likud bloc to power.[38]

The new Israeli prime minister, Menachem Begin, initially appeared to be somewhat flexible on the Golan issue, and the guidelines of the new Likud government pointed in that direction also with regard to other occupied Arab territories: they stated that Israel would be ready to participate, without preconditions, in the Geneva Peace Conference on the basis of UN Resolutions 242 and 338 (whose formula had been 'territories for peace').[39]

But as a matter of fact Begin strongly rejected the Syrian (and American) notions of a united Arab delegation in Geneva, of a Palestinian entity/homeland in the West Bank and Gaza, as well as of a total withdrawal from the Golan Heights. Significantly, Egypt's President Sadat, although again calling for total Israeli withdrawal from the occupied territories, continued his rivalry with Asad, objected to a united Arab delegation in Geneva, and still preferred to sign a separate agreement with Israel, without any linkage to Syria.[40] Indeed, the Egyptian and Israeli leaders Dayan and Tuhamy started to hold secret talks in Morocco, in September 1977, to discuss a bilateral agreement without American and Syrian involvement and outside the Geneva conference.[41]

The United States–Soviet joint communiqué of 1 October 1977—which called for a comprehensive settlement of the Middle East problem in the framework of the Geneva conference—obviously threatened these Israeli–Egyptian talks, particularly by giving Syria (and the USSR) a certain veto power over a separate agreement between Cairo and Jerusalem. Israel, with the help of friends in Washington, exercised strong pressure on the Carter administration; this, together with Dayan's diplomatic skills, produced an American–Israeli working paper, dated 5 October 1977. This paper was more in line with Israel's (and Egypt's) desire to conduct bilateral negotiations with the Arab parties (after an opening plenary session in Geneva) rather than that of Syria (and the USSR), which in fact insisted on controlling all other Arab parties, notably Egypt. Consequently, Asad found himself let down (if not betrayed) by Carter, while Sadat was more encouraged to make a separate deal with Begin.[42] Following his historic journey to Jerusalem in November 1977, Sadat signed the Camp David accords with Begin and Carter in September 1978, which led to the Egyptian–Israeli peace treaty of March 1979, and indeed to the collapse of Asad's diplomatic-political strategy towards Israel.

IRAQ, JORDAN, AND THE GREATER SYRIAN DESIGN

The Iraqi Alternative

Yet from 1974, even before the culmination of Sadat's peace strategy towards Israel, but following Sadat's first disengagement with Israel, Asad endeavoured to create strategic alliances with other Arab nations as alternative options (or as additional partners) to the Syrian–Egyptian axis. Iraq, the north-eastern neighbour, had obviously been his prior choice because of its unique combination of military and economic power, which could provide strategic depth for Syria, as well as because of its Baʿthist regime, which, it could be supposed, shared with Baʿthist Syria notions of Arab unity and the struggle against Israel. As early as September 1968,

Asad, as Syrian defence minister, had sought to establish an 'eastern front command' with Iraq (and Jordan) and in 1969 he arranged for 6,000 Iraqi troops to enter Syria and conduct joint military manœuvres with the Syrian army.

During the 1973 war, at Asad's request, Iraq sent two armoured and one infantry division to help Syria fight Israel on the Golan front. Baghdad, however, recalled this force immediately after Syria accepted UN Resolution 338, labelling Damascus 'defeatist' and accusing it of recognizing Israel. Asad then made several attempts in 1974 and 1975 to settle his differences with the Iraqi regime and establish a union between the two countries. But Baghdad rejected Asad's offers while denouncing his readiness to 'make peace with the Zionist enemy'. Damascus reacted by depicting the Iraqi regime as 'rightist', 'fascist', 'splitting Arab solidarity', etc.[43]

In December 1977, following Sadat's journey to Jerusalem, Asad renewed his efforts to form a new inter-Arab alliance—the 'Tripoli Bloc'—with Iraq and other radical Arab regimes. But the Iraqis insisted again that Syria disavow UN Resolutions 242 and 338 and, when Asad refused, they left. But in October 1978, following the Camp David accords, Iraq's President Ahmad Hasan al-Bakr suggested working closely with Asad in foiling the Camp David accords. By late October 1978 Asad and Bakr signed in Baghdad a charter for 'Joint National Action' which provided for the 'closest form of unity ties' including 'complete military unity' as well as 'economic, political, and cultural unification'. It depicted this 'historical pan-Arab step' as a serious search 'for greater strength in confronting the present Zionist onslaught against the Arab nation'.[44]

Subsequently, in early November 1978, an Arab summit convened in Baghdad, warning Sadat against signing a peace treaty with Israel and offering him $5 billion a year for ten years if he renounced the Camp David accords. The summit also promised Syria $1.8 billion a year for ten years, Jordan $1.2 billion, the PLO $150 million, the occupied territories $150 million, and Lebanon $200 million. Sadat rejected the offer and in March 1979 he signed a peace treaty with Israel. Unity talks continued between Asad and Saddam Hussein, Iraq's strong man, who officially succeeded al-Bakr as president in July 1979. Asad rejected Iraqi demands for a full merger between the two states and for immediate deployment of Iraqi troops in Syria. He advocated a step-by-step approach, possibly fearing Iraqi domination,[45] perhaps also a new war with Israel. Consequently by summer 1979 the unity talks were suspended by Iraq, after an alleged discovery of a Syrian plot to overthrow Saddam Hussein. In 1980 Iraq expelled the Syrian ambassador in Baghdad after the alleged discovery of another Syrian plot; Syria retaliated in the same fashion. And with the outbreak of the Iraq–Iran war a while later, Syrian–Iraqi relations sank to their lowest ebb, as Damascus sided with Teheran against Baghdad in that long and devastating war.

Asad's Greater Syria Strategy

Alongside his attempts to enlist Iraq's co-operation in his political-military strategy towards Israel, Asad made special efforts to create a 'Greater Syria' strategic alliance with Lebanon, Jordan, and the Palestinians. Such an alliance, it would seem, would be relatively easy to form and dominate, more crucial to Syria's defensive/offensive system vis-à-vis Israel, and could also manageably integrate into a larger regional Arab framework such as the 'Fertile Crescent' (which also comprises Iraq).

From a historical-geographical point of view, the region of Greater Syria has for centuries included the present-day territories of Syria, Lebanon, Jordan, the West Bank, Gaza, and Israel. During certain periods under Arab and Muslim rule, this region also constituted a political-administrative unit, and in modern times it became accepted as a political-ideological concept: initially in the mid-1860s by Christian Lebanese intellectuals, who were followed in the 1930s by Antun Sa'adah's 'Syrian Nationalist Party' (PPS; subsequently known as SSNP). On the Muslim Arab side, the Hashemite Amir (later King) Faysal, who ruled Syria during 1918–20, considered Greater Syria as the core of a larger Arab union, while his brother Amir (later King) Abdallah of Transjordan (later Jordan) in the early 1940s designed a scheme to unify Greater Syria under his rule.[46]

To the extent that Asad has been influenced by the ideological-historical concept of Greater Syria, he has publicly regarded this region as a nucleus of larger Arab unity. And even though he would have liked the region to be unified under his domination, his pragmatic goal was to establish a political-military strategic structure of Greater Syria states and entities under his leadership. Damascus could then become a new regional power centre vis-à-vis its Arab rivals—Cairo and Baghdad—as well as against its major foe in Jerusalem.

Syrian Attempts to Influence Jordan

Of the three potential partners for a Greater Syrian alliance, Jordan was the most important component during the 1970s and beyond, but also the hardest to tackle. Having the longest border with Israel among the 'confrontation states' and the best-trained Arab army, Jordan could block or delay an Israeli outflanking movement via the north or, conversely, could serve as an important springboard in an offensive against Israel. In addition, the pro-Western Hashemite kingdom might be useful in bringing American pressure to bear on Israel to return the West Bank to Jordan, so rendering the Jewish state more vulnerable.

As far as King Hussein was concerned, an alliance with Syria could offer important assets, but also serious liabilities. On the one hand, he was keen to avoid belligerent relations with his powerful Syrian neighbour and to enlist the backing of Damascus against the PLO's claim to the West Bank. But, on the other hand, Hussein might have been concerned lest an alliance with Syria could drastically diminish his manœuvring ability among the other major Arab states, and particularly undermine his delicate relations with Israel.[47] Consequently, Hussein would not submit for too long to the embrace of the northern lion (Asad) and would counterbalance Syria's influence by playing the Iraqi card and/or maintaining his tacit strategic alliance with Israel.

As already pointed out, on the eve of his ascent to power Asad, as Syria's defence minister and air force commander, denied air cover to the Syrian armoured units dispatched by Jadid's government in September 1970 to help the Palestinian rebels in Jordan overthrow King Hussein. Asad took this unusual step because he feared *inter alia* that Syrian military intervention would alienate King Hussein. On the eve of the October 1973 war, he indeed appealed to Hussein to open a 'third front' against Israel. Hussein declined to do so and instead sent two brigades to the Golan front, while earlier, on 25 September 1973, he came secretly to Israel to warn Prime Minister Golda Meir personally that Syria and Egypt were preparing a war against the Jewish state.[48] After the war, in December 1973, Jordan participated in the Geneva conference, despite Syria's negative position, whereas Syria supported the PLO as the sole representative of the Palestinian people at both the Algiers (November 1973) and the Rabat (October 1974) summits—to Jordan's detriment. Subsequently, Asad assured Hussein that Syria did not fully share the PLO position against Jordan and that he would work to achieve a compromise between the two rivals. Referring to the Jordan–PLO rift since 'Black September' 1970, Asad remarked, for example, in June 1975:

I said at the Rabat conference . . . that the responsibility concerning the 1970 events was shared by King Hussein, the Palestinian resistance, and other Arab countries. . . . But even if we assume that it was the responsibility of one party, must Arab history stop at that September? Our interests and rules of life require us to overcome this complex and act to further the essential interests of our nation.[49]

Around the same time, Asad proposed the establishment of a tripartite Syrian–Jordanian–Palestinian federation or at least co-ordination among these three parties. But, unable to contrive a bridge between Hussein and Arafat, Asad directed his efforts towards creating two parallel military-political alliances, one with Jordan and one with the PLO, putting his main trust in the former. (During 1976 Syrian–PLO relations also sharply worsened.) Thus, taking advantage of Jordan's inter-Arab isolation following the Rabat summit, in April 1975 Asad suggested to Hussein the establishment of a Joint Supreme Leadership Council. And during his subsequent state visit to Amman (it was the first visit of a Syrian head of state for eighteen years), Asad referred to Syria and Jordan as 'one people, one country, one army'. In July 1975 Asad and Hussein also agreed to create a Supreme Jordanian–Syrian Joint Committee to prepare the integration (*takamul*) of the two countries in the political, military, economic, cultural, and educational fields. During the following two years a series of steps were indeed taken in these fields towards Syrian integration with Jordan. The process apparently went so well—alongside Syrian achievements in Lebanon—as to prompt Asad in late 1977 to reveal his long-term design: the creation of a Greater Syria federation under his leadership, composed of Syria, Lebanon, Jordan, and the West Bank.[50]

At this juncture, however, Jordan's relations with Syria began to show signs of strain, developing into an open rift by late 1980. Among the main reasons for this development were the improvement in Syrian–PLO relations and Syria's intense opposition to Sadat's peace initiative. Although King Hussein was displeased that he was not consulted regarding the Egyptian move, he tacitly backed it in anticipation of settling the West Bank–Palestinian issue in accordance with Jordan's interests. Subsequently, even though he opposed the Camp David accords and the Egyptian–Israeli peace treaty, King Hussein refused to yield to Asad's pressure, allowed members of the Syrian Muslim opposition to operate in Jordan, and sided with Baghdad in the renewed Syrian–Iraqi conflict.[51] In an attempt to bring Hussein back under Syrian influence, Asad deployed his troops along the Jordanian border in December 1980, while resorting to terrorist actions against Jordanian leaders and officials. At the same time, Syrian leaders and officials attacked King Hussein and his regime as 'illegitimate' and 'alien,' calling for the overthrow of the Jordanian monarchy. Asad himself declared in April 1981:

We and Jordan are one country, one people. . . . The Jordanian people now have nothing to do with the decision made by the Jordanian regime. And the day will come, perhaps very soon, when the Jordanian people will regain their right to make decisions. . . . King Hussein will discover that we are one people and that his majesty was no more than a passing, dark and rainless cloud in our historical march.

King Hussein, however, was not intimidated by Asad's threats, and late in 1980 he deployed his troops along the Syrian border to counter the Syrian military build-up. In 1985, following the Hussein–Arafat confederation agreement, Syria resumed its terrorist actions against Jordanian targets in Jordan and abroad. In reaction, Jordan radio attacked 'the fascist-sectarian regime in Syria . . . [that] has set up special apparatuses for terrorism, assassination and crime against those who oppose it in the Arab arena.'[52]

NOTES

1. Quandt, *Decade*, 188, 235, 237, 239; Karsh, *The Soviet Union*, 13–14, 17; Rabin, *Pinkas Sherut*, 427, 438, 451.
2. Rabin, *Pinkas Sherut*, 424. Cf. Allon, *Behatira*, 157–8; Peres's statement cited by UPI, 19 Aug. 1974.
3. Rabin, *Pinkas Sherut*, 442, 447, 471, 475, 496. Cf. Quandt, *Decade*, 262; UPI, 2 June 1975.
4. Allon, *Kelim*, 133–5, 170.
5. See respectively Israeli Ministry of Foreign Affairs, *Defenceless*. Three complaints by the Government of Israel respecting grave violations of the 1949 Geneva POW Convention, Jerusalem, Dec. 1973; idem, *Syrian Standards of Chivalry* (with the Arabic text), Jerusalem, 22 June 1975.
6. See respectively *Skira Hodsheet*, June 1974, 28 ff.; Seale, *Asad*, 245. Cf. Memo NSC, 27 May 1975, DD 10, 2803 (1990).
7. Confidential, Dec. 1976, DD No. 779, 1984, 15–16, 25. Cf. Allon, *Behatira*, 157, 192; idem, *Kelim*, 128–9, 133; M. Dayan, *On the Peace Process* (Hebrew; Tel Aviv, 1988), 91. On the Israeli policy of creating Jewish settlements in the Golan see also Erez, *Dayan*, 117; Galili, 252–4, 268; S. Peres, *Ka'et mahar* (Jerusalem, 1978), 48.
8. For Arabic and English sources and for more details, see Ma'oz, *Asad*, 104–6

and n. See also Asad's remarks in the Baʿth 12th National Congress, 1975. See also President Ford Library, WHCF, Box 48, Co. 146, Letter of Muhammad al-Halabi, speaker of the Syrian parliament, 27 June 1975.

9. Baʿth 12th National Congress, 1975; cf. 'Statement of the National Leadership on the Activities of the 12th National Congress of the Arab Socialist Baʿth Party (Damascus, 1975), in A. Drysdale and R. A. Hinnebusch, *Syria and the Middle East Peace Process* (New York, 1991), 112.

10. See citations in Maʿoz, *Asad*, 106, and 302 and n. Cf. M. Z. Diab, 'Syria's Objectives and its Conceptions of Deterrence, Defence and Security' draft study presented to United States Institute of Peace (n.d.), 10–11.

11. See Maʿoz, *Asad*, 49; cf. Drysdale and Hinnebusch, *Syria*, 108, 11; *New York Times*, 18 Dec. 1974; NA, DOS Background Notes, Syria, Apr. 1974.

12. Maʿoz, *Asad*, 105 and n.

13. Asad's interview with *Al-Ahram*, 5 July 1974. For details, see Maʿoz, *Asad*, 107, 110 ff.

14. *Jaysh al-Shaʿb*, 29 Apr. 1975.

15. Asad's interview with BBC TV, Radio Damascus, 8 Sept. 1975; Asad's interview with *Newsweek*, 22 Sept. 1975; *New York Times*, 18 Dec. 1975; *Time*, 2 Dec. 1975; cf. Maʿoz, *Asad*, 103 ff.

16. Quandt, *Camp David*, 97; cf. E. Haber, E. Yaʿari, and Z. Schiff, *Shnat hayona* (Tel Aviv, 1980), 46.

17. Seale, *Asad*, 304.

18. Maʿoz, *Asad*, 145.

19. Ibid. 95, 97; cf. Rabin, *Pinkas Sherut*, 428.

20. *Public Papers of the President of the United States Richard Nixon, 1974* (Washington, 1975), 516.

21. Tad Szule, *The Illusion of Peace* (New York, 1978), 783; cf. Edward Sheehan, 'Step by Step in the Middle East', *Foreign Policy*, 22, (spring 1976); Kissinger, *Years*, 1135; Seale, *Asad*, 248; Quandt, *Decade*, 248.

22. For these and other citations and their sources, see Maʿoz, *Asad*, 100 and n.

23. *Washington Post*, 5 Mar. 1975. Cf. Maʿoz, *Asad*, 101.

24. See respectively Kissinger, *Years*, 1134; Seale, *Asad*, 248; Z. Schiff, 'Dealing with Syria', *Foreign Policy*, 55 (summer 1984), 92–112. See also Rabin, *Pinkas Sherut*, 437.

25. See Seale, *Asad*, 247; Quandt, *Decade*, 279; Rabin, *Pinkas Sherut*, 492–5; *New York Times*, 12 Oct. 1976.

26. Rabin, *Pinkas Sherut*, 475; Quandt, *Decade*, 273. Cf. Ford Library, WHCF Box 48, 16 Aug. 1974.

27. See respectively M. Gazit, *Report from Israel*, 16 (June 1990); *Boston Herald*, 25 July 1976. But cf. *Public Papers of the President of the United States Gerald Ford*, 1975, ii (Washington, 1977), 1914 (26 Nov. 1975).

28. Karsh, *The Soviet Union*, 17 ff.; G. Golan, *The Soviet Union and Syria Since the Yom Kippur War*, Research Paper 21 (Jerusalem: Hebrew University, 1977), 13, 21–2; *Pravda*, 14 Oct. 1975.

29. Rabin, *Pinkas Sherut*, p. 503; interview with Rabin in *Ma'ariv*, 14 Apr. 1976; *The Times*, 13 Sept. 1976. Cf. Ma'oz, *Asad*, 137–8; Ford Library, WHCF CD 71, Box 27, 13 Apr. 1976.

30. *Washington Post*, 2 Dec. 1976; *Time*, 17 Jan. 1977.

31. W. B. Quandt, *Camp David: Peacemaking and Politics* (Washington: Brookings Institute, 1986), 30. Ibid., *passim*, for an excellent account of Carter's Middle Eastern policy.

32. Seale, *Asad*, 296; Ma'oz, *Asad*, 139. See also *al-Ba'th*, 17 Feb. 1977 and *Tishrin* 11 Mar. 1977—articles by Jubran Kurriya.

33. Quandt, *Camp David*, 57–8; cf. J. Carter, *The Blood of Abraham* (Boston, 1985), 72.

34. Drysdale and Hinnebusch, *Syria*, 115.

35. Full text of the interview in the author's possession. Cf. *Washington Post*, 2 Dec. 1976; *Tishrin*, 21 Mar. 1977.

36. See respectively Quandt, *Camp David*, 107; Ma'oz, *Asad*, 140, quoting Carter's accounts.

37. Quandt, *Camp David*, 45. On Rabin's official position regarding the Arab–Israeli settlement, see also Rabin, *Pinkas Sherut*, 508 ff.

38. Cf. Quandt, *Camp David*, 62, 58. For other more substantial reasons, see Sachar, *A History*, 28 ff.

39. See respectively I. Rabinovich, 'Israel, Syria and Jordan', paper presented at the Council on Foreign Relations, New York, Oct. 1989; Y. Nedava (ed.), *The Arab–Israeli Conflict* (Hebrew; Ramat Gan, 1983), 273; cf. Quandt, *Camp David*, 79; A. Na'or, *Begin bashilton* (Tel Aviv, 1993), 18–19, 92, 95–6, 119, 122.

40. Quandt, *Camp David*, 79 ff., 96 ff.; Ma'oz, *Asad*, 144–6; Seale, *Asad*, 294 ff. Cf. Haber, *Shnat hayona*, 193; *New York Times*, 18 Nov. 1975.

41. Erez, *Dayan*, 113–14; Quandt, *Camp David*, 109 ff.; Seale, *Asad*, 299 ff.; Na'or, *Begin*, 137–8.

42. Cf. Erez, *Dayan*, 119; Quandt, *Camp David*, 130 ff., Seale, *Asad*, 300 ff. See also *Public Papers, Jimmy Carter, 1977*, ii (1978), 1728; ibid. *1978*, i (1979), 544.

43. Ma'oz, *Asad*, 112 and n.

44. Text in *Journal of Palestine Studies*, 8/2 (1979), 200–2; see also Ma'oz, *Asad*, 146–7; Seale, *Asad*, 312–13.

45. For a different version, see Phebe Marr, *The Modern History of Iraq* (Boulder, Colo. 1985), 231.

46. For more details and references, see Ma'oz, *Asad*, 113–14. See also D. Pipes, *Greater Syria* (London, 1990), 3 ff.

47. For a more detailed analysis, see Ma'oz, *Asad*, 115.

48. General (ret.) E. Zeira in *Yediot Ahronot* and Z. Schiff in *Ha'aretz*, 15 Sept. 1993. For a further account see E. Zeira, *The Yom Kippur War: Myth versus Reality* (Hebrew; Tel Aviv, 1993).

49. Asad in an interview with *al-Hawadith* (Lebanon), 26 June 1975.

50. For more details and sources, see Maʿoz, *Asad*, 115–19. See also an interview with the Syrian deputy foreign minister, *al-Hadaf* (Kuwait), 28 Apr. 1977.
51. For more details and sources, see Maʿoz, *Asad*, 118–19 and n.; A. Susser, *Between Jordan and Palestine* (Hebrew; Tel Aviv, 1983), 178 ff.
52. Pipes, *Greater Syria*, 139–40; cf. Maʿoz, *Asad*, 119, 172.

8

The Struggle over Lebanon and the Palestinians

SYRIA'S BID TO CONTROL LEBANON AND THE PALESTINIANS

With Jordan's refusal to integrate into Asad's Greater Syria strategy, his remaining potential partners were Lebanon and the Palestinians. Both these parties, being politically and militarily much weaker than Jordan, could, it seemed, be easily influenced if not dominated by Damascus and serve its regional strategic interests, notably vis-à-vis Jerusalem. For generations Damascus had considered Lebanon as the western part of Syria, arbitrarily and artificially carved off by the French Mandate; Damascus thus had never established diplomatic relations with Beirut. In addition to its economic importance—much Syrian trade passed through the port of Beirut—democratic Lebanon constituted an antithesis to the authoritarian Syrian regime and a main haven for Syrian opposition groups; hence the ambition of Damascus to control it. More crucially, Lebanon has been a highly important component in the Syrian strategic-military confrontation with Israel: the Biqaʿ valley being a natural invasion route for the Israeli army to take towards Damascus and central Syria, whereas southern Lebanon could serve as a springboard for a Syrian military offensive or Syrian-sponsored guerrilla/terrorist operations against northern Israel, notably by Palestinian organizations.[1]

With regard to the Syrian attitude towards the Palestinians, as in the case of Lebanon, Damascus had long considered the whole of Palestine as southern Syria, usurped by the Zionist-Israeli enemy, and thus calling for total liberation. The Palestinian issue has indeed been a cornerstone in Syrian pan-Arab and anti-Israel strategy. And, as already pointed out, various Syrian governments, notably the Baʿthist regimes, rendered military, logistic, and diplomatic support to Palestinian armed organizations, notably the Fatḥ/PLO, in their struggle against Israel.

Yet, although Damascus considered itself as 'the lung from which Palestinian activity draws breath', Syrian rulers, particularly Asad, have sought to control the PLO as well as other Palestinian organizations, and make them instruments of the inter-Arab and anti-Israeli policies of Damascus. And when the PLO, despite its long-standing strategic alliance with Damascus, strove to preserve a certain degree of independence from Syria (as well as from other Arab states), it was harshly persecuted.[2] Except for short periods, Damascus was careful not to employ Palestinian guerrillas from the Golan Heights against Israel, but rather encouraged them to operate from Jordanian and Lebanese territories. But again, when PLO actions clashed with Syrian national interests or priorities, Damascus would take strong measures against the PLO. Such fluctuations in Syrian–Palestinian relations occurred particularly in Lebanon from the early 1970s, following the elimination of the PLO in Jordan in September 1970 and the transfer of its headquarters and bases to Lebanon. For the next five years Syria gave substantial military and diplomatic support to the PLO, while Asad depicted himself as the great champion of the Palestinian cause. In many speeches and interviews he stressed that the liberation of Palestine was the most crucial issue for the Arabs, even more important than the occupied Golan; and that the PLO represented the Palestinian people and only it could define Palestinian rights and aspirations.[3] Indeed, at the October 1974 Rabat summit, Asad, as we know, was a leading supporter of the decision to recognize the PLO as the sole representative of the Palestinian people. In March 1975 Syria offered to form a joint Syrian–PLO political and military command, apparently in an attempt to institutionalize control over the Palestinian movement.

In fact, the considerable Syrian backing helped the PLO in Lebanon to become an important military and political factor which presented a potential challenge to the weak Lebanese government, and thus contributed to the outbreak of the civil war in 1975. Ironically, however, the PLO role in that war threatened Syrian designs in Lebanon and consequently led to severe conflicts between Asad and Arafat.

While supporting the PLO and certain radical Muslim groups, Asad sought to work also with the new conservative Christian Lebanese president, Sulayman Franjiyya, in order to extend Syrian influence, if not protectorate, over the country. Stressing the 'special historical relations between Lebanon and Syria'—'their two peoples are more than brothers'—Asad managed in the early 1970s to secure a degree of military cooperation with the Lebanese government.[4]

Syrian influence in Lebanon increased considerably after the 1973 war, with Asad's soaring prestige in the region. During his visit to Lebanon in January 1975—the first of a Syrian head of state in eighteen years—Asad was warmly welcomed as the 'hero of the Golan in his second homeland, Lebanon'. After discussing 'military co-operation' against Israeli 'aggression' with the Lebanese leaders, Asad announced that Syria will support Lebanon 'with her military, political and economic resources . . . in order to enable her to withstand and act against the aggression, and to maintain her sovereignty and territorial integrity'. Reportedly, Asad and Franjiyya signed a secret agreement whereby Syria would send troops to Lebanon and train the Lebanese army; Asad also remarked that Franjiyya was 'the only Lebanese president who would immediately agree to sign a treaty unifying his country with Syria should I ask him to do so'.[5]

However, Asad's growing prestige in the region not only gave him a powerful leverage on the Lebanese government, but greatly contributed to the strengthening of the Muslim-leftist elements in Lebanon, organized in the 'Lebanese National Movement' under the leadership of the Druze chief Kamal Junblatt. This Lebanese National Movement had also been radicalized by the increasing number of Israeli raids against PLO targets in Lebanon (in reaction to growing terrorist activity by Palestinian groups), while drawing military and political support from various Palestinian guerrilla organizations. In contrast, deeply concerned that the Lebanese–Palestinian radical alliance might overthrow the Christian Lebanese regime, Christian Maronite groups, notably the Phalangists and the National Liberals, became highly belligerent towards those anti-establishment forces. Consequently, a single violent clash between Phalangist militiamen and pro-Syrian Palestinian commandos on 13 April 1975 in a Christian quarter of Beirut soon developed into armed clashes in various parts of Lebanon between Maronite militias and Muslim radicals, assisted by Palestinian militant groups. The Lebanese civil war had begun.

SYRIA AND THE LEBANESE CIVIL WAR

Without dealing with the various aspects of this civil war, which have been fully described and analysed in several studies,[6] it is relevant to our theme mainly to examine the involvement of and confrontation between Syria and Israel during the phases of this war until its termination in 1985.

During the first phase, from April 1975 until early 1976, Damascus refrained from direct military intervention to bring the Lebanese internal conflict to a halt. Syria was then still involved in the peace process under American auspices and did not wish to antagonize Washington. Perhaps Asad was also unaware of the conflict's depth, and preferred to use mediation in order to stop the fighting. But rather than achieving a settlement, he contributed indirectly to stepping up the civil war. He continued to supply substantial quantities of arms to radical Palestinian guerrilla organizations, which were transferred in part to the militant Lebanese groups. On 19 January 1976 Damascus also dispatched two brigades of the Syrian-controlled PLA (Palestine Liberation Army) to Tripoli (in Lebanon) and Zahla to defend the Lebanese–Palestinian radical forces against Christian attacks.

Indeed, worried about the growing strength of these anti-establishment forces, and motivated by other strategic and political considerations, Christian Maronite forces for the first time also attacked Palestinian refugee camps in and around Beirut. These attacks provoked the mainstream PLO—which until then had been only marginally involved in the fighting—openly to join forces with the radical Muslim-Druze groups, and in fact the PLO became the major fighting power in the Lebanese–Palestinian radical alliance. This alliance destroyed Christian villages and small towns in northern and eastern Lebanon and captured several Christian townlets south of Beirut.

At that juncture, in February 1976, Asad, fearing further deterioration of the civil war, initiated a plan to settle the conflict by issuing a 'constitutional document', which, while improving the position of the Sunni Muslims, essentially preserved the old status quo in the political system. Simultaneously, the Lebanese–Palestinian agreements of 1969 and 1973—limiting Palestinian activities in Lebanon—were reconfirmed under a new Syrian–Lebanese understanding. Those measures now became Syrian official policy and were formally adopted by President Franjiyya and other Christian Maronite leaders, but rejected by the Lebanese–Palestinian radical alliance. Kamal Junblatt, the alliance leader, accused Asad of intending 'to dominate Lebanon and domesticate the Palestinians . . . to turn Lebanon into a satellite state without having to fight it.'[7]

Indeed, against the background of the Israeli–Egyptian Sinai 2 agreement, Asad apparently intended to integrate Labanon into his Greater Syria strategic design (as discussed above) and calculated that it would be easier to achieve that goal with the weak Christian-led conservative government. Asad possibly felt that the ascendancy of a strong Lebanese–PLO axis, under the charismatic leadership of Kamal Junblatt, was likely to bring about a radical government which would be independent of Syrian influence and might also form an alliance with radical Iraq against Damascus. Furthermore, in Asad's view, a Muslim–PLO military advantage over the Christian Maronites was likely to split Lebanon and provoke Israeli intervention aiming at creating a 'second [Christian] Israel':

A decisive military action [by the radical axis] . . . would open doors to every foreign intervention, particularly Israel's intervention. Let us all visualize the magnitude of the tragedy which might ensue if Israel were to intervene and save [Christian] Arabs from other [Muslim] Arabs. . . . The partitioning of Lebanon is an old Zionist aim . . . [it] would acquit Israel of the charge of racism . . . when Lebanon is partitioned between Christians and Muslims Israel will say: 'Where is racism? Israel is based on religion, and in Lebanon there would be states, or statelets, based on religion.'[8]

Asad possibly also wished to demonstrate to the United States, Israel's ally, that Syria, acting alone, was able to restore order in Lebanon, and thus prevent Israeli military intervention. Consequently, Asad switched sharply away from his long-term ideological backing, and military support, of the Palestinian organizations and Lebanese left, and applied military pressure against them, while denouncing Junblatt's and Arafat's motives.[9] And following his indirect military intervention in early 1976 (by means of the Syrian-controlled PLA), on 1 June 1976 Asad dispatched regular armoured and commando units to fight the Lebanese–Palestinian radical forces in various parts of Lebanon, apparently with the aim of imposing *Pax Syriana* in the country.[10]

But these radical forces bravely fought back the Syrian troops, inflicting heavy losses on them and blocking their advance in several places. Asad was deeply hurt by these setbacks and by the PLO's so-called attempt to turn Lebanon into a 'second Vietnam' for Syria. In one of his major speeches, on 20 July 1976, he said *inter alia*:

The Palestinian resistance is currently fighting for the accomplishment of the objectives of others [the Lebanese left] and against the interests and goals of the Palestinian Arab people . . . He [Arafat] wants to liberate Juniyya and Tripoli [in Lebanon] and does not want to liberate Palestine even if he so claims.

And on an earlier occasion Asad told Arafat: 'You do not represent Palestine more than we do. There is neither a Palestinian people nor a Palestinian entity, there is only Syria . . . and Palestine is an inseparable part of Syria.'[11]

Following futile attempts to reach agreement with the Palestinians, the Syrian army, in co-ordination with Maronite militias, renewed its attacks against the PLO and the Lebanese radicals. Among the targets were also several Palestinian refugee camps, such as Tallal Za'tar, which was brutally attacked, and many of its inhabitants massacred, by Maronite militiamen with Syrian sanction.[12]

Finally, the Syrian army, continuing its military offensive, defeated the PLO–Lebanese leftist alliance by mid-October 1976 and assumed control in large parts of Lebanon. On 16 March 1977 Kamal Junblatt was assassinated, allegedly by Syrian agents, and the anti-Syrian alliance consequently disintegrated.[13] A few months later, however, Damascus made separate rapprochements with Junblatt's son, Walid, and with the PLO leader Yasir Arafat. The reasons for these new moves were to demonstrate to the Syrian public and to the Arab world that Syria was still the guardian of the Lebanese left and particularly of the 'Palestinian resistance';[14] and, more importantly, to mobilize these radical forces against the disillusioned Maronites and their new, formidable, ally—Menachem Begin, Israel's new prime minister.

THE ISRAELI CHALLENGE IN LEBANON

Against the background of Israel's threat of intervention in the 1970 Jordanian crisis, and in view of its strategic advantage following the Sinai 2 agreement, Asad was worried lest Israel should move forces into Lebanon, in reaction to the Syrian military encroachment in early 1976. To avert such an action, Asad already in late 1975 sought American approval for his intervention in Lebanon and a guarantee that Israel would not interfere. The United States, however, did not at that juncture support Syrian military action in Lebanon, fearing that this might trigger a fresh Israeli–Syrian armed conflict. As Asad revealed later, on 16 October 1975 the American ambassador to Damascus (Richard Murphy) had told him that 'Israel will consider the intervention of foreign [i.e. Syrian] armed forces [in Lebanon] a very grave threat.' And in January 1976 in reaction to Foreign Minister Khaddam's statement that Syria would not hesitate to annex Lebanon, should it be partitioned, the Americans warned both Syria and Israel against intervention in Lebanon.[15]

Subsequently, however, the Ford administration changed its policy and tacitly backed Syrian action in Lebanon, following Asad's constitutional reform for Lebanon of February 1976. The United States now believed that only Syria could stop the Lebanese civil war, bring about a construc-tive solution, curb the Lebanese–Palestinian radical alliance, and possibly join an American-sponsored Arab–Israeli peace process, thus also reduc-ing Soviet influence in the region.[16] (Soviet leaders tried in vain to stop the Syrian offensive against the PLO–Lebanese axis.) Significantly, Asad was not content with American backing only and in April 1976 he asked King Hussein of Jordan to seek the consent of Israel's prime minister, Yitzhak Rabin, to a Syrian military intervention in Lebanon that would not jeop-ardize Israel's security interests.[17]

Despite Israel's concerns lest Syria should assume control in Lebanon, deploy its army there, and pose a strategic threat along the Lebanese–Israel border, Rabin and Israeli army commanders also saw important merits in such a Syrian deployment: it would divert Syrian army units from the Golan and engage them in an exhausting war against the PLO, Israel's enemy. And, although feeling sympathy for the Lebanese Christians 'who are struggling for their lives against the fanatic Muslim nationalist chauvinism', Rabin refused to involve the army directly in fighting the Christian's war in Lebanon. He rather preferred 'to help them help themselves' and let them also benefit from Syrian backing.[18]

As a result of these considerations, and with American mediation, a secret understanding was reached between Rabin and Asad in April–May 1976, whereby Syrian ground forces in Lebanon would not move south of the Sidon–Jezzin/Khuna line (the 'Red Line'); that the Syrian army would not use its air force against the Lebanese Christians; that it would not be equipped with surface-to-air missile batteries; and that Syria should withdraw its forces from Lebanon after pacifying it.[19]

The Maronite–Likud Alliance

Syria, however, did not withdraw its army from Lebanon following the (interim) end of the civil war and the restoration of internal order in late 1976. During 1977 the Maronite leaders became increasingly apprehen-sive that Syria intended to continue its control over Lebanon, attempting to disarm the Christians of their heavy weapons and renewing its alliance with the PLO and Lebanese left.[20] The establishment of the new Likud government in Israel in mid-1977 substantially encouraged the Maronites in opposing these Syrian designs. (The main anti-Syrian leaders were Bashir Jumayyil, the commander of the 'Lebanese Forces' [Maronite militias] and Camille Chamoun, leader of the Lebanese [Christian] Front.) They put their trust in Mr Begin.

Israel's new prime minister, Menachem Begin, indeed considered the Christian–Lebanese issue not merely in political and humanitarian terms, as did his predecessor, but also from an ideological and political-strategic point of view. He believed that Israel's mission as a Jewish state was to help the Christians fight against their 'fanatic' Muslim enemy, who intended to eliminate them.[21] Begin also regarded Christian Lebanon as Israel's ally in the common struggle against the Syrian threat, unlike Rabin, who had reached an understanding with Asad regarding Lebanon.

Initially, however, Begin followed Rabin's policy of supplying the Christian Maronites in northern Lebanon with light weapons and military training.[22] But, as regards southern Lebanon, Begin's government expanded its support of local Christian-led militia, and in September 1977 for the first time ordered direct armoured intervention to assist this militia in a pre-coordinated attack against a PLO position near Marj Ayun.

Since the 'Red Line' agreement, southern Lebanon had become a haven for the Palestinian guerrilla/terrorist organizations, being independent of Syrian control—ironically owing to Israel's deterrence vis-à-vis Damascus. The southern Lebanese militia, however, was unable to prevent all PLO raids against Israel, and in reaction to a Palestinian terrorist attack on a bus on a northern highway, the Israeli army carried out a large-scale offensive (the Litani operation) against the PLO military infrastructure south of the River Litani in mid-March 1978. The army was careful not to attack nearby Syrian positions, while the Syrians also refrained from interfering on the PLO side. Both Syria and Israel were determined to avoid a direct military clash.[23]

Nevertheless, the militant Maronite leaders, in and around Beirut, were apparently encouraged by Israel's activist policy in southern Lebanon, and its growing support of the local Christian militia (which now became the 'Southern Lebanese Army'—SLA), as well as by Begin's deep sympathy for their cause, expressed also by increasing military supplies. And, in February 1978, while starting their military struggle against the Syrian 'occupation', Bashir Jumayyil and Camille Chamoun renewed their endeavours to enlist direct Israeli intervention against the Syrian army in Lebanon. But in an August 1978 meeting in Israel, Begin turned down the Jumayyil–Chamoun request, although he undertook to order Israeli air intervention should the Syrian air force attack Christian Lebanese positions.

Significantly, a month earlier, on 6 July 1978, in reaction to Syrian ground attacks on Christian forces in Beirut, Israeli air force jets flew over

Beirut, while armoured units were deployed in the Golan. Begin and other Israeli leaders declared that Israel would not remain idle in view of the 'genocide' being carried out against the Lebanese Christians.[24] To be sure, the Maronite leaders shrewdly, or even deviously, utilized Begin's perception of their plight as 'genocide', as well as his commitment to employ the air force in their defence—and this in order to provoke Syrian attacks and thus draw Israel into a military confrontation with the Syrian forces in Lebanon.

The case in point occurred in Zahla, the central (Christian) town of the Biqaʿ valley (in eastern Lebanon) a strategic region which had been under Syrian control since 1976. Exploiting Syria's regional weakness in the wake of the Egyptian–Israeli peace treaty (1979) and its difficulties in Lebanon, Bashir Jumayyil, the Phalangist leader, assumed control in Zahla late in 1980, amidst armed clashes with Syrian military units. In April 1981, when the Syrian forces, not without Phalangist provocation, tried to evict the 'Lebanese forces' (Phalangists) from the city by military and diplomatic means, Bashir asked for Israeli help. According to a senior Israeli officer and political analyst, Bashir's reports to Israel were 'exaggerated and false . . . regarding the genocide, as it were, which was committed against them [the Christians by the Syrian army] . . . aiming at dragging Israel into a battle against Syria'. Nevertheless, Begin was deeply moved by the Christian clamours and reportedly said: 'What is being done to the Christians in Lebanon today, is exactly what the Nazis did to the Jews in the 1940s in Europe.'[25]

And as Syrian military pressure mounted and Syria also employed combat helicopters against the Christians, the Israeli air force shot down two Syrian transport helicopters near Zahla on 28 April 1981. Syria promptly reacted by introducing ground-to-air missiles in the Zahla region, and by deploying additional long-range missiles in Syrian territory along the Lebanese border. The tacit 1976 Syrian–Israeli understanding was thus broken by both sides, their confrontation over Lebanon was revived, and led, among other factors, to the 1982 war in Lebanon.

Towards the 1982 War in Lebanon

As a matter of fact, the 1976 Syrian–Israeli understanding had already been eroded since July 1978, when Israeli war-planes flew over Beirut as a warning to Damascus against attacking the Christians. During the first half of 1979, Israel, responding to the serious Palestinian terrorist actions in Israel (such as in Maalot and Nahariya), carried out several military operations north of the Red Line, including air and naval bombardment of Palestinian guerrilla bases. And when, for example, on 27 June 1979 Syrian war-planes tried to intercept Israeli planes over Sidon, five Syrian jets were shot down.[26]

Still, until 1981, the Likud government was relatively careful to avoid major military clashes with the Syrian forces in Lebanon, for the following main reasons: Begin did not wish to jeopardize the peace process with Egypt, namely the 1978 Camp David accords and the 1979 peace treaty; nor did he wish to antagonize the Carter administration, which was strongly opposed to growing Israeli involvement in Lebanon as well as to renewed Israeli–Syrian confrontation in the region. Moreover, even within Begin's cabinet, senior members—Defence Minister Weizman and Deputy Prime Minister Yadin, and possibly also Foreign Minister Dayan (as well as the military intelligence)—objected to the deepening of Israeli ties with, and commitments to the Christian Phalangists, lest they should draw Israel into a major collision with Syria.

All those constraints, however, were removed by 1981, following the resignation of Weizman and Dayan from Begin's cabinet. Begin also assumed the defence portfolio until Ariel Sharon was appointed to this position in August 1981. Yitzhak Shamir, another hardline leader, became foreign minister, while the new militant chief of staff, Rafael Eytan, completed the circle of Israeli decision-makers who were determined to help the Lebanese Christians actively and prevent Syrian domination of Lebanon. As General Eytan wrote later:

During the term of Menachem Begin as defence minister the relations with the Christians in Lebanon were further tightened, not only owing to Israeli political and military reasons, and not merely because he [Begin] believed, like me, in the need to prevent the takeover of Lebanon by the Syrians and the [Palestinian] terrorists . . . but also because Begin was highly sensitive to the humanitarian aspect of Israel's commitment to prevent a genocide in Lebanon.[27]

However, in addition to these motives, the Begin government, in its new assertive, or aggressive, policy towards Syria, was also influenced by external developments. Apart from the peace treaty with Egypt, which gave Israel a freer hand in its confrontation with Syria, the new Reagan administration in Washington (January 1981) led Begin to believe that the United States now considered Israel as a major regional ally in a joint containment strategy vis-à-vis the 'evil Soviet empire' and its Syrian and Palestinian allies. Indeed, the new American secretary of state, General

Haig, is said to have depicted the Syrian military activities in Zahla as a 'Soviet conspiracy', and on his visit to Israel in April 1981 he stressed the link existing between the USSR and the PLO. Begin responded by emphasizing the common position of the United States and Israel towards Syria and the PLO, and added that the Syrians had better withdraw from Lebanon, since they no longer constituted a pacifying force. Several weeks later, during an election rally, Begin boasted that if American special envoy Philip Habib were not able to remove the Syrian missiles from the Zahla region, 'we shall indeed remove them', adding: 'The Syrians are afraid of the Israeli army. Asad, Asad, beware Asad! Yanush [General Ben-Gal, the commander of the IDF Northern Command] and Raful [Eytan, the chief of staff] are ready.'[28]

The Golan Law

Moreover, not only was Begin now disposed (and Sharon certainly determined) to dislodge the Syrian army from Lebanon, he was also apparently prepared to further aggravate the Israeli–Syrian conflict by formally annexing the occupied Golan Heights. Already in the spring of 1981 Begin publicly declared that as long as he was prime minister, Israel 'would not give up any territory of Judaea and Samaria [the West Bank], Gaza Strip, and the Golan Heights to foreign rule.'

In the autumn of 1981 Begin was contemplating extending Israeli sovereignty over the Golan in response to the earlier demands and pressures of an Israeli Golan lobby which also included Labour Party activists and *kibbutzim*. (Rabin, Peres, and Allon were among seventy Knesset members who signed a petition against a future Golan withdrawal.) Begin also calculated that such a move in the Golan would mitigate the opposition of many Israelis to the return of the remaining parts of Sinai to Egypt and the dismantling of the Jewish settlements there—all of which was due in April 1982. Finally, Begin assumed that the United States and the USSR, then deeply engaged in the Polish crisis, would not intervene against Israel's decision to change the status of the Golan. In his speech in the Knesset presenting the Golan Law (on 14 December 1981), Begin alleged that for many generations the Golan had been part of Eretz Israel (the Land of Israel), that it was essential to Israel's security, and that it was unlikely that the Golan would one day be returned to Syria, being, as it was, the most extreme Arab country, and rejecting Israel's existence within any boundaries. Begin added, however, that the application of

'Israeli law, jurisdiction, and administration' to the Golan Heights should not close the options for negotiations with Syria and would not prevent border changes in the future.[29]

Begin's arguments were accepted by (only) sixty-three Knesset members, who voted for the Golan Law, but were rejected by the friendly American administration, which promptly announced the 'temporary suspension' of the newly signed American–Israeli strategic co-operation agreement and of some $300 million in projected arms sales to Israel.

THE 1982 WAR AND ITS AFTERMATH

The angry American reaction to the Golan Law did not deter Begin from embarking on another major hostile action against Syria that was not compatible with American interests or policies ('Israel is not a "banana republic",' Begin told American Ambassador Lewis in reaction to the suspension of the strategic co-operation agreement). This move—attacking the Syrian forces in Lebanon in the course of the June 1982 war—like the enactment of the Golan Law, was made by Israel without previous Syrian provocation and contrary to the American position. In fact, even the initial offensive in Lebanon ('Peace of Galilee' operation) ostensibly directed against the PLO bases in southern Lebanon, was not fully compatible with American policy. Already on 24 July 1981, following two weeks of artillery duels between the Israeli army and PLO positions in southern Lebanon, Special Envoy Philip Habib achieved a cease-fire agreement between the two warring parties. Subsequently, the United States endeavoured to settle the overall Lebanese crisis through a comprehensive scheme whereby Syria would withdraw its forces from Lebanon, including the missile batteries from Zahla; the PLO would withdraw its heavy weapons from southern Lebanon; and Israel would terminate its military presence in the SLA strip.

But none of these parties was inclined to accept the American proposals. The PLO continued its terrorist operations against Israel from other regions—but not from southern Lebanon, according to their interpretation of the July 1981 cease-fire agreement; Israel, on its part, considered such operations a breach of the agreement and, in view of the expanding PLO military infrastructure in Lebanon, Ariel Sharon, the new defence minister (since August 1981) started at once to prepare a large military operation (initially named 'Oranim') against the Lebanese-based PLO, whose artillery attacks had virtually paralysed northern Israel in July 1981. Sharon also considered the Syrian occupation of Lebanon as not only harmful to the Christian community but dangerous to Israel's security, and to his own strategic design in the region. He thus planned to expel the Syrian army from Lebanon, destroy the PLO infrastructure there (as well as in the West Bank), and establish an independent, pro-Israeli Lebanese government under Bashir Jumayyil's leadership.[30]

The American administration, although sharing certain of Israel's concerns (and aware of its war preparations), was inclined to accept only a 'limited' Israeli reaction against the PLO, provided that there was a provocation of 'internationally organized' dimensions. It is not clear whether or not Haig warned Sharon and Begin against a large-scale operation in Lebanon.[31] The leaders of the Israeli Labour opposition and even several Likud ministers were opposed to such an operation; but neither they nor the American administration were able to stop Sharon and Begin from carrying out their plan.

The pretext to launch the 'Peace of Galilee' operation was the assassination attempt on 3 June 1982 by a Palestinian terrorist (of the Abu Nidal group) on the Israeli ambassador in London, Shlomo Argov, who was severely wounded and paralysed. As expected—and even preconceived by Israeli military leaders—the air force reacted, on 4 June, by heavily bombing southern Lebanon and west Beirut, causing many casualties; and this time the PLO riposted by shelling northern Israel. This was indeed the signal for the beginning of the 1982 Lebanon war, starting on 6 June.[32]

Different versions exist regarding the goals and parameters of the 1982 war, notably its territorial limits and whether or not attacking the Syrian forces and pushing them out of Lebanon was one of Israel's aims. Officially, the main purpose was to destroy the PLO's infrastructure in southern Lebanon. And, according to Sharon's plan, approved by the Israeli cabinet on 5 June, the territorial limits of the operation would be 40 kilometres from the Israeli border (being the effective range of the PLO's artillery). Concerning the Syrian forces in Lebanon, on 6 June the cabinet issued a statement which *inter alia* reads: 'During the operation the Syrian army will not be attacked unless it attacks our forces.' In the same vein, Begin appealed to Asad in a Knesset speech on 8 June:

We do not want war with Syria. From this podium I call on President Asad to instruct the Syrian army not to attack Israel's soldiers, in which case they [the Syrian troops] would not be hurt at all. Essentially, we do not wish to harm anybody; we want only one thing, that nobody should any longer hit our settlements in Galilee. . . . We do not want any clash with the Syrian army. If we reach the 40-kilometres line from our northern border, that work would be done, all fighting would stop. I deliver this call to the ears of Syria's president. He knows how to keep an agreement; he signed a cease-fire agreement with us and kept it. He did not permit Syria and the [Palestinian] terrorists to act. If he acts in this spirit now in Lebanon, no Syrian soldier will be attacked by our soldiers.[33]

Whether or not Begin was sincere in his appeal to Asad, and was fully aware of the real war goals and their repercussions, Sharon's and Eytan's design certainly differed from Begin's statement. First, with regard to the operation's range: according to Eytan: 'There was never, in the government decision . . . a definition of kilometres for the implementation of the military action, neither 40 nor 45, no less and no more. . . . In the map that I presented to the ministers the arrows clearly showed the intention: they reached the Beirut–Damascus road [which is far beyond 40 km.].' Eytan, in fact, on 6 June ordered certain army units to land (by sea) north of Sidon, namely, beyond the 40 km. limit. And on the same day, he issued COS Command No. 1 which reads:

The IDF will attack the [Palestinian] terrorists and destroy their infrastructure . . . will be on call to join the Christians in *northern Lebanon* and will be on call to *destroy the Syrian army in Lebanon*.[34] [my italics]

Indeed, how could the army attack the PLO bases and headquarters in the eastern and central section of Lebanon (and in Beirut) and also reach the Beirut–Damascus road, without clashing with the Syrian forces, which were deployed in those sections and around Beirut? Obviously, the Sharon–Eytan war aims were not only to destroy the PLO infrastructure in the whole of Lebanon and establish a pro-Israeli Lebanese government, but inevitably also to defeat the Syrian forces and push them out of the country.[35] Whether or not the Israeli cabinet approved Sharon's design in advance, or *post factum* (which is more likely), by advancing along certain strategic routes towards Syrian positions, the Israeli army provoked the Syrian forces to open fire first. As General Ben-Gal, the Israeli commander in the Jezzin region, remarked after the war: 'From a legalistic point of view, the Syrians fired the first shell, but did they have any choice?'[36]

In fact, the Syrian leaders, although well aware of Israeli military preparations, were surprised by the magnitude and timing of the operation, while their forces in Lebanon were neither sufficient nor prepared to face the massive Israeli offensive. Until 8 June the Syrians forces were careful not to provoke Israeli attacks on their positions and only engaged the advancing forces with sporadic fire. The Syrians were even ready to put up with the destruction of the PLO bases in southern Lebanon; but when the Israeli army advanced towards the strategic town of Jezzin, the Syrian army launched an abortive counter-attack and also introduced more ground-to-air missile batteries into the area. Simultaneously, on 7 and 8 June, there were two attempts by the American envoy Philip Habib and by Begin, via Washington, to reach an Israeli–Syrian settlement in Lebanon, but these were apparently foiled by Sharon. On his orders, on 9 and 10 June massive air and ground attacks were launched on the Syrian missile batteries and on an armoured division in the Biqaʿ valley—aiming at reaching the Beirut–Damascus highway. But, despite the Syrians' heavy losses in armour and aircraft, the Israeli army was unable to reach the Beirut–Damascus highway and other strategic positions in the Biqaʿ valley until 11 June. This was because of the following main factors: (*a*) the outnumbered Syrian forces, notably the air force and the commando units, fought well and managed to hold up the advance until the cease-fire on 11 June; (*b*) diplomatic pressure by the United States, culminating in the cease-fire, also prevented the army, which made certain grave mistakes, from reaching the Beirut–Damascus road.[37]

Yet, despite the American-imposed cease-fire and growing domestic criticism in Israel, Sharon and Eytan, without Begin's pre-approval,[38] on 12 June ordered the army to move towards the western section of the Beirut–Damascus road and to besiege the Lebanese capital. The military and diplomatic campaign over Beirut, which involved further Israeli–Syrian fighting, as well as heavy Israeli bombardments, resulted by mid-August 1981 in an Israeli victory and Syrian and PLO defeat. According to an American-sponsored agreement, which had been co-ordinated with Syria and Saudi Arabia, all Syrian troops and PLO fighters evacuated Beirut, and on 23 August Bashir Jumayyil, the pro-Israeli Maronite leader, was elected as the new Lebanese president.

Asad's Predicament and Recovery

The partial evacuation of the Syrian troops from Lebanon and the election of Bashir Jumayyil, the anti-Syrian leader, as president were the culmination of the humiliating military and political defeat of Syria at the hands of Israel. Indeed, despite its courageous defensive fight, the Syrian army suffered severe losses: 400 soldiers killed, 1,400 wounded, 145 tanks destroyed, and 100 planes shot down.[39] None of the neighbouring Arab countries sent any troops to help the Syrian army in Lebanon, which officially also embodied the 'Arab deterrence force', approved by inter-Arab decisions in October 1976. Nor did Moscow extend military assistance to Damascus, despite the Soviet–Syrian friendship and co-operation treaty of October 1980. In addition, Washington again demonstrated its anti-Syrian policy, and not only by backing Israel's demands to oust the Syrian forces from Beirut: on 1 September 1982, a day after the final departure of the Syrian army from Beirut, the United States president announced his new diplomatic initiative regarding the establishment of Palestinian self-rule in the West Bank and Gaza in conjunction with the Jordanian kingdom. This plan, which was designed to bring Jordan and the Palestinians (not the PLO) into the Arab–Israeli peace process, did not mention the Golan issue at all and threatened to further isolate Syria in the region.[40]

In any case, Syria's inter-Arab isolation had increased since the early 1980s, when in late 1981 it rejected the peace plan of Saudi Crown Prince (later King) Fahd. And although later, in September 1982, it accepted a new version of that plan,[41] Syria's relations with Saudi Arabia and other Arab states significantly worsened because of its support of Iran in its war with Iraq (see below).

Simultaneously, a renewed, grave conflict developed between Syria and the PLO, mainly concerning three issues. First, in 1981 the PLO accused Syria of fresh attempts to control its actions in Lebanon. And in 1982, despite the Syrian–PLO joint strategic agreement (of April 1982) vis-à-vis the imminent Israeli attack, the PLO accused Syria of deliberately failing to help the Palestinian forces against the Israeli offensive in south Lebanon and in Beirut. Secondly, in contrast, Syria accused the PLO of failing to co-ordinate its military and political actions with it during the Lebanese war, and of trying to join the peace process with Israel in 1981 and 1982. Thirdly, Damascus also accused the PLO of assisting the militant Muslim opposition in Syria (and in Tripoli, Lebanon) in its violent struggle to topple Asad's regime.[42]

Indeed, alongside his acute regional-external predicament, since 1977 Asad had faced growing domestic Muslim-led popular unrest (partly because of his initial alliance with the Lebanese Christians). During 1981 and early 1982 this evolved into an open militant Islamic rebellion against the Ba'th regime. In reaction, in early February 1982 the Syrian army bombarded the rebellion's centre in Hama, destroying large parts of the city and killing between 10,000 and 30,000 inhabitants.[43]

Consequently, by late 1982, Asad's regime was not only deeply hated and seen as illegitimate by many Syrians, but it was also ostracized by other Arab peoples and regimes, as was reflected, with a certain bias, in a *fatwa* (religious ruling) which was issued in 1983 by a group of Iraqi *ulama* (religious leaders):

Hafiz al-Asad, the oppressive tyrant of Syria, bears the blame for the present fate of the [Arab] nation . . . particularly the fate of the Palestinian movement . . . because of the series of crimes he has committed against the Syrian people, the Palestinian people and the Iraqi people . . . in Tall Zaʿatar, in Hama, in Tadmur prison [in Syria] . . . in the Biqaʿ [and because of] the material, moral and military aid he extends to the Khomeini regime.[44]

This juncture indeed constituted the worst setback in Asad's political life as both his domestic and his regional policies painfully collapsed, while Israel posed a serious threat to Syria's security. On the one hand, the Golan had been formally annexed and the Israeli army was deployed some thirty miles south of Damascus; and on the other, Lebanon practically became Israel's satellite, while Israeli troops were stationed some twenty-five miles west of Damascus.

Asad, however, did not give up, and tenaciously fought back on all fronts, notably against the grave Israeli challenge. Indeed, as we shall see later on, he subsequently stepped up his efforts to reach a strategic balance with Israel, but managed to achieve only part of his goal. In Lebanon, however, Asad's struggle against Israel's presence and influence was more successful: by means of a guerrilla/terrorist war of attrition, carried out by proxies, he brought about both the withdrawal of the Israeli army and the establishment of a Syrian protectorate over the country.

To begin with, on 14 September 1982 Bashir Jumayyil, the pro-Israeli ('Zionist agent') president of Lebanon, was assassinated, apparently by a Syrian agent.[45] In reaction, the Israeli army occupied the western section of Beirut, while the Maronite 'Lebanese Forces' entered the Sabra and Shatila Palestinian refugee camps near Beirut, and massacred the inhabitants, under the umbrella of Israel's military presence.[46] This act aroused sharp criticism against the Israeli government, both at home and in the world, and brought about the withdrawal of the army from Beirut. Together with Bashir's assassination, this withdrawal contributed to the undermining of Israel's strategic position in Lebanon. True, Bashir's successor and brother, Amin Jumayyil (who was by no means pro-Israeli), signed a political agreement with Israel on 17 May 1983, with United States encouragement, despite Syrian intimidation (Asad said of the agreement: 'worse than the Camp David accords . . . part of the American–Zionist plan to dominate [the region]'). This agreement formally ended the state of war between the two countries and provided various security arrangements for Israel in southern Lebanon. But it was not a peace treaty nor did it entail diplomatic relations between Beirut and Jerusalem; and it also committed Israel to withdraw its forces from Lebanon within a few months.[47]

In any event, Israel decided in early September 1983 unilaterally to withdraw its forces south to the River Awali, regardless of the May 1983 agreement. This, because the army had been caught since May 1983 in cross-fire fighting in the Shuf mountains between Lebanese Maronite forces and the Syrian-backed Druze militias. At the same time the Israeli government, with Moshe Arens replacing Sharon as defence minister, had become disillusioned with Amin Jumayyil's rule, which was neither pro-Israel nor stable.

To be sure, Syria not only supported the Druze militia against its Maronite enemy, but also employed several other Lebanese and Palestinian organizations in a systematic endeavour to drive the Israeli forces, as well as American and French units (of the multilateral force) out of Lebanon, and reimpose Syrian control in Beirut. Thus, from April to September 1983, the pro-Iranian Lebanese-Shi'i militant organization Hizballa committed, apparently under Syrian direction, a series of suicide assaults against Israeli, American, and French targets: on 18 April the American Embassy in Beirut was attacked by a car bomb, killing 63 people; and on 23 October, American and French barracks were destroyed by Shi'i suicide squads, claiming the lives of 241 American and 58 French soldiers. Likewise, on 4 November 1983, a similar assault was carried out against the Israeli military headquarters in Tyre, killing 28 people.[48]

Consequently, in February 1984, while the Americans and French pulled their units out of Beirut, Amin Jumayyil abrogated the May 1983 agreement with Israel, thus accepting Syrian orders. Damascus, however, was not content only with the recovery of its predominance in Beirut, subsequently also acknowledged by Washington. Damascus (and Teheran) continued to use the various militant organizations in Lebanon (including now also the moderate Shi'i Amal movement) in order to oust the Israeli army also from southern Lebanon. Thus, following a tough guerrilla campaign which claimed the lives of many Israeli soldiers (and heavy material losses), the Israeli government, now under Shimon Peres, decided early in 1985 to evacuate the army from Lebanon, without reaching any political or security agreements with Beirut. (Israel, however, unilaterally created a six-mile wide security belt along the border, under the control of the SLA.)[49]

Asad was now in a position to snub Begin—who had already resigned as prime minister in September 1983 (apparently having been deeply disturbed over the heavy loss in lives incurred during the Lebanese war). In early May 1985 the Syrian leader stated, *inter alia*:

Israel assumed that the invasion [of Lebanon] would become a rural journey . . . which would result in turning Lebanon into an Israeli protectorate. . . . We all remember Begin's words on the invasion day, telling the Israelis: your security is safeguarded for forty years. Yet, he did not succeed in assuring their security even for forty days.[50]

It can thus be concluded that the Israeli–Syrian struggle over Lebanon which started in 1978, following Begin's coming to power, ended in 1985 in a painful setback for Israel and a substantial advantage to Syria. In addition to heavy casualties in lives and economic assets, Israel lost its political influence in most of Lebanon, while contributing to the anti-Israeli radicalization of the Shi'i community in the south. Even the PLO infrastructure in that region, which had been destroyed in 1982, was partly reconstructed after 1984, while in the West Bank and Gaza the seeds of the Palestinian *intifada* ('uprising', starting in late 1987) had been sown, owing also to the 1982 war. Finally, the Lebanon war, in addition to affecting Israel's image in the international community and its relations with Egypt, caused a grave split and an ongoing trauma within Israeli-Jewish society.

In contrast, Syria managed not only to force the Israeli army out of Lebanon, by proxy, while redeploying its own forces and missile batteries in strategic locations, but, by means of political manipulation, assassination, and intimidation, it also gradually extended its influence over most Lebanese power centres, and ultimately formalized its indirect domination in Lebanon through the 1989 Ta'if agreement (see below).

However, Asad's success in turning Lebanon into a Syrian satellite state constituted the only single gain in his ambitious regional and anti-Israeli Greater Syria strategic design. Indeed, after failing by the late 1970s to keep Jordan in Syria's strategic orbit, in 1982–3 Asad totally alienated the PLO leader, Yasir Arafat, when the Syrian leader did not even attempt to defend the PLO bases in Lebanon, created a split in the Fath organization, and deported Arafat from Damascus. And although Damascus continued to control several rejectionist Palestinian organizations, it largely lost its influence over the mainstream Palestinian movement in Lebanon, Jordan, the West Bank, and the Gaza Strip. In sum, the Syrian–Israeli struggle over Lebanon also contributed to enhancing

Asad's strategic design as conceived since the late 1970s, namely: the doctrine of strategic balance with Israel and the strategic alliance with revolutionary Iran, both intended to strengthen Syria's regional position and counterbalance Israel's strategic advantage. Thus, the initial Israeli victory in the Lebanon war motivated Damascus to increase its military power substantially in order to reach military parity with Israel. Damascus also strengthened its relations with Teheran in a joint effort to employ the Lebanese Shi'i organizations in guerrilla warfare against Israeli troops in Lebanon. Yet, as we shall see later on, Asad's new strategic designs largely failed to materialize by 1988, causing him thereafter to seek a political settlement with Israel.

NOTES

1. Cf. A. I. Dawisha, *Syria and the Lebanese Crisis* (London, 1980), 38; Ma'oz, *Asad*, 123–4; Mustafa Tlas, *al-Ghazu al-isra'ili li-Lubnan* (Damascus, 1983), 199.
2. Details and sources, in Ma'oz, *Asad*, 119 ff.; Ma'oz and Yaniv, 'On a Short Leash', 191 ff.
3. See e.g. *al-Nahar*, 17 Mar. 1971; *al-Sayyad*, 13 Dec. 1973; *Newsweek*, 1 June 1974. See also Shemesh, *Entity*, 213 ff.
4. Asad's interviews with *al-Nahar*, 17 Mar. 1971 and with *al-Anwar*, 10 Aug. 1972. See also R. Avi-Ran, *Syrian Involvement in Lebanon, 1975–1985* (Hebrew; Tel Aviv, 1986), 15 ff.; Dawisha, *Syria*, 38.
5. See respectively Damascus Radio, 6 Jan. 1975; Beirut Radio, 3 and 5 Jan. 1975; *al-Yawm* (Lebanon), 5 Jan. 1975; K. Junblatt, *I Speak for Lebanon* (London, 1982), 11.
6. For elaborate accounts of the background and development of the Lebanese civil war, see Junblatt, *I Speak*; K. Salibi, *Crossroads to Civil War* (Delmar, NY, 1976); W. al-Khalidi, *Conflict and Violence in Lebanon* (Cambridge, Mass., 1979); M. Deeb, *The Lebanese Civil War* (New York, 1980); I. Rabinovich, *The War for Lebanon* (Ithaca, NY, 1984); I. Harik, *Lebanon: Anatomy of Conflict* (Hanover, Pa., 1981); Dawisha, *Syria*; Avi-Ran, *Syrian Involvement*; Y. Evron, *War and the Intervention in Lebanon: The Israeli–Syrian Deterrence Dialogue* (Baltimore, 1987); M. Hudson, 'The Palestinian Factor in the Lebanese Civil War', *Middle East Journal*, 32 (1978), 261–78.
7. Junblatt, *I Speak*, 81–2, 86.
8. Ma'oz, *Asad*, 127–8, citing Asad's speech of 20 July 1976; cf. Dawisha, *Syria*, 103–6.

9. K. Paqraduni, *al-Salam al-mafqud* (Beirut, 1984), 19, 36. Asad's speech, Damascus Radio, 20 July 1976; *Jaysh al-Sh'ab*, 15 June 1976.

10. Details in Dawisha, *Syria*, 99 ff.; 135 ff.; Avi-Ran, *Syrian Involvement*, 31 ff. Cf. *Jaysh al-Sh'ab* 2 Sept. 1976.

11. See Ma'oz, *Asad*, 129, 114 and n.

12. *Al-Muharrar* (Lebanon), 16 Aug. 1976; Seale, *Asad*, 284; Dawisha, *Syria*, 138.

13. Baghdad Radio, 18 Mar. 1977; Seale, *Asad*, 288–9; Rabinovich, *The War*, 77; Ma'oz, *Asad*, 128.

14. Cf. Asad's interview, *Jaysh al-Sh'ab*, 16 Nov. 1976 and 26 Oct. 1977; Paqraduni, *al-Salam*, 213; cf. *al-Ba'th*, 30 July 1976.

15. See respectively Asad's speech, Damascus Radio, 20 July 1976, cited in Ma'oz, *Asad*, 127; interview with Khaddam in *al-Ray al-'Am* (Kuwait), 7 Jan. 1976; cf. Seale, *Asad*, 278; and Avi-Ran, *Syrian Involvement*, 62–3.

16. Ma'oz, *Asad*, 137; Avi-Ran, *Syrian Involvement*, 63; cf. Seale, *Asad*, 278–9.

17. Author's interview (29 Sept. 1993) with Gideon Rafael, former director-general of Israel's Ministry of Foreign Affairs, who carried the messages from Hussein to Rabin via Foreign Minister Allon.

18. Rabin, *Pinkas Sherut*, 502–3; cf. Avi-Ran, *Syrian Involvement*, 66–7; Schiff, *Peace*, 24–6.

19. Avi-Ran, *Syrian Involvement*, 67; Schiff, *Peace*, 26. Cf. Rabin, *Pinkas Sherut*, 503; Ma'oz, *Asad*, 138.

20. *Al-Nahar al-arabi* (Paris), 10 July 1977; *Time*, 22 Nov. 1976; Avi-Ran, *Syrian Involvement*, 90 ff.; Dawisha, *Syria*, 135 ff.

21. Cf. A. Na'or, *Begin*, 240–1.

22. Rabin, *Pinkas Sherut*, 503; R. Eytan, *Story*, 154.

23. Na'or, *Begin*, 245–6; Avi-Ran, *Syrian Involvement*, 121–2; E. Weizman, *The Battle for Peace* (Hebrew; Tel Aviv, 1982), 256–7.

24. Avi-Ran, *Syrian Involvement*, 111–12; Na'or, *Begin*, 247; Eytan, *Story*, 189–90; Sachar, *A History*, 169; Dawisha, *Syria*, 191–3.

25. Avi-Ran, *Syrian Involvement*, 133–4, 139–40; cf. Na'or, *Begin*, 248, 255; Rabinovich, *The War*, 114 ff.; Ma'oz, *Asad*, 144.

26. Dawisha, *Syria*, 192; Avi-Ran, *Syrian Involvement*, 137–8.

27. Eytan, *Story*, p. 189; Na'or, *Begin*, 239–40, 246–9; Avi-Ran, *Syrian Involvement*, 141–2.

28. Na'or, *Begin*, 225, 249–50; Avi-Ran, *Syrian Involvement*, 142.

29. Na'or, *Begin*, 232–3; Sachar, *A History*, 149–50.

30. Avi-Ran, *Syrian Involvement*, 148–9; Na'or, *Begin*, 265–8; Sachar, *A History*, 172; Ma'ariv, 25 June 1982. For another version see Seale, *Asad*, 371 ff.

31. For various versions see Sachar, *A History*, 174; Seale, *Asad*, 375–6; Rabinovich, *The War*, 123 ff; Na'or, *Begin*, 267 ff.; R. Tanter, *Who's at the Helm: Lessons of Lebanon* (Boulder, Colo., 1990), 111–13.

32. Na'or, *Begin*, 271 ff.; Avi-Ran, *Syrian Involvement*, 150 ff.; Rabinovich, *The War*, 132 ff. For more accounts and documents on the 1982 war, see R. Avi-

Ran, *The War of Lebanon: Arab Documents* (Hebrew; Tel Aviv, 1987); Paqraduni, *al-Salam*; Tlas, *al-Ghazu*; Z. Schiff and E. Ya'ari, *Milhemet Sholal* (Hebrew; Jerusalem, 1984); Tanter, *Who's at the Helm*, 107 ff.

33. Na'or, *Begin*, 283, 287, 292; Rabinovich, *The War*, 121–2; Seale, *Asad*, 379.

34. Eytan, *Story*, 210–11; Na'or, *Begin*, 287–9.

35. Na'or, *Begin*, 267, 271, 284–5, 291; Avi-Ran, *Syrian Involvement*, 151–2; Rabinovich, *The War*, 122, 137; Seale, *Asad*, 380; Ma'oz, *Asad*, 166.

36. Cited in Na'or, *Begin*, 295.

37. For details see Tlas, *al-Ghazu*; Schiff and Ya'ari, *Milhemet Sholal*; A. Yaniv and R. Lieber, 'Personal Whim or Strategic Imperative', *International Security*, 8/2 (1983), 117–42.

38. Na'or, *Begin*, 307–309, 312; Avi-Ran, *Syrian Involvement*, 164–5.

39. Avi-Ran, *Syrian Involvement*, 162; Schiff and Ya'ari, *Milhemet Sholal*, 204.

40. Seale, *Asad*, 402 ff.; Drysdale and Hinnebush, *Syria*, 193; Ma'oz, *Asad*, 167–8.

41. Drysdale and Hinnebush, *Syria*, 202; Seale, *Asad*, 403.

42. Ma'oz, *Asad*, 167–8.

43. *Egyptian Gazette*, 23 Mar. 1982; *Observer*, 4 May 1982; *al-Dustur* (London), 19 Mar. 1983. For a comprehensive account of the Hama massacre, see Ma'oz, *Asad*, 159 ff.; see also Seale, *Asad*, 323 ff.

44. Cited in Ma'oz, *Asad*, 168 and sources.

45. Avi-Ran, *Syrian Involvement*, 175 and sources; Seale, *Asad*, 391–2.

46. On the massacre of Sabra and Shatila and its consequences, see Seale, *Asad*, 392–3; Rabinovich, *The War*, 144–6; Sachar, *A History*, 195 ff.

47. Damascus Radio, 1 Aug. 1983. On the Israel–Lebanon agreement, see also Avi-Ran, *Syrian Involvement*, 186–7; Seale, *Asad*, 408–10; Ma'oz, *Asad*, 169.

48. Avi-Ran, *Syrian Involvement*, 210; Ma'oz, *Asad*, 173.

49. On Israeli losses and the decision to pull out of Lebanon, see *Jerusalem Post*, 1 Apr. 1984; *Yediot Ahronot*, 31 May 1985; Avi-Ran, *Syrian Involvement*, 211–15; Seale, *Asad*, 410 ff.; cf. Eytan, *Story*, 331–2; Na'or, *Begin*, 314–15.

50. *Al-Ba'th*, 5 May 1985, quoted in Avi-Ran, *Syrian Involvement*, 224.

9

Asad's Strategic Design

THE EVOLUTION OF ASAD'S REGIONAL STRATEGY

Since coming to power, Asad has been gripped, perhaps obsessed, by the need to achieve a balance of power with Israel. Apart from his declared ideological commitment to fight and destroy the 'Zionist entity', Asad's practical political attitude towards Israel has largely derived from his strategic thinking. Considering the Jewish state as a predominant regional power, Asad has sought to counterbalance Israel's superiority as a pre-requisite for either a military confrontation or a political settlement between the Arab world/Syria and Israel. As he stated in 1981: 'If the military balance is needed to liberate the land and repel the aggression, it is equally needed to implement a just peace ... peace could never be established between the strong and the weak.'[1]

Yet although assigning a major role to his country in the military and political struggle with Israel, Asad, until the late 1970s, regarded the power balance with Israel in pan-Arab terms. Initially he visualized the Cairo–Damascus axis as the core of Arab military and political power, around which other Arab nations (notably Saudi Arabia) should mobilize their economic resources, and their diplomatic support. And despite the Arab military defeat in the 1973 war, perhaps because of it, Asad continued to adhere to his concept; during the 1974 Rabat summit he defined it for the first time as a 'strategic balance' (*al-tawazun al-istratiji*) between the Arab states and Israel.[2]

Asad indeed continued to consider Egypt as a corner-stone of the Arab equation; and even though Sadat signed another separate agreement with Israel (Sinai 2 of September 1975), for a few more years Asad endeavoured to form a joint all-Arab front, including Egypt, in order to negotiate a political settlement with Israel from a position of strength. Simul-taneously, as discussed above, Syria sought to create alternative strategic alliances with Iraq, Jordan, Lebanon, and the PLO, but by 1979 it still remained regionally isolated and threatened. The March 1979 peace agreement between Sadat and Begin finally disengaged Egypt from the

Arab–Israeli dispute and exposed Syria to the menace of a right-wing Israeli government. This government, as we know, threatened Syria from the west, through Lebanon, since 1978, and from the south, by continuing to occupy and settle the Golan Heights. On the eastern border of Syria, Iraq became a serious challenge in 1979, extending its influence also in Jordan on the south-eastern Syrian border. And in 1980 Iraq, still a potential Syrian ally against Israel, started a devastating war against Iran, thus, in Asad's words, 'departing from the Arab–Israeli struggle for not a short period'.[3] Consequently, from 1979 Asad for the first time developed a new regional strategy seeking primarily to enable Syria, independently of other Arab countries, to encounter the Israeli threat, and, with Iran's help, also to topple Saddam Hussein and bring Iraq back to a new anti-Israeli alliance.

At the core of Asad's strategic doctrine was first the need to gain 'military parity' with Israel. In quantitative terms this required a substantial increase in Syrian troops and divisions. For vis-à-vis Israel's 158,000-strong regular army plus 450,000 reservists in 1978, Syria, according to Syrian military analysts, had only 227,000 troops in regular service and 212,000 reservists.[4] But in Asad's view Syria, with its great human potential (about 10 million in 1980), could enlist 900,000 to 1 million soldiers, whereas Israel, with barely 4 million people, had already reached the limits of its army growth.[5] Regarding the qualitative aspects of the military balance, Syria sought to obtain more advanced Soviet weapons and improve training with the help of Soviet experts. To these ends, in October 1980 Damascus, for the first time, signed a treaty of 'Friendship and Co-operation' with Moscow, which in Asad's words was 'an important factor in securing the strategic balance between us and Israel'.[6]

Yet in Asad's view that strategic balance ought to be based not only on military power, but also on a stable political regime, a cohesive society, and a sound economy. As he remarked on several occasions: 'In the strategic balance there are many elements: political, military, cultural, and economic. . . . Syria must be strong, of course, and its strength is based on the power and firmness of its people.'[7]

The goals of the strategic balance were as follows: first, to deter the Israeli army from attacking Syria and to defend it against an Israeli assault or, in Asad's words, 'We bought these arms in order to use them in defending ourselves . . . They [the Israelis] must remember that Israeli towns are within our artillery range, and most Israeli towns are within the range of other weapons of ours.'[8] Secondly, and equally important, was the aim of recovering the occupied Golan Heights and liberating the

Palestinian territories, at least those which had been occupied in 1967, that is, the West Bank and Gaza. Apparently this aim could be achieved either by war or through a political settlement. But while Asad would not rule out a political settlement with Israel, albeit on his terms, he did not emphasize this option within his new doctrine of strategic balance. What he did stress was the military option in the struggle against Israel. For example, when asked late in 1982, 'Is it possible to fight Israel and defeat it?' Asad answered: 'Why not? . . . affairs of nations are measured in long range. There are many examples: the Vietnamese, the Algerians . . . we should not despair because for several years we have not defeated Israel, which is equipped with American arms. Certainly we shall achieve a victory.' Similarly, in his address to the newly elected Syrian People's Assembly on 27 February 1986, Asad said:

If the Israelis work to put the Golan within their borders, we will work to put the Golan in the middle of Syria and not on its borders . . . The opening of fire by Israeli security men in your villages . . . will only increase our hatred for the historical enemy and augment our determination to fight it through the end. History will record that the Golan was the climax of the disaster for the Israelis.[9]

In an attempt to understand Asad's motives for emphasizing the military-combatant line, it can be assumed that by the late 1970s and early 1980s he could not visualize that the Golan could be recovered by political-diplomatic means alone. For, following its separate peace treaty with Egypt, Israel enjoyed the increasing support of the United States and became more and more belligerent towards Syria. In 1981 Israel and the United States signed a strategic co-operation agreement which, in Asad's words, 'directly puts US forces . . . against us . . . and on the side of the Israeli forces'.[10] A few months later Israel formally annexed the Golan, and in mid-1982 it invaded Lebanon and attacked the Syrian army there without previous Syrian provocation.

These events, followed by the establishment of a pro-Israeli, anti-Syrian Lebanese government, further threatened the strategic-security interests of Damascus, and led Asad to enhance his military build-up. Indeed, three new armoured divisions were created in the Syrian army after 1982, bringing it by 1985–6 to about half a million regular soldiers, with ten combat divisions. This huge army received large quantities of modern Soviet arms, including T-72 tanks, MiG-29 planes, SS-21 ground-to-ground missiles, etc. Some 6,000 Soviet experts helped in training and modernizing the Syrian forces.[11]

But although by 1985–6 Syria had probably reached military parity with Israel in quantitative terms, and was thus capable of effectively defending itself and of deterring the Israeli army from launching an offensive against Damascus, it was nevertheless far from achieving a strategic balance with Israel or being capable of launching a successful all-out attack against the Jewish state. The only viable military option that Syria had at that juncture was a war of attrition against Israel, similar to that of the post-1973 period. And, in fact, during 1983 and 1984, Damascus, aware of Israel's high sensitivity to losses in life,[12] carried out a proxy guerrilla war against the Israeli troops in Lebanon, leading to the withdrawal of the Israeli army in 1985.

This type of war, accompanied by terrorist attacks on Israeli (and also American and Jordanian) targets in Europe, was aimed at damaging Israel's morale and social fabric, while it boosted Syria's prestige and encouraged it to work towards reaching full strategic parity with Israel. To be sure, Asad considered his doctrine of strategic balance as a long-term design, and possibly believed that it could be realized and bear fruit in the foreseeable future. As he said in mid-1983: 'Time is on our side . . . the just solution for the big problem in this region will be achieved only when a strategic balance between us and Israel is reached.'[13]

Asad indeed stressed that his design was not limited to Syria's confrontation with Israel, but included the all-Arab/regional struggle against Israel, led by Syria, or in his own words (in 1983):

Israel does not want Syria alone but the entire Arab homeland. The Israelis want Jordan because it is part of Palestine. . . . The Israelis want Iraq because their promised land should extend from the Nile to the Euphrates. . . . Israel also wants the Arabian peninsula . . . Egypt . . . Lebanon and Sudan . . . [therefore] if Syria collapses, the entire region will follow. We see the danger as it is, but some of our brothers [Arab leaders] do not see that as we do. . . . Syria is the only hope of the Arab world.[14]

Such a statement certainly reflected Asad's ideological rather than pragmatic position, and it was aimed at restoring his domestic legitimacy as a pan-Arab leader, following his brutal repression of the 1982 Muslim rebellion in Hama, as well as his severe setback in Lebanon. Moreover, at that juncture, Asad greatly needed to reinforce his pan-Arab image for yet another reason: to explain and justify his alliance with Persian-Islamic Iran in its war with Arab-Baʿthist Iraq. This extraordinary alliance, tenaciously pursued by Asad against many odds, indeed became an important component of his new regional strategy, notably vis-à-vis the two hostile major powers—Israel and Iraq.

SYRIA AND IRAN: THE UNHOLY ALLIANCE

During 1975–6, Asad had already endeavoured to improve Syria's relations with the Iranian monarchy under the Shah, in an attempt both to undermine the March 1975 Algiers treaty between Iran and Iraq and the close strategic relations between Iran and Israel.[15] But, having failed to change the Shah's position, in 1977 Asad began to support the Iranian Shi'i Islamic opposition, calling also on the assistance of the Shi'i Lebanese leader, Imam Musa al-Sadr. While offering Imam Khomeini, the leader of the Iranian opposition, refuge in Syria, Damascus provided military training and arms to Iranian rebels in guerrilla bases in Lebanon and Syria.[16]

Damascus was the first Arab country to hail the new Islamic revolutionary regime in Teheran in 1979, while Asad, who was promptly invited to visit Iran, sent Vice-President Khaddam in August of that year in order to establish new strategic relations with the Islamic regime.[17] Initially and essentially, the Damascus regime regarded revolutionary Iran as highly significant in Syria's doctrine of strategic parity with Israel, especially after the Egyptian 'defection' from the conflict. In Asad's words:

This revolution introduced important changes in the strategic balance . . . from regional and global points of view [it] supports the Arabs, without hesitation, in action for the sake of liberating our occupied lands . . . How can we be allowed to lose a great achievement and lose a country like Iran of the Islamic revolution . . . with all its human, military, and economic potential?[18]

Indeed, in a joint Syrian–Iranian communiqué signed in Damascus on 27 April 1980, both parties undertook to act in an atmosphere of friendship and mutual understanding, and stressed the need to oppose the Camp David accords and strengthen the united front 'against Israel, the Egyptian regime and the US'.[19]

But the Iraqi invasion of Iran in September 1980, which started the long and devastating Gulf War, caused a serious setback to the new Syrian strategy. Asad and other Syrian leaders harshly denounced the Iraqi invasion and depicted it as 'the wrong war':

. . . waste of the Arab potential . . . in the confrontation against Israel . . . [From the beginning we] believed that this invasion was expected, planned to create a new enemy for the Arab nations, an enemy that was placed on the same level as Israel. This situation would make us distribute our forces between the front of the real enemy . . . and the Iranian front.[20]

Consequently, for some eight years Damascus extended military, strategic and diplomatic support to Teheran in its war against Baghdad, anticipating the defeat of the hostile Iraqi regime (but not the state) as: 'An Iranian victory in the Gulf war will allow for the establishment of the three states—Iran, Iraq, Syria—as the principal front against the Zionist state of Israel.'[21]

Yet, short of this grand design, Syria expected that an Iranian victory would weaken, if not topple, Saddam Hussein's regime and diminish its potential to dominate the Fertile Crescent. And, in addition to enjoying a generous supply of Iranian oil, Damascus used its alliance with Teheran in order: (*a*) to influence Saudi Arabia and other Arab oil states to further their financial contributions to Syria; (*b*) to legitimize Asad's Ba'thist–Alawi rule in Syria; and (*c*) to mobilize the support of the Shi'i community in Lebanon and employ its armed organization against the Israeli military presence in southern Lebanon.

But, as things turned out, only the last goal was successfully realized: using the Hizballa as well as other Lebanese and Palestinian guerrilla/terrorist groups in a war of attrition against Israeli troops in Lebanon, Damascus caused the Israeli withdrawal in 1985. This was the only significant achievement of the Damascus alliance with Teheran, and indeed of Syria's confrontation with Israel in Lebanon. Otherwise, this strategic alliance proved to be a liability rather than an asset to Syria's regional position and domestic situation. For, in addition to its failure to legitimize Asad's rule in the eyes of the conservative Syrian Muslims, the association with revolutionary Iran deepened Baghdad's hostility towards Damascus, and intensified Syria's isolation in the Arab East. Not only did all the Arab states refrain from helping Syria during the 1982 Israeli invasion of Lebanon; many of them, notably Jordan and the Arab Gulf states, remained alienated from Damascus, and continued to support Iraq. Indeed, despite Syrian objections, the November 1987 Arab summit in Amman expressed solidarity with Iraq in its war with Iran; and, for the first time since Egypt's expulsion from the Arab League following its peace treaty with Israel, individual Arab states were permitted to restore full diplomatic relations with Cairo.

It would seem, then, that these resolutions not only reflected criticism of Syria's support for Iran, but also weakened the all-Arab antagonism towards Israel, paving the way for the readmittance of Egypt to the Arab League in May 1989, and thus indirectly acknowledging Egypt's peace with Israel and signalling that the Iranian menace was far more dangerous and devastating than the Israeli one. This indication may also be seen in the initial refusal of the Arab summit to discuss essentially the Arab–Israeli conflict, not the Iraqi–Iranian war.

Nevertheless, the 1987 Amman summit, unwilling to alienate Syria, adopted a resolution expressing collective Arab solidarity and committing the entire Arab potential to achieving strategic parity [for Syria] with Israel. It also pledged $2.25 billion of Arab money to Syria, partly to be paid immediately and mostly to be delivered in instalments, contingent upon Syria's implementation of the summit resolutions.[22]

THE FATE OF SYRIA'S STRATEGIC BALANCE WITH ISRAEL

At that juncture, however, Damascus was still far from reaching a strategic balance with Israel, not only because of the shift of the Arab potential towards the Gulf War. Syria's major global ally and principal supplier of weapons, the USSR, had dramatically changed its policy towards the Syrian quest for strategic balance with Israel. During Asad's visit to Moscow in April 1987 the new Soviet leader, Gorbachev, told him bluntly that 'the reliance on military force in settling the Arab–Israeli conflict has completely lost its credibility.' Gorbachev also told Asad that the USSR would no longer support Syria's doctrine of strategic parity with Israel, and urged him to seek a political settlement to the conflict, with Soviet help.[23] And, if this serious setback was not sufficient to affect Syria's military potential, the end of the Iran–Iraq war in summer 1988, to Baghdad's advantage, further weakened Syria's strategic posture vis-à-vis Israel.

True, by 1986 Damascus had succeeded in achieving military parity with Israel in quantitative terms, as discussed above. But qualitatively the Syrian army was still far from matching the Israeli army, notably its air force. As far as strategic weapons were involved, the long-range missiles and chemical warheads acquired by Syria could by no means match Israel's nuclear arsenal and strategic missiles.[24] Furthermore, Syria's huge military build-up (absorbing some 65 per cent of the yearly budget) contributed, along with other factors, to a severe economic crisis in 1986 and afterwards. This in turn forced Damascus to make major cuts in defence spending, including the reduction of the army's size.[25]

Nevertheless, despite all these difficulties, Asad and other Syrian leaders and analysts have not ceased to promote their doctrine of strategic balance with Israel[26] (while the Syrian army has continued to absorb new weapons and to modernize). In their analysis of this doctrine, Syrian leaders and writers again and again pointed out the importance of the

social, economic, political, cultural, scientific, and psychological compo-
nents, in addition to military strength, in Syria's quest for strategic balance with Israel. However, they would now also stress other crucial
prerequisites for reaching this strategic balance: (*a*) Arab solidarity or
unity and the mobilization of the all-Arab potential—human, material and
military—against the enemy; and (*b*) strategic alliances with other powers—notably the USSR—to obtain military, political, economic, and
moral support vis-à-vis Israel's strategic alliance with the United States,
and its nuclear capability.

In an attempt to evaluate Syria's new position, it may be suggested that
the Syrian leaders were now endeavouring to justify (but not to admit)
their inability to reach strategic balance with Israel by the absence of
suitable inter-Arab and global conditions. First, as we know, the Arab
world was divided over the Iran–Iraq war, and neglected its conflict with
Israel. Egypt continued its peace with the 'Zionist enemy', and even the
PLO started to seek a political settlement with Israel. Secondly, the Soviet
Union reduced its military aid to Syria, demanded hard currency for arms
deliveries, and urged Asad to abandon his doctrine of strategic balance
with Israel.

Consequently, while indicating the serious difficulties in reaching this
strategic balance, Asad emphasized in his speeches that the struggle
against Israel 'cannot be measured in days, months, or years . . . It is a
very long and hard struggle', that may last generations. Among the historic examples that he cited was the Arab [should be: Muslim] struggle
against the Crusaders ('they were defeated after two hundred years'),
the Algerian war against France, and the Vietnamese war against the
United States. Similarly, Israel was depicted by Asad and Syrian writers
as a formidable enemy supported by American imperialism ('the Satanic
alliance') and given unlimited American aid. It had also exploited the
'submissive Egyptian regime' and the 'Palestinian rightists [PLO]
dragged to the quagmire of betrayal', in order to control Arab lands 'from
the Nile to the Euphrates'. Asad also warned against the illusion that
Israel wished to make peace with the Arabs. 'Israel wants the submission
of the Arabs, not peace with the Arabs' (*Israi'l turid bi-istislam al-Arab, la-
salam al-Arab*).[27]

To compound Israel's evil and dangerous image, Asad and other leaders resorted again and again to crude anti-Zionist propaganda such as the
equation of Israel with Nazism, racism, and aggression. Even school
textbooks in the late 1980s continued to depict Israel as an aggressor and

the usurper of Arab Palestine (the Israelis are described as armed people with 'ugly faces as devils' faces').[28]

This Syrian line of anti-Israeli indoctrination and propaganda was intensified since early 1988 also in conjunction with the Palestinian *intifada* against Israel, which broke out in Gaza and the West Bank in December 1987. This uprising obviously gave Damascus an opportunity to denounce Israel's alleged colonialist and aggressive conduct towards Arabs. Equally important: the *intifada* was highlighted by Damascus as an important element in its doctrine of strategic balance with Israel:

In the light of the *intifada* of stones in Palestine, the desire for achieving a strategic balance has gained another proof for its truth. . . . Palestine is Syria and Syria is Palestine . . . the Syrian army will remain the army of the Arab nation . . . we shall persist in achieving a strategic balance with the Zionist enemy.[29]

Nevertheless, despite these warlike and militant statements, in 1987, 1988, and 1989, Asad also reaffirmed that strategic parity was the basis of Syria's struggle to 'achieve a comprehensive peace', and that only when Israel realized that it no longer enjoyed military superiority would it 'respond to the requirements of a just peace'. These requirements were Israel's withdrawal from the occupied Arab territories, recognition of the Palestinians' right to self-determination and statehood, the convocation of an international conference under United Nations auspices, wielding full powers, and the participation in this conference of a united Arab delegation.[30]

The questions that should now be addressed are: what was Israel's position regarding these requirements, and what were Israel's reactions to, and impact on, Syria's doctrine of strategic balance during the 1980s?

ISRAEL'S STATUS QUO POLICIES

Broadly speaking, Israel's governments, both Likud and Labour (as well as the Israeli public), continued during the 1980s to reject these Syrian conditions for a 'comprehensive peace'. Not only did they believe that Damascus was truly opposed to peace with Israel, but also that it still posed a serious threat to the security of the Jewish state. The manifestations of these positions were, according to Israel: (*a*) Asad's doctrine of strategic balance and the enormous Syrian military build-up, with Soviet

help: all of which might lead to a Syrian attack in the Golan; (*b*) the
Damascus-engineered guerrilla/terrorist warfare against Israel, by proxy,
in Lebanon during the 1980s, and in Europe, notably the attempt to blow
up an El-Al plane in London airport in April 1986; (*c*) Syria's endeavours
to undermine Jordanian and PLO moves towards a political settlement
with Israel, as well as towards a Jordanian–Palestinian confederation; (*d*)
Syria's continued militant declarations against Israel. Israel reacted to
these Syrian deeds and words by issuing stern warnings, displaying force,
and augmenting its military-strategic power.

Nevertheless, Israel's positions regarding Syria, like Syrian attitudes
towards Israel, were not monolithic. There were certain differences between Likud and Labour (and within the parties) and each of them held
somewhat different positions while in government than when in opposition. Neither ruled out a peace agreement with Syria and their leaders
have periodically and publicly stated Jerusalem's desire to make peace
with Damascus. But both Likud and Labour insisted that Israel should
negotiate directly with Syria, without any linkage to other Arab parties,
notably the PLO.

Israeli governments were initially prepared to give up part of the Golan,
but not all of it, in return for full peace and normalization with Syria,
although the Likud governments hardened their position on the Golan
issue during the 1980s. For example, following his advent to power in
1977, Prime Minister Begin declared that 'Israel will remain in the Golan
Heights, but in the framework of a peace treaty we will be ready to
withdraw our forces from their present line to a [new] line that will be a
permanent boundary.'[31]

Subsequently, however, Begin adopted a more inflexible position
against the background of Syria's alleged attempts to dominate Lebanon
and 'exterminate the Christians', and its massive military build-up with
modern Soviet weapons in preparation for reaching a strategic balance
with Israel and for possible military actions against it.[32] Consequently, on
14 December 1981, upon Begin's suggestion, the Knesset passed the
Golan Law, which applied Israeli law, jurisdiction, and administration to
that area. Begin reportedly told his cabinet that among the reasons for his
decision was the conviction that Syria was not ready to make peace with
Israel and continued to manifest a hostile, uncompromising attitude towards the Jewish state. Begin, however, also said in the Knesset that the
Golan Law should not close the options for negotiations with Syria and
would not prevent border changes in the future.[33]

Significantly, already in 1980 not a few members of the Labour Party and its *kibbutz* movement demanded the extension of Israeli sovereignty over the Golan, and the Labour Knesset members voted for the 1981 Golan Law (11 voted against, including Rabin and Peres). For, in point of fact, many Jewish settlements had been established during the Labour government's period of office up till 1977. Several more settlements were added after Likud's ascendancy in 1977 and, in late 1981, a new Golan development project envisaged building a few more regional centres and adding several thousand new settlers in the Golan.[34]

To be sure, those Israeli actions, which were criticized by the United States and European countries, provoked strong Syrian verbal reactions, as well as an appeal to the Security Council to have Israel abrogate the Golan Law. Israel not only ignored these Syrian requests, but, as we know, invaded Lebanon in June 1982 and attacked the Syrian army there, thus encouraging Syria's endeavours to increase its military build-up greatly, as part of its doctrine of strategic balance with Israel. Syria, indeed, organized three new armoured divisions, partly equipped with T-72 Soviet tanks, modernized its air force with MiG-23 planes, and added SS-21 long-range ground-to-ground missiles to its arsenal, as well as SA-5 long-range anti-aircraft missiles.[35]

Syria's massive military build-up as well as the proxy war of attrition against the Israeli troops in Lebanon since 1983 caused deep misgivings among Israelis and also had an impact on the government. In August 1983 Prime Minister Begin announced his resignation, largely owing to the heavy losses in life among Israeli soldiers in Lebanon. He was succeeded by Yitzhak Shamir, a former leader of the Lehi (Stern Gang) during the British Mandate and a hardline anti-Arab politician. Nevertheless, the growing domestic criticism of the Lebanon war and the resulting severe economic crisis led to the collapse of Shamir's government and to new national elections.[36]

But even though the Labour alignment won the 1984 elections, it was unable to establish a coalition and was obliged to form a 'national unity' government with the Likud. According to the Labour–Likud agreement, Peres, the Labour leader, would initially serve as prime minister, while Shamir would revert to his earlier position in the Begin government as foreign minister. After twenty-five months, the two would reverse roles, while Rabin would serve as defence minister under both.

Peres's first decisions as prime minister (with Rabin's support) were: to withdraw the Israeli troops from Lebanon, to cut the defence budget, and to rehabilitate the economy. Yet Israeli leaders sternly warned Syria not to interpret these decisions as signs of weakness: Rabin, for example, said (in

September 1985) that it would be a 'fatal mistake' for Syria to launch a war against Israel, under the illusion that Damascus had achieved a strategic balance with Jerusalem.[37]

Possibly in order to underline its deterrent capability, on 19 November 1985 Israel shot down two Syrian MiG-23s over Syrian territory after they had approached an Israeli surveillance aircraft flying over Lebanon. Damascus promptly moved its anti-aircraft missiles up to the frontier and into the Lebanese Biqaʿ valley, challenging Israel's control of Lebanese air space. After American diplomatic intervention, the missiles were pulled back from the Biqaʿ but not from Syrian territory close to the Lebanese border, thus curtailing Israel's surveillance flights over Lebanon. Syria (and the USSR) also publicly warned Israel against attacking these missile batteries.[38]

Tension between Jerusalem and Damascus continued to mount during 1986, bringing the two parties almost to the brink of war in the spring. On 4 February 1986 Israeli fighters forced down a Libyan plane carrying a Syrian delegation led by the assistant secretary-general of the Baʿth Party, Abdallah al-Ahmar, to Damascus. The plane was later permitted to resume its flight, but, according to Seale, Syria 'vowed revenge'. And on 17 April 1986 an attempt was made, apparently by a Syrian agent, to place a bomb aboard an El-Al aircraft, carrying some 400 passengers, on a flight from London airport.[39] At that period Syria was apparently involved in several more international terrorist actions, while continuing to receive more Soviet weapons, to conduct large military manœuvres, and to make threatening speeches against Israel.

Israeli leaders were seriously concerned that Syria might attempt to launch a limited war in order to snatch back the Golan, or part of it, and accordingly they warned Asad against such an attempt. For instance, depicting Asad as 'the most extremist Arab world leader . . . trying to amass power to defeat Israel', Prime Minister Peres stated, in March 1986, that Israel was prepared to fight back, but preferred to make peace with Syria. Similarly, Defence Minister Rabin said, in May 1986, that 'Syria should know that it has not reached military parity with Israel [and] . . . in the long run Syria alone is not a match for Israel. I have no doubt we will win such a war . . . [but] we are not interested in an escalation.'[40]

To be sure, at that juncture neither Israel nor Syria were interested in escalation and fighting, although each side was concerned about the other's intention to start a war, owing to domestic difficulties. Asad was well aware that Syria had not yet achieved a strategic balance with Israel and was likely to be badly defeated in the event of war, causing huge destruction and even the collapse of the regime. Peres and Rabin also realized that, although Israel was likely to defeat Syria in a war, it would suffer heavy human and economic casualties. As ʿAbd al-Halim Khaddam, Syria's foreign minister, remarked: 'The Israelis are aware that their next war will by no means be a limited war, nor would it be a picnic.'[41]

But, whereas Peres and Rabin in their public statements endeavoured in 1986 to defuse the mounting tension with Syria, Foreign Minister Shamir publicly advocated a military (air) strike against Syria, like that of the United States in Libya (on 15 April 1986), in order to induce Damascus to stop supporting terrorism.[42]

Nevertheless, as a matter of fact, Israel refrained from attacking Syria even after Shamir became prime minister in October 1986, and despite alleged Syrian-sponsored guerrilla/terrorist operations, mostly from Lebanon. Thus, for example, a hang-glider attack on an Israeli army base near Qiryat Shmona (Upper Galilee) in late November 1987, by the Syrian-based Jibril group, did not provoke an Israeli air strike against Syrian targets. Shamir only accused Damascus of granting haven and assistance to the 'terrorists', and said that Israel would draw the 'necessary conclusions' from that event.[43] Further guerrilla/terrorist attacks from Syrian-controlled Lebanon against Israeli targets during the following years again merely drew accusations from Israeli leaders of indirect Syrian involvement; periodically, however, Israeli air force and armoured units would attack guerrilla/terrorist bases in various parts of Lebanon, including several situated near Syrian positions, or near the Syrian border.[44]

Even though such operations were aimed at inducing Syria to stop the guerrilla attacks from Lebanon, Israel avoided clashing with Syrian forces or downing military planes in, or over Lebanon, and in fact tolerated Syria's dominance over most of that country. The main reasons for this Israeli policy were, first, that the government, under the influence of Defence Minister Rabin, did not wish to entangle itself in a war with Syria, either in the Golan or in Lebanon. The lingering trauma of the Lebanese war and the heavy losses which could be expected in another war—also among the civilian population—from Syrian long-range missiles were further factors that deterred Israeli political and military leaders from attacking Syria. Secondly, Israel was heavily engaged, from late 1987, with the Palestinian *intifada* in the West Bank and Gaza, which was more crucial, politically, economically, and as regards morale, than the sporadic actions emanating from Lebanon.[45] At the same time, Israel sought to improve its relations with Egypt and bring about a political settlement with Jordan regarding the Palestinian problem, while maintaining a strong deterrence vis-à-vis Syria, thus prolonging the regional isolation of Damascus, and sustaining the Israeli–Syrian status quo.

In any event, Jerusalem was able to avoid a major military clash with Damascus and for several more years it managed also to sustain the status quo with Syria over the Golan Heights, despite a fresh American attempt to bring about a change. Indeed, in 1988 the raging Palestinian *intifada* aroused the United States' concern and motivated it to seek again a solution to the Palestinian problem within a comprehensive Arab–Israeli settlement. American Secretary of State George Shultz, induced by Egypt's President Mubarak, in February 1988 adopted a fresh initiative to achieve such a settlement on the basis of UN Resolutions 242 and 338. Prime Minister Shamir, however, rejected this move, publicly saying that the exchange of territory for peace was foreign to him. Defence Minister Rabin similarly declared that he did not regard Syria under Asad as a partner for peace and that the issue of peace for territories was therefore irrelevant as far as Syria was concerned.[46]

On the other hand, Asad (and the Syrian media) strongly attacked Shultz's initiative as implying 'capitulation', being incompatible with a 'just and comprehensive peace' and designed to serve Israeli interests. And, while presenting the Syrian version of a just peace, Asad continued to uphold the notion of strategic parity as a means of struggle against the 'expansionist and aggressive Zionist entity'.[47]

In conclusion, by the late 1980s, the positions of Israel and Syria with regard to the Golan and the Arab–Israeli conflict were very far apart and highly asymmetric. Damascus insisted on Israel's total withdrawal from all occupied Arab lands, including the Golan, and the establishment of a Palestinian state in the West Bank, East Jerusalem, and Gaza, as preconditions for a 'just and comprehensive peace'. Jerusalem, in contrast, called for peace with the Arab states on the basis of UN Resolutions 242 and 338, but refused to withdraw from the Golan, the West Bank, and Gaza, let alone recognize Palestinian rights to self-determination and statehood.

At the same time, however, Syria and Israel were at that juncture in a state of mutual military deterrence, even though Jerusalem continued to maintain a clear strategic advantage over Damascus. This mutual deterrence, although not eliminating the risks of another war, could potentially also provide for a political settlement, given suitable circumstances or developments. Such developments indeed occurred during the late 1980s and early 1990s, inducing Syria in particular to moderate its preconditions and gradually seek a political settlement with Israel. Those developments or new circumstances were mainly Syria's failure to achieve strategic parity with Israel, its domestic economic difficulties, and regional inter-Arab isolation, as well as the disintegration of the USSR and the emerging global predominance of the United States, under the new Bush leadership. This last development certainly also had an impact on Jerusalem's position regarding a political settlement with Damascus, but the Shamir–Likud government still refused to trade the Golan for a peace with Syria. It was only after the Labour Party came to power in the summer of 1992 that Israel offered to give up territories in the Golan in return for a full and genuine peace with Syria.

NOTES

1. Asad's address to the 'Revolutionary Youth', 1 Oct. 1981; *al-Ba'th* (Damascus), 3 Feb. 1985. For a detailed study of Asad's strategy see M. Eisenstadt, *Arming for Peace? Syria's Elusive Quest for 'Strategic Parity'* (Washington, 1992).

2. According to Syrian Vice-President Khaddam, in an interview with *al-Mustaqbal*, 17 May 1986, 17.

3. Damascus Radio, 7 Nov. 1980; cf. *Jaysh al-Sh'ab*, 1 Nov. 1980.

4. *Tishrin*, 25 Feb. 1988. Cf. *al-Safir*, 23 Apr. 1980; *Tishrin*, 9 Aug. 1981, article by Ayyubi, *Tishrin*, 30 May and 10 Oct. 1981.

5. Asad's address to the teachers' convention, Damascus Radio, 15 Mar. 1980.

6. Asad's interview and speech, Damascus Radio, 9 Mar. 1981, 17 Sept. 1981. Also ibid. 17 Sept. 1982; Syrian foreign minister's interview, *al-Mustaqbal* 6 Feb. 1982.

7. See respectively Asad's interviews with Italian TV, Damascus Radio, 25 Feb. 1982; with the *Observer*, Damascus Radio, 7 Mar. 1982; with Soviet TV, Damascus Radio, 27 Apr. 1986. Cf. *al-Ba'th*, 22 Oct. 1985; *al-Iqtisad* (Damascus), July 1980; *al-Mustaqbal*, 6 Feb. 1982.

8. See respectively Damascus Radio, 15 Nov. 1985 and 17 Sept. 1982. Cf. *Tishrin*, 19 May 1980; *al-Ray'* (Amman), 7 Apr. 1980.

9. See Ma'oz, *Asad*, 182–3, citing Syrian sources.

10. Asad's interview and speech, Damascus Radio, 9 Mar. 1981, 17 Sept. 1982; see also Damascus Radio, 17 Sept. 1982. See also *al-Ba'th*, 6 Oct. 1981; *al-Thawra*, 5 Nov. 1981. See also *The Concluding Statement of the Eighth Congress*

of the Ba'th party in the Syrian Region (Arabic; Ba'th Party National Command, Damascus, 1985).

11. Ma'oz, *Asad*, 59, 179, citing various sources. See also *International Herald Tribune*, 23 Mar. 1983 and 17 Dec. 1986; *al-Majalla* (Saudi Arabia), 16 Oct. 1985; P. Seale, *Observer*, 29 May 1983.

12. *Jaysh al-Sh'ab*, 1 July 1985.

13. Asad's interview, Damascus Radio, 23 June 1983.

14. See Asad's speeches, Damascus TV, 1 Oct. 1983. See also *Jaysh al-Sh'ab*, 15 May 1984; *al-Majalla* (Saudi Arabia), 23 July 1983; Damascus Radio, 18 Nov. 1984 and 20 Jan. 1985. Cf. *al-Istratijiyya al-Nidaliyya* . . . (Ba'th Party, Damascus 1981).

15. See e.g. *Jaysh al-Sh'ab*, 6 Jan. 1976; *al-Thawra*, 12 Dec. 1985.

16. M. Zonis and D. Brumberg, *Khomeini: The Islamic Republic of Iran and the Arab World* (Cambridge, 1987), 37–8; J. Alpher, 'The Khomeini International', *Washington Quarterly* (autumn 1980), 61.

17. C. Moss Helms, *Iraq: Eastern Flank of the Arab World* (Washington, 1984), 179; *FBIS*, 16 Aug. 1979. See also D. Govrin, 'The Syria–Iran Relations during the Iran–Iraq War, 1980–8', Occasional Paper (Jerusalem: Hebrew University, 1993), 3–4.

18. M. Tlas (ed.), *Kadhalika qal al-Asad* (Damascus, 1984), 389–90, cited in Govrin 'Syria–Iran Relations', 4; cf. al-Ayyubi in *Tishrin*, 23 Aug. 1980; *Jaysh al-Sh'ab*, 1 May 1984; *The Concluding Statement of the Ba'th Party, 1985*.

19. *Journal of Palestine Studies*, 12 (1980), 196–7.

20. Asad's speech, Damascus Radio, 7 Nov. 1980; Asad interview with French TV, 18 Nov. 1984, in *FBIS*, 20 Nov. 1984, 42; see also *Tishrin*, 7 Nov. 1980 and 30 May 1988; *The Concluding Statement of the Ba'th Party, 1985*.

21. The Syrian oil minister, Associated Press, 30 Apr. 1987. For full accounts of Syrian support of Iran see Moss Helm, *Iraq*, 179 ff.; Y. Hirschfeld, 'The Odd Couple: Ba'athist Syria and Khomeini's Iran', in Ma'oz and Yaniv, *Syria under Asad*, 105 ff.; R. King, *The Iran-Iraq War*, Adelphi Papers, 219 (London, 1987), 41.

22. *The Economist* (London), 14 Nov. 1987, 14, 62.

23. Karsh, *Soviet Union*, 92; H. Cobban, *The Superpowers and the Syrian–Israeli Conflict* (Washington, 1991), 38.

24. Cf. A. H. Cordesman, *The Arab–Israeli Military Balance and the Art of Operations* (Washington, 1986), 45 ff.; *International Herald Tribune*, 17 Dec. 1986; *Ha'aretz*, 27 Nov. 1986; Z. Schiff, *Ha'aretz*, 18 Mar. 1986. On Syrian perceptions regarding Israel's nuclear capability see *Tishrin*, 10 Aug. 1981, 19 Sept. 1985, 5 Mar. 1988, and 16 May 1988; *al-Thawra*, 24 Nov. 1982.

25. *Washington Post*, 15 Nov. 1986; *al-Dustur* (London), 31 Mar. 1986; A. Cowell, 'Trouble in Damascus', *New York Times Magazine*, 1 Apr. 1990. Cf. Drysdale and Hinnebusch, *Syria*, 44 ff.; D. Hopwood, *Syria, 1945–86: Politics and Society* (London, 1988), 112–14.

26. See e.g. *al-Ba'th*, 28 Jan. and 13 Feb. 1988; *Tishrin*, 3 and 27 Jan. 1988, 6 and 7 Mar. 1988, 14 May 1988.

27. *Tishrin*, 9 Mar. 1988; for other references regarding the new dimensions of the strategic balance, see also *Tishrin*, 27 Jan. 1988 and 6 Mar. 1988. Cf. *The Concluding Statement of the Ba'th Party, 1985.*

28. *This is Our Land* (Arabic; Readings for the fifth grade, part 2), by Sulayman al-Isa *et al.* (Syria, The Public Institute for Publications and Textbooks, 1988/9), 43–5. *Al-Ba'th*, 4, 10, and 17 Jan. 1988, 10 Feb. and 10 Mar. 1988; *Tishrin*, 29 June 1988.

29. *Tishrin*, 6 Feb. 1988; *al-Ba'th*, 13 Feb. 1988; cf. ibid. 18 and 21 Feb. and 10 Mar. 1988.

30. References in *MECS* (1987), 84–5; 1988, 100–1; 1989, 84.

31. I. Rabinovich, 'Israel, Syria and Jordan', in Drysdale and Hinnebusch, *Syria*, 114.

32. *Ha'aretz*, 13, 16, and 29 Apr. 1981; [General, ret.] A. Tamir, *Hayal shoher shalom* (Tel Aviv, 1988), 145.

33. *Ha'aretz*, 15 and 22 Dec. 1981; Na'or, *Dayan*, 232–3.

34. *Ha'aretz*, 11 and 12 Dec. 1980, 15 Dec. 1981, 23 May 1986. On the Israeli public position regarding the Golan, see *Ha'aretz*, 29 Dec. 1985.

35. Z. Schiff, *Ha'aretz*, 7 and 10 Jan., 21 Apr. 1983; *Ma'ariv*, 9 Dec. 1983 (interview with Israel's chief of military intelligence); see also Ma'oz, *Asad*, 179; *New York Times*, 10 May 1986; Seale, *Asad*, 398–9.

36. For details see Sachar, *A History*, 282 ff.

37. *Ma'ariv*, 11 Sept. 1983; *Ha'aretz* (Tel Aviv), 11 Sept. 1985. On Israel's defence budget cut, see H. Cobban, *The Superpowers*, 64 ff.

38. Seale, *Asad*, 473; *Ha'aretz*, 16 and 20 Dec. 1985.

39. Details in Seale, *Asad*, 473 ff. Cf. Ma'oz, *Asad*, 174; *Ha'aretz*, 8 May 1986; *Middle East Journal*, 41 (1987), 79.

40. IDF Radio, 11 Mar. 1986; *Ha'aretz*, 12 and 19 Mar. 1986; *New York Times*, 10 May 1986. See also *Sunday Telegraph*, 9 Mar. 1986; *Yediot Ahronot*, 16 May 1986; *New York Times*, 19 May 1986. Cf. Cobban, *The Superpowers*, 69 ff.

41. Damascus Radio, 10 May 1983. Cf. *New York Times*, 10 and 19 May 1986; A. Yaniv, 'A Syrian–Israeli Detente', *Middle East Insight*, 5/5 (Jan.–Feb. 1988), 27 ff.

42. *Ha'aretz*, 28 Apr. 1986. Cf. Shamir Statement in *Ha'aretz*, 18 Dec. 1985. See also *Ma'ariv*, 11 May 1986.

43. *Middle East Journal*, 42 (1988), 275; *Ha'aretz*, 27 Nov. and 1 Dec. 1987.

44. *Financial Times*, 28 Apr. and 5 May 1988; *International Herald Tribune*, 25 Oct. 1988 and 28 May 1989; *Ha'aretz*, 18 Aug. 1989.

45. For a detailed analysis of certain issues, cf. Cobban, *The Superpowers*, 65 ff., 91 ff. See also *Ha'aretz*, 7 Mar. 1986; *Davar*, 30 Oct. 1987; Tamir, *Hayal*, 9–10; *Middle East Journal*, 42 (1988), 277.

46. See W. B. Quandt, *Peace Process: American Diplomacy and the Arab–Israeli Conflict since 1967* (Washington: Brookings Institution, 1993), 364 ff.; *Ha'aretz*, 8 June 1988.

47. *Al-Ba'th*, 10 Jan., 10, 21 and 29 Mar., and 6 Apr. 1988; *Tishrin*, 9 Mar., 14 May, and 29 June 1988.

10

Syria, Israel, and the Peace Process

ASAD RE-EMBARKS ON THE
POLITICAL-DIPLOMATIC TRACK

Whereas Israel persisted in its status quo policy regarding Syria and the Golan until mid-1992, from 1988 Syria revived and expanded its strategy of achieving a political settlement of the Arab/Syrian–Israeli conflict, albeit on its terms, and without renouncing its military reinforcement. Indeed, in certain respects this policy represented the continuation of the two-track strategy that Asad had initiated since his rise to power in 1970, and particularly after the 1973 war, the simultaneous development of military option and the use of diplomacy in order to regain the Golan Heights as well as other occupied Arab territories, and also implement the national rights of the Palestinian people.

During the mid-1970s Asad had given preference to the political-diplomatic option because of Syria's military weakness and other severe difficulties. Despite their initial successes, Syria and Egypt were defeated by Israel in the 1973 war; subsequently Egypt was inclined to sign a separate agreement with Israel, leaving Syria exposed to the Israeli threat. Later, in 1976–7, Damascus was drawn into the Lebanese quagmire, leading to further military and economic embarrassments. Consequently, while attempting to create a 'Fertile Crescent' or a 'Greater Syria' strategic alliance vis-à-vis Israel, Asad also endeavoured to co-ordinate a diplomatic campaign with Egypt and Saudi Arabia aimed at gaining American backing for the Syrian version of a 'just and comprehensive' solution to the Arab–Israeli conflict.

A similar strategy, although bolder and more advanced, has gradually been developed by Asad since 1988, under still greater Syrian constraints than in the mid-1970s: Syria's failure to achieve a strategic balance with Israel; its regional isolation and vulnerability following the end of the Iraq–Iran war; a severe economic crisis; and particularly the dramatic change in the global configuration with the disintegration of the Soviet Union and the emergence of the United States as the single major super-

power. Thus, while for the first time since 1978 starting to emit conciliatory signals towards Egypt, and further strengthening its relations with
Saudi Arabia, Syria from early 1988 cautiously sought a rapprochement
with the United States aiming to reinforce its regional position, improve
its economic situation, and settle its conflict with Israel, with American
and Arab diplomatic support. In the process, for the first time and with
American persuasion, Damascus adopted, notably in mid-1991, more
flexible positions regarding the settlement of the Arab–Israeli conflict.
Simultaneously, however, throughout 1988 (and beyond) Syria continued
to develop its military power and to conduct a strident propaganda campaign against Israel.[1]

To begin with, Damascus gradually and carefully sought to mend
fences with Washington and Cairo, although not with Jerusalem. For
example, the Syrian media aggressively attacked the peace initiative of
American Secretary of State George Shultz (in February 1988) as 'worse
than the Camp David accords'; but at the same time they also said, 'If
Shultz wants a just peace the door is well known and he can enter it
peacefully.' In fact, Shultz conducted several frank talks with Asad and
other Syrian leaders in Damascus in late February, early April, and early
June 1988.[2] Asad pointed out to Shultz that Syria was interested in a 'just
and comprehensive peace' (according to its own definition) and not in
partial or interim solutions (although reportedly Asad had told Senator
Arlen Specter in early February 1988 that he was ready to discuss peace
with Israel in return for the Golan and without any linkage to the
Palestinian problem).[3] And even though the American position regarding
a comprehensive peace and the Israeli withdrawal from the Golan was
closer to the Syrian position than to the Israeli one, Shultz and Asad failed
to reach an understanding, as the gap between them remained wide, and
Shultz was interested in the Palestinians rather than the Syrians.[4]

Asad, however, did not have a viable alternative to American backing,
since the Soviet Union under Gorbachev had continued, during 1988–9,
to urge him to seek a political settlement of the Arab–Israeli conflict and
to relinquish 'illusions about a military option' against Israel.[5] Consequently, although still considering the USSR as a strategic ally, Damascus
tilted more and more towards Washington, particularly after the beginning of 1989, when George Bush started his presidential term. Encouraged by the fact that Bush had been elected without the support of the
Jewish vote, Damascus expected that the United States, 'as a superpower
directly responsible for international security and peace should give up its
Zionist point of view, put an end to the Zionist danger . . . force the

Zionist enemy to withdraw from the occupied territories, and execute the international decisions to achieve just and true and comprehensive peace in the region.'[6]

President Bush and Secretary of State James Baker were indeed critical of Israel's policies in the occupied territories, and urged it to seek a comprehensive settlement to the Arab–Israeli conflict on the basis of United Nations Resolutions 242 and 338, meaning peace in return for territories. At the same time the United States also assured Syria that it intended to achieve a comprehensive solution on all fronts, including the Golan, on the basis of those resolutions, and subsequently, according to the American Ambassador in Damascus, initiated a new 'framework for action and co-operation with Syria'.[7]

Adopting more flexible positions during 1989, Syria also expressed its support for Resolutions 242 and 338, at the same time making a gradual rapprochement with Egypt, the only Arab nation to have signed a formal peace treaty with Israel on the basis of those resolutions. Already in December 1988, after a decade of bitter anti-Egyptian propaganda, Asad publicly stated that he 'acknowledged the importance of Egypt in the Arab arena' and that Syrian–Egyptian co-operation had always been compatible with the interests of the Arab world. The Syrian media likewise adopted a positive attitude towards Egypt and in May 1989 Damascus no longer objected to the readmittance of Egypt to the Arab League.[8]

In mid-December 1989 flights were resumed between Damascus and Cairo, and two weeks later full diplomatic relations were restored between the two countries. In mid-July 1990 Asad paid his first official visit to Cairo for thirteen years, and on departing he said: 'We are ready to join the peace process and we accept UN Resolutions 242 and 338 and we still call for a just and comprehensive peace.'[9]

By making these significant moves Asad sought not only to consolidate Syria's regional position and obtain inter-Arab backing in his sharp rivalry with Iraq. He also aimed at forging a common front with Egypt (as well as with Saudi Arabia and Jordan) vis-à-vis Israel's persistent refusal to withdraw from the Golan, and its attempts to conclude separate deals with the Palestinians and with Jordan. Asad kept sending more messages reflecting Syria's readiness to find a peaceful solution to the Arab–Israeli conflict.

These messages were directed particularly to the Bush administration as the only power able to induce Israel to negotiate a comprehensive settlement and pull back from the Golan, and/or render Syria economic assistance, and have its name erased from the list of countries supporting international terrorism. During 1990 Asad and other Syrian leaders thus continued their dialogue with American officials and politicians, leaving them with the strong impression that Syria was adopting more flexible positions regarding peace with Israel. For example, former President Carter met Asad in Damascus on 14 March 1990 and subsequently told reporters in Israel that Asad had authorized him to say that he was ready to negotiate directly with Israel under the auspices of an international conference, and that he was also prepared to have the Golan demilitarized after it was returned to Syria. Asad himself denied Carter's message, although he did not disavow his own assertion to Senator Specter (in January 1990) that Syria no longer insisted that a peace conference be convened by the five permanent members of the UN Security Council and that it agreed that only the United States and the Soviet Union should participate in a peace conference (a position which Israel was also inclined to accept).[10] At this juncture it must be stressed that Asad's new flexible position regarding a peace conference by no means reflected willingness to make full peace with Israel or to accept its legitimacy in the region. Nor did his continuing dialogue with the Americans mean that he trusted Washington's readiness to drop its support for Israel and force it to withdraw from the Golan.

Indeed throughout 1988, 1989, and 1990 Asad and other Syrian leaders and media continued to depict Israel as a neo-Nazi entity, 'tirelessly seeking by expansion, manipulation, brutal force, or subtle play to bring under its sway the land mass between the Nile and the Euphrates'.[11] Asad and his media organs also continued to criticize the United States, although in milder terms during 1989 and 1990, for supporting Israel and supplying it with modern weapons; for facilitating the immigration of Soviet Jews to Israel as well as supposedly preparing to broker a separate deal between Israel and the Palestinians as a substitute for a comprehensive settlement.[12]

FROM THE END OF THE COLD WAR TO THE END
OF THE GULF WAR: THE IMPACT ON SYRIA

Nevertheless, as an experienced and pragmatic statesman, Asad continued to realize that only Washington could help him out of his strategic, political, and economic predicaments. This, particularly since his veteran ally, the Soviet Union, under Gorbachev had further reduced its military and diplomatic support for Syria, while improving relations with Israel and the United States. Thus, for example, during the first four years of Gorbachev's tenure (1985–9) Moscow cut its military deliveries to Damascus from $2.4 billion to $1.3 billion per year (compared to the years 1977–84); still refused to supply SS-23 long-range strategic missiles; and asked Syria to repay its military debt and pay in cash for some of the new deliveries. These measures indeed reflected Gorbachev's 'new thinking' regarding the Syrian–Israeli conflict, which *inter alia* requested Damascus to replace its concept of 'strategic balance' by a 'balance of interests' with Israel, within a peaceful settlement of the conflict. As Soviet Foreign Minister Shevardnadze told his Syrian hosts on an official visit in February 1989:

Movement towards this noble goal is only possible given the rejection of strong arm approaches in politics and the transfer from confrontation to dialogue, from rivalry to codevelopment and the search for a balance of interests . . . The new thinking is powerfully knocking at the door of the Near East too. It is time to build the bridges of mutual understanding and peaceful coexistence in this region too.[13]

Gorbachev and Shevardnadze also offered Soviet help in achieving Syrian–Israeli (and Palestinian–Israeli) 'balance of interests' by re-establishing consular and subsequently diplomatic relations with Israel, meeting Israeli leaders, and allowing some 400,000 Soviet Jews to emigrate to Israel.[14]

Asad and other Syrian leaders and the media ostensibly continued to hail Soviet–Syrian friendship and Moscow's support of Syria's defensive capability and its policy regarding a just and comprehensive settlement of the Arab–Israeli conflict.[15] For, even though Asad was no doubt deeply concerned about and highly critical of the new Soviet policies, he could not afford to relinquish the remaining significant military and diplomatic support of Moscow; he intended to use it to the utmost, in view of the changing global and regional circumstances. Yet he also acknowledged that 'Israel, more than other nations, drew benefits from the [new] global changes. It renewed relations with several states and its influence in-creased in several states . . . [including] the Socialist States.' Israel was also becoming stronger owing to the immigration of Soviet Jews, who according to Asad were descendants of the Khazars (a Turkish tribe that lived in the Lower Volga basin and partly converted to Judaism in the late eighth century), who had never been inhabitants of Palestine.[16]

In sum, despite its rapprochement with Washington and Cairo and its more flexible approach to the Arab–Israeli conflict, Damascus was still by mid-1990 in a markedly disadvantageous position vis-à-vis Jerusalem. Israel indeed enjoyed a large strategic edge over Syria, substantial American military and financial support, and a better international backing. It had also initiated a peace plan (May 1989) which aimed at reaching agreements with the Palestinians and Jordan while ignoring Syria and the Golan issue. The Bush administration was inclined to back this plan, to Syria's prejudice.

Paradoxically and unexpectedly, the person who indirectly helped Asad to emerge from this predicament and win a 'breakthrough' in Syrian–American relations was Saddam Hussein of Baghdad, the sworn enemy of Damascus. Indeed, the Iraqi invasion and conquest of Kuwait in August 1990 gave Asad a rare opportunity to improve immensely his relations with Bush as well as his regional and international standing; this, provided Syria became an ally in the war against Saddam's Iraq. Not surprisingly, Asad, the cool-headed strategist, was prepared to compromise his pan-Arab Baʿthist ideology by joining American and British 'imperialism' in a shattering offensive against a fellow Arab Baʿthist country, which presented itself as the great defender of Arabism and Islam versus 'infidel' Western imperialism, Zionist Israel, and 'reactionary' Arab regimes. To be sure, Asad and his controlled media endeavoured to condemn Iraq's invasion of Kuwait as a blow to Arab solidarity and to the Palestinian issue, declaring that it was 'used by the Zionist enemy in exploiting to the utmost the crisis to acquire economic, military and political support for Israel from the United States . . . As for the Palestinian cause, it had receded. It no longer occupies the first priority of some Arabs.' Similarly, Asad tried both to explain and to hail the nationalist mission of Syria in the Gulf crisis: 'We are the ones serving Arab nationalism . . . we are doing what might prevent the brother [Iraq] from attacking his brother [Kuwait] and this helping both of them.'[17]

Whether or not Asad succeeded in ideologically justifying his decision to send troops to fight alongside American, European, and Arab forces against the Iraqis in Kuwait, his tangible benefits—strategic, economic, and political—were certainly large. In addition to seeing his dangerous rival Saddam badly defeated, Asad was able to secure his grip on Lebanon by crushing the 'rejectionist' Maronite leader General Aoun (ʿAwn) in October 1990 with tacit American approval, and signing (on 22 May 1991) a 'treaty of brotherhood, co-operation and co-ordination' with Lebanon's President Elias Hrawi. Affirming the Taʿif accords of 1989, this treaty gave Syria *de facto* control over Lebanese security and foreign affairs.[18] Taking advantage of Arafat's predicament caused by his initial support of

Saddam's invasion of Kuwait, Syria also managed to resume its influence—albeit only for a certain period—over the PLO regarding the peace process with Israel. Thus, after years of ferocious denunciation of 'deviationist' PLO policy of allegedly inclining towards separate negotiations with Israel (since 1988),[19] Syria made the PLO adopt its own stance: Arafat announced in early June 1991 that 'the Palestinian and Syrian viewpoints are identical' and that the 'PLO would not go to a peace conference without Syrian participation.'[20]

At that juncture Syria was indeed better prepared to participate in a peace conference with Israel, but not only thanks to its influence over the PLO and Lebanon. More important was the fresh American policy or commitment to bring about a comprehensive settlement of the Arab–Israeli dispute, Syria being an important party to such a settlement. Bush had probably already made such a commitment to Asad during their meeting in Geneva on 23 November 1990 to discuss Syrian participation in the war against Iraq. Asad very likely asked at that meeting for an American undertaking to support a comprehensive settlement whereby Israel should totally withdraw from the Golan and agree also to find a solution to the Palestinian problem. It is not known what exactly Bush's position was, but according to a press release by the White House the two leaders 'discussed the overall Middle East peace process and the importance of moving ahead with UN resolutions on the Palestinian issue'. According to a Syrian source, Bush and Asad 'dealt as well with [the] issue of [the] Arab–Israeli conflict and stressed the necessity of reaching a just and comprehensive solution on the basis of UN resolutions . . . 242 and 338.'[21] And on 6 March 1991, following the American victory over Iraq, President Bush addressed a joint session of Congress, saying: 'We must do all that we can to close the gap between Israel and the Arab states and between Israelis and Palestinians. . . . A comprehensive peace must be grounded in United Nations Security Council resolutions 242 and 338 and the principle of territory for peace.' Subsequently, Secretary of State James Baker made several trips to the Middle East, and from his 'first round of talks it seems as if an effort was under way to bring Syria into the process'.[22] Early in June 1991 Bush sent letters to leaders of Arab states and Israel spelling out his ideas for convening a peace conference in the autumn. The first positive reply came on 14 July from Asad, and Bush depicted it as 'a good response and breakthrough from what we know about it'.[23]

Asad indeed was now ready to take another big leap within his renewed strategic decision of 1988 to reach a political solution to the Arab–Israeli conflict, with maximum American support and with minimum Syrian concessions. The end of the Gulf War, like the end of the Cold War—both in favour of the United States—boldly underlined Syria's constraints in its confrontation with Israel. First and foremost, Asad again and finally realized that his doctrine of strategic balance with Israel had failed and that Syria did not have and was not likely to build in the foreseeable future a credible military option against Israel. This, not only because of the significant cuts in Soviet military supplies, but also in view of the clear superiority of American weapons as demonstrated in the Gulf war. And since Israel possessed certain types of those weapons (let alone nuclear capability) it certainly enjoyed a clear military advantage over Syria. Secondly, the grave undermining of Iraqi military power greatly weakened Syria's potential 'strategic depth' vis-à-vis Israel, while the continued alliance of Damascus with Teheran could not provide Syria with either a military option or a nuclear capability in a reasonable space of time.

True, the military relationship with Iran was still important to Syria in order to signal that it could develop a war option if the diplomatic process failed. For the same reason Damascus continued its military build-up and spent the $2 billion it had received from the Gulf states after the war to purchase SCUD-C missiles from North Korea and T-72 tanks from Czechoslovakia.[24] But undoubtedly Syria was not then prepared to go to war; it intended to negotiate a political settlement with Israel from a position of military strength.

Indeed, by mid-1991 Asad had evidently opted for a political settlement of the Middle East conflict, believing that only the United States could and would help implement it according to his interpretation of UN Resolutions 242 and 338. As Asad told Lally Weymouth of the *Washington Post* in late July 1991:

The current [American] administration is seriously oriented toward pushing the peace process forward. This seriousness has never been felt by us before . . . So we can make efforts without feeling these efforts will be futile. . . . The U.S. was concentrating on the importance of peace for the region and the world and certainly we shared that view. We [emphasized] that peace must be based on U.N. resolutions [242 and 338]. . . . The U.S. has not given any assurances, it only reaffirmed its commitment to [these] U.N. resolutions. . . . We are not asking for more than this. . . . The United States has not recognized the Israeli annexation of the Golan. It rejected this annexation and the other countries of the world have taken similar attitudes.[25]

Probably to help the United States help Syria realize its expectations, Asad was now ready to accept American terms for a peace conference which he had previously rejected. As we know, Syria had demanded a fully pledged international peace conference under UN Security Council sponsorship, to meet only after an advance commitment by Israel to withdraw from all occupied territories. At such a conference, whose resolutions would be binding, the Arab parties were to negotiate with Israel jointly rather than separately, and indirectly rather than directly. The Palestinian people were to be represented by the PLO and be entitled to establish an independent state in the Gaza Strip and the West Bank, including East Jerusalem. Now, however, under the new terms, Syria agreed to convene a regional conference under American and Soviet sponsorship with only a passive UN observer; and following the opening of the conference to conduct *direct negotiations with Israel.* Syria also dropped the demand that Israel must commit itself in advance to withdraw from the occupied territories and to agree to Palestinian statehood. Instead these issues were to be discussed during the conference, where the 'Palestinian problem must be resolved'.[26]

To be sure, notwithstanding these significant changes, Damascus continued to insist on a total Israeli withdrawal from all occupied territories, the Golan, southern Lebanon, the Gaza Strip, and the West Bank, including East Jerusalem, and on the implementation of Palestinian national rights. As Syrian Vice-President ʿAbd al-Halim Khaddam said on the eve of the Madrid peace conference (October 1991): 'Not a single Arab participating in the peace process can sell out one inch of the occupied territories or a single right of the national Palestinian rights.'[27]

Similarly Damascus at that juncture had not changed its position regarding the meaning of its peace with Israel. In return for these territories Syria was ready to offer a 'peace' to Israel which in fact stopped short of full recognition and normalization, diplomatic relations, and the like, and could be interpreted as no more than a non-belligerency agreement. In late July 1991, for example, Asad evaded the question whether or not he accepted 'the existence of a Jewish state in the Middle East'. Other Syrian leaders emphasized both before and after the Madrid conference that peace with Israel should include neither diplomatic relations nor economic co-operation. For example, at the Madrid conference, when Khaddam was asked about Syria's position on Israeli attempts to attend a meeting in Turkey on regional water problems, he said: 'Israel has no right to a single drop of water in the region. It is absolutely unacceptable for Israel to be a party to any arrangements on water or any other issues in the region.'[28]

Probably this stiff Syrian refusal, at that time and in subsequent years, to recognize Israel's legitimacy and agree to full normal peace relations with it represented not only Syria's unchanged ideological stance, but also a bargaining position in the negotiation process. For, as a matter of fact, Israeli governments continued until June 1992 to overlook the positive changes in Syria's position and were not prepared to give up the Golan Heights (let alone the West Bank) even for full peace with Syria.

ISRAEL'S UNCHANGED POSITIONS

Already in 1988 both Prime Minister Shamir and Defence Minister Rabin (serving in a national unity government) rejected Secretary of State George Shultz's initiative to convene an international conference with the participation of the five permanent members of the Security Council as well as the relevant Arab countries, including Syria. This peace conference was expected to discuss a final settlement of the Arab–Israeli conflict on the basis of UN Resolutions 242 and 338, which would also entail Israel's withdrawal in, or from, the Golan. Labelling the international conference 'a disaster', Shamir argued that Israel's withdrawal from Sinai had completed its commitment to withdraw from occupied Arab territories, according to UN Resolution 242; he also said that Israel would continue to establish Jewish settlements in 'Judaea and Samaria' and in the Golan.[29] Yet, following the collapse of Shultz's initiative and the election of George Bush as president, in early 1989 Shamir and Rabin drafted plans for a political settlement with the Palestinians and with Jordan on the basis of the Camp David accords (1978). These plans were formulated in an official Israeli 'Peace Initiative of 15 May 1989' which *inter alia* called for 'the establishment of peaceful relations between Israel and those Arab states which still maintain a state of war with it for the purpose of promoting a comprehensive settlement for the Arab–Israeli conflict'.

However, this document did not include any reference to Syria or to the Golan,[30] and the Israeli government's position of ignoring the Syrian Golan problem persisted for a few more years, even though certain Israeli Arabists, including some former senior intelligence officers, assessed that Damascus was interested in a political settlement with Jerusalem, and warned against excluding Syria from the peace process. As Israel's former chief of military intelligence, General (ret.) Shlomo Gazit said in a press interview in February 1989: 'If we reach an agreement on the West Bank and the Palestinian issue that leaves the Syrian problem open, it will blow up in our faces sooner or later.'

To be sure, the main reason for the refusal of the Israeli government and indeed of most Israeli Jews to include Syria in the peace initiative continued to be strategic, but was also strengthened by a deep psychological motivation. As indicated in a press interview: 'Gazit . . . believe[s] that Israelis have created a "mythos" about the importance of the Golan Heights in the state's strategic security that makes discussion about any compromise with Syria close to impossible.' Hence, 'the consensus of Israelis concerning the Golan is at least as great as it is concerning Jerusalem' (according to an Israeli settler in the Golan). His view was basically confirmed by Israel's chief poll-taker Hanoch Smith, who concluded in March 1991 that public opinion polls since 1967 had periodically shown that some 90 per cent of Israeli Jews wished to retain the Golan.[31] Significantly, many members and leaders of the Israeli Labour Party were perhaps more reluctant than Likud people to give up the Golan, not only because of strategic considerations and psychological motives, but also because many of the settlements in the Golan has been established by, and were affiliated to, the Labour movement. Thus, as already mentioned, Rabin, in reaction to the Shultz initiative, stated in June 1988 that he did not regard Syria under Asad as a partner for peace, and that the issue of peace for territories was therefore irrelevant as far as Syria (or the Golan) was concerned. Similarly, in December 1989, while Syria was signalling a new positive attitude toward a political agreement with Israel, Rabin declared: 'We don't see a change in the Syrian position.' And in June 1990 (and again in April 1991), despite further signs of Syrian flexibility, Rabin—now in the opposition—repeatedly said that he would rather retain the Golan even if this prevented peace with Syria than make peace with Syria and relinquish the Golan.[32]

Nevertheless, in view of the Syrian–American rapprochement in the late 1990s, and the positive Syrian response to the new American peace initiative in June 1991, the Israeli Labour Party (now out of power) adopted more flexible positions regarding the Golan Heights. Already in March 1991 Shimon Peres, the Labour Party chairman, said that he did not rule out a 'territorial compromise' with Syria in the Golan; this, according to the formula 'territories for peace'. But he added: 'not all the territories'. Similarly, in late 1991 the Labour Party adopted a new platform regarding Syria and the Golan, which stated somewhat ambiguously:

The peace treaty with Syria will be based on Security Council Resolutions 242 and 338, whose meaning is the principle of territorial compromise within a framework of a full and viable peace in which the security needs of Israel will be provided for . . . in any peace agreement with Syria and the [accompanying] security arrangements. . . . Israel's [military] presence and [civilian] settlement and militarily in the Golan Heights . . . will continue.

The only senior Labour leader who was explicit about this issue was Ezer Weizman; he advocated the Egyptian–Sinai model for Syria and the Golan.[33]

In contrast, the new Likud-led Israeli government ('the most right-leaning government in Israeli history') did not change its hardline positions regarding the Golan, although by mid-1991 it was acknowledging the new Syrian policy towards peace with Israel.

Thus, although Likud leaders stated in July 1990 and March 1991 that Israel was prepared to negotiate with Syria without preconditions, in August 1990, Prime Minister Shamir told representatives of the Golan settlers that 'our presence in the Golan is eternal'; and in July 1991 he said: 'I don't believe in territorial compromise . . . our country is very tiny. The territory is connected to our entire life—to our security, water, economy.'[34] Yet several Likud ministers and Knesset members apparently felt uncomfortable with Shamir's uncompromising line vis-à-vis the new, more flexible Syrian position regarding negotiations with Israel. This was particularly the case following Asad's letter to Bush of 14 July 1991, which, as we know, for the first time expressed Syria's willingness to take part in direct negotiations with Israel. Foreign Minister David Levy and Defence Minister Moshe Arens said in reaction that if it appeared that there was indeed a change in the Syrian position, Israel should consider changing its position as well. Even Shamir, for a while comparing Asad to Sadat, later acknowledged that a positive change had occurred in Asad's attitude; but he also indicated that Asad was not manifesting any willingness to make peace with Israel, and that 'in any case we shall oppose any territorial compromise . . . the entire world knows Israel's position that the Golan Heights is by law an inseparable part of the state [of Israel].'[35]

To be sure, these ambivalent reactions to Asad's bold diplomatic move of 14 July 1991 indicated that the Israeli government was probably caught by surprise and put on the spot. Certain officials such as Yossi Ben

Aharon, Director-General of the prime minister's office and Shamir's chief aide, tried to dismiss the Syrian move as 'a trick designed to push Israel to the corner . . . [adding] we will show them who is going to eventually find himself in the corner.' He also depicted the Syrian regime as totalitarian, dealing in terrorism and drugs, and keeping its Jews as hostages. Probably Ben Aharon's remarks were partly a reaction to the Syrian media's provocative assertions such as: 'The entire world attests that this response [Asad's letter to Bush] has turned enemy calculations upside down and rendered Shamir's government unable to continue the campaign of deception in which Arabs are portrayed as unwilling to make peace.'[36] Ben Aharon's reaction partly reflected the continuous hardline position of Shamir's government regarding the Golan.

Thus, in order to underline its determination not to relinquish the Golan, on 21 July 1991 the Israeli government published a plan to double the Jewish population in the Golan, enhancing economic development and creating more jobs there. And while the Israeli chief of staff, General Barak, publicly stressed the vital importance of the Golan to Israel's security, sixty-nine Knesset members—including Labour members—signed a document in which they promised to maintain Israel's sovereignty over the Golan.[37] In contrast, 'senior military sources' reportedly said that although the Golan Heights had a crucial strategic value, it would be a mistake to rule out negotiations with Syria, as the political process might engender a real chance of getting another Arab country out of the circle of hostility surrounding Israel. A few Likud Knesset members advocated returning part of the Golan for peace with Syria, but insisted on retaining the West Bank and Gaza. Such a position was at that juncture perhaps more widespread among Likud than Labour members. The latter preferred to hold on to the Golan and give up Gaza and part of the West Bank.[38]

The public debate regarding the Golan notwithstanding, the Israeli government's major concern was the United States, not Syria. After a series of talks with Baker, in June 1991 Shamir rejected Bush's proposal for a Middle East peace conference on the assumption that Asad would also turn it down. But subsequently Shamir had to re-evaluate his position in the light of Asad's positive response in July. Shamir and his colleagues possibly suspected that Bush had promised Asad to force Israel to withdraw from the Golan within the framework of a peace agreement. Reacting to such a scenario, Israeli Defence Minister Arens said: 'The USA is not capable of promising such a thing. We are in the Golan Heights, not the Americans,' and Binyamin Begin said in a Knesset debate: 'As an arm is part of the body, so is the Golan to the state of Israel.'[39] Other officials indicated that President Bush should be aware of President Ford's commitment (in a letter of 1 September 1975) to Israel's then prime minister, Rabin, regarding Israel 'remaining on the Golan Heights' even within a peace agreement with Syria. Reportedly Baker told Shamir in July 1991 that the United States would continue to honour the terms of this letter and possibly gave other assurances concerning Israel's security and economy.[40] As it happened, Israel at that time was awaiting American assurances on the $10 billion in loan guarantees for settling Soviet–Jewish immigrants; and in order to obtain those assurances and avoid confrontation with Washington on the peace process, on 1 August 1991 Shamir announced his conditional acceptance of the American proposal for a peace conference in October (pending the list of Palestinian negotiators with whom Israel would agree to meet); and on 22 October 1991 the Israeli cabinet voted to go to the Madrid peace conference due to open on 30 October.

It would appear that this decision, although significantly supported by a large majority of Israelis,[41] was rather tactical, aiming at throwing the ball back into the Syrian court and avoiding American accusations of obstructionism. Yet, to make sure that his own line would prevail, Shamir himself assumed leadership of the Israeli delegation to the Madrid conference, causing his more pragmatic foreign minister David Levy to forgo the event (which was to be attended by Arab foreign ministers).

Dismayed by the Israeli decision to accept the American proposal (and later to attend the Madrid conference), the Syrian media denounced it as 'no more than a manoeuvre intended primarily to get Israel out of its dilemmas, which resulted from the sincere Syrian response to international peace efforts'.

In sum, on the eve of the Madrid conference the declared positions of both Syria and Israel did not show promising signs of a peaceful settlement. The Syrian government, allegedly presenting a unified Arab position, stressed its adherence to UN Resolutions 242 and 338 and demanded full Israeli withdrawal from the entire Golan as well as from all Arab territories occupied in June 1967, notably the West Bank, Gaza, and East Jerusalem ('Palestine comes before the Golan Heights').[42] In return Syria was prepared to agree to peace, which in fact meant non-belligerency, without recognition of Israel's legitimacy and with no diplomatic relations and normalization.

Israel, in contrast, demanded full peace with diplomatic relations and the like, but refused to relinquish the Golan (and other occupied territories, let alone East Jerusalem). While continuing to expand Israeli settlements in the Golan (even in October 1991), Shamir would not budge from his earlier statements in March and July 1991:

> The Syrians will tell us that they want the Golan Heights and we shall tell them No! . . . Undoubtedly the Golan Heights is part of Israel. . . . This is the government's position. . . . Resolution 242 has nothing to do with the Golan. . . . If the Syrians were to bring up in the negotiations the subject of withdrawal from the Golan Heights, they should know our answer.[43]

Whether or not these divergent Israeli and Syrian positions were merely of a declarative bargaining nature,[44] they were essentially presented at the Madrid peace conference and also in the subsequent bilateral negotiations, during the first months of 1992.

THE MADRID PEACE CONFERENCE AND PROCESS: SYRIA CHANGES COURSE

The Madrid peace conference opened on 30 October 1991 under the joint chairmanship of Bush and Gorbachev and with the participation of Israel, Syria, Lebanon, and a joint Jordanian–Palestinian delegation, as well as representatives of the UN and the European Community. In its opening speech, as well as at subsequent sessions, Syria manifested its traditional hostile ideological attitude towards Israel: it did not acknowledge Israel's legitimacy, attempting to forge a joint Arab position and minimize direct deliberations with the Israeli delegation. Thus, while stressing Syria's genuine desire for a 'just and comprehensive peace' based on UN resolutions, Foreign Minister Faruq al-Shara', in his opening speech, sharply attacked Israel for its aggression since 1948 against the Arabs, notably the Palestinians, its inhuman and unjust behaviour in the occupied territories, as well as its settler-colonialist nature and its distorted, illegitimate claim for Jewish sovereignty in Palestine. Producing and waving a photo of the young Shamir, whom he called 'a terrorist' (under the British mandate in Palestine), al-Shara' insisted that 'not one inch' of the Golan Heights, the West Bank, the Gaza Strip, and 'Arab Jerusalem' should remain in Israeli hands.[45] He also announced Syria's refusal to attend the multilateral talks on regional issues, in which Jordan, the Palestinians, and several Arab states agreed to participate. Presumably al-Shara' did not approve of these pragmatic decisions by the Jordanians and the Palestinians; nor did he like their conciliatory speeches at the Madrid conference opening session. Damascus indeed made great efforts during and after the conference to exercise control over the positions of the other Arab parties, notably the

PLO, but failed. Nor was Syria able to involve the United States in the negotiations in order to apply pressure on Israel to accept the principle of withdrawal from the occupied territories before any progress could be made.[46]

Israel, in contrast, manifested a mixture of rigid and positive positions both at Madrid and in the subsequent bilateral talks with Syria. In his opening speech in Madrid Shamir appealed for peace between Israel and the Arab states, for Arab recognition of Israel's legitimacy, as well as for the building of confidence between the parties. He omitted assertions of Israeli claims with respect to the Golan Heights, Jerusalem, the West Bank, and Gaza, and did not rule out eventual Israeli withdrawal from some of the territory occupied in 1967. On the other hand, Shamir depicted Syria as 'one of the most oppressive tyrannical regimes in the world' and demanded that the Arabs should renounce *jihad* (holy war) and the PLO covenant, and end violence and terrorism.[47] Similarly, Yossi Ben Aharon, Shamir's aide and head of the Israeli delegation to the Syria–Israel talks, apparently accused Syria of anti-Semitism: during one of the bilateral sessions he threw onto the table a copy of an anti-Jewish book written by Mustafa Tlas, Syria's defence minister and a close comrade of Asad.[48]

Nevertheless, after several rounds of bilateral talks, mostly in Washington, during which the positions of both sides remained far apart, the atmosphere surrounding the talks improved and some progress was made. The Syrian delegates also professed an interest in discussing peace, not only territory, while the Israelis suggested that Israeli withdrawal was not excluded.[49]

Subsequently, in March 1992, the Syrian delegation for the first time adopted a more positive position, talking about now recognizing Israel and reaching a peace agreement (though not a 'treaty') with it, provided that Israel was prepared to withdraw from the entire Golan Heights, as well as from other occupied territories. As Muwaffaq al-Allaf, head of the Syrian delegation, publicly said in Washington on 6 March 1992:

The Arabs are saying to Israel . . . we want to settle the conflict with you . . . we are ready to make peace with Israel, with all the attributes of that peace, and we hope that you in your turn . . . [will] implement withdrawal from the territories that you have occupied in 1967, in order to make that peace, and those peaceful relations of the future Middle East, possible between you and us.

Al-Allaf would not describe the attributes of peace with Israel, but he gave (in his definition) 'positive' answers to the following three questions put to him: 'Is Syria ready to end the conflict with Israel? Is Syria ready to recognize Israel in its pre-1967 border? Is Syria ready to sign a peace treaty with Israel?' The answer to the first question was direct: 'I tell you, yes, we want to end the conflict with Israel.' To the second question: 'Yes . . . if a comprehensive settlement ended Israel's occupation of all Arab territories, then we would be talking about a situation of regional co-operation, economic co-operation, other co-operation, and how can you have that co-operation without mutual recognition and mutual acceptance?'

Finally, the third question was answered in a rather evasive and unclear way: 'When you make peace between all the Arab partners and Israel you will not just say a word, you have to have an instrument registered at the United Nations . . . that means the answer to all your three questions is positive, but subject to a basic Israeli answer that they are ready to withdraw completely from the Arab territory . . . Because relinquishing the land Israel occupied in 1967 [al-Allaf said in his opening remarks] would permit discussion of how to ensure security for Israel not based on geography and on territory but based on acceptance and agreements and international guarantees and the outcome would be peace.'

Throughout his talk al-Allaf stressed that by peace he meant 'comprehensive peace' with all Arab parties, and he also remarked: 'The Israelis are very allergic to the concept of comprehensive peace . . . They always ask us to confine ourselves to relations and to a settlement between Syria and Israel. . . . [and regarding the notion of territory for peace] the Israelis respond with the principle of peace for peace.'[50]

Al-Allaf essentially reiterated these points in another lecture in Washington on 10 May 1992, with a few nuances:

The equation of peace is that Israel withdraws from the territories it occupied and the Arabs accept to establish peace with Israel. When that understanding and agreement is achieved, it has to be translated into an instrument . . . whatever you call that instrument, whether it is an agreement, whether it is an accord, it is an instrument which shall really put your agreement into writing officially . . . What is the difference between accord, agreement, or treaty? I do not see any difference myself.

In sum, by the spring of 1992 Syria made a very significant move towards Israel by being publicly prepared, for the first time, to recognize it and its security needs, forgo the past, 'become good neighbours', and finally to sign a peace agreement, the attributes of which still remained unclear. All this, provided Israel withdrew from all Arab territories occupied in 1967 and according to UN Resolutions 242 and 338 agree to a comprehensive settlement of the Arab–Israeli conflict. It should be pointed out at this juncture that even Hafiz al-Asad, on the occasion of starting his new term as Syria's president on 12 March 1992, alluded to the new Syrian approach in his generally mild speech: 'It is known that Syria was the one which opened the road for peace by positively respond-ing to the American initiative which is based on Resolutions 242 and 338 and the principle of land for peace . . . Israel does not want peace . . . is the enemy of peace.'[52]

To be sure, the Israeli public has longed for peace with Syria and other Arab nations for years, but the Shamir government adhered to its old rigid position. Syrian Foreign Minister al-Shara' indicated this already in November 1991, when he surprisingly said 'that he believed that the Israeli people desired peace, but their government was blocking the way . . . Israel is a special case where the government is more hawkish than the people. In the Arab world it is just the opposite—we are more flexible than the Arab people.'[53]

Indeed, Shamir's right-wing government rejected the Syrian con-ditions for a comprehensive peace and particularly for an Israeli with-drawal from all occupied territories. Perhaps Shamir was prepared to withdraw from a small part of the Golan, but not from the entire Heights, nor the West Bank, let alone from East Jerusalem. He possibly continued to interpret UN Resolutions 242 and 338 as not being applicable to the Golan (or the West Bank). As the spokesperson for the Syrian delegation to the peace talks publicly complained to Washington on 27 April 1992: 'One of the points they [the Israeli delegation] raised was that Resolution 242 is just a set of non-binding principles . . . Mr Ben Aharon [head of Israel's delegation] himself gave a statement which said that Israel's objective is to reach a peace treaty with Syria, but without any with-drawal.'[54]

NOTES

1. For numerous references see the Syrian newspapers *al-Ba'th*, *Tishrin*, *al-Thawra*, and Damascus Radio for the year 1988–9. Cf. F. Lawson, 'Syria' in R. Brynen, *Echoes of the Intifada* (Boulder, Colo., 1991), 217–19.
2. See respectively Damascus Radio, 18 and 20 Feb. 1988; *Ha'aretz*, 26 Feb. 1988, citing Richard Murphy. See also *al-Ba'th*, 15 and 18 Feb. 1988.

3. See respectively *al-Ba'th*, 6 Apr. 1988; *Ha'aretz*, 7 Feb. 1988; *US News and World Report*, 14 Mar. 1988, 14.
4. Cf. G. P. Shultz, *Turmoil and Triumph* (New York, 1993), 1025 ff.; *Ha'aretz*, 25 Feb., 5 Apr., and 7 June 1988; *Ma'ariv*, 26 Feb. 1988.
5. *Al-Qabas* (Kuwait), 27 Jan. 1989. See also Drysdale and Hinnebusch, *Syria*, 166–7. Cf. *Yediot Ahronot*, 2 and 9 June 1988; *Ha'aretz*, 20 Feb. 1989.
6. *Tishrin*, 21 Jan. 1989. *MECS* (1990), 124.
7. *Yediot Ahronot*, 23 May and 11 July 1989. Cf. Drysdale and Hinnebusch, *Syria*, 196 ff.
8. See *Ha'aretz*, 23 Dec. 1988; *Middle East Journal*, 43 (1989), 286; cf. *Tishrin*, 9 Feb. and 16 May 1989; *Newsweek*, 1 May 1989, 17; *Yediot Ahronot*, 20 Jan. 1989; *Ha'aretz*, 4 May 1989.
9. *New York Times*, 15 and 17 July 1990, 29 Dec. 1989; *Tishrin*, 12 and 17 Dec. 1989; *Yediot Ahronot*, 3 May 1990.
10. *MECS* (1990), 123; *Ha'aretz*, 19 Mar., 2 and 3 June 1990; a letter from Senator Arlen Specter to Neil Abrams, dated 31 Jan. 1990 (in author's possession). See also *Yediot Ahronot*, 19 Jan. 1990.
11. P. Seale, 'Asad: Kibitzing on Syria's Grand Master', *International Herald Tribune*, 19 May 1989; interview with Asad, *Time*, 3 Apr. 1989. Asad's speech, 8 Mar. 1990, Damascus Radio; for more examples see: *al-Ba'th*, 4 and 10 Jan., 10 and 18 Feb., 14 May, 29 June 1988; *Tishrin*, 9 Mar. and 11 Apr. 1989; Damascus Radio, 19 Sept. and 23 Nov. 1990.
12. *International Herald Tribune*, 19 May 1989; Radio Damascus, 8 Mar. and 31 July 1990; *al-Ba'th*, 5 Jan., 21 Feb., 21 Apr. 1988. *Tishrin*, 9 May, 17 July 1988 and 10 and 18 Oct. 1989. Damascus Radio, 27 July 1990 and 29 Oct. 1990.
13. See T. P. Hannah, *At Arms Length: Soviet–Syrian Relations in the Gorbachev Era*, Washington Institute Policy Paper, (Washington, 1989), 25. For more details regarding the changes of Soviet policy in the political and military arenas, see ibid., *passim*; also *Ha'aretz*, 13 Dec. 1988. Cf. Drysdale and Hinnebusch, *Syria*, 162 ff.
14. Hannah, *At Arms Length*, 13–14; J. Schreiber, 'Major Soviet Shift', *Jerusalem Post*, 9 Nov. 1988; *Financial Times*, 21 Dec. 1988; cf. *Tishrin*, 11 Apr. 1988. See also R. O. Freedman, 'Continuity and Change in Soviet Policy toward the Middle East', Occasional Paper (Jerusalem: Hebrew University, 1989).
15. See e.g. *al-Ba'th*, 22 Feb., 5 Apr. 1988; *Tishrin*, 16 May 1988, 9 Mar., 1 Apr., 4 Dec. 1989; Asad's speech, Damascus Radio, 8 Mar. 1990. Cf. A. Cowell, 'Trouble in Damascus', *New York Times Magazine*, 1 Apr. 1990, 33.
16. Asad's speech, Damascus Radio, 8 Mar. 1990. See also *Syria and Gulf Crisis* (Damascus; Dar al-Ba'th, n.d. trans. Ahmad Fayez Ayashi), 11; *MECS* (1990), 124; cf. *al-Ba'th*, 5 Aug. 1990; Drysdale and Hinnebusch, *Syria*, 169 ff.
17. *Syria and Gulf Crisis*, 15, 27, 37, 41; for other accounts of the Iraqi invasion of Kuwait and its impact on Syria and Israel *see Harb al-Khalij* (Arabic; Damascus, 1992); R. O. Freedman (ed.), *The Middle East after Iraq's Invasion of*

Kuwait (Gainesville, Fla., 1993), 237 ff.; J. Alpher (ed.), *War in the Gulf: Implications for Israel* (Tel Aviv University, Jaffee Center, 1992); D. Pipes, *Damascus Courts the West: Syrian Politics 1989–1991* (Institute for Near East Policy, Washington, 1991). See also Damascus Radio, 8, 14, 30 Aug. 1990.

18. Cf. Pipes, *Damascus Courts*, 27. For the text of the treaty see ibid. 71 ff. Cf. M. Ma'oz. 'Brit Surya Levanon', *Yediot Ahronot*, 23 May 1991. Cf. J. K. Cooley, 'Asad in Beirut . . .', *International Herald Tribune*, 19 May 1991; *al-Masira* (Lebanon), 29 July 1991.

19. See e.g. *Tishrin*, 29 June, 4 July 1988, 9 Mar. 1989. Cf. Drysdale and Hinnebusch, *Syria*, 134–5; Quandt, *Peace Process*, 367 ff.

20. Pipes, *Damascus Courts*, 25, citing Arab sources. See also *Ma'ariv*, 16 July 1991.

21. See respectively *International Herald Tribune*, 24–5 Nov. 1990, 1; *Syria and Gulf Crisis*, 15.

22. Quandt, *Peace Process*, 396, 399, 402; see also *New York Times*, 18 Apr. 1991.

23. *Washington Post*, 16 July 1991. See also *New York Times*, 15 July 1991; *Ma'ariv*, 17 July 1991; *Tishrin*, 30 July 1991.

24. A. Shalev, 'The Outlook for Substantive Syrian–Israeli Negotiations', in Alpher (ed.), *War in the Gulf*, 267–8; M. Ma'oz, 'Is Syria Preparing a War against Israel?', *Yediot Ahronot*, 22 Mar. 1991; interview with P. Seale, *Ha'aretz*, 4 June 1991; *al-Hayat*, 19 Aug. 1991.

25. *Washington Post*, 29 July 1991; cf. *New York Times*, 15 and 21 July 1991; *Newsweek*, 1 July 1991 (interview with Faruq Shara', Syrian foreign minister); *al-Hayat*, 9 July 1977; *Ha'aretz*, 26 July 1991; *al-Masira* (Lebanon), 29 July 1991. See also Asad's interview for ABC TV, cited in *Tishrin*, 21 Sept. 1991.

26. See M. Ma'oz, 'Syrian–Israeli Relations and the Middle East Peace Process', *Jerusalem Journal of International Relations*, 14/3 (1992), 12 ff.; cf. Asad's interview with *Washington Post*, 29 July 1991.

27. *FBIS*, 10 Oct. 1991, 27; cf. Asad's interview with *Washington Post*, 29 July 1991; cf. Damascus Radio, 22 July, 6 Aug. 1991; *New York Times*, 28 Oct. 1991.

28. See respectively Asad's interview with *Washington Post*, 29 July 1991; *FBIS*, 10 Oct. 1991; cf. *al-Hayat*, 28 Aug. 1991; and *Peacewatch* [Institute for Near East Policy, Washington], 8, 31 Oct. 1991.

29. *Ma'ariv*, 26 Feb. 1991; *Ha'aretz* 4 and 5 Feb. and 1 and 2 Mar., 5 Apr. 1988; cf. Shultz, *Turmoil*, 1024 ff.

30. For the text see *Jerusalem Post*, 15 May 1989; *Yediot Ahronot*, 11 Mar. and 15 May 1989.

31. See respectively E. R. Fletcher, 'The Quiet Border', *Jerusalem Post Magazine*, 3 Feb. 1989; *New York Times*, 24 Mar. 1991; cf. *Yediot Ahronot*, 26 Jan. 1990; Z. Schiff, *Peace with Security*, 75–6.

32. See respectively *Ha'aretz*, 8 June 1988; *New York Times*, 24 Dec. 1989; *Yediot Ahronot*, 19 June 1990 and 4 Apr. 1991; *Ma'ariv*, 4 Aug. 1991. See also Shalev, 'The Outlook', pp. 271–2.

33. See respectively *Ha'aretz*, 22 Mar. 1991; *Spectrum* (Labour Party monthly), Dec. 1991, 11. *Ma'ariv*, 1 Mar. 1991. Cf. *Davar*, 26 Feb. 1991; *Ha'aretz*, 22 Sept. 1991.

34. See respectively M. Feuerwerger, 'Israel, the Gulf War and its Aftermath', in Freedman (ed.), *The Middle East after*, 238; Israel Radio, 7 Aug. 1990; *Yediot Ahronot*, 19 Mar. 1991. See also *New York Times*, 17 July 1991; Quandt, *Peace Process*, 402; *Yediot Ahronot*, 17 July, 19 Sept., and 6 Dec. 1990; *Ha'aretz*, 23 Sept. 1990.

35. See *New York Times*, 17 July 1991; *Ma'ariv*, 16, 24, and 30 July 1991; *Ha'aretz*, 26, 27 July 1991; Israel Educational TV, 30 July 1991.

36. See respectively *Ha'aretz*, 26 July 1991; *Ma'ariv*, 25 July 1991; *Tishrin*, 18 July 1991; cf. *al-Hayat*, 19 Aug. 1991; Damascus Radio, 19 July 1991; *Yediot Ahronot*, 23 Nov. 1990 and 14 Mar. 1991.

37. *Ha'aretz*, 21 July 1991; Israel Radio, 14 Mar., 23 July, and 6 Aug. 1991. See also *Yediot Ahronot*, 20 Mar. 1991; *Ma'ariv*, 23 July and 1 Aug. 1991.

38. See respectively Israel Radio, 23 July 1991; Shalev, 'The Outlook', 271–2; Ma'oz, 'Syrian–Israeli Relations', 14; Feuerwerger, 'Israel, the Gulf War', 247. Cf. *Yediot Ahronot*, 22 Mar. and 19 Apr. 1991; *Ma'ariv*, 30 July 1991.

39. *Ma'ariv*, 21 and 23 July 1991. See also *Ha'aretz*, 20 and 22 July 1991; *Washington Post*, 16 July 1991; *New York Times*, 15, 17, and 21 July 1991. Cf. Y. Olmert, 'The Syrian Position', in *The Negotiation between Israel and Syria*, (Hebrew; Bar Ilan University, 1993), 5.

40. Israel Radio, 20 July 1991; *Davar*, 28 July 1991; *Ma'ariv*, 22 and 30 July 1991. Cf. Quandt, *Peace Process*, 402. For the text of Ford's letter see ibid. 441–2; *New York Times*, 17 July 1991.

41. *New York Times*, 28 Oct. 1991; cf. Feuerwerger, 'Israel, the Gulf'. 247.

42. Damascus Radio, 5 Aug. 1991. See also ibid. 3 and 6 Aug., 2 and 7 Oct. 1991; *New York Times*, 29 Oct. 1991. Cf. *Washington Post*, 31 July 1991.

43. See respectively *Yediot Ahronot*, 19 Mar. 1991; *Ma'ariv*, 30 July 1991. See also Israel Radio, 4 Oct. 1991; *New York Times*, 17 July and 20 Oct. 1991.

44. Cf. J. L. Rasmussen and R. B. Oakley, *Conflict Resolution in the Middle East: Simulating a Diplomatic Negotiation between Israel and Syria* (Washington: United States Institute of Peace, 1992).

45. CNN and Israel TV, 31 Oct. 1991; *The Times* and *Financial Times*, 1 Nov. 1991; cf. *al-Ba'th*, 25 Dec. 1991.

46. Cf. Quandt, *Peace Process*, 404–5; *New York Times*, 10 and 19 Nov. 1991; *Peacewatch*, 9 and 10, 1 and 8 Nov. 1991; 12, 5 Dec. 1991. See also *Independent*, 31 Oct. 1991; *al-Ba'th*, 29 Jan. 1992.

47. *Independent*, 2 Nov. 1991; Feuerwerger, 'Israel, the Gulf War', 247; *Peacewatch*, 7, 31 Oct. 1991; *New York Times*, 2 Nov. 1991 (the full text of Shamir's address).

48. Interview with Yossi Olmert, a member of the Israeli delegation to the talks with Syria, *Ha'aretz*, 7 Aug. 1992.

49. *Peacewatch*, 14, 13 Dec. 1991; 16, 20 Dec. 1991; cf. *al-Ba'th*, 29 Jan. 1992.

50. Israel Ministry of Foreign Affairs, unclassified document, 6 Mar. 1992. Cf. *Washington Post*, 3 Mar. 1992.
51. Israel Ministry of Foreign Affairs, unclassified document, 10 May 1992. Cf. *al-Quds* (Jerusalem), 9 May 1992.
52. Damascus Radio, 12 Mar. 1992; *International Herald Tribune*, 19 Mar. 1992. Cf. interview with Olmert, *Ha'aretz*, 7 Aug. 1992.
53. *International Herald Tribune*, 5 Nov. 1991.
54. Israel Ministry of Foreign Affairs, unclassified document, 27 Apr. 1992. Cf. *Peacewatch*, 27, 5 Mar. 1992.

Peace Negotiations

CHANGES IN RABIN'S POSITION

The Israeli Labour Party, as we know, has adopted a different interpretation of UN Resolutions 242 and 338: accepting the principle of 'territorial compromise within the framework of full and viable peace', but also insisting that Israeli settlement and military control in the Golan should continue even if there were peace with Syria. To be sure, several senior members of the party, particularly those who belonged to the Knesset Golan lobby, are categorically opposed to any compromise in that region. At one stage they were headed by Shlomo Hillel, former Speaker and one of Labour's candidates for the presidency.

Ezer Weizman, former minister in the Likud and Labour governments (and president since 1993) has maintained a totally different position. At a press conference held early in March 1991 he proposed to American Secretary of State Baker:

Go to Damascus and tell President Asad that we are ready to talk with him about a peace agreement identical to the peace agreement with Egypt, namely, regarding the Golan Heights. It is clear to me that Asad's reply would be: there can be no agreement with me outside the Palestinian issue. Then I would reply, this is also my understanding, and I am prepared to part with Judaea and Samaria [the West Bank] in return for peace, and within special arrangements that will assure security. Tell Asad that Syria, Lebanon, and Jordan and the Palestinians are in one package. We are talking about a wide [comprehensive] peace. The Syrians will lead the process in co-operation with Egypt.[1]

In view of these divergent Labour Party attitudes, it is clearly worth while examining the evolution of Rabin's position, since, as prime minister since June 1992, he has led the peace negotiations with the Arab nations, notably with Syria. On the one hand, Rabin has a long record of mistrust and antagonism towards the Syrian regime and Hafiz al-Asad. As we saw above, on the eve of the June 1967 war Rabin, then chief of staff, openly called for toppling the Ba'th regime in Damascus, and in June 1988, as defence minister, he declared that he did not regard Syria under

Asad as a partner for peace. Further, following his assertions in 1990 (and subsequently) that he would not give up the Golan even in the context of a peace treaty with Syria, Rabin made another belligerent statement in February 1991: 'We told [Syria] "if you use ground-to-ground missiles against Tel Aviv, Damascus will be destroyed. You launch missiles on Haifa, neither Damascus nor Aleppo will survive." '

On the other hand, Rabin said in late 1991 that Israel could talk with Syria ('already in 1949 we met the Syrians') and that Syria 'has already kept the separation of forces agreement for seventeen years, since May 1974'.[2] And on the eve of the 1992 elections, he said: 'There is limited room for territorial compromise . . . [and I] would be willing to return some of the land to Syria. . . . There might be other compromises . . . like leasing the land.'[3]

It would appear, then, that notwithstanding his belligerent attitude towards Syria, Rabin has recognized not only that without Syria there cannot be a stable and durable Arab–Israeli peace, but that in return for peace with Damascus, Jerusalem would be required to relinquish almost the entire Golan Heights. Or, in his own words, 'Asad will not settle for less than what Sadat got.' This, as Rabin frequently explained, was due to Begin's commitment to return the whole of Sinai and remove all the settlements there, all of which established a negative precedent regarding the Golan.[4]

Yet, as we know, Rabin considered the Golan an important strategic asset and was also attached to the settlements there, many of which are affiliated with the Labour Party. Therefore he wished to see the Golan/Syrian issue deferred as long as possible, and eventually to reach a 'territorial compromise' with Syria in return for peace. As for this 'compromise', Rabin apparently expected to secure American backing, mainly on the basis of Ford's letter to him of September 1975. He felt further encouraged when President Bush, in his speech at the opening of the Madrid conference, referred to the concept of 'territorial compromise' between Syria and Israel. 'This was the first utterance of an American president since the Six Day War in such a form,' said Rabin on 1 November 1991, but he also added that: 'the solution to the Israeli–Syrian problem is much more complex and complicated than . . . the Israeli–Palestinian problem.' This, since the Palestinian issue, unlike the Syrian, could, it seemed to him, be settled in a two-phase process before reaching final status.

Consequently on 19 April 1992 Rabin stated that, if he were to be elected prime minister, he would work to grant autonomy to the Palestinians in the West Bank and Gaza 'within six months to a year' . . . whereas peace with Syria must wait until the end of the process, and 'it is highly doubtful whether a comprehensive peace [i.e. including Syria] will be reached in my lifetime.' Indeed, following his election as prime minister, Rabin announced that he would first work towards implementing Palestinian autonomy 'within six to nine months', and leave the Syria–Golan issue for the final stages of negotiations.[5] In making such a statement, he perhaps believed that to realize Palestinian autonomy would be more acceptable to the Israeli public than to relinquish the Golan. Apart from the difficulty of simultaneously negotiating on two crucial issues, it can be assumed that by first hastening on the Palestinian track Rabin intended to put pressure on Asad to meet Israel's terms regarding the 'territorial compromise' or be left behind.

Apparently in reaction, Asad staged a show of strength by encouraging, in July 1992, further Hizballa terrorist/guerrilla attacks against Israeli targets, and ordering, in mid-August, a test firing of an advanced SCUD-C missile. Former Chief of Staff Gur, now Israel's deputy defence minister, threatened to storm Damascus should Syria launch missiles against Israel, while Rabin expressed scepticism regarding Asad's peace intentions.[6] Subsequently, however, with the mediation of Secretary of State Baker (and President Mubarak), both Rabin and Asad adopted more positive attitudes towards Israeli–Syrian negotiation, while President Bush promised Rabin, in August 1992, to support the loan guarantees to Israel and to maintain its qualitative military superiority—to Syria's dismay.[7] Recognizing also that Syria could undermine the Israeli–Palestinian track, Rabin sought to improve the atmosphere. He mentioned the possibility of an interim settlement whereby Israel would give up a few kilometres in the Golan. Furthermore, Israel's newly appointed chief negotiator with the Syrian delegation, Professor Itamar Rabinovich, announced for the first time, on 24 August 1992, that Israel considered UN Resolution 242 to be applicable also to the negotiations with Syria.

Bushra Kanafani, spokesperson for the Syrian delegation in Washington, praised the new Israeli approach as 'constructive' and reflecting a fresh 'political mentality', while the Syrian media manifested a more sceptical attitude.[8]

ASAD'S AND RABIN'S INDIRECT DIALOGUE

Earlier that month Syria initiated its own positive, constructive signal regarding the peace process with Israel. Professor Muhammad Aziz Shukri, dean of the Law faculty at Damascus University—a government-controlled institute—in a lecture at the Washington Institute for Near East Policy, spelled out for the first time that Syria was willing to give Israel the kind of peace it was requiring. First Professor Shukri repeated Syria's known demands: 'Israel must withdraw from all Arab occupied territory . . . and recognize the rights of the Palestinians.' Regarding the Golan, Shukri did not leave any room for doubt: 'Not an inch of the Golan is for sale or lease . . . even a lease would be admitting Israel has some rights to the land.' Then he added: 'The solution must be comprehensive. Peace treaties can be signed separately, but simultaneously. . . . Syria accepts the idea of mutual security arrangements.' But Shukri's key sentences were: 'The state of war between Israel and Syria should be ended legally and completely, and replaced with a state of peace. This should be peace in the widest sense imaginable, including mutual recognition, normalization of relations, diplomatic exchange, economic co-operation, social co-operation, etc.'[9]

True, Professor Shukri was not speaking officially for his government, but as a respectable scholar in an autocratic country like Syria, he could not have made statements incompatible with the official line. Thus, even if his lecture was a trial balloon, it could possibly have indicated Syria's intentions regarding peace with Israel. Furthermore, Asad himself responded positively to the new Israeli line. In a speech to a visiting Druze delegation from the Golan on 9 September 1992, Asad talked for the first time about his concept of peace: 'the peace of the brave, the peace of knights, real peace, a peace that lives, endures, and guarantees the interests of all'. But he added that in return for a peace settlement, Syria demanded 'each centimetre of the Golan'. Syria's chief negotiator, Muwaffaq al-Allaf, explained later to his Israeli counterparts that by 'peace of the brave . . . of knights', Asad was not referring to relations between Salah-al-Din (Saladin) and the Crusaders in the twelfth century, but to a comprehensive and respectable peace taking a brave person to implement and maintain with a knight's honour. Allaf himself reportedly said to the Israeli delegation, in late August 1992, that Syria was ready to sign a contractual peace with Israel and to discuss diplomatic relations. Syria's minister of foreign affairs, Faruq al-Shara', took another significant step when he announced, also for the first time, on 23 September 1992 in New York, that Syria was prepared to sign a 'total peace' with Israel in return for Israel's withdrawal from the occupied Arab lands.[10]

Israeli reactions to these important Syrian statements varied. Foreign Minister Peres depicted Asad's words as 'almost sensational'; he suggested opening an 'informal channel' of talks with Syria, and reportedly also advocated, in private, an Israeli withdrawal from the Golan in return for peace with Syria. Deputy Defence Minister Gur said that Syria's readiness to make peace with Israel seemed serious and that it was important for Israel to examine that opportunity very thoroughly. Rabin also considered Asad's statement as 'important progress', but was not yet ready to accept the Syrian terms and to change his concept of 'territorial compromise'. In his address to a special meeting of the Knesset, Rabin said (amidst strong protests from right-wing members): 'Our intention is indeed to thoroughly exploit that chance, but not on the assumption that in return for peace we give everything; certainly the precedent of the peace with Egypt should not be repeated. The government has a mandate and it will conduct negotiations in order to achieve full peace, while preserving the territorial-security assets as much as possible.' Reportedly Rabin instructed his chief negotiator with Syria to explore whether Syria was ready to sign a contractual peace treaty that would include all elements of normalization (diplomatic relations, open borders, trade and tourism); and whether Syria would agree to de-link this treaty from the need to achieve progress on other fronts. If Syria's response was positive, an attempt would then be made to negotiate an 'agreement in principle' that would cover three areas: the nature of peace; the applicability of UN Resolution 242, including the clauses on Israeli withdrawal; and the need for mutual security arrangements.[11]

In short, Rabin's position can be summarized in a few sentences:

We shall not enter into any territorial discussion with the Syrians before they say in a loud voice to us and to the people in Syria that peace for them means embassies, open borders, and normalization. Peace with Syria must stand on its own feet and must not be conditioned on agreements with other states [parties] with whom we negotiate. . . . Israeli forces cannot come down from the Golan until it is manifestly clear that the Syrian people—from top to bottom—have come to accept that the conflict with Israel is finally over.

In an attempt to explain Rabin's new strategy, it can be assessed that apart from American and Egyptian inducements to advance on the Syrian track, Rabin himself believed that a strategic change had occurred in Damascus towards Israel; and that, unlike the Palestinians, 'Syria is a clear address with a householder who is capable of taking decisions.' True, Rabin was not convinced that Damascus had undergone an ideological transformation and a change of heart ('peace does not mean love for the other nation'), but he was determined to examine thoroughly the chances for peace with Syria. He argued that if this was not done, a stalemate would occur and this could 'bring sooner or later a danger of war . . . I have experienced enough wars and wish to live with a clear conscience that we have done everything for the sake of peace.' Yet Rabin demanded that Asad provide proof that he seriously sought peace: 'I do not have X-rays to examine a person's intentions . . . I judge on the basis of moves, deeds, and expressions, and this component is greatly missing on the part of Syria.'[12] Specifically, Rabin wanted Asad to convince him and the Israeli public of his peaceful policies by clearly spelling out his readiness for genuine peace with Israel, and making gestures, such as meeting with Rabin; or broadcasting 'a speech on Syrian television by President Hafiz Asad to his own people, advocating peace and coexistence with Israel'.[13] Only then would Rabin possibly commit himself to the principle of complete withdrawal from the Golan, although the final phase of the withdrawal would only be implemented when Syria established normal, peaceful relations with Israel.

In sum, at that juncture Rabin sought both to throw the ball back into Asad's court, and to prepare the Israeli public for concessions in the Golan. Meanwhile, the right-wing parties and the Golan settlers organized a series of demonstrations and protests in reaction to Rabin's conciliatory remarks towards Syria. He was sharply attacked, particularly after he was reported to have told a delegation from the Golan settlements that within a framework of peace with Syria 'it is not terrible if only thirteen settlements [out of thirty] will remain on the Golan Heights.' He was labelled a 'traitor' who 'deceived the people' and who did not have a 'mandate from the people' to give up parts of the country.[14] Significantly, several senior members of the Labour Party and of the Shinui Party also expressed their concern that, if the Golan returned to Syria, Israel's security and water resources (from the River Banyas) could be seriously threatened by a hostile, untrustworthy Baʿthist regime.[15]

In return, Rabin repeatedly stressed that Israel would not negotiate any territorial issues before the population was convinced that Asad and his people were ready for full and genuine peace and normalization. At the same time, Rabin pointed out over and over again that he did not see 'any preparation and manifestation of readiness by the [Syrian] president and the regime there to prove to Israel that they are truly ready for peace . . . Syria's president has not done even 1 per cent of what President Sadat did to convince the peoples in Israel and in Syria that he wants peace.'[16] Rabin complained that Asad refused to meet him or even to participate in a proposed TV satellite interview on the NBC network. He also criticized Syria for providing a base and backing for the ten militant Palestinian organizations and the Hizballa—all of whom are opposed to peace with Israel.[17]

Indeed, from Israel's viewpoint, Asad was doing very little at that period to convince the Israelis that he was ready for genuine peace and normalization, nor was he systematically preparing his own people for conciliation with Israel. True, Asad and other Syrian leaders, as well as the media, repeatedly stressed Syria's desire for peace, occasionally using the terms 'peace of the brave', 'an honourable peace', and on a few occasions advocating the study of the 'arts of peace', or indicating that Syria's 'struggle for peace' was no less important than any other struggle.[18] Yet these expressions did not always refer directly to Israel, which continued, in late 1992, to be frequently denounced in the Syrian media as rejecting or obstructing peace, as well as being aggressive and expansionist.[19] Syrian leaders (and media) did not miss a chance to stress that the Middle East peace should be 'just and comprehensive', entailing Israel's total withdrawal (*insihab kamil wa-shamil*) from all occupied Arab lands including East Jerusalem.[20]

Asad himself would not elaborate on his notion of 'total peace', and refused to meet with Rabin. He continued to insist on a prior Israeli commitment to total withdrawal from the Golan, as well as on the 'comprehensiveness' of any peace agreement, referring to the all-Arab conflict with Israel. It is very likely that Asad was prepared to accept Rabin's terms for peace and normalization in principle, and to implement them in the course of time, provided Israel agreed to his terms for peace. For although peace and normalization with Israel are certainly not compatible with Ba'thist pan-Arab tenets, or with his own ideological beliefs, Asad has recognized that he has no better alternative. Yet, in order to convince his own people, long indoctrinated on anti-Israeli lines, to accept Israel, he needed to demonstrate to them that he was forcing Israel to withdraw from all occupied Arab lands, notably the entire Golan; and that he was the only Arab leader since 1948 capable of achieving national rights for the Palestinians. Apart from his ideological motives, Asad also had strategic considerations behind his peace terms: on the one hand, he sought to push back the Israeli forces from their Golan positions, some 35 miles from Damascus, down to the pre-1967 armistice lines along the Hula and Jordan valleys; and on the other, he has sought not only to maintain his control in Lebanon, but also to cast his influence over a Palestinian entity or state (and possibly also Jordan); this, by helping both to get back their territories and/or national rights.

Consequently, Asad could not afford to commit himself to peace and normalization with Israel before these strategic and ideological objectives were achieved.

At the same time Asad continued to strengthen his army and to maintain his alliances with Iran, the Lebanese Hizballa, and the various militant Palestinian organizations, in order to achieve the following objectives: to enhance his leverage on the peace negotiations; to prevent or obstruct separate agreements between the PLO, or Jordan, and Israel, and to signal Syria's intention to develop a military option in the event that the peace negotiations collapsed.[21] To be sure, this Syrian policy, which represented a continuation of Asad's two-track strategy, was directed not only towards Israel, the PLO, and Jordan. Asad was also sending a message to President Bush that Syria was the key to peace or war in the Middle East. In addition to joining the American-led coalition in the Gulf War, Damascus had made several important concessions in the peace process, in accordance with Bush's requests; and it now expected American support for its position, otherwise the peace process could be undermined and Syria might use its alliance with Iran and the rejectionist organizations to destabilize the Middle East.

ASAD, RABIN, AND CLINTON

Nevertheless, despite continuing American military and financial assistance to Israel (which was criticized by Damascus), Asad considered President Bush's policy as empathetic, if not sympathetic, towards Syria. But following Clinton's victory in the November 1992 elections, Syrian leaders and media expressed anxiety regarding his Middle East policy (apparently in view of his record as a supporter of democratic Israel and his aversion to dictatorships and 'terrorist states' such as Syria). Syria's chief negotiator, Muwaffaq al-Allaf, complained, for example, that 'it seems that Israel, thinking that the Clinton administration is likely to be inclined to satisfy its ambitious endeavours now [will try] to bring about a standstill until the new administration takes office.'[22] Allaf also accused Israel of 'attacking Lebanon [Hizballa targets] . . . without justification or provocation'. Israel, in turn, had earlier blamed Syria for encouraging Hizballa's actions against Israel in order to remind Clinton that Asad was the 'Arab master of war-and-peace decisions'.[23]

Thus, by the end of 1992, following the Clinton victory and two more rounds—seven and eight—of the Arab–Israeli peace talks, the Syrian–

Israeli negotiations were at a standstill, despite the significant progress achieved during round six (from 24 August to 24 September 1992): while Israel had stated that UN resolution 242 was applicable to the Golan Heights and had given priority to the negotiation with Syria, Syria declared its readiness for 'total peace', for a 'peace agreement' with Israel and made other positive gestures such as permitting Syrian Jews to travel abroad.[24] But on the core issues, the Syrian definition of peace and the extent of the Israeli withdrawal, a wide gap still existed between Damascus and Jerusalem, beyond the chicken-and-egg argument over what came first. Whereas Israel was ready to withdraw *in* the Golan in return for a separate, full peace and normalization with Syria, Syria insisted on a *total* Israeli withdrawal from the entire Golan, southern Lebanon, the Gaza Strip, and the West Bank, including 'Arab Jerusalem'. Syria also insisted that the peace should be comprehensive, on all Arab fronts, and particularly include the implementation of the Palestinian rights to statehood as well as to the return of the 1948 refugees to their homes in pre-1967 Israel.[25]

Were these positions tactical or strategic, bargaining or final? What were both Asad's and Rabin's expectations from the new Clinton administration? Asked, in late 1992, whether they were optimistic regarding the prospects of peace, Asad said, 'I am inclined to be optimistic. The prospects are better because of the international climate and because of the increased number of Israelis who want peace.' Rabin was more sceptical: 'I hope it [peace] will be achieved. I don't know if it will be [reached] in my lifetime.' To be sure, both Asad and Rabin at that juncture recognized that the prospects of peace in the Middle East, notably between Syria and Israel, would depend to a large extent on the position of the incoming American president, Bill Clinton. Each of them had been preparing for Clinton's mediation, as described concisely and wittily by Leslie Gelb:

Obstructed by America's presidential campaign, the Syrian fox, President Assad, and the Israeli ox, Prime Minister Rabin, have been playing a daring game of peace. Sometimes publicly, sometimes secretly, both always ambiguously and cleverly in their different ways. . . . The Assad–Rabin peace formula is old: land for peace. What's new is that each leader has positioned himself to make a deal. The diplomatic trick for the mediator is to maneuver both into saying the magic words simultaneously and with substance.[26]

The Clinton administration began its term on 20 January 1993 and already in early February the new Secretary of State Christopher was assigned to 'revitalize' the peace process which had been suspended for several months, not only because of the divergent positions of the Arab and Israeli delegations but because of their inclination to wait for the new American administration's involvement. On 17 December 1992, following the kidnapping and killing of an Israeli police officer inside Israel by the Islamic Palestinian Ḥamas group, Israel deported some 400 Ḥamas leaders and activists to southern Lebanon. This action triggered widespread international criticism and intense Palestinian violence in the occupied territories, and caused a long delay in the resumption of the peace talks. (At a meeting of Arab foreign ministers in Cairo on 24 December it was said that the expulsion of the Palestinians [Ḥamas members] jeopardized but did not warrant ending the Middle East peace process.[27])

Significantly, in contrast to the PLO position, Syrian Foreign Minister Faruq al-Sharaʿ, after his meeting with Christopher, said on 21 February 1993 that Syria would not link the return of the Palestinian deportees to the renewal of the peace negotiations, because a peace settlement was more important. The Lebanese foreign minister, Faris Buwayz, apparently following Syrian directives, expressed a similar position, while his prime minister, Rafiq al-Hariri, had said a month earlier that his government was willing to conclude a peace treaty with Israel.[28]

Thus, even though he had valid cause to blame Israel for thwarting the peace process, and in spite, or because of, his concern about the pro-Israeli line of the new Clinton administration (and its Middle East team), Asad was determined to demonstrate his adherence to the peace negotiation under American auspices, pursuing a legalistic and a practical approach based on UN Resolutions 242 and 338 and on the Egyptian–Israeli precedent. Asad expected Clinton to follow the path of previous American administrations and support the Syrian position, and he continued to send positive signals towards the United States regarding his peaceful intentions and his hopeful expectations that an agreement would be achieved, with American backing.[29]

Thus, in order to facilitate the acceptance of his notions of a comprehensive peace and of total Israeli withdrawal, Asad for the first time, in early 1993, introduced the ideas of a gradual Israeli withdrawal and of possible different paces in the parallel Israeli–Arab negotiating tracks.[30] He also made further remarks, including some to his own public, regarding his desire for peace and his acceptance of Israel's existence. For example, in an address to Syrian religious leaders on 18 March 1993, at the end of the Ramadan fast and after Christopher's visit, Asad indicated that the 'struggle for peace is much harder than our war cam-

paigns . . . the developments in the world are very difficult for us . . . and
we in Syria must be aware of this and fulfil our obligations in order to be
more assured about our present and future . . . the future of our children
and grandchildren.'[31] In early May 1993 Asad gave an exclusive and
important interview to Patrick Seale for *al-Wasat*, an Arabic weekly
published in London. Expressing his doubts that the Israeli government
wished to make peace, and reiterating Syria's principles for a comprehensive peace, Asad made several significant comments such as: 'During the
past two years [there has been] a good support for peace efforts in Israel
and certainly it will have an influence on Israeli rulers.' Asked by Seale
whether he agreed to Israel's existence in the region, Asad answered that
he supported the Palestinian and Arab 'new position . . . that Palestine
consists of both the Arabs and the Israelis'. Equally important were Asad's
remarks related to the linkage between the various negotiation tracks. He
said that there could be varying speeds in the different tracks that might
produce agreements at different times; but these agreements should be
subject to a comprehensive settlement or 'the collective interests of all'
[Arabs, to be approved by Syria].[32] Asad's remarks were possibly directed
to give the impression that Syria would not object to separate bilateral
agreements between other Arab delegations and Israel, on condition that
they did not harm Syrian interests and were compatible with the goal of a
comprehensive settlement.

It can safely be assumed that besides his attempt to win (or regain)
American support for his position, Asad was endeavouring, through this
interview and similar utterances, to achieve other objectives as well: (*a*) to
'throw the ball into the Israeli court', by manifesting a flexible, new
position to the Israeli public and inviting official Israeli response to the
new Syrian position ('but we have not yet received a reply from them [the
Israelis]'); (*b*) to prevent a separate deal between Israel and the Palestinians (and also Jordan), thus leaving Syria in the cold; and (*c*) at the
same time to assure the PLO that Syria would not sign a separate agreement with Israel, leaving the Palestinians behind:

It is a known fact that the rulers in Tel Aviv topped by Yitzhak Rabin are
relentlessly seeking to divide the ranks of Arab negotiators. During the eighth
round, they hinted that there was progress in the Syrian–Israeli talks, and that an
agreement was imminent. Today they are playing the same game by speaking
about progress on the Palestinian track. . . . Syria could have reached a bilateral
agreement with Israel long ago . . . [but] Syria has repeatedly said that it is concerned with Jerusalem, the West Bank, and southern Lebanon in the same way as
it is concerned with the Golan.[33]

It was indeed obvious that Rabin was continuing, during the first half of 1993 and beyond, to try to make progress on the Syrian track, perhaps even to strike a deal with Asad. This, in line with his strategy of separate peace agreements, in response to Syria's peace proposals and in view of the initial refusal of the Palestinian delegation to resume negotiations until the Ḥamas deportees were returned.

Apparently to indicate Israel's strong inclination to conclude a peace agreement with Syria and also prepare their public for such a development, both Rabin and Peres, in early 1993, conveyed optimism about an imminent peace with Syria. In an interview on the eve of Israel's Independence Day (late April 1993), Rabin is reported to have said that there is a risk in 'descending from the Golan', like the risk taken in the withdrawal from Sinai.[34] If Rabin's statement was correctly reported, it indeed for the first time represented a signal that he was considering a total withdrawal from the Golan Heights in return for a bilateral full peace agreement with Syria. To corroborate this assumption, it should be pointed out that around the same time Rabin changed his previous motto 'withdrawal on the Golan, not *from* the Golan' to a more flexible one, namely, the extent (or 'depth') of Israeli withdrawal would depend on the extent ('depth') of the Syrian peace. This could be interpreted as readiness for full withdrawal from the Golan in return for full peace and normalization with Syria (but with no linkage to other Arab parties).[35]

But despite these public (tactical?) statements, the Syrian and Israeli delegations, which resumed their talks in Washington on 27 April (round nine), were unable over the next two rounds to settle their basic differences. The Israeli delegation, while acknowledging progress in the negotiations, continued essentially to ask their Syrian counterparts for an explicit definition of 'full peace', recognition of Israel's security needs, and public statements and gestures (by Asad) to convince public opinion in both Israel and Syria of the need and desirability of peace. Israeli negotiators also asked that Syria clarify its position regarding the linkage between the Syrian–Israeli settlement and a comprehensive Arab–Israeli settlement. Only then would Israel be prepared to discuss the extent of its withdrawal from the Golan.[36] The Syrian delegates, in contrast, continued to insist on Israeli commitment to full withdrawal from all territories occupied in 1967 as a precondition for a 'full peace' between the Arabs and Israel, whose nature they still refused to define.[37]

Thus, by mid-July 1993 (following round ten) neither Syria nor Israel were ready to say the magic words, peace and normalization or total withdrawal, respectively, although Damascus continued to send more positive signals of its readiness to sign a peace agreement compatible with Israeli expectations. Jerusalem, however, did not show any inclination to give up the entire Golan, and renewed its previous attempts at manœuvring Syria into accepting Israeli terms for peace, namely: withdrawal from the major part of the Golan, but not from the entire region; and de-linking the Golan–Syrian issue from the Palestinian–Israeli settlement. Rabin possibly expected that he could achieve these aims by resuming his initial policy of summer 1992: first to implement Palestinian autonomy or self-rule in Gaza and the West Bank, deferring the settlement with Syria to a juncture where Israel could negotiate from an advantageous position. Presumably Rabin resorted to his initial strategy towards Syria not only out of his own convictions and his deep concern lest a large majority of Israeli Jews refuse to accept withdrawal from the entire Golan even for peace with Syria.[38] The secret negotiations being held in Oslo at that time between Israeli and PLO representatives presented prospects for a breakthrough, thus again motivating Rabin to give preference to the Palestinian track over the Syrian.

Apparently in reaction to Rabin's declared refusal to give up the entire Golan in return for peace, Asad again resorted to his old tactics of exerting military pressure on Israel through southern Lebanon. During the first two weeks of July 1993 the Syrian-directed Hizballa and the Syrian-controlled Jibril group ('Popular Front for Liberation of Palestine— General Command') launched several attacks, including Katyusha rockets, against Israeli targets in southern Lebanon and northern Israel, killing five soldiers and wounding eight. Israel responded with a large-scale artillery and air bombardment against terrorist/guerrilla positions and villages in southern Lebanon. In this operation (named *Din veHeshbon* or 'Accountability'), which lasted seven days, some 50 to 70 'terrorists' and 114 civilians were reportedly killed, 400 to 500 wounded, and several hundred thousand Lebanese villagers fled their homes. With American mediation, an understanding was reached in early August between Syria, Lebanon, and Israel whereby Damascus and Beirut undertook to prevent the launching of Katyusha rockets from Lebanon into Israel[39] (although not against the Israeli-held security zone in southern Lebanon). Israel undertook not to attack Lebanese civilians in the course of its military actions against Hizballa targets.

This new Syrian–Israeli understanding demonstrated not only that Damascus was capable of restraining the Hizballa and held the key to stability in the region; it also indicated that Asad was not interested in a military showdown, but rather in a political settlement. As Rabin admitted in late August: 'Today there is a greater chance for the achievement of stability in Lebanon, as well as progress towards peace with Syria.' Asad himself had earlier given yet another sign of his peace strategy. In a written message to the Syrian army on its anniversary in early August, he said: 'We are in the battle for peace and we conduct it with the same ability that we displayed in conducting the military battles. Our positions in the peace battle will not be less courageous than those in the battlefield.'[40]

Nevertheless, with the resumption of the next round of Arab–Israeli peace talks in late August 1993, a breakthrough towards peace did not occur between Syria and Israel, partly because an Israeli–PLO breakthrough took place earlier in Oslo on 19 August, and thus the Syrian–Israeli negotiations were not to produce any substantial results for many more months.

THE OSLO ACCORD AND ITS REPERCUSSIONS

On the very day that round eleven of the Arab–Israeli peace negotiations started in Washington, on 31 August 1993, Israel and the PLO announced the conclusion of the Oslo accord of 19 August 1993, consisting of a 'Declaration of Principles on Interim Self-Government Arrangements', as well as a statement of mutual recognition between Israel and the PLO. This accord, publicly and officially signed by Rabin and Arafat on 13 September 1993 (in the White House), undoubtedly represented a historical breakthrough in the Palestinian–Israeli conflict and indeed in Arab–Israeli relations. Without dwelling upon the provisions of the accord,[41] which is not within the scope of the present work, it is certainly both relevant and significant to examine the repercussions of the Israeli–PLO rapprochement on the Syrian–Israeli peace process.

To begin with, the Oslo accord did not include any reference to the Syrian–Israeli track, only vaguely to the 'current Middle East peace process'. But Arafat (who did not mention Syria in his White House speech) and other PLO leaders explained that this accord did not constitute a separate agreement with Israel, but a 'disengagement agreement . . . similar to the disengagement on the Syrian, Lebanese, [?] and Egyptian fronts', part of a comprehensive agreement with all the Arab nations.[42] Rabin, on the other hand, speaking in the Knesset, described this accord as 'a bilateral agreement . . . not conditioned on what we achieve with Lebanon, Syria, and Jordan . . . [and] it is preferable to have a partial withdrawal in Gaza than a [total] evacuation of the Golan, at this stage, and in the future . . . it leaves us freedom of maneuverability toward them [Syria, Lebanon and Jordan].'

No wonder, then, that Asad was taken aback by the Oslo accord, which gave Israel a considerable tactical advantage and undermined his strategy regarding the Syrian–Israeli negotiations. Yet Syria's main criticism was directed against the PLO for reaching a 'partial solution' which 'came as a surprise to the Arab governments because there was no prior co-ordination.'[43] Indeed, whereas Syria had obviously not expected Israel to co-ordinate the Oslo accord with it and was probably not surprised by this move, it was deeply disturbed by the PLO's independent action. On the face of it, the PLO–Israel agreement was of an interim nature and essentially did not contradict Syria's diplomatic strategy of allowing for parallel progress in negotiations between other Arab parties and Israel, provided that the final peace settlement was comprehensive and approved by Damascus. Furthermore, Damascus itself, as discussed above, repeatedly stressed the vital need for a solution of the Palestinian problem, demanding this as part of a settlement with Israel, in line with both its Arab ideological concepts and its regional strategic aims.

Nevertheless, as we know, since the emergence of Fatḥ/PLO in the mid-1960s, alongside periods of ideological consensus and strategic alliance, there have been even longer periods of strategic and tactical differences, tensions and armed clashes, between Syria and the PLO. These arose essentially as a result of Syria's consistent endeavours to control the PLO and make it an instrument of its inter-Arab and anti-Israeli policies, vis-à-vis the PLO's efforts to retain its 'independent decision-making' concerning the conflict with Israel.[44]

This pattern of some strategic and tactical co-ordination set against a greater conflict of interests between Syria and the PLO continued even after 1988 against the background of parallel Syrian and PLO attempts to reach a political settlement with Israel through diplomatic means. Thus, when American Secretary of State George Shultz was engaged in his peace initiative in early 1988, Damascus tried to mend fences with the PLO, apparently in order to present a common front vis-à-vis Shultz, and prevent the PLO from accepting a separate deal with Israel, possibly in conjunction with Jordan. Hence, for the first time after his expulsion from Syria (and Lebanon) in June 1983—against the background of the Syrian–PLO conflict in Lebanon—Arafat was invited to meet Asad in Damascus on 25 April 1988. The PLO was reportedly permitted to resume its activities in Syria, and some 2,000 Palestinians were released from Syrian gaols. Yet, at their meeting, Arafat mentioned independent Palestinian decision-making, and Asad responded that Syria and Palestine were inseparable and that independent decision-making would terminate whenever it was incompatible with Syrian national interests.[45]

In fact, Syrian–PLO relations again deteriorated, apparently owing to further independent actions by the PLO which did not suit Syria's policies: its continuous endeavours to rebuild a power-base around Sidon and Tyre in Lebanon; its inclination towards Egypt; as well as its positive signal towards Israel (reflected in a document published by Arafat's adviser, Bassam Abu Sharif, in mid-June 1988). Reportedly, in July 1988 Arafat labelled Asad and his comrades 'Zionists who talked Arabic', in reaction to Syrian allegations that the PLO was prepared to accept mere self-rule in the occupied territories.[46] Subsequently, the PLO took further important decisions without previously consulting Damascus: on 15 November 1988 the Palestine National Council (PNC) proclaimed an independent Palestinian state in the West Bank and Gaza and, for the first time, implicitly recognized Israel by accepting UN partition resolution 181 (of November 1947); and in December Arafat on two occasions (including an address to the UN General Assembly) stated that the PLO accepted Israel's existence, rejected terrorism, and offered a peaceful settlement. Damascus vaguely supported the announcement of a Palestinian state, but several Syrian-based Palestinian organizations denounced the PNC action. The Syrian government itself (as well as the Israeli) rejected the new US–PLO dialogue which had been initiated by Washington following Arafat's above-mentioned statement to the UN Assembly in Geneva (on 13 December 1988).[47]

Damascus continued to oppose sharply and denounce the PLO's separate peace *démarche* towards Israel during 1989–90, denying its right to represent Palestinian opinion.[48] The Syrian–PLO disagreement reached another peak when Arafat supported the invasion of Kuwait (in August 1990) by Saddam Hussein, Asad's sworn enemy.

Following the defeat of Iraq in mid-1991, the PLO—discredited and vulnerable—sought a new rapprochement with Syria and undertook not to pursue the peace process without it.[49] However, on the eve of the Madrid peace conference, while insisting that the Palestinian problem must be solved within a general peace settlement, Syria did not insist that the PLO should represent the Palestinians at the conference. Asad reportedly said in August 1991 that Arafat was making every possible mistake, while Faruq al-Shara' advocated replacing Arafat by another leader. Nevertheless, Asad agreed to receive Arafat officially in Damascus on 19 October 1991 to co-ordinate their positions on the Madrid conference;

and subsequently it was agreed that neither party would sign a separate peace settlement with Israel.[50]

However, despite the ostensible improvement in their relations, the mutual distrust between Syria and the PLO persisted, particularly following the election of Rabin as prime minister and his attempts to manœuvre between the two. Syria was apparently not pleased with Palestinian participation in the multilateral talks with Israel, which it boycotted. Damascus continued to manifest uncompromising positions, perhaps harder ones than the PLO, regarding Palestinian issues such as the removal of Jewish settlements from the West Bank and Gaza, the inclusion of East Jerusalem in a Palestinian state, as well as the right of the 1948 refugees to return to their homes in Israel. Nor did Damascus cut short its support of the militant Palestinian organizations which rejected the peace process.[51]

Significantly, when Vice-President 'Abd al-Halim Khaddam was asked by an interviewer to comment on Arafat's deprecation of Syria's support of the Palestinian rejectionist groups, he said: 'I have the impression that Mr Arafat has lost a lot of his brain as a result of his airplane accident.' And, in reaction to Arafat's alleged claim to part of the Golan [al-Hamma?] to be included in the Palestinian state, Khaddam declared: 'This only proves again that he has gone crazy. He has become unbalanced. Yes, write that, this is exactly what ['Abd al-]Halim Khaddam thinks and says.'[52]

No wonder, then, that these Syrian attitudes did not prevent the PLO from making a deal with Israel behind Syria's back, probably because Arafat recognized that Asad would not approve of the Oslo accord if consulted beforehand. Indeed, Arafat went to Damascus only after the accord was signed, to seek Asad's *post-factum* approval. Asad, however, neither adhered nor openly objected to the agreement, but said that he would not obstruct it. Yet Asad also admitted that the Oslo accord caused him 'painful surprise' and 'heartache': first, because Arafat had not reported his secret negotiations to Syria and to Egypt in advance, even though he had undertaken to co-ordinate his moves with the other Arab parties. Secondly, because 'the Palestinian problem is the problem of all the Arabs . . . of Egypt and Syria (that had sacrificed too much for the Palestinian cause) . . . Palestine for us is like any other part of Sham [Greater Syria].' Third, because Arafat acted hastily, he did not bargain sufficiently; consequently 'the agreement caused much damage in the Palestinian arena . . .' [and] 'only Israel gains . . . it strives to isolate each Arab party . . . in order to impose its will.' Asad added that he had no intention of thwarting the resistance of the Palestinian rejectionist organizations to the Oslo accord; and hinted also that Arafat might pay with his life for his individualist conduct. ('Arafat does not distinguish between himself and the Palestinian cause.')[53]

It would thus appear that the PLO–Israeli agreement placed Asad in an inferior tactical position vis-à-vis Rabin, reinforcing his suspicions of Israel's intentions: Rabin was now again pressing for an advance on the Palestinian track (and also the Jordanian), expecting to squeeze more concessions from Syria. Asad also could not rely much on Arab help, except for verbal and diplomatic support from Mubarak. Consequently, President Clinton remained the only party from whom Asad could expect political backing.

But not only was Clinton preoccupied at that juncture with the problems of Somalia and Bosnia, he refused to urge Rabin to recognize Syrian sovereignty in the Golan, or commit himself to total withdrawal from it. He reportedly asked Asad to resume the peace talks which Syria had suspended following the Oslo accord, and to give Israel a chance to implement its agreement with the PLO.[54] Thereafter, in several months' time Clinton would become actively involved in advancing the Syrian–Israeli negotiations, also through personal meetings with Asad and Rabin, perhaps in order to conclude a declaration of principles between Syria and Israel whose outline had possibly been agreed upon, with Christopher's mediation, in late July–early August 1993. This would possibly include a total, but phased, Israeli withdrawal from the Golan, with security arrangements, in return for full peace and normalization with Syria, to be implemented gradually.[55]

Meanwhile, to demonstrate his interest in the Syrian–Israeli issue, Clinton met with Faruq al-Shara' in Washington in early October, and Rabin in mid-November 1993, talked by phone with Asad several times, and arranged to meet him in Geneva in mid-January 1994. He also dispatched Dennis Ross, head of the American peace team, and Christopher, to Damascus and Jerusalem in mid-October and in early December 1993 respectively, to prepare the ground for the resumption of the Syrian–Israeli peace talks. Simultaneously, as a gesture of goodwill, in December 1993 Washington allowed the transfer of three American-made commercial aircraft from Kuwait to Syria (while Israel received fifty used American F-16 fighter planes at a large discount).[56]

But all these moves did not change Rabin's position: during that period, from October to early December 1993, not only did he give priority to the Palestinian track while belittling the Syrians' role, he also demanded that Damascus conduct secret negotiations with Israel while making public gestures towards it; and that Asad should not obstruct Israel's tacit agreement with Jordan (of 14 September 1993). Asad, for his part, rejected the request for secret talks, promoted another Hizballa attack on the Israeli-controlled security zone in southern Lebanon in mid-November, and obtained a commitment from King Hussein to avoid signing a separate peace treaty with Israel.[57]

Asad, on the other hand, also made a few gestures towards Israel and the US: he promised to allow American investigators to determine the fate of the Israeli soldiers missing since the 1982 Lebanese war; he also offered exit permits to the remaining Syrian Jews (about 1,000), and told visiting American senators that he was seeking a comprehensive peace with Israel, 'even a half-literate will understand the meaning of the peace that I refer to' (said Asad). 'Abd al-Halim Khaddam took a further step towards indicating the meaning of that peace: 'Recognition (*i'tiraf*) and normalization (*tatbi'*) are included within the framework of the peace concept, which is now the subject of negotiations . . . the contents of peace and what would the relations look like in a state of peace with Israel are subject to negotiation.'[58] Other Syrian leaders and the media stressed that peace was a 'strategic choice' for Syria, but reiterated the notion of a 'just and comprehensive peace', entailing total Israeli withdrawal from all occupied Arab territories, including East Jerusalem, and the recognition of the Palestinians' legitimate rights. They also accused the Israeli government, although not the Israeli people, of using deception, evasion, tricks, games, slackness, and manœuvres to avoid making peace, and alleged that Israel, and Arafat too, were not credible even regarding the Oslo accord. In this respect the Syrian media raised high expectations that the United States and President Clinton as 'a full partner and an honest broker', holding the 'key to peace', should exert pressure on Israel to comply with UN Resolution 242, regarding total withdrawal from the Golan and other occupied Arab lands.[59] To these Syrian expectations one should add Asad's hope that Clinton would promise to give Syria economic aid and to erase its name from the list of countries supporting international terrorism, in order to obtain foreign loans and investments.

To be sure Washington did not intend at that juncture to remove Syria from the list as long as Damascus was hosting terrorist groups and having dealings with drug traffickers. Yet Clinton sought to continue the process of rapprochement with Asad, initiated by Bush, in order to strengthen the 'dual containment' of Iran (Syria's ally) and of Iraq (Syria's foe) and promote the Arab–Israeli peace process. Regarding the latter issue, Washington certainly expected that the Clinton–Asad summit would contribute to a resumption of peace negotiations between Syria (and Lebanon) and Israel, and towards the establishment of a 'comprehensive, just, and durable peace' in the Middle East.[60]

Israeli leaders, notably Rabin and Peres, were not too pleased with the Clinton–Asad meeting and its prospects, since they still preferred to advance first along the Palestinian (and Jordanian) track, and continued also to be concerned about the lack of domestic support regarding withdrawal from the Golan. Indeed, in a professional public opinion survey conducted in Israel during mid-January 1994 (partly after the Clinton–Asad meeting) most respondents were unwilling to give back the Golan area in return for full peace and security arrangements. Among those who shared this position were not a few Labour Party members, including Knesset members.[61] Nevertheless, Rabin and Peres were willing to advance on the Syrian track and upgrade the level of talks, provided that Asad would give Clinton 'the magic words', namely, peace and normalization with diplomatic relations, open borders, trade, and the like.[62]

THE CLINTON–ASAD SUMMITS AND THE JORDANIAN–ISRAELI PEACE TREATY

As a matter of fact, at his meeting with Clinton in Geneva on 16 January 1994 Asad did not publicly and precisely say the 'magic words' that Rabin awaited, but instead used terms that further indicated his 'strategic choice' (*khiyar istratiji*) in favour of real peace with Israel in return for Israeli execution of UN Resolutions 242, 338, and also 425 (concerning southern Lebanon). He had been spelling out several of these terms since 1992, but others were significantly new, clear, and forthcoming.

Thus, although Asad did not refer to, and even evaded, the notion of 'normal diplomatic relations with Israel, including open borders and tourism', he spoke for the first time about 'normal [or regular] peaceful relations [*'alakat silm 'adiyya*]', 'real and durable peace', and 'respectable peace'. In addition to his previous expressions, 'peace of the brave' and, obviously, 'just and comprehensive peace', Asad referred to the joint efforts (made together with the United States) 'to put an end to the Arab–Israeli conflict and reach a comprehensive and true peace that will enable the peoples of the region to concentrate on their growth and progress . . . [in] a new era of security and stability'. Finally he said, in response to a question, that 'we are ready to sign peace now.' No less important was Clinton's understanding or interpretation of Asad's message regarding the nature of peace, which went beyond the public statements of the Syrian leader himself. When he was asked: 'Do you feel that you have a firm commitment from President Asad to normalize relations with Israel? And by that I mean open borders, free trade and diplomatic relations,' Clinton responded:

The short answer is yes. I believe that President Asad has made a clear, forthright, and very important statement on normal relations. Now, in order to achieve these relations, a peace agreement has to be negotiated in good faith and carried out. But this is an important statement—the first time that there has been a clear expression that there will be a possibility of that sort of relationship.

In addition, Clinton not only stressed that 'Syria is the key to the achievement of an enduring and comprehensive peace', but also supported Asad's concept 'that there still would have to be a comprehensive peace in which the issues affecting Lebanon, the issues affecting Jordan, and the issue relating to the PLO would—in addition to the Syrian issues—all be resolved.'

It would indeed appear that Clinton was not only expressing his own personal commitment to Middle East peace, but was also deeply impressed with Asad's commitment to peace with Israel (Vice-President Gore depicted it as a huge 'breakthrough'). Placing Asad at the centre of the peace process and helping him to put the onus for new movement on Rabin, Clinton expected Israel in particular to adopt new 'crucial decisions' on the 'question of relating withdrawal to peace and security'.[63] In this respect the United States now urged Israel to discuss the withdrawal issue during renewed talks with Syria. This in fact represented paragraph 5 in the Syrian working paper of August 1992—which the Israeli delegation had since evaded.[64]

Yet in the next two rounds of talks (from 24 January to 25 February 1994), the gap between Syria and Israel still appeared wide. Syria criticized Rabin's decision to carry out a Golan referendum (see below) and repeated its demand for discussion of paragraph 5 of its 1992 document regarding Israeli withdrawal from the entire Golan. The Israeli delegation responded by again asking Syria to clarify the nature of the peace and normalization that it envisaged and to make public gestures in order to convince the Israeli population that Damascus was seriously aiming at real peace.

Consequently, despite certain positive gestures and statements by both parties, the Syrian–Israeli bilateral negotiations were temporarily sus-

pended in late February, also as a result of three events. First, on 7
February four Israeli soldiers were killed in southern Lebanon in an
exchange of fire with Hizballa guerrillas. Israel responded with air attacks
in Lebanon, and for another week further military action was taken by
both sides. Syria blamed Israel for alleged aggression. Secondly, the
Israeli–PLO Cairo agreement of 9 February 1994, regarding the Palestinian Authority and security arrangements in Gaza and Jericho, was sharply
criticized by Syria and created new tensions between Syria and Israel.
Thirdly, the massacre on 25 February of some thirty Muslim Arab wor-
shippers in Hebron by a Jewish settler caused the suspension of all Arab–
Israeli peace talks. The Syrian media blamed Israel for the massacre as
well as for the bomb explosion in a Maronite church in Juniyya a few days
later.[65]

Nevertheless, these adverse events notwithstanding, the Syrian–Israeli
peace talks slowly advanced since the Clinton–Asad summit, mainly
through American mediation and in unpublicized meetings between the
two ambassadors in Washington.[66] At the same time, both Israeli and
Syrian leaders made various efforts to demonstrate or signal to each other,
and particularly to Washington, their adherence to peace, and prepare
their publics for it. But both Rabin and Asad tried also to shift the onus,
and squeeze concessions from, one another, through the United States
and also by using other regional actors—Egypt, Jordan, Lebanon, and the
PLO. And, in fact, Rabin and Peres now undertook more initiatives than
Asad, who by and large adhered to his basic position.

Thus on 26 January 1994 Rabin said that 'our negotiations with Syria
have been . . . serious and open and progress has even been made. However, I call on President Asad to walk the extra mile in order to meet us in
the middle of the road to peace.' And on another occasion, Rabin remarked that he trusted Asad more than Arafat and that the Syrian regime
was more stable than the Egyptian one. A week before, Rabin and
Weizman sent their condolences to Asad after his son, Basil, was killed in
a car accident on 21 January.[67]

Earlier, on 18 January 1994, Rabin suggested to the Knesset through
Deputy Defence Minister Gur that 'in the event that the territorial price
demanded from us in the Golan Heights is significant, the government
will bring the matter to a referendum.' By this proposal Rabin sought first
to neutralize domestic opposition, and to prepare the public for a substantial withdrawal on the Golan, perhaps even from the entire area; and
secondly, to throw the ball back into Asad's court and induce him to make
peace gestures that the Israeli public could not ignore, thereby helping

Rabin to gain domestic support for his Syrian policy. Rabin himself admitted that the referendum

aims at signalling to Asad that he should also be more forthcoming [lit. elasticize his position] if he wishes to reach a settlement with Israel. . . . I have been disappointed by Asad because I expected him [to say] clearer things [words] on normalization . . . a warmer expression of his readiness for peace. . . . Asad has not done 2 per cent of what President Sadat did to convince the people of Israel that he means real peace.

Nevertheless, Rabin pointed out that in Asad's position 'there is enough fuel' to resume the new round of talks with Syria, and that Damascus had signalled to Jerusalem that it was prepared to reach a separate peace agreement with it; this agreement would, however, be linked also to a settlement with Lebanon, a Syrian condition that Rabin now accepted.[68]

Rabin and now also Peres, besides some left-wing ministers, went on to make further favourable comments concerning the peace process with Syria. Military leaders were apparently also mobilized to support this line. In addition to the chief of staff, who commended Asad's new approach, the chief of military intelligence told a cabinet meeting on 23 January 1994 that Syria was now prepared to move towards full peace and normalization with Israel.[69] Reiterating his analysis in March 1994 in a press interview, this officer also indicated that diplomatic relations with Israel were included in Syria's notion of peace. He added that the negotiations with Syria were indeed the key to reaching a comprehensive settlement in the Middle East, and that Asad was likely to keep an agreement with Israel (as long as it suited his interests). Similar views were expressed by Edward Djerejian, former American ambassador to Syria and a veteran Asad watcher, as well as by Dr al-Baz, Mubarak's chief political adviser, in interviews with an Israeli newspaper.

Around the same period, Rabin said, for the first time, that the Clinton–Asad meeting 'gave signs of hope', and that when Israel started significant negotiations with Syria, the time for 'painful decisions' would come, and the Israelis would do 'what is required from us', provided the Syrians would do 'what is required from them'. Rabin concluded: 'I hope that Asad will respond accordingly and we shall be able to sign a peace treaty with Syria by the end of the year [1994].'[70]

Reportedly Rabin and Foreign Minister Peres have finally recognized that 'the price of peace with Syria is clear-cut', namely an Israeli withdrawal from the entire Golan Heights in return for full peace and normalization with Syria, and consequently also with Lebanon, Jordan, and other

Arab countries. Peres, who had previously manifested some criticism regarding the Syrian position, has now voiced his support for an early breakthrough with Syria. In March–April 1994 he instructed his experts to prepare a position paper dealing with security arrangements in the Golan within the framework of peace with Syria. Rabin again publicly expressed his readiness to uproot Jewish settlements in the Golan in return for peace, and directed the army and the Mossad to prepare a draft proposal for a 'peace package' with Syria.[71]

Asad's response was no different to his previous positions, although he continued to make further gestures towards Israel while preparing his people for normalization with it. Thus, his statement at the Geneva summit regarding a normal peace with Israel was fully transmitted, together with Clinton's remarks, in the press and television. Following the resumption of the Syrian–Israeli talks in Washington on 24 January 1994, the Syrian media commented that the negotiations with Israel were being held in 'a positive and encouraging atmosphere'.[72] And, despite the suspension of these talks in late February, after the Hebron massacre, Damascus for the first time allowed a large delegation of Arab-Israeli citizens to visit Syria, to convey their sympathy to Asad following his son's death. He delivered a long talk to this delegation, mildly criticizing Israel's attitudes, and stressing Syria's contribution to the 'complete peace'. Asad did not rule out the resumption of the peace talks which had been suspended after the Hebron massacre.

Other Syrian officials also announced that the suspension of those talks related only to the current round, and that the (peace) process would continue, although there was a need to exert American and international pressure on Israel. Indeed, despite further media accusations of alleged Israeli responsibility for the massacre, and following the Security Council resolution denouncing it, Asad advocated the resumption of the Arab peace talks with Israel.[73]

In the event, the bilateral Syrian–Israeli talks did not resume in late April 1994 in Washington but, following Rabin's visit to Clinton in mid-March, the American president held telephone talks with Asad and instructed Secretary Christopher to travel to the Middle East in late April in an attempt to bridge the gap between Jerusalem and Damascus. In preparation for this American visit, Asad endeavoured to co-ordinate a common position regarding Israel with other Arab leaders, notably Mubarak, but without significant success.[74] Yet his main efforts were obviously directed towards the United States. Although criticizing its continuous military and economic support of Israel and its pro-Israeli and anti-Syrian inclinations, Damascus expected Washington to fulfil its commitment to the peace process and exercise pressure on Israel to accept real peace and total withdrawal.[75]

Christopher met Rabin in Jerusalem on 29 April 1994 (and subsequently Asad in Damascus) and was asked to deliver to Asad an Israeli 'peace package' which reportedly consisted of the following elements:

1. Israel will withdraw in the Golan in three stages over a period of five to eight years, parallel to three phases of peace and normalization with Syria.

2. In the first stage, Israel will withdraw from three Druze villages in the north-east adjacent to the cease-fire line with Syria, and in return Syria will establish diplomatic relations with Israel, and exchange ambassadors.

3. During the second stage, Israeli settlements will be evacuated, and full normalization will be implemented between the two states.

4. In the third stage, Israel will complete its withdrawal (although it would not specify the final line of withdrawal).

5. A variety of security arrangements will be implemented, including demilitarization and reduction of troop concentrations—largely on the Syrian side—as well as creating early-warning stations and deploying an international force to supervise the security arrangements.

The Syrian media flatly rejected the Israeli peace proposal, mainly because it did not include a clear-cut commitment to total withdrawal to the pre-1967 lines: Faruq al-Shara' even depicted it as a 'stupid proposal'.[76] Yet Asad himself, although disappointed by the Israeli offer, did not regard it as a non-starter. He reportedly suggested his own plan to Christopher, including the following items:

1. Israel should rescind the Golan Law of 1981 and recognize Syrian sovereignty in the Golan.

2. Israel must withdraw from the entire Golan Heights within a short period [two years?], followed by full peace with Israel (but with no mention of diplomatic relations).

3. Peace with Israel should be part of a comprehensive peace with all Arab confrontation nations.

4. Security arrangements should be symmetrical.

5. Syria will be ready (following Israel's withdrawal) to discuss elements of normalization, such as diplomatic and economic relations.[77]

It would thus appear that the Israeli 'peace package' and the Syrian response, although not representing a breakthrough, nevertheless contributed to narrowing the gap between the positions of both parties, and evidently to reinforcing the American stance as a mediator, or broker, between Damascus and Jerusalem. Yet, in their competition to win the support of the United States for their respective agendas, Jerusalem retained the upper hand over Damascus. Despite its diplomatic efforts and practical steps, Syria was still unable to have its name removed from the American list of countries supporting terrorism and dealing in narcotics.[78] In contrast, Israel continued to request and to obtain advanced American weapons[79] and to secure full American backing for its separate political agreements with the PLO (and later also with Jordan), which were sharply opposed by Syria. Thus, for example, on 4 May 1994, in the middle of his two-phase shuttle between Jerusalem and Damascus, Christopher, as a chief co-sponsor, attended the signing of the Cairo agreement between Israel and the PLO regarding the implementation of the Gaza–Jericho accord. (Significantly or insensitively, unlike Mubarak, Arafat, and even Peres, Christopher, in his speech, did not refer to Syria as a future partner for peace with Israel.)[80]

Even though Washington was convinced that Asad was prepared to grant Israel full peace and normalization in return for the entire Golan—a trade-off which the Americans probably accepted—Clinton and Christopher have apparently refrained from pressing Rabin to commit Israel openly to full withdrawal from the Golan. Being aware of his domestic constraints regarding the Golan issue, the American leaders have backed Rabin's gradual, cautious way of both signalling to Damascus and preparing the Israeli public for giving up the entire Golan in return for full peace with Syria. This, by making more pointed political statements on the Golan/Syrian issue; advancing the peacemaking process with the PLO and with Jordan, as well as by taking steps to safeguard Israel's future security, with massive American military aid.

Thus, between Christopher's three visits to the region (in May, July, and August 1994), Rabin said in Jerusalem on 22 June 1994 that Syria was acquiring a large arsenal of long-range missiles and if 'there will not be a territorial compromise with Syria within three, five to seven years, there will be war with it, not peace'. He also pointed out that Menachem Begin gave up the entire Sinai for peace with Egypt. Earlier, Egypt's President Mubarak said that Rabin had told him that Israel was prepared to withdraw fully from the Golan in return for full peace with Syria (Rabin denied Mubarak's works). Again Peres suggested, on 22 June, that Israel should be prepared to withdraw fully from the Golan in return for good security arrangements and reconciliation with the Arab world within a new regional order.[81]

On 14 July 1994, a few days before Christopher's visit to Israel and Syria, Peres for the first time made a highly significant statement regarding the Golan: 'We have acknowledged Syrian sovereignty on the Golan Heights, time after time,' In that context, Peres also mentioned the Israeli government's resolution of 19 June 1967, offering to withdraw the army to the international boundary with Syria in return for full peace, the safeguarding of Israel's security, and the uninterrupted flow of the River Jordan headwaters. Peres later implied in the Knesset that there was a need to change the 1981 Golan Law (which, in fact, meant the annexation of the Golan to Israel) and that he believed that more than half of the Knesset was prepared to make such a change.[82]

Peres's statements, possibly co-ordinated with Rabin, clearly signified Israel's positive response to some of Asad's major peace conditions, or at least demonstrated its readiness to give up the entire Golan in return for peace. Reportedly, by the end of July 1994, Rabin delivered to Asad through Christopher a new proposal for a Syrian–Israeli peace treaty on the model of the Egyptian–Israeli peace agreement of 1979, namely: total Israeli withdrawal from the Golan (including the settlements) to the international boundary, in stages and within three years; following the first stage, Syria and Israel will establish diplomatic relations and open their borders to tourists from both countries; in addition to the demilitarization of the Golan, security arrangements beyond the borders will be asymmetric, in proportion to the size of each country[83] (meaning more extensive on the Syrian side).

Parallel to these fresh diplomatic moves, Israel, with American blessing and possibly co-ordination, initiated several bilateral agreements with Jordan, notably a mutual non-belligerency declaration (in Washington on 25 July 1994), aiming *inter alia* at further inducing Syria to make an advance on the peace process with Israel. This, by signalling that King Hussein was conducting an independent policy regarding his relations with Israel, and that Syria was likely to be left out of the peace process and its benefits, if Asad continued to adhere to his uncompromising line.

To be sure, in his deliberations with Christopher and Mubarak, as well as in public statements, Asad has continued to stress Syria's adherence to peace with Israel. But he insists, despite Israel's new signals, that it must commit itself to total withdrawal to the pre-1967 cease-fire line (which extends beyond the international boundary and includes the strategic area of al-Hamma or Hamat Gader); that the Israeli withdrawal from the Golan, southern Lebanon (and other occupied Arab lands) must be completed within one year; that normalization will be established only follow-

ing the total Israeli withdrawal; and that the security arrangements beyond the Syrian–Israeli border will be symmetrical.[84]

Simultaneously, however, Damascus has shown certain signs of
flexibility, while taking further steps to prepare the Syrian public for
peace. It signalled that it was ready to discuss a phased Israeli withdrawal
from the Golan, provided Israel commits itself first to total withdrawal.
Damascus also took certain measures to curb Hizballa activities in
Lebanon against Israel, and permitted a few Israeli journalists carrying
non-Israeli passports to visit Syria. And in May and July Syrian television
transmitted uncut the signing ceremonies in Washington and Cairo between Israeli, Jordanian, and Palestinian leaders respectively. Asad also
told Clinton and Christopher that he did not object to the Rabin–Hussein
joint declaration signed in the White House on 25 July 1994 (which was
also attended by a Syrian diplomat), since he considered it as part of the
comprehensive peace process which included Syria, and was orchestrated
by the United States.[85] Nevertheless Asad was very unhappy about the
PLO–Israeli and the Jordanian–Israeli interim agreements and criticized
both Arafat and Hussein. But while he ceased to insist on the linkage
between the settlement of the Golan–Lebanon issues and the Palestinian
solution, Asad expected King Hussein not to sign a final peace accord with
Israel before the conclusion of a Syrian–Israeli agreement. To his deep
dismay, however, Jordan and Israel stepped up bilateral negotiations and,
with American encouragement and sponsorship, concluded a final peace
treaty on 26 October 1994. Asad now not only lost his automatic veto over
Hussein's crucial move, but was further exposed to Israeli pressure. He
was particularly angered by Hussein's consent to lease back to Israel for
twenty-five years part of Jordan's territory in the Arava, which had been
settled by Israelis. Labelling Hussein's concession 'blasphemy', Asad was
presumably worried that Israel would use this leasing provision as a
precedent for the agreement on the Golan.[86]

At any rate, Syrian leaders continued to insist on total Israeli withdrawal from the Golan (and southern Lebanon) within one year, but
simultaneously made further conciliatory references regarding the nature
of peace with Israel. Thus, in a press conference in London on 8
September 1994, Faruq al-Shara‘ said for the first time that 'Syria is
prepared to offer Israel a warm peace including full diplomatic relations
between the two countries in exchange for [i.e. following] full withdrawal
from the Golan Heights.' Two days later, Asad for the first time told the
Syrian parliament that he would honour the 'objective requirement of
peace', namely normal relations with Israel, which hopefully would be

achieved in the near future.[87] Similarly, on 7 October 1994, Faruq al-Shara' gave an unprecedented exclusive interview (in Washington) to Israel television, in which he said that 'we are interested in real peace . . . [with Israel] as soon as possible'. Finally on 27 October 1994, in his second meeting with Clinton (in Damascus) within a year, Asad reiterated phrases which he had used before but added new expressions:

I also affirmed to President Clinton the readiness of Syria to commit itself to the objective requirements of peace through the establishment of peaceful normal relations with Israel in return for [i.e. after] Israel's full withdrawal from the Golan to the line of June 4 1967 and from the south of Lebanon . . . [it will be] a peace that prevails throughout the region and enables its peoples, Arabs and Israelis, to live in security, stability and prosperity.[88]

Despite these positive public statements, the Israeli government would not commit itself to total withdrawal from the Golan, but proposed a different agenda for the peacemaking process with Syria. Already in early September 1994, Rabin outlined the phases of a peace agreement which entailed an initial 'very partial' Israeli pull-back from the four Druze villages in the Golan. This would be followed by a three-year test period during which there would be 'full normalization in relations with Syria, including embassies'. Subsequently, there would occur 'a significant Israeli withdrawal' within 'a comprehensive peace package' to be approved by a referendum.[89]

It would appear then that this guarded Israeli stance represented a regression from the previous forthcoming positions held by Rabin and Peres; in particular Rabin's ambiguous stand concerning the extent of Israeli withdrawal did not match Syria's clear statements regarding 'normal peace relations' and 'warm peace including full diplomatic relations'.

It is likely that what appeared to be Rabin's new position was influenced by the growing opposition in Israel, including in his own party, to a full withdrawal from the Golan. He was possibly worried that peace with Syria, involving the relinquishing of the entire Golan, would not be approved in a referendum and would thus cause the collapse of his government. In addition given Israel's separate agreements with the PLO and Jordan, Rabin possibly tried to squeeze more concessions from Asad concerning the terms of peace, for example, leasing from Syria the strategic regions of Mount Hermon and the Golan ridge,[90] in a deal similar to Israel's arrangement with Jordan (which was apparently agreed upon by early October 1994). Or perhaps Rabin tried to pressure Asad to accept the Egyptian–Sinai model, namely to agree to full normalization, including diplomatic relations, with Israel following the first phase of Israel's withdrawal in the Golan.

Undoubtedly, Asad lost much of his bargaining power, not only owing to Rabin's peace agreement with Hussein, but also in view of the newly established economic and diplomatic ties between Israel and several Arab states in North Africa and the Persian Gulf. In order to contain, or even reduce, Israel's growing influence, and to strengthen his own bargaining position, Asad has endeavoured to enlist the diplomatic support of Mubarak and King Fahd (of Saudi Arabia). Yet his main effort has been directed towards gaining the backing of Clinton to his negotiations with Israel. Thus, in his meeting with Clinton in Damascus on 27 October, 1994, Asad apparently persuaded the American president that Syria was ready for full peace with Israel in return for full Israeli withdrawal from the Golan. And, while refusing to condemn publicly Islamic terrorism against Israel, Asad reportedly agreed to extend the period of Israeli withdrawal to more than one year, and to expand normalization (but still without establishing diplomatic relations), after the first phase of Israel's withdrawal. Asad also undertook to continue the unpublicized talks between the Syrian and Israeli ambassadors in Washington, which had been going on for several months. These talks were also attended from November 1994 by senior military officers from Syria and Israel, including the chiefs of Staff Hikmat Shihabi and Ehud Barak. In these military talks the Israeli and Syrian officers discussed security arrangements, including the deployment of American troops on the Golan, but did not reach any agreement.[91]

Following a three-month suspension of the bilateral talks, the negotiations between Syria and Israel were resumed in March 1995 under the shadow of a growing awareness by both parties that time is running out owing to the forthcoming 1996 national elections both in Israel and the United States.

NOTES

1. *Yediot Ahronot*, 1 Mar. 1991; cf. *Ma'ariv*, 8 Aug. 1991. For Mr Hillel's position see *Ma'ariv*, 23 Oct. 1991.
2. See respectively *Ha'aretz*, 25 Feb. 1991; *Ma'ariv*, 4 Nov. and 23 May 1991.
3. See respectively *International Herald Tribune*, 26 Apr. 1992; *Independent*, 6 June 1992.

4. *Maʿariv*, 29 Oct. 1991; Schiff, *Peace with Security*, 78–9; A. Eldar, 'A New Political Agenda' [Hebrew], *Haʾaretz*, 3 July, 1992; *Haʾaretz*, 26 Aug. 1992; *Yediot Ahronot*, 10 Sept. 1992.

5. See respectively *Yediot Ahronot*, 1 Nov. 1991 and 19 Apr. 1992; *Financial Times*, 25 June 1992; cf. *Haʾaretz*, 3 July and 23 Aug. 1992.

6. *Maʿariv*, 14 Aug. 1992; *Haʾaretz*, 23 Aug. 1992. Cf. *Tishrin*, 14 July 1992; *al-Baʿth*, 30 July 1992.

7. *Haʾaretz*, 21 July and 23 Aug. 1992; *Peacewatch*, 39, 21 Aug. 1992. Cf. Quandt, *Peace Process*, 407. Cf. Damascus Radio, 18 and 20 Aug. 1992; *Maʿariv* 22 July 1992.

8. *Haʾaretz*, 25 Aug. 1992. Damascus Radio, 22 and 26 Aug. 1992.

9. *Peacewatch*, 38, 5 Aug. 1992; Israel Ministry of Foreign Affairs, unclassified document, 4 Aug. 1992.

10. See respectively *Yediot Ahronot*, 10 and 24 Sept. 1992; *Haʾaretz*, 31 Aug. 1992; *Peacewatch*, 40, 14 Sept. 1992; *al-Safir*, 24 Sept. 1992. Cf. interview with Usama al-Baz, Mubarak's chief adviser, *Yediot Ahronot*, 30 Aug. 1992; *al-Wasat*, 18 Sept. 1992. Damascus Radio, 26 Sept. 1992.

11. See respectively *Yediot Ahronot*, 10 Sept. 1992; *Haʾaretz*, 10, 13 and 15 Sept. 1992; *Peacewatch*, 40, 14 Sept. 1992; 43, 25 Sept. 1992. See also *Maʿariv*, 11, 22, and 27 Sept. 1992.

12. Citations from *Maʿariv*, 22 and 27 Sept. 1992; *al-Hamishmar* (Tel Aviv), 23 Sept. 1992; Martin Indyk and Robert Satloff, 'Washington VI: In Search of a Breakthrough', *Peacewatch*, 40, 14 Sept. 1992; *Maʿariv*, 27 Sept. 1992; cf. *Yediot Ahronot*, 8 Dec. 1992; *Haʾaretz*, 10 Sept. 1992.

13. I. Rabinovich, 'Israel's Approach to Negotiations with Syria', *Peacewatch*, 42, 22 Sept. 1992. See also *Yediot Ahronot*, 1 and 2 Oct. 1992.

14. *Yediot Ahronot*, 10 Sept. 1992; *Maʿariv*, 10 Sept. 1992; *Haʾaretz*, 13 Sept. 1992.

15. See e.g. an article by General (ret.) A. Qahalani (Labour MK and a prominent figure in the 1973 war) in *The Negotiation between Israel and Syria* (Hebrew; Bar Ilan University, 1993), 9–14; Y. Porath [professor of Middle Eastern Studies and senior member of the Shinui Party], 'Not to Give up the Water Resources' [Hebrew]. *Haʾaretz*, 25 Sept. 1992; A. Lynn [former Labour MK], 'The Golan Heights is not the Sudeten Region' [Hebrew], *Davar*, 18 Oct. 1992.

16. See respectively interview with Rabin, *Maʿariv*, 27 Sept. 1992; *Yediot Ahronot*, 26 Nov. 1992; Rabin interview in *Time*, 30 Nov. 1992, 32. See also *Maʿariv*, 11 and 22 Sept. 1992; *Yediot Ahronot*, 2 Oct. 1992.

17. *Yediot Ahronot*, 1 Oct., 16 Nov., and 8 Dec. 1992; Rabin interview in *Time*, 30 Nov. 1992, 32.

18. *Al-Baʿth*, 2 Aug. and 30 Sept. 1992; *al-Thawra*, 8 and 20 Nov. 1992; Damascus Radio, 26 Sept. 1992. See also *al-Baʿth*, 30 July and 2 Aug. 1992; cf. *al-Hayat*, 26 Nov. 1992.

19. Cf. *al-Baʿth*, 30 July, 20 Aug. and 19 Nov. 1992; *al-Thawra*, 2 Aug. 1992;

Damascus Radio, 9 and 22 Aug., 25 Oct., 1992. *Tishrin*, 28 Oct. and 4 Nov. 1992; Associated Press Report, 28 Oct. 1992.

20. *Tishrin*, 14 July 1992; *al-Ba'th*, 18 Oct. 1992; Damascus Radio, 26 Aug. and 26 Sept. 1992; interview with Syria's Vice-President Khaddam on Radio Monte Carlo, 16 Nov. 1992; interview with Muwaffaq al-Allaf, *al-Quds al-Arabi* (London), 17 Nov. 1992.

21. Cf. *al-Ba'th*, 30 July and 7 Aug. 1992; *Tishrin*, 28 Oct. and 29 Nov. 1992; see also interview with Khaddam on Radio Monte Carlo, 16 Nov. 1992. For a detailed examination of Syrian military build-up in the early 1990s, see Eisenstadt, *Arming for Peace?*

22. Interview with Muwaffaq al-Allaf in *al-Quds al-Arabi* (London), 17 Nov. 1992. See also Khaddam's interview on Radio Monte Carlo, 16 Nov. 1992. *Tishrin*, 9 Nov. 1992; *al-Ba'th*, 3 Dec. 1992; *al-Hayat*, 4 Mar. 1993. Cf. Y. Olmert, *Toward a Syrian–Israeli Peace Agreement* (Institute for Near East Policy, Washington, 1994), 22.

23. See respectively Allaf's interview, 17 Nov. 1992; R. Satloff, 'The Arab–Israeli Talks: Peace for November 3', *Peacewatch*, 45, 29 Oct. 1992. See also 'Signals from Two Old Foes', *Time*, 30 Nov. 1992, 30–3; *Washington Post*, 19 Nov. 1992.

24. *Foreign Policy Bulletin* (Washington), 3/1 (July–Aug. 1992), 70; *Rus al-Yusuf* (Cairo), 1 Dec. 1992.

25. Allaf's interview, 17 Nov. 1992; interview with Asad in *The Times*, 30 Nov. 1992; interview with Khaddam in *Il Giornale* (Milan), 14 Dec. 1992. Cf. 'Reported Text of Syria's Proposed Joint Statement of Principles, October 26, 1992', *FBIS*, 28 Oct. 1992.

26. See respectively 'Signals from Two Old Foes', *Time*, 30 Nov. 1992, 32, 33; L. H. Gelb, 'Double Dare', *New York Times*, 12 Nov. 1992.

27. *Middle East Journal*, 47 (1993), 312. For more details, see ibid. 311 ff.

28. *Middle East Journal*, 47 (1993), 479, 483. *Middle East International*, 5 Mar. 1993, 8.

29. *Al-Hayat*, 4 Mar. 1993; Damascus Radio, 1, 16, and 19 May 1993.

30. Cf. L. H. Gelb, 'Assad's Surprise', *New York Times*, 4 Mar. 1993; *Ha'aretz* (Tel Aviv), 26 Jan. 1993.

31. Damascus Radio, 18 Mar. 1993; *FBIS*, 19 Mar. 1993, 48. Cf. *Yediot Ahronot*, 5 Mar. 1993.

32. *Al-Wasat*, 67, 10 May 1993, 12–20; *Ha'aretz*, 24 May 1993. Cf. E. Ya'ari, 'The Problem with Asad', *Jerusalem Report*, 6 May 1993, 31; *Yediot Ahronot*, 12 May 1993. Cf. *FBIS*, 10–16 May 1993, 45–52.

33. See respectively Damascus Radio, 1 May and 18 Mar. 1993; Asad's interview, *al-Wasat*, 10 May 1993.

34. *Ma'ariv*, 25 Apr. 1993. See also *Yediot Ahronot* (Tel Aviv), 8 Dec. 1992 and 4 May 1993; *FBIS*, 19 Jan. 1993.

35. Interview with Rabin, *Yediot Ahronot*, 4 May 1993; cf. Y. Marcus, 'Return of Golan: Rabin's Victory, Likud's Loss', *Ha'aretz*, 30 Apr. 1993; Rabin to Israel

Radio, 4 June 1993.
36. See I. Rabinovich, 'The Politics of Patience', *Policywatch* [Institute for Near East Policy Washington], 3 June 1993; 'Smile When You Say Peace', *New York Times*, 19 May 1993; 'A Sharper Peace Message is Required', *Ha'aretz*, 25 May 1993.
37. London MBC TV in Arabic, 30 Apr. 1993; Damascus Radio, 3 and 5 May 1993 as cited in *FBIS*, May 1993, 8–10; *Davar*, 7 May 1993; *Ma'ariv*, 16 May 1993.
38. See a public poll by Gallup (Israel) which shows that in Apr. 1993, 63% of Israelis rejected withdrawal from the Golan even for peace with Syria, along the Egyptian model. *Ma'ariv*, 5 Apr. 1993. Cf. *Ha'aretz*, 19 July 1993.
39. See Z. Schiff, 'Asad bohen et Rabin', *Ha'aretz*, 16 July 1993; also *Ha'aretz*, 2, 4 and 8 Aug. 1993; *Near East Report* [Washington], 24, 19 July 1993. Cf. T. W. Seelye, 'Syria and the Peace Process', *Middle East Policy*, 11/2 (1993), 109.
40. See *Near East Report*, 34, 23 Aug. 1993; *Ha'aretz*, 4 Aug. 1993.
41. Text of the draft accord in *Yediot Ahronot*, 31 Aug. 1993; *Ha'aretz* and *New York Times*, 1 Sept. 1993. For statements, comments, and reactions regarding the Oslo agreement, see also *Ha'aretz*, 14 Sept. 1993; interview with Arafat on Radio Monte Carlo, in Arabic, 1 Sept. 1993; see also *FBIS*, 1 and 2 Sept. 1993.
42. See interviews with Arafat and Mahmud Abbas on Radio Monte Carlo, 1 Sept. 1993.
43. See respectively *Yediot Ahronot*, 31 Aug. 1993; *New York Times*, 1 Sept. 1993; Asad's interview with *al-Akhbar* (Cairo), 20 Sept. 1993.
44. See relevant sections in Chs. 5, 7, and 8 above. See also Ma'oz, *Asad*, 119ff.; Shemesh, *Entity*, 62–6, 112, 203–5, 277–9.
45. *Ha'aretz*, 2 May 1988; *Middle East Journal*, 42 (1988), 640. See also F. Lawson, 'Syria', 225–6.
46. Lawson, 'Syria', 228–30, 220. See also T. Hanf, *Co-existence in Wartime Lebanon* (London, 1993), 318, 619; *Middle East Journal*, 42 (1988), 646; ibid., 43 (1989), 77; *Tishrin*, 29 June and 4 July 1988.
47. *Middle East Journal*, 43 (1989), 249, 250, 252, 253; cf. Quandt, *Peace Process*, 372–5.
48. *Middle East Journal*, 43 (1989), 464, 667; Drysdale and Hinnebusch, *Syria*, 234–5; *Ha'aretz*, 5 Nov. 1989.
49. *Middle East Journal*, 45 (1991), 651–2; *Ma'ariv*, 16 July 1991; *Ha'aretz*, 16 June 1991.
50. *Ma'ariv*, 6 Aug. and 16 Oct. 1991; *Middle East Journal*, 46 (1992), 294; cf. *al-Quds al-Arabi* (London), 17 Nov. 1992.
51. *Tishrin* and *al-Thawra*, 2 Aug. 1992; Damascus Radio, 9 Aug. and 24 Oct. 1992; *al-Quds al-Arabi* (London), 17 Nov. 1992; Radio Monte Carlo, 16 Nov. 1992, interview with Khaddam.
52. *Il Giornale* (Milan), 14 Dec. 1992.
53. See respectively interview with Asad in *al-Akhbar*, 16 and 21 Sept. 1993; and

with American PBS TV, 2 Oct. 1993; See also *Ha'aretz*, 21 Sept., 3 and 5 Oct. 1993; *Yediot Ahronot*, 23 Sept. 1993; *al-Ba'th*, 21 Sept. 1993; *Tishrin*, 21 Oct. 1993; *The Middle East* (London), 230 (Dec. 1993), 18 ff.

54. Cf. interview with Asad in *al-Akhbar*, 20 Sept. 1993; *Ha'aretz* and *Yediot Ahronot*, 18 Oct. 1993; *Tishrin*, 4 Nov. 1993; *Ha'aretz*, 5 Nov. 1993; *al-Hayat*, 12 Nov. 1993; Damascus Radio, 17 Nov. 1993; *New York Times*, 10 Dec. 1993.

55. Cf. *Ha'aretz*, 4 Oct. 5, 12, 19, 21, and 22 Nov., 10, 17, and 24 Dec. 1993; *The Times*, 23 Nov. 1993.

56. *Los Angeles Times*, 6 Dec. 1993; *New York Times*, 10 Dec. 1993; *Ha'aretz*, 21 and 22 Nov. 1993.

57. See respectively *Ha'aretz*, 7, 17, 21, 22, and 23 Nov., 6 Dec. 1993; *The Times*, 23 Nov. 1993; *Jerusalem Report*, 13 Jan. 1994, 13: *Jerusalem Post*, 15 Sept. 1993.

58. See respectively *Los Angeles Times*, 6 Dec. 1993; *New York Times*, 10 Dec. 1993; *Time*, 20 Dec. 1993; *Ha'aretz*, 18 and 19 Dec. 1993; Khaddam to *al-Hayat*, 5 Jan. 1994.

59. Faruq al-Shara' to Damascus Radio, 9 Dec. 1993 and to *al-Hayat*, 3 Dec. 1993; also *al-Hayat*, 18 Dec. 1993 and 14 Jan. 1994; Muwaffaq al-Allaf to *al-Ray* (Jordan), 20 Dec. 1993 and to Egyptian TV, 16 Dec. 1993. See also *al-Ba'th*, 12, 14, 15, 19, 23, and 29 Dec. 1993 and 3 Jan. 1994; *al-Thawra*, 11 Nov., 11, 15, 19, and 21 Dec. 1993; *Tishrin*, 10 Dec. 1993; Damascus Radio, 8, 13, 22, and 27 Dec. 1993.

60. Cf. *International Herald Tribune*, 15–16 Jan. 1994; *Ha'aretz*, 10 and 22 Dec. 1993, 14 Jan. 1994.

61. A. Arian, *Israeli Security and the Peace Process: Public Opinion in 1994* (Tel Aviv, Mar. 1994), 16–17; *Ha'aretz*, 17 and 21 Nov. and 5 Dec. 1993; *Yediot Ahronot*, 24 Jan. 1994; *Ma'ariv*, 28 Jan. 1994.

62. C. Haberman, 'Awaiting "Magic Word" on the Golan Heights', *International Herald Tribune*, 15–16 Jan. 1994; *Ha'aretz*, 5 Dec. 1993 and 16 Jan. 1994.

63. For the full Arabic text of the Clinton–Asad press conference, see Syrian TV, 16 Jan, 1994; *al-Safir*, 18 Jan. 1994. See also *Ma'ariv* and *Ha'aretz*, 17 Jan. 1994; R. Satloff, 'Asad's Geneva Success', *Policywatch*, 111, 19 Jan. 1994; *New York Times* and *Washington Post*, 17 Jan. 1994. For Syrian comments on Asad's success in the summit, see Damascus Radio, 18 Jan. 1994; *Tishrin*, 17 Jan. 1994.

64. On this working paper and Israel's reaction, see Damascus Radio, 1 Sept. 1993; *al-Wasat*, 18 Sept. 1992; *Ha'aretz*, 6 July and 21 Nov. 1993. See also *al-Bilad* (Amman), 19 Jan. 1994.

65. See respectively Israel TV, 8 Feb. 1994; *Ha'aretz*, 15 and 17 Feb. 1994; *Los Angeles Times*, 19 Feb. 1994; Israel Radio, 14 Feb. 1994; *al-Ba'th*, 13 Feb. 1994; *Yediot Ahronot*, 28 Feb. 1994; *al-Safir*, 19 and 22 Feb. 1994; Damascus Radio, 23 and 28 Feb. 1994; *Tishrin* and *al-Ba'th*, 28 Feb. 1994.

66. *Ha'aretz*, 26 Jan. 1994; *al-Hamishmar* (Tel Aviv), 26 Jan. 1994; *Yediot*

Ahronot, 21 Jan. 1994.

67. See respectively 'Excerpts from speech by Prime Minister Yitzhak Rabin to the Parliamentary Assembly of the Council of Europe, Strasbourg, 26 January 1994'; unclassified document, Israel Ministry of Foreign Affairs, 27 Jan. 1994; *Ma'ariv*, 24 Jan. 1994; *Yediot Ahronot*, 2 and 25 Feb. 1994; *Los Angeles Times*, 19 Feb. 1994; *Near East Report*, 31 Jan. 1994.

68. See respectively *Ha'aretz*, 18, 20, and 26 Jan. 1994; *al-Hamishmar* (Tel Aviv), 20 Jan. 1994; *Ma'ariv*, 27 Jan. 1994; see also *Near East Report*, 24 Jan. 1994; *al-Bilad* (Amman), 19 Jan. 1994; Lebanon Radio, 17 Jan. 1994.

69. *Al-Hamishmar* (Tel Aviv), 21 Jan. 1994; *Ma'ariv*, 24 and 26 Jan. 1994. Cf. Peres's speech, 2 Feb. 1994; *Peacewatch*, 2 Feb. 1994.

70. See respectively *Ha'aretz*, 16 and 17 Mar. 1994; *Yediot Ahronot*, 25 Mar. and 18 Feb. 1994; *International Herald Tribune*, 17 Mar. 1994.

71. *Ha'aretz*, 25 and 29 Mar., 1, 5, 15, 17, 18, and 22 Apr. 1994. See also *Yediot Ahronot*, 8 and 18 Apr. 1994; *Ma'ariv*, 4 Apr. 1994; *New York Times*, 22 Apr. 1994.

72. *Al-Thawra*, 30 Jan. 1994 cited in *Ha'aretz*, 31 Jan. 1994. See also *Yediot Ahronot*, 21 Jan. 1994.

73. Damascus Radio, 28 Feb., 2, 5, 9, and 19 Mar. 1994; *al-Ba'th* and *Tishrin*, 20 Mar. 1994.

74. Damascus Radio, 9 Mar. and 2 Apr. 1994; *Tishrin*, 2 Apr. 1994; *Ha'aretz*, 25 Mar., 5 and 6 Apr. 1994.

75. Damascus Radio, 17, 23, 25, and 31 Mar., 3, 5, and 19 Apr. 1994; *al-Hayat*, 22 and 23 Mar. 1994; *al-Sharq al-Awsat* (London), 26 Mar. 1994; *al-Ba'th*, 29 Mar. 1994; *al-Thawra*, 9 Apr. 1994.

76. *Ha'aretz* and *Ma'ariv*, 29 Apr., 1 and 2 May 1994; *Yediot Ahronot*, 1 and 2 May 1994; Damascus Radio, 29 and 30 Apr. 1994; *al-Ba'th*, 3 May 1994.

77. *Al-Hayat*, 26 May 1994; *Ha'aretz*, 3 and 17 May 1994; cf. French News Agency, Damascus, 1 May 1994.

78 *Al-Wasat*, 11 Apr. 1994; cf. *Ha'aretz*, 1 May 1994; *Yediot Ahronot*, 2 May 1994.

79. *Ha'aretz*, 1, 6, 8, 19, and 20 May 1994; *Middle East Dialogue*, 16 June 1994; cf. *Syria Times*, 7 May 1994; *Tishrin*, 10 May 1994.

80. *Ha'aretz*, 5 May 1994; on the negative Syrian attitude towards the Cairo agreement, see e.g. *Tishrin* and *al-Thawra*, 5 May 1994.

81. See respectively *Ha'aretz*, 31 May, 22, 23, and 29 June 1994.

82. Ibid. 15 and 20 July 1994.

83. Ibid. 28 and 29 July and 5 and 12 Aug. 1994.

84. Cf. Faruq al-Shara' to Radio Monte Carlo, 2 June 1994; *al-Ba'th* and *Tishrin*, 21 July 1994; *Ha'aretz*, 28 July 1994.

85. See respectively *New York Times*, 29 July 1994; *Philadelphia Inquirer*, 14 May 1994; *al-Ba'th*, 28 July 1994; *Ha'aretz*, 22 June, 19, 21, and 28 July 1994; *Yediot Ahronot*, 22 July and 1 Aug. 1994.

86. Cf. *International Herald Tribune*, 19 Oct. 1994.

87. See respectively *FBIS*, 8 Sept. 1994; *Ha'aretz*, 8, 11 Sept. 1994; cf. *Ha'aretz*,

4 Sept. 1994; *Yediot Ahronot*, 8 Sept. 1994; *New York Times*, 11 Sept. 1994.

88. See respectively *Ha'aretz*, 9 Oct. 1994; Reuter News Agency from Damascus, 27 Oct. 1994.

89. *Ha'aretz*, 8 Sept. 1994; *Washington Post*, 9 Sept. 1994.

90. Cf. *Ha'aretz*, 7 Oct. 1994. On the opposition in Israel to a total withdrawal from the Golan, see *Ha'aretz*, 11, 13 Sept, and 4 Oct. 1994.

91. *Ha'aretz*, 28, 31, Oct, 6 Nov. 25, 30 Dec. 1994, and 1 Jan. 1995; *Yediot Ahronot*, 29 Dec. 1994.

From War to Peace?

The transformation of Syrian–Israeli relations from war to peace has not yet been completed; and the process will probably continue for more years to come since it does not derive from any profound changes in the long-term and deep-seated causes of the conflict and war between the two nations, particularly the historical, cultural, ideological, and psychological causes. Ba'thist Syria, for example, has not yet relinquished its role as the seedbed of Arabism, committed to Arab unity and to the historic struggle against the allegedly alien and expansionist Zionist movement, embodied in the State of Israel. Many Syrians still consider the wars with Israel in 1948, 1967, and certainly in 1956 (Sinai–Suez) and 1982 (in Lebanon) as evident manifestations of Israel's territorial and colonial ambitions. And even if Israel withdraws from the Golan, southern Lebanon, and the West Bank, not a few Syrians and other Arabs may fear Israel's imputed tendency to dominate its Arab neighbours by means of its greater military and economic power.

Similarly, many Israeli Jews regard the wars with Syria, particularly in 1948 and 1973, as well as Syria's attempt to divert the River Jordan headwaters, as clear proof of its declared design to destroy the Jewish state. They deeply suspect that if Syria regains the Golan it will resume its hostile actions against Israel, aiming at undermining its security and well-being.

These mutual feelings of suspicion, hatred, and fear, as well as the vicious cycle of armed clashes, have periodically been fostered rather than mitigated by Syrian rulers and by certain Israeli governments to serve their respective policies. Thus, Syrian rulers, particularly from the Ba'thist–Alawi minority groups, have used the conflict with Israel to strengthen their domestic legitimacy and control, as well as to enhance their regional influence, especially in Lebanon, Jordan, and among the Palestinians.

In comparison, some Israeli governments initially, and to some extent later, made use of Syrian (and all Arab) belligerency in order to forge a new nation-state, and subsequently to establish new Jewish settlements in the Golan Heights (as in other occupied Arab territories) and to justify military and political intervention in Lebanon.

As for some major characteristics of the Syrian–Israeli conflict itself: broadly speaking, during most of this long and bitter dispute Jerusalem has maintained a military upper hand and a strategic advantage over Damascus, thanks to its more cohesive society, stronger economy, advanced technology, and superior army, equipped since the 1960s with sophisticated American weapons (not to mention nuclear capability). Except in the 1973 war and perhaps in 1948, Damascus has not constituted a strategic threat to the very existence of Israel, notwithstanding intense ideological motivation, military coalitions with Egypt and with other Arab states, and massive Soviet weaponry. The major Syrian menace to Israel has been in military attrition and disruption of civilian life, by way of shooting across the border, and through guerrilla/terrorist actions, initially carried out by Palestinian proxies (in the 1960s) and later also by Lebanese-Shi'i surrogates (since the 1980s). This type of Syrian warfare largely contributed to the eruption of the 1967 war, but conversely also to the forced withdrawal of Israeli troops from Lebanon in 1985.

To be sure, Syria, over a long period, has established a powerful military force with the declared aim to wage war against Israel in order to liberate Palestine and since 1967 also the Golan. But owing to Israel's strategic-military advantage, the major role of the Syrian military build-up was in fact to deter Israel from attacking Syria and to defend Damascus against an Israeli offensive. This has been the case since the Syrian reverses in 1973, and especially in Lebanon in 1982. Significantly, the concept of deterrence/defence constituted the core of Asad's doctrine of strategic balance with Israel, which developed from the late 1970s and was pursued especially after the collapse of Soviet military backing of Syria.

Furthermore, the expanding Syrian army has been used by Asad since 1974 also in order to negotiate a political settlement with Israel, from a position of military strength, and on Syrian terms. This policy arose out of Syria's strategic constraints—external and domestic—and its need for American diplomatic and economic support. Particularly since 1988, Damascus, under Asad's leadership, assigned priority to a political settlement with Israel, paving the way for Syria's participation in the 1991 Madrid peace conference.

That important shift in Syrian strategy stemmed from the following constraints: Syria's failure to achieve a strategic balance with Israel; the sharp change in Soviet policy towards the Syrian–Israeli dispute; the end of the Cold War, with America's superiority; the end of the Iraq–Iran war to Iraq's advantage; and the severe economic crisis in Syria caused largely by its arms race with Israel.

Israel, for its part, maintaining strategic military superiority and enjoying, by and large, American backing, for a long time refused to relinquish the Golan in return for a political settlement with Syria. Most Israeli Jews also developed a new Golan ethos, viewing it as part of Israel and as the object of new settlement ventures, owing to its strategic importance and the potential Syrian threat. Only after the ascendancy of the Labour–left coalition in June 1992, and with American inducement, has Israel become prepared to give up most of the Golan, perhaps the whole of it, in return for full peace and normalization with Syria.

In addition to securing ongoing American support, to its strategic advantage, reducing the Syrian potential military threat (underlined by its ballistic missiles and strategic alliance with Iran), Jerusalem expects to gain further benefits from peace with Damascus, such as: Syrian action to disarm and curb the Hizballa in Lebanon; to help settle Palestinian refugees who have lived in Syria and Lebanon since 1948; to abolish the Arab economic boycott against Israel; and to generate diplomatic and economic relations between most Arab states and Israel.

Syria itself was initially prepared to sign only a non-belligerency agreement with Israel in return for a total withdrawal from the Golan Heights and southern Lebanon and the implementation of the Palestinians' national rights. But since late 1992 Asad has been ready to conclude a full peace agreement with Israel on the above-mentioned terms, expecting, moreover, that the United States would induce Israel to give up the entire Golan, and remove Syria's name from the list of countries supporting terrorism, in order to help it develop its economy. Indeed, Syria in recent years has been simultaneously developing its economy while continuing its military build-up, as Israel has been doing, more successfully, for longer.

In sum, the leaders of both countries have taken strategic decisions to end the state of war between their nations, and improve their well-being, but also to continue increasing their military arsenals. And even though both the Syrian and the Israeli governments have gradually and cautiously started to prepare their peoples for a new era of peace, their major historic task and challenge is still ahead: to transform a political agreement between the two governments into genuine peace and normalization between the two peoples by shattering the psychological barrier of mistrust, hate, and fear through education, cultural exchange, and economic co-operation. Undoubtedly those tasks are likely to be very difficult to carry out, particularly in Syria with its authoritarian, minority-led regime, centralized economic system, and partisan-ideological orientation. Yet, a final settlement of the Palestinian problem, and the advent of a more positive atmosphere in Arab–Israeli relations, may at least help gradually to heal the ravages of the past half-century and cultivate trends of peaceful coexistence among the peoples of the region.

BIBLIOGRAPHY

A. ARCHIVES

Great Britain

Public Record Office, Foreign Office (FO 371) dispatches to and from Beirut, Damascus, and Tel Aviv 1948–62.

Israel

1. Israel State Archives, Jerusalem. Documents for the period 1947–60 regarding Israel–Syria.
2. Israel Defence Forces (IDF) Archives; Ben Gurion Diary.
3. Ben Gurion Archives, Sde Boker, Israel.

United States

1. National Archives (NA), Washington. Documents from the Department of State (DOS), 1948–61.
2. President Gerald Ford's Library, Ann Arbor (various documents).
3. Declassified Documents (DD) from the White House, Department of State, CIA, National Security Council.

B. PUBLISHED DOCUMENTS

1. Ba'th Party documents, pamphlets and circulars (various dates).
2. *Divrey Haknesset* (Knesset Records, Hebrew), vols. 23–63 (Jerusalem, 1957–72).
3. Israel State Archives (ISA), *Documents on the Foreign Policy of Israel*, i–vii. *1948–1952* (Jerusalem, 1981–92).
4. *Policies and Interests of the USSR in the Middle East, 1945–66*, ed. Y. Ro'i, part I-II (Tel Aviv, 1969–70).
5. *Public Papers of the President of the United States Richard Nixon, 1974* (Washington, 1975).
6. *Public Papers of the President of the United States Gerald Ford, 1975* (Washington, 1977).
7. *United Nations Yearbooks* and *Supplements*.
8. United States, *Foreign Relations of the United States* (*FRUS*), ix. *1952–1954* (Washington, 1986); xiii. *1955–1957* (Washington, 1988).

C. NEWSPAPERS AND PERIODICALS (SELECTED LIST)

1. *Egypt*—Cairo: *al-Ahram; Egyptian Gazette.*
2. *Great Britain*—London: *Daily Telegraph; Financial Times; Guardian; al-Hayat* (Arabic); *Independent; Sunday Times; The Times; al-Wasat* (Arabic).
3. *Israel*—Tel Aviv: *Davar; Ha'aretz; Hamizrah Hehadash* (Israel Oriental Society); *Ma'arachot; Ma'ariv; Skira Hadsheet* (IDF); *Yediot Ahronot.*
4. *Lebanon*—Beirut: *al-Anwar; al-Jarida; al-Hayat; al-Mustaqbal; al-Nahar; al-Safir; al-Sayyad.*
5. *Syria*—Damascus: *Alif Ba; al-Ba'th; Jaysh al-Sh'ab* (military); *al-Ma'rifa; al-Munadil; al-Thawra; Tishrin.*
6. *United States*: *Los Angeles Times; Newsweek; New York Herald Tribune; New York Times; Time; Washington Post.*

D. BOOKS AND ARTICLES (SELECTED LIST)

ABU IYAD [pseud.], *Filastini bila hawiyya* (Kuwait, n.d.).

ABU JABER, KAMEL S., *The Arab Ba'th Socialist Party* (Syracuse, NY, 1966).

AFLAQ, MICHEL, *Fi sabil al-Ba'th* (Beirut, 1959).

ALLON, YIGAL, *Behatira lashalom* (Tel Aviv, 1989).

—— *Kelim shluvim* (Tel Aviv, 1980).

ALPHER, JOSEPH (ed.), *War in the Gulf: Implications for Israel* (Tel Aviv: University, Jaffee Center for Strategic Studies, 1992).

ANTONIUS, GEORGE, *The Arab Awakening* (London, 1961).

AL-AQQAD, SALAH, *al-Mashriq al-arabi, 1945–1958* (Cairo, 1966).

ARIAN, ALAN, *Israeli Security and the Peace Process: Public Opinion in 1994* (Tel Aviv, Mar. 1994).

AL-'ARIF, 'ARIF, *al-Nakbah* (Beirut, 1956).

ARNON-OHANA, Y., *Falahim bemered ha'aravi be-Eretz Yisrael, 1936–1939* (Tel Aviv, 1978).

ARONSON, SHLOMO, *The Politics and Strategy of Nuclear Weapons in the Middle East* (Albany, NY, 1992).

AVI-RAN, REUVEN, *Syrian Involvement in Lebanon, 1975–1985* (Tel Aviv, 1986; in Hebrew). English edn., Boulder, Colo., 1991.

—— *The War of Lebanon: Arab Documents* (Tel Aviv, 1987; in Hebrew).

AL-'AZM, KHALID, *Mudhakkirat* (Beirut, 1973).

BAR-LAVI, ZE'EV, *The Hashemite Regime 1949–1967 and its Position in the West Bank* (Tel Aviv, 1981; in Hebrew).

BAR'ON, ARYE, *Moshe Dayan and the Yom Kippur War* (Tel Aviv, 1992; in Hebrew).

BAR-ON, MORDECHAI, *Gaza Gates* (Tel Aviv, 1992; in Hebrew).

BAR SIMAN-TOV, YACOV, 'The Limits of Economic Sanctions', *Journal of Contemporary History*, 23 (1988), 425–43.

—— *Linkage Politics in the Middle East: Syria between Domestic and External Conflict, 1961–1970* (Boulder, Colo., 1983).

BAR YAʿACOV, NISSIM, *The Israel–Syrian Armistice* (Jerusalem, 1967).

BARTOV, HANOCH, *Dado, 48 Years and 20 Days* (Tel Aviv, 1978).

BAR ZOHAR, MICHAEL, *Ben Gurion* (Tel Aviv, 1968; in Hebrew).

BEN-TZUR, ABRAHAM (ed.), *The Syrian Baʿath Party and Israel* (Givat Haviva, 1968).

BRECHER, MICHAEL, *The Foreign Policy System of Israel* (London, 1972).

BURNS, EDSON L. M., *Between Arab and Israeli* (London, 1962).

CAPLAN, NEIL, *Futile Diplomacy*, i and ii (London, 1983–6).

CARTER, JIMMY, *The Blood of Abraham* (Boston, 1985).

COBBAN, HELENA, *The Palestinian Liberation Organization* (Cambridge, 1984).

—— *The Superpowers and the Syrian–Israeli Conflict* (Washington, 1991).

COHEN, HAYYIM, *The Jews in the Middle Eastern Countries* (Jerusalem, 1972; in Hebrew).

COPELAND, MILES, *The Game of Nations* (New York, 1969).

CORDESMAN, ANTHONY H., *The Arab–Israeli Military Balance and the Art of Operations* (Washington, 1986).

DAM, NIKOLAOS VAN, *The Struggle for Power in Syria* (London, 1979).

DAWISHA, ADEED ISAM, *Syria and the Lebanese Crisis* (London, 1980).

DAYAN, MOSHE, *Avney Derekh* (Tel Aviv, 1967).

—— *Mapa hadasha, yehasim aherim* (Tel Aviv, 1969).

—— *On the Peace Process* (Tel Aviv, 1988; in Hebrew).

—— *The Story of My Life* (New York and London, 1976).

DEEB, MARIUS, *The Lebanese Civil War* (New York, 1980).

DEVLIN, JOHN F., *The Baʿth Party: A History* (Stanford, Calif., 1976).

Dirasat Tarikhiyya . . . li-Nidal Hizb al Baʿth (Damascus, 1972).

DODD, CLEMENT H., and SALES, MARY E. (eds.), *Israel and the Arab World* (London, 1970).

DRYSDALE, ALASDAIR, and HINNEBUSCH, RAYMOND A., *Syria and the Middle East Peace Process* (New York, 1991).

EBAN, ABBA, *Pirkey Haim* (Tel Aviv, 1978).

EISENSTADT, MICHAEL, *Arming for Peace? Syria's Elusive Quest for 'Strategic Parity'* (Washington, 1992).

EREZ, YAʿACOV, *Conversations with Moshe Dayan* (Tel Aviv, 1981; in Hebrew).

EVRON, YAIR, *War and the Intervention in Lebanon: The Israeli–Syrian Deterrence Dialogue* (Baltimore, 1987).

EYTAN, RAFAEL, *The Story of a Soldier* (Tel Aviv, 1985; in Hebrew).

FREEDMAN, ROBERT O. (ed.), *The Middle East after Iraq's Invasion of Kuwait* (Gainesville, Fla., 1993).

FRY, MICHAEL G., and RABINOVICH, ITAMAR (eds.), *Despatches from Damascus* (Tel Aviv, 1985).

GALILI, ISRAEL, *Bemoqdey ʿasiya vehakhraʿah* (Tel Aviv, 1987).

GAZIT, MORDECHAI, *The Peace Process, 1969–1973: Efforts and Contacts* (Jerusalem, 1983).

GAZIT, SHLOMO (ed.), *The Middle East Military Balance 1992–1993* (Tel Aviv, 1993).

GOLAN, GALIA, *The Soviet Union and Syria since the Yom Kippur War*, Research Paper 21 (Jerusalem: Hebrew University, 1977).

—— *Yom Kippur and After* (Cambridge, 1977).

HABER, EYTAN, YA'ARI, EHUD, and SCHIFF, ZE'EV, *Shnat hayona* (Tel Aviv, 1980).

HAMEIRI, YEHEZKEL, 'The Question of the DMZ along the Israeli–Syrian Border, 1949–1976', MA thesis, Haifa University, 1978 (in Hebrew).

HANF, THEODOR, *Co-existence in Wartime Lebanon* (London: Centre for Lebanese Studies, 1993).

HARIK, ILIYA F., Lebanon: *Anatomy of Conflict* (Hanover, Pa., 1981).

HARKABI, YEHOSHAFAT, *The Arabs' Position in their Conflict with Israel* (Tel Aviv, 1968; in Hebrew).

—— 'The Armistice Agreements—in Retrospect', *Ma'arachot* (July 1984) (in Hebrew).

HEIKAL, MUHAMMED H., *The Road to Ramadan* (New York, 1975).

HELMS, CHRISTINE MOSS, *Iraq: Eastern Flank of the Arab World* (Washington, 1984).

HERZOG, CHAIM, *The Arab–Israeli Wars* (New York, 1982).

—— *The War of Atonement* (Boston, 1975).

HOPWOOD, DEREK, *Syria, 1945–1986: Politics and Society* (London, 1988).

HOROWITZ, DAN, *Israel's Concept of Defensible Borders* (Jerusalem, 1975; in Hebrew).

HUDSON, MICHAEL C., 'The Palestinian Factor in the Lebanese Civil War', *Middle East Journal*, 32 (1978), 261–78.

HUREWITZ, JACOB COLEMAN, *Diplomacy in the Near and Middle East* (Princeton, 1956).

JUNBLAT, KAMAL, *I Speak for Lebanon* (London, 1982).

AL-JUNDI, SAMI, *Arab wa-Yahud* (Beirut, 1968).

—— *al-Ba'th* (Beirut, 1969).

KARSH, EPHRAIM, *The Soviet Union and Syria* (London, 1988).

KAYALI, GHALIB, *Hafiz al-Asad—qa'id wa-risala* (Damascus, 1977).

KERR, MALCOLM M., *The Arab Cold War* (London, 1965).

KEDOURIE, ELIE, 'The Bludan Congress on Palestine, September 1937', *Middle Eastern Studies*, 17 (1981), 107–25.

KHADDURI, MAJID, 'The Scheme of Fertile Crescent Unity', in R. A. Frye (ed.), *The Near East and the Great Powers* (Cambridge, Mass., 1951), 137–77.

AL-KHALIDI, WALID, *Conflict and Violence in Lebanon* (Cambridge, Mass., 1979).

KHOURI, FRED J., *The Arab–Israeli Dilemma* (Syracuse, NY, 1970).

—— 'Friction and Conflict on the Israeli–Syrian Front', *Middle East Journal*, 17 (1963), 14–34.

—— 'The Jordan River Controversy', *Review of Politics*, 27 (1965), 32–57.

—— 'The Policy of Retaliation in Arab–Israeli Relations', *Middle East Journal*, 20 (1966), 435–55.

KHOURY, PHILIP S., 'Divided Loyalties? Syria and the Question of Palestine 1919–1939', *Middle Eastern Studies*, 21 (1985), 324–48.

—— *Syria and the French Mandate* (Princeton, 1987).

—— *Urban Notables and Arab Nationalism* (Cambridge, 1983).

KIMCHE, DAVID, *The Last Option* (Tel Aviv, 1992; in Hebrew).

KING, RALPH, *The Iran–Iraq War*, Adelphi Papers, 219 (London, 1987).

KISSINGER, HENRY, *Years of Upheaval* (Boston, 1982).

Al-Kitab al-Urduni al-abyad (Amman, 1947).

LAQUEUR, WALTER Z., *The Israel–Arab Reader* (London, 1968).

LAWSON, FRED, 'Syria', in R. Brynen (ed.), *Echoes of the Intifada* (Boulder, Colo., 1991).

LEVY, AVIGDOR, and RABINOVICH, ITAMAR, *Soviet Policy, the Syrian Communists and Intra-Ba'thi Politics, 1963–1971* (Tel Aviv, 1979).

LONGRIGG, STEPHEN HELMSLEY, *Syria and Lebanon under French Mandate* (London, 1958).

LOUIS, WILLIAM M. R., and OWEN, ROGER (eds.), *Suez 1956* (Oxford, 1989).

LUNTZ, YOSEF, 'The Diplomatic Contacts between the Zionist Movement and the Arab Nationalist Movement', *Hamizrah Hehadash*, 12 (1962), 212–29 (in Hebrew).

MANDEL, NEVILLE J., *The Arabs and Zionism before World War I* (Berkeley, 1976).

MA'OZ, MOSHE, 'Alawi Military Officers in Syrian Politics', in H. Zvi Schriffin (ed.), *Military and State in Modern Asia* (Jerusalem, 1976), 277–97.

—— *Asad, the Sphinx of Damascus: A Political Biography* (London and New York, 1988).

—— 'Attempts at Creating a Political Community in Modern Syria', *Middle East Journal*, 22 (1972), 389–404.

—— 'The Background of the Struggle over the Role of Islam in Syria', *New Outlook*, 16 (May 1973), 13–18.

—— 'Syrian–Israeli Relations and the Middle East Peace Process', *Jerusalem Journal of International Relations*, 14 (1992), 1–21.

—— and YANIV, AVNER, 'On a Short Leash: Syria and the PLO', in M. Ma'oz and A. Yaniv (eds.), *Syria under Assad* (New York, 1986), 191–205.

MARR, PHEBE, *The Modern History of Iraq* (Boulder, Colo., 1985).

MAYER, THOMAS, 'Arab Unity of Action and the Palestine Question 1945–1948', *Middle Eastern Studies*, 22 (1986), 331–49.

MEIR, GOLDA, *My Life* (Tel Aviv, 1975; in Hebrew).

Middle East Record (MER), i. *1960* (Tel Aviv, n.d.); ii. *1961* (Tel Aviv, n.d.); iii. *1967* (Tel Aviv, 1971).

MORRIS, BENNY, *Israel's Border Wars* (Oxford, 1993).

MORRIS, MARY, *New Political Realities and the Gulf, Egypt, Syria and Jordan* (Santa Monica, Calif., 1993).

AL-MUʿALIM, WALID, *Suriyya, 1918–1958* (Damascus, 1985).
Mudhakkirat al-zaʾim al-shahid al-duktur ʿAbd al-Rahman Shahabandar (Amman, n.d. [1947?]).
MUSLIH, MUHAMMAD, 'The Golan: Israel, Syria and Strategic Calculations', *Middle East Journal*, 47 (1993), 611–32.
MUSTAFA, KHALIL, *Suqut al-Jawlan* (Amman, 1970).
NAFURI, AMIN, 'The Syrian Army in the 1948 War', *Maʿarachot*, 279–80 (May–June 1981), 30–2 (Hebrew translation of the Arabic original).
NA'OR, ARYE, *Begin bashilton* (Tel Aviv, 1993).
NEDAVA, Y. (ed.), *The Arab–Israel Conflict* (Ramat Gan, 1983; in Hebrew).
The Negotiation between Israel and Syria (Bar Ilan University, 1993; in Hebrew).
Nidal al-Baʿth, 1943–1949 (Beirut, 1963).
Nidal Hizb al-Baʿth, 1943–1975 (Damascus, 1968).
Nidal al-Shʿab, i. *1943–1949*, (Beirut, 1963).
NIMROD, YORAM, *Mey meriva* (Givat Haviva, 1966).
NIXON, RICHARD, *The Memoirs of Richard Nixon* (London, 1978).
OLMERT, YOSSI, *Toward a Syrian–Israeli Peace Agreement* (Washington Institute, 1994).
PALMER, MONTE, 'The United Arab Republic: An Assessment of Failure', *Middle East Journal*, 20 (1966), 50–67.
PAPPE, ILAN, *The Making of the Arab–Israel Conflict, 1947–51* (London and New York, 1992).
PAQRADUNI, K., *al-Salam al-mafqud* (Beirut, 1984).
PARKER, RICHARD B., 'The June 1967 War: Some Mysteries Explained', *Middle East Journal*, 46 (1992), 177–97.
PERES, SHIMON, *Kaʿet mahar* (Jerusalem, 1978).
—— *Qela David* (Jerusalem, 1970).
PETRAN, TABITHA, *Syria* (London, 1972).
PIPES, DANIEL, *Damascus Courts the West* (Washington Institute for Near East Policy, 1991).
—— *Greater Syria* (London, 1990).
PODET, ALLEN H., 'Husni al-Barazi on Arab Nationalism in Palestine', in E. Kedourie and S. Haim (eds.), *Zionism and Arabism in Palestine and Israel* (London, 1982), 173–7.
PORATH, YEHOSHUA, *Bemivhan hamaʾase hapoliti* (Jerusalem, 1985).
—— *The Emergence of the Palestinian Arab Nationalist Movement* (Tel Aviv, 1970; in Hebrew). English edn., London, 1974.
—— *From Riots to Rebellion* (London, 1976; in Hebrew).
QASMIYYA, KHAYRIYYA, *al-Hukuma al-arabiyya fi Dimashq* (Damascus, 1971).
—— (ed.), *Falastin fi mudhakkirat fawzi al-Qawwuqji* (Beirut, 1975).
QUANDT, WILLIAM B., *Camp David: Peacemaking and Politics* (Washington, 1986).
—— *Decade of Decisions* (Berkeley, 1977).
—— 'Lyndon Johnson and the June 1967 War', *Middle East Journal*, 46 (1992), 198–228.

—— *Peace Process: American Diplomacy and the Arab–Israeli Conflict since 1967* (Washington, 1993).

—— JABBER, F., and LASCH, A. MOSELY, *The Politics of Palestinian Nationalism* (Berkeley, 1973).

RABIN, YITZHAK, *Pinkas Sherut* (Tel Aviv, 1979).

RABINOVICH, ITAMAR, *The Road Not Taken* (Jerusalem, 1991; in Hebrew).

—— *Syria under the Ba'th, 1963–1966* (Jerusalem, 1972).

—— *The War for Lebanon* (Ithaca NY, 1984).

RAFAEL, GIDEON, *Besod leumim* (Jerusalem, 1981).

—— *Destination Peace* (New York, 1981).

AL-RAZZAZ, MUNIF, *al-Tajriba al-murra* (Beirut, 1967).

RO'I, YAACOV (ed.), *Policies and Interests of the USSR in the Middle East, 1945–1966* (Tel Aviv, 1969–70).

SACHAR, HOWARD MORLEY, *A History of Israel*, ii (New York, 1987).

SAFADI, MUTA, *Hizb al-Ba'th* (Beirut, 1964).

SAFRAN, NADAV, *From War to War* (New York, 1969).

—— *The United States and Israel* (Cambridge, Mass., 1982).

SA'ID, AMIN, *al-Thawra al-arabiyya al-kubra* (Cairo, 1934).

—— *al-Jumhuriyya al-arabiyya al-muttahida* (Cairo, 1959).

SALIBI, KAMAL S., *Crossroads to Civil War* (Delmar, NY, 1976).

SASSON, ELIYAHU, *Baderekh el hashalom* (Tel Aviv, 1978).

SAUNDERS, HAROLD H., *The Other Walls* (Princeton, 1991).

SAYEGH, FAYEZ ABDALLAH, *Arab Unity* (New York, 1958).

SCHIFF, ZE'EV, 'Dealing with Syria', *Foreign Policy*, 55 (summer 1984), 92–112.

—— 'Dispute on the Northern Border', *New Outlook*, 6 (Jan. 1963), 10–19.

—— *October Earthquake* (Tel Aviv, 1974).

—— *Peace with Security: Israel's Minimal Requirements in Negotiations with Syria* (Washington, 1993).

—— and YA'ARI, EHUD, *Milhemet Sholal* (Jerusalem, 1984).

SCHOENBAUM, DAVID, *The United States and the State of Israel* (New York, 1993).

SCHULTZ, GEORGE P., *Turmoil and Triumph* (New York, 1993).

SEALE, PATRICK, *Asad: The Struggle for the Middle East* (London, 1988).

—— *The Struggle for Syria* (London, 1965).

SEELYE, T. W., 'Syria and the Peace Process', *Middle East Policy*, 11: 2 (2 Nov. 1993), 104–9.

SELA, AVRAHAM, 'The Question of Palestine in the Inter-Arab System', Ph.D. diss., Hebrew University, Jerusalem, 1986 (in Hebrew).

—— 'Syria and the Palestine Question', *Ma'arachot* (July 1984), 46–51 (in Hebrew).

—— *Unity within Conflict: The Arab Summit Conferences* (Jersualem, 1982; in Hebrew).

SEYMOUR, MARTIN, 'The Dynamics of Power in Syria', *Middle Eastern Studies*, 6 (1970), 35–47.

SHALEV, ARYEH, *Co-operation under the Shadow of Conflict* (Tel Aviv, 1989; in Hebrew).

—— *Shalom vebitahon baGolan* (Tel Aviv, 1993).

SHALOM, ZAKI, 'Hitnagdut Ben-Gurion ve-Sharett la-tviot ha-teritorialiot me Y'israel 1949–1956', *Iyunim Bitkumat Israel*, 2 (1992), 197–213.

SHAMIR, SHIMON, 'The Collapse of Project Alpha', in W. M. Roger Louis and Roger Owen (eds.), *Suez 1956* (Oxford, 1989), 73–100.

SHARETT, MOSHE, *Yoman Ishi* (Tel Aviv, 1978).

SHAVIT, YAʿACOV, 'Meshihiyut, utopia ve-pesimiyut bishnot hahamishim', *Iyunim Bitkumat Israel*, 2 (1992), 56–78.

AL-SHAZLY, SAʿAD, *The Crossing of the Suez* (San Francisco, 1980).

SHEEHAN, EDWARD, 'Step by Step in the Middle East', *Foreign Policy*, 22 (spring 1976), 3–70.

SHEFFER, GABRIEL, 'Inclusive Solutions versus Moderation', in *Zionism and the Arab Question* (Jerusalem, 1979), 119–62 (in Hebrew).

—— *Resolution versus Management of the Middle East Conflict: A Reexamination of the Confrontation between Moshe Sharett and David Ben Gurion* (Jerusalem, 1980).

SHEMESH, MOSHE, *The Palestinian Entity, 1959–1974* (London, 1988).

SHLAIM, AVI, 'Conflicting Approaches to Israel's Relations with the Arabs: Ben Gurion and Sharett 1953–1956', *Middle East Journal*, 37 (1983), 180–201.

—— 'Husni Zaim and the Plan to Resettle Palestinian Refugees in Syria', *Journal of Palestine Studies*, 15 (1986), 68–90.

SMITH, CHARLES D., *Palestine and the Arab–Israeli Conflict* (New York, 1988).

SULTAN, ALI, *Ta'rikh Suriyya 1918–1920* (Damascus, 1986).

SUSSER, ASHER, *Between Jordan and Palestine* (Tel Aviv, 1983).

SZULE, TAD, *The Illusion of Peace* (New York, 1978).

TAMIR, AVRAHAM, *Hayal shoher shalom* (Tel Aviv, 1988).

TANTER, RAYMOND, *Who's at the Helm? Lessons of Lebanon* (Boulder, Colo., 1990).

Al-Taqarir al-muqaddama ila al-mu'tamar al-qawmi al-thamin (Damascus, 1967).

TEVETH, SHABTAI, *Moshe Dayan* (Jerusalem, 1973; in Hebrew).

TIBAWI, ABDUL LATIF, *A Modern History of Syria* (London, 1961).

TLAS, MUSTAFA, *al-Ghazu al-isra'ili li-Lubnan* (Damascus, 1983).

—— (ed.), *Kadhalika qal al-Asad* (Damascus, 1984).

TORREY, GORDON HOWARD, *Syrian Politics and the Military* (Columbus Oh., 1964).

TROEN, SELWYN ILAN, and SHEMESH, MOSHE (eds.), *The Suez–Sinai Crisis 1956* (New York, 1990).

WEIZMAN, EZER, *On Eagles' Wings* (New York, 1976).

YANIV, AVNER, 'Syria and Israel: The Politics of Escalation', in M. Maʿoz and A. Yaniv (eds.), *Syria under Assad* (New York, 1986), 157–78.

—— 'A Syrian–Israeli Detente', *Middle East Insight*, 55 (Jan.–Feb. 1988), 27–33.

—— and LIEBER, ROBERT J., 'Personal Whim or Strategic Imperative', *International Security*, 8/2 (1983), 117–42.

ZAK, MOSHE, *Israel and the Soviet Union* (Tel Aviv, 1988; in Hebrew).

ZEIRA, ELIE, *The Yom Kippur War: Myth versus Reality* (Tel Aviv, 1993; in Hebrew).

ZONIS, MARVIN, and BRUMBERG, DANIEL, *Khomeini: The Islamic Republic of Iran and the Arab World* (Cambridge, Mass., 1987).

INDEX